The Inarticulate Renaissance

Language Trouble in an Age of Eloquence

Carla Mazzio

PENN

UNIVERSITY OF PENNSYLVANIA PRESS

PHILADELPHIA

Published by
University of Pennsylvania Press
Philadelphia, Pennsylvania 19104-4112

Printed in the United States of America on acid-free paper
10 9 8 7 6 5 4 3 2 1

Library of Congress Cataloging-in-Publication Data

Mazzio, Carla.
The inarticulate Renaissance : language trouble in an age of eloquence / Carla Mazzio.
    p. cm.
    Includes bibliographical references and index.
    ISBN: 978-0-8122-4138-9 (hardcover: acid-free paper)
  1. English literature—Early modern, 1500–1700—History and criticism.   2. Eloquence in literature.   3. English language—Early modern, 1500–1700—History.   4. Speech and social status—England—History—16th century.   5. Speech and social status—England—History—17th century.   6. Speech in literature.   7. Silence in literature.   8. Rhetoric, Renaissance.   9. Speech, Intelligibility of.   I. Title.
PR418.E45 M39 2009
820.9'003 22

                                                      2008032141

CONTENTS

ILLUSTRATIONS

NOTE ON THE TEXT

With the exception of regularizing the letter *s* in Renaissance texts, I typically preserve the spelling and punctuation used in editions cited. In some cases, I have capitalized the initial letter in a quotation silently when called for by the sentence structure. Although I use contemporary editions of most of the dramas that I discuss, I cite the Early English Books Online facsimiles of Nicholas Udall's *Ralph Roister Doister,* a play that has become increasingly rare in anthologies of Renaissance drama, and Thomas Tomkis's *Lingua,* a play much in need of a critical edition. All quotations from those plays, located by signature rather than act, line, and scene number, can be easily searched through the transcribed texts also available on Early English Books Online. Finally, I have shortened a number of titles in the notes and bibliography.

INTRODUCTION

THE TITLE OF this book, *The Inarticulate Renaissance,* may well seem oxymoronic.

For what place could the inarticulate possibly have had in a period of English literary history so long defined by the humanist revival of classical eloquence, the flourishing of the vernacular as a basis for literary and dramatic invention, and the Reformation of the Word through Protestant politics and poetics? Such titanic cultural forces, which have helped students, scholars, and teachers to understand the "Renaissance" in England as a distinct field of study, have also made it difficult for those same students, scholars, and teachers to see, hear, and grapple with the "inarticulate" as a central dimension of developing language practices and ideologies in the culture and drama of the period. Historical and literary-critical generalizations about the Renaissance as an "age of rhetoric" in which the dominant intellectual keynote was "the pursuit of eloquence" (from *eloqui,* to speak out),[1] are of course still invaluable to any approach to the period. But at the same time, such generalizations have had the power to overwrite an alternative history of involuted speech forms lodged in language practices, textual formations, and cultural phenomena that seemed, to many in the sixteenth century, antithetical to individual and communal coherence.[2] This alternative history can enable us to see literary innovation from an "inarticulate" perspective, where playwrights, in particular, fostered alternative forms of communal involvement precisely by staging, rather than burying or disavowing, such involutions of the word.

Challenges posed to the establishment of coherent speech communities in the spheres of religion, humanism, law, historiography, and vernacular development in sixteenth-century England foreground the inarticulate as a central subject of cultural history. In each of these fields, we see new attempts to distinguish between articulate and inarticulate, intelligible and unintelligible forms of speech and writing. These attempts set the stage for what we now understand as a Renaissance in England defined by both humanist ideals of persuasion and Reformation ideals of plain speech—and for the historical amnesia about particular persons, communities, and linguistic forms coded as unintelligible or ineffectual. By analyzing the historical attitudes toward mumbling, lexical and syntactic confusion, and other forms of ineffectual elocution, as they both informed and were recast through Renaissance dramas, this book directs attention to the inarticulate as a subject of dramatic development. It demonstrates how incoherence was not just the bad "other" to rhetorical fluency or plain speech but also as a site where meanings and emotions disavowed by dominant cultural formations could be voiced and thought through. Rather than simply asking how individuals and communities shaped their worlds in and through the power of rhetoric or even ordinary language, it is important to ask what it might have meant, on both the dramatic and the historical stage, to speak indistinctly: to mumble to oneself or to God; to speak unintelligibly to a lover, a teacher, a neighbor, or a court of law; to experience verbal incoherence in situations of passionate extremity or cognitive superflux, or to be utterly dumbfounded in the face of new words, persons, situations, and things. In pursuing these leads, *The Inarticulate Renaissance* argues for the affective and conceptual potential of the disabled utterance, aiming through a historical analysis to give the inarticulate a place in our understanding of Renaissance culture.

Departures from rhetorical competence, in both sacred and secular contexts, could be seen as enabling new forms of thinking, feeling, and acting. This premise is drawn largely from the study of drama as a particular medium through which cultural formations of the inarticulate became most audible and subject to public scrutiny. Drama is of course a medium that always involves communal situations of interaction and interlocution. Tensions constituting dramatic affect typically reflect the fault lines of communication, rifts in the production of shared meanings and imagined communities. While drama is thus a charged locus for the representation and imaginative transformation of cultural concerns about speech as a vehicle for communal and interpersonal exchange, it is also a curious medium through which forms of inarticulateness are given a "place" in the history of thought and emotion.[3] This is not simply because, as Peter Burke has observed, "playwrights exploited sociolects for comic effect, representing marginal communities as funny foreigners who do not know how to speak."[4] In Renaissance drama, verbal incapacity or incoherence subtends whole constellations of affect within diverse socioeconomic communities: we find suitors rendered lexically confused in the face of the beloved, courtiers or avengers acting out failures of expressive capacity and verbal negotiation, and scholars alienated by the inability of their language to be used or comprehended by others, or sometimes even by themselves. In the chapters that follow, lovers, courtiers, revengers, and scholars, as well as mumblers, hearing-impaired aristocrats, and not-so-marginalized "foreigners," emerge as theatrical constructs that at once reflect and reconfigure historically specific understandings of just what constituted effective and ineffective speech. Crucially, forms of linguistic deficiency on stage will be examined not simply in terms of "faults" of individual speakers marginalized from rhetorical culture by region, rank, gender, profession, or by compromised ethical and affective states, but in terms of historically specific fault lines of discourse out of which many of these characters arguably emerge.[5]

Being inarticulate is often conditioned by social contexts that, if undetected or unexamined, can lead to injurious forms of internalization; to the pathos of "feeling inarticulate" rather than a condition of knowing that one is unacknowledged or uninterpolated into a community of legitimate speakers. What "we suppose to be inarticulate or unsignificant sounds" among even animals, reads Philemon Holland's 1603 translation of Plutarch's *Moralia*, is but a matter of limited human perception.[6] Those unable to acknowledge the "lamentable and trembling voice," the "praiers, supplications, pleas & justifications of these poore innocent creatures," simply cannot fathom a "language" other than their own, leading to unjust and injurious divisions between the human and the inhuman or the subhuman.[7] Since this was of course often the case in human-to-human encounters, part of our task will be to examine how "inarticulate or unsignificant sounds" were deemed such; and how the codification of distinct and indistinct speech informed social assumptions about who did, and who did not, count in scenes of interlocution. For being inarticulate—as the citation from Plutarch also suggests—often involved an attempt to speak, whether to others or to oneself. The inarticulate is thus largely aligned in this book with representations of speech or sound-making rather than silence.[8]

Silence, however, could also encode conceptions of inarticulate speech.

The famous image of Harpocrates, the classical god of silence with his lips conspicuously sealed, for example, was glossed by Plutarch as a sign of "mens language as touching the gods, being yet new, unperfect, and not distinct nor articulate."[9] The figure fusing Hermes, the god of speech, and Harpocrates, the god of silence, in Achille Bocchi's *Symbolicarvm qvaestionvm* suggests as much (Figure 1). For there we see not only a tension between speech and silence, embodied in one and the same figure, but also silence aiming to quell an imminent storm in the upper region of the air—the well-known element of communication and intellection—which, configured in strong vertical lines around the candelabra, clearly threatens to dampen hermeneutic illumination.

Thus, silence often can serve as a powerful cover story for otherwise discomforting, because inchoate, if not always dark and stormy, forms of expression. The conception of silence as a convenient hiding place for the otherwise

Figure 1. Hermes as Harpocrates, Achille Bocchi, *Symbolicarvm qvaestionvm, de vniverso genere, quas serio ludebat, libri qvinqve* (Bologna, 1574). Typ 525.74.223 C, Department of Printing and Graphic Arts, Houghton Library, Harvard College Library.

dumbfounded, or inarticulate, speaker, was registered as a commonplace in 1597: for if "Silence is a sweet Eloquence," it could enable even "fooles in their dombnes" to be "accounted wise."[10] In the material that follows, concerns about incomprehensible speech at times shade over into concerns about "silence." When the very phrase "a kinde of vnsensible and vnarticulate silence" was used by the preacher John King in 1594, for example, it was to define a species of self-talk rather than what we might now consider "silence," as in one who might "mutter to himself, as the philosophers in the Poet, humming within themselves."[11] The inarticulate here, as elsewhere in this book, marks something between, but not reducible to either, speech and silence. An earlier allusion to the "inarticulate voice" in William Fulke's *Praelections vpon the sacred and holy Reuelation of S. John* (1573) indexed a rather roaring and "rude crie wtout vnderstanding"—which was invoked, in this instance, as a counterpoint to Christ's comparatively articulate (albeit furious and lionlike) roar in Revelation.[12] Fulke's gloss to Revelation 10:3 ("And he cried with a loude voice, as when a lyon roreth") reads, "Although I do not thinke that he vsed an inarticulate voice . . . he thretned horrible vngeance to the wicked, wt an imperiouse & angry voice." The curious qualification, "Although I do not thinke," opens up at least the possibility of a sacred and inarticulate "roar"; of an "inarticulate voice" that might be "vsed" for the expression of moral outrage.[13]

The fact that the quotations above from King and Fulke are not referenced in the *Oxford English Dictionary*, which dates these uses and senses of "inarticulate" later than both, suggests, on perhaps the smallest of scales, how the inarticulate remains an underarticulated facet of language use and language history in the English Renaissance. While variants of the English verb and adjective "articulate" were, from the early sixteenth-century, terms for speech, the word was typically used in reference to the fifth division of rhetoric, *pronunciation*, simply to index clarity and audibility of phonemic units. When Thomas Elyot, for example, wrote in *The boke named the Gouernour* (1531) of "English . . . cleane, polite, perfectly and articulately pronounced," the word signified distinct pronunciation.[14] The opposite of articulate here is not simply silence but rather, as in the cases above, indistinctly pronounced speech. *"Articulatly, sounding euery syllable, and staying at euery pointe,"* reads Richard Huloet's *Dictionarie* (1572), in an entry that grounded the English word in the Latin *articulim,* meaning joint by joint, also point for point, distinctly.[15]

At the same time, the root of "articulate" in the Latin *artus*, or "joint," could invoke a world in or "out of joint"[16] in the anatomy of grammar.[17] As Ferdinand de Saussure put it, "In Latin *articulus* means a member, part, or subdivision of a sequence; applied to speech, articulation designates either the subdivision of a spoken chain into syllables or the subdivision of the chain of meanings into significant units."[18] In terms of this latter sense of *articulus* as grammatical structure, it might be well said that the English Renaissance was seriously "inarticulate," because the vernacular was thought to be without the "joining" structures of what Sir Philip Sidney called "differences of *Cases, Genders, Moods, & Tenses*" so central to the classical languages of Latin and Greek.[19] While many writers of the Tudor period thought English grammar deficient for humanist projects of imitation, speech located at the nexus of classical and vernacular organization could prove vividly inarticulate in ways that spurred dramatic innovation; engendering *pathos* through scenes of representational *sparagmos*, a "tearing apart" of language.

As the anonymous author of the 1602 English academic play *Narcissus* put it, "angry grammar" makes the "tottering tongue to stammer."[20] Such tottering and stammering was often dramatized in plays composed for students at grammar schools and universities, where problems of pronunciation were often wedded to problems of grammar and elocution. In one of the most vivid examples of the period, when Latin grammar becomes the subject of the vernacular drama *Heteroclitanomalonomia*, the scene is violent and disarticulated. Priscian, the classical grammarian, inaugurates the plot with a bloodied head, describing "hott warres" between nouns and verbs in this Renaissance "Grammar-Land" where verbs "have lost their limbes": "some verbes grew hoarse . . . / Some lost their Active some their passive voyce."[21] "Vox," a character with respiratory as well as epistemological issues, declares, "I have scant breath to speake the thing at large / wch was ear while committed to my charge" (72–73). And "Queen Oratio" enters "in teares . . . wth blood besmeare[d]" (80), soon stating, "I feele that Barbarisme nighe approaches" (90), as she mourns the ruins of representation, witnessing a battlefield rife with scattered "legges," "armes," and "yea bodies" (92–93). Beyond the irregularities of Latin grammar, this play draws upon the problem of English as a vehicle for translation and communal formation. In many of the plays explored in this book, in and beyond the genre of academic drama, dramatic action itself is mobilized by such cleavages in linguistic or grammatical coherence. We will see ruptures of clean speech creating a channel for the flow of new affects. When brought into the foreground of the theatrical agon, the rhetorical insufficiencies alongside the ideals of the period could be mobilized to investigate forms of thought and feeling both beyond, and deep within, officially sanctioned rhetorics and grammars of culture.

The perils as well as the pleasures of rhetoric have become familiar to Renaissance scholars, particularly through extensive investigations by such critics as Terence Cave, Wayne Rebhorn, Patricia Parker, and Anne Coterrill, who focus in various ways on the vulnerable as well as the virtuosic dimensions of the "digressive voice" in sixteenth-century literary culture.[22] So, too, commonplace tropes of inarticulate passion have become familiar through studies of English poetry, and of the lyric in particular as a genre that put pressure on what it meant to express oneself in words.[23] But *copia* or *digressio,* and indeed eloquent expressions of ineloquence, are one thing,[24] while the history and dramatic representation of verbal *sparagmos* or outright unintelligibility are another. For what do we make of fundamental problems in the formation of speech communities that were thought at the time to resist recuperation through available practices and technologies of the word? In the developing field of law we find a case in point. According to Abraham Fraunce, a Tudor humanist, translator, and dramatist turned legal scholar in the 1580s, the unwieldy, because trilingual and textually disorganized, field of law—itself in "vaste volumes confusedly scattered"—created a crisis in public oratory to the extent that the public rhetorician "neyther himselfe can well vnderstand his vniointed discourse, nor the hearers conceaue his vncohaerent iangling."[25]

However hyperbolic this claim may seem to us now, the location of inarticulate ("vniointed") speech in *textual* conditions of production and reception, and in learned professional spheres such as law, is worth taking seriously. According to Fraunce, while juridical discourse suffered incoherence due to "such variety of borrowed words, wherein our law is written," even those textual forms so often understood by book historians as vehicles for informational rationalization, such as "Alphabetical breuiaries" (or the "A.B.C. abridgement"), actually led to textual and oratorical material being "torne and dismembred."[26] The English jurist Sir Edward Coke followed the same path, observing, "This I know, that abridgements in many professions haue greatly profited the Authors themselues; but as they are vsed haue brought no small preiudice to others. . . . certaine it is that the tumultuarie reading of Abridgements, *doth cause a confused iudgement, and a broken and troubled kind of deliuerie or vtterance.*"[27] Here "confused iudgement" and "broken" and "troubled . . . vtteraunce" are lodged in the very conditions of print and professional reading practice.[28] Possible remedies abounded, as we will see. Fraunce himself would follow Ramus (Pierre de la Ramée, the French educational reformer) by calling for the elevation of logic over rhetoric in order to expunge oratorical "iangling" from the public domain. But I invoke these examples in order to emphasize the extent to which the inarticulate was a phenomenon linked to particular textual as well as oral cultures of the Renaissance, and to stress the extent to which the two intersected.[29] The distinctly textual substrates of inarticulate speech will become important in this book. As we will see, oral and aural phenomena such as mumbling, babbling, and rhyming without reason (Chapters 1 and 2), confused or unintelligible elocution (Chapter 3), and even the sighs, groans, and vivid inarticulacy of lovers (Chapter 4), were all, if in varied ways, entwined with issues of print and developing textual cultures of the sixteenth century. Because drama involved the often conspicuous interplay of oral and textual forms, it became a potent medium for the representation of the halts and starts of spoken words mired in a rapidly developing textual culture.

Indeed, if the inarticulate was for Fraunce a product of a textual culture too "confusedly scattered" for the grounding of coherent speech, it nonetheless found a place on the stage.[30] The specter of "vnioynted discourse" that Fraunce aimed to expunge from public oratory functioned centrally even in his own Latin comic drama, *Victoria* (c. 1583), where the detritus of learned rhetoric accumulated new meanings on the stage.[31] This play and others examined in this book mobilized compromised forms of oratorical performance so that they might "speak," as it were, to processes of social exchange otherwise obscured by the clear transmission and reception of spoken language. When variants of the phrase "I don't understand what you're saying" ("Quod dicis, Onophri, non agnosco" or "non ego intelligo") resound throughout Fraunce's *Victoria*, we are invited to investigate the logic of unintelligibility as it might generate bafflement and break consensual networks of exchange. The extent to which reading practices could confound communal intelligibility is another of the central points of *Victoria*, which closes with an often incomprehensible pedant staying up all night, poring over Theodore Zwinger's "tables" in order to compose a simple epithalamion.[32] Since Zwinger's *Theatrum Vitae Humanae* (1565), while containing dichotomous or "Ramist" charts ("tabulis"), had no guide to pagination and sprawled forth in no fewer than fourteen hundred folios,[33] what Fraunce's play promises is yet more unintelligible speech the following day. If an overwhelming, because underrationalized, textual culture was Fraunce's bane as a legal scholar, it was his boon as a dramatist.[34] His own play threw the learned and textual grounds of uncommon speech forms into vivid relief and gestured toward states of thought and feeling otherwise eclipsed by comprehensible speech.

The halting effect of the inarticulate utterance, when detached from a simplifying logic of blame, could provide an entryway into the exploration of previously undisclosed structures of feeling. This sudden disruption in the flow of communication could expose the exclusionary logic integral to established communities of linguistic exchange, revealing the logic of affect—of hurt feelings, awkwardness, vulnerability, and alienation—with regard to codes of language and interaction. Failures of spoken communication often expose the constraining coordinates of what Erving Goffman has called "interactional ritual." Goffman's sociological investigations into the deep structure of "talk" are particularly germane here, especially his insights on heightened forms of awareness enabled precisely by uncomfortable moments when interactional encounters meet with sudden "disenchantment": "Disenchantment with an interaction may take the form of preoccupation, self-consciousness, other-consciousness, and interaction consciousness. These forms of alienation have been separated for purposes of identification. In actual conversation, when one kind occurs the others will not be far behind."[35]

This insight can help us to see how disruptions in conversational encounters might produce not only shame, awkwardness, alienation, or a sense of participatory insufficiency but also a heightened awareness of the (suddenly disrupted) protocols governing selves and others, as speakers may be occupied or preoccupied with, or oblivious to, demands of sociolinguistic decorum. Talk not understood may appear as a kind of "self-talk," but even this can be productive, as Goffman puts it, in posing a "threat to intersubjectivity: it warns others that they may be wrong in assuming a jointly maintained base of ready mutual intelligibility among all persons present."[36] It can, in other words, challenge consensus and expand the field of apperception in social interaction. The potential for heightened awareness in the face of interactional failure becomes all the more vivid as we move from "actual" to staged "disenchantments" in dramas when new enchantments with linguistically imagined communities meet with equal and opposite forms of disenchantment. Because drama was a genre that licensed the dense exploration of forms of language gone awry in communal interactions, playwrights were able to expose the internal logic of failed speech acts in ways that informing cultural discourses would, more often than not, find threatening to their purpose.

In order to resist the seductive appeal of coherence by which my analysis might reduce the term "inarticulate" to a single theory of meaning, I provide a variety of conceptually related but historically diverse approaches to the topic at hand. I focus on a series of cognate problems, ordered chronologically; I consider dramatic responses to, and reformulations of, treatments of inarticulateness in Reformation polemic and humanism (Chapters 1 and 2); in vernacular, legal, and foreign language debates (Chapter 3); in approaches to language acquisition made newly available through print culture (Chapter 4); and in medical, philosophical, and antitheatrical discourses about language and sensation (Chapter 5). These historical discourses are treated not simply as a backdrop to dramatic innovation but also as zones in which protocols of speech were often put under serious pressure.

Chapter 1, "The Renaissance of Mumbling," focuses on new ways of distinguishing between the intelligible and the unintelligible utterance in religious and humanist contexts. I examine, in particular, how the Reformation idealization of vernacular plainness as a vehicle of scriptural and liturgical translation found its diabolical antitype in Catholic Latin "mumbling." In Protestant polemic, the Catholic liturgy was deemed unintelligible both for individual utterance and for communal participation. Yet the Protestant emphasis on "mumbling" Catholics at once constituted a co-optation of late medieval intra-Catholic concerns about distinct pronunciation and enabled Tudor polemicists to disavow problems of coherence within their own newly forming modes of vernacular translation, transmission, and communal formation. Accusations directed against Latin "mumblers" (and against the nonsensical rhyming said to be associated with the Catholic liturgy) and the reduction of Catholicism to a species of unredemptive *orality*, I argue, helped to displace conflicts within a vernacularism that reformers defined as both common and bibliocentric. Such polemic generated a rhetoric of comic unintelligibility that would inform a range of anti-Catholic vernacular dramas. At the same time, Protestant humanists such as Thomas Wilson began to convert anti-Catholic polemic into a vehicle through which bad *English* pronunciation might be banished from the scene of the "common." Here we see the other side of Reformation polemic, in which competing and unintelligible voices within England become subject to disavowal through comic satire.

In *Ralph Roister Doister,* the play by Nicholas Udall I examine in Chapter 2, this disavowal is reversed: Protestant and humanist ideologies become subject to the same comic irony to which they subjected Catholics and "common" English folk. The chapter, entitled "From Fault to Figure: The Case of Madge Mumblecrust," shows how Udall grants a unique form of agency and cognition to the mumbling Madge Mumblecrust, a character drawn straight out of the tradition of Protestant polemic *against* Catholics. By unhinging verbal "error" from a logic of blame, Udall demonstrates how flawed and oblique forms of utterance could trump both humanist and Protestant approaches to effective speech. Interactional and communicative failures in the play provoke a number of impasses. These moments of blockage become for Udall opportunities to encourage a deeper and more expansive form of listening than was allowed by approaches to speech that Udall wrote about at length elsewhere. Here we begin to see how Tudor vernacular drama could thrive on disenchantments with the very rhetoric that informed it; the play itself was informed by both classical comic drama and religious polemic. This double-edged attitude toward English discourse encouraged a heightened awareness of otherwise buried forms of social interaction. Enchantment and disenchantment were of course mutually constituting, but they could collide in ways that generated alternatives to rhetorical protocols. Udall's drama mined phenomena of disabled speech in both religious and humanist contexts but offered an expanded, ethically capacious understanding of just what constituted intelligible and unintelligible speech.

The first two chapters thus explore how religious and humanist controversy about intelligible and unintelligible speech became a locus for vernacular dramatic innovation, which questioned the very distinctions informing assumptions about who did, and did not, count as arbiters of meaning.[37] Chapter 3, "Disarticulating Community," turns to the inaugural revenge drama in England, Thomas Kyd's *The Spanish Tragedy*, which featured perhaps the period's most dramatic instance of a disarticulated subject and a disarticulated community. Hieronimo's "autoglossotomy" (he bites off his own tongue) and wildly chaotic playlet, *Soliman and Perseda*—staged in an amalgam of Greek, Latin, French, and Italian—can easily be interpreted as a testament to an emergent Protestant English nationalism defining itself as distinct from so much Catholic Iberian confusion. Against this common reading, however, I argue that Kyd's play was engaged with a range of distinctly *English* concerns about linguistic incoherence that were integral to debates about vernacularism, legal rhetoric, and chronicle historiography. By situating the play in terms of the work of Richard Mulcaster—who headed the Merchant Taylor's School where Kyd studied—and other writers concerned about the incoherent status of the enriched vernacular as well as legal language, I argue that Hieronimo's polyglot playlet, followed by his spectacular lingual ejection and suicide by penknife, signaled a profound ambivalence about an increasingly alienated and scattered tongue used to shape common language as well as common law. Linguistic sparagmos constituted a tragedy that hit home. The question of linguistic incoherence meets, in the play, with a related question of plot *coherence*; thus I close by suggesting that *The Spanish Tragedy* reflected ironically on calls, by scholars of the period, for the cultivation of logical methods through which to counter the often incoherent language practices operative in legal practice, vernacular drama, and chronicle historiography. Kyd's Hieronimo turns away from shared language practices through which law and history might be socially negotiated and mobilizes, instead, his own peculiar logical method to construct an eerily coherent but deadly dramatic "plot." As he deploys logic to lend coherence to his tragic playlet and to his world, he stands as an internal antitype for Kyd's experimental but more nuanced mode of dramatic composition, which drew on seemingly disjointed languages, time periods, genres, sources, styles, plots, and forms of address in order to produce a more productive model of inarticulate theater. Through Hieronimo, Kyd took a canny form of revenge on those who would kill off what I have called the "inarticulate Renaissance" in the name of logical coherence.

Chapter 4, "Acting in the Passive Voice," further examines problems inherent in using logical method to rationalize spoken language. It does so by situating problems of speech in Shakespeare's *Love's Labour's Lost* in terms of the methods for language acquisition, practice, and development that were available in late sixteenth-century print culture in the form of textbooks, dictionaries, bilingual guides to translation, and models for love lyrics. One might imagine that the abundance of love lyrics and pedagogical manuals in print would have enabled readers to experience a liberating expansion of expressive resources. Shakespeare instead exposes the ways in which print could lead to dramatically compromised oral utterance, rendering scholars and lovers more passive because they were subject to textual forms that organized their emotions into templates that were hard to convert into effective speech and action. At the same time, Shakespeare exposes the affective consequences of print organization and transmission itself: extensive lists, catalogues, and conspicuously reproduced tropes of affective utterance move imagined speakers further away from particularized contexts, thereby constituting a "melancholy of print." Whereas English humanists typically presented rhetoric as a means for effecting social change, my emphasis in this chapter on "acting in the passive voice" enables me to examine dimensions of rhetoric that worked against this humanist agenda, stimulating dramatic investigations into the textual structure of affect. These structures are most visible in characters unable to "move" (in both senses of the word—to move others emotionally, and to move themselves forward into imagined plots) because they are stuck in awkward positions of vocal passivity and affective self-reference.

The final chapter, "Feeling Inarticulate," takes as its subject two plays that in many ways draw together the concerns examined in the book. Thomas Tomkis's *Lingua,* an academic play performed at Cambridge University in about 1602, and Shakespeare's *Hamlet,* also performed at Cambridge about the same time, both reimagine forms of inarticulate speech integral to religion, humanism, legal rhetoric, vernacular expansion, historiography, and print culture. While I index these issues, this chapter also moves beyond the discursive register to consider the place of the senses, particularly the sense of touch, in the dramatic representation of the inarticulate. Turning to the relationship between language and sensory perception on stage, I examine aspects of the extralinguistic by focusing on the peculiar status of touch as a vehicle for communication in both plays. I first consider medical and philosophical approaches to the faculty of touch—a form of sensory-emotional perception—in which words and methods failed to do the job of clear description. In classical and Renaissance taxonomies of the senses, touch was considered the faculty most resistant to representation, to articulation by means of objectification, reification, and classification. The attention playwrights paid to the complexity of feelings, grounded in forms of touch that exceeded available taxonomies of sensation and representation, gestured toward the difficulty, within available lexicons, of producing a language that could acknowledge interpersonal vulnerability. Touch as a complex and representationally resistant phenomenon was maligned by Renaissance antitheatricalists, who often reduced the sensory-affective dimensions of touch to the dangers of bodily injury. Conversely, Tomkis's *Lingua* and Shakespeare's *Hamlet* expose the theatrics of bodily injury as an altogether too easy way of making touch "speak," and both plays thus evoke the possibility for subtler forms of touch to ground a complex and ethically expansive sense of communal vulnerability. By doing so, the plays gesture toward nonrational dimensions of human experience through which communities could acknowledge a subtext of shared vulnerability without pinning it down discursively or ideologically. With a reading of *Hamlet*, I close by arguing for an "inarticulate Shakespeare" in the most positive senses mapped throughout the book.

One might, obviously, use other sources and methods to explore the conceptual and affective potential of the inarticulate utterance in the Renaissance, so it is worth saying a word about my choice of materials. One might, for example, consult classical texts on the history of speech disorders, which often aligned problems of speech with complex forms of thinking and feeling. In the Hippocratic *Precepts*, which was rediscovered in the Renaissance, "Unclearness of speech (*asaphie glōssēs*) . . . comes from an affection (*pathos*), or from the ears (*ôta*), or from saying other things before saying what has already been thought," or, as a 1595 commentary on Hippocrates reads, "*Irascentes enim balbutiunt* (men growing angry do in fact stutter)."[38] Attending to such diagnostic treatments of speech could offer a way to understand cognitive and affective dimensions of linguistic indistinction, linked here in the Hippocratic tradition with conditions of superflux: speech interrupted by escalating fury, humoral disequilibrium, physiological impairment, or the intrusion of the as-yet-unthought into spoken language. Jeffrey Wollock's *The Noblest Animate Motion: Speech, Physiology, and Medicine in Pre-Cartesian Linguistic Thought* (1997) approximates this approach, but Wollock's study is best understood as a comprehensive *guide* to speech disorders in classical and Renaissance thought that could spark future research into irrational dimensions of thought and feeling often indexed by disordered or disabled speech, not simply in the medical but also in the literary discourses of the Renaissance.[39] On the other hand, such materials offer insight into early conceptions of individual pathology without necessarily shedding light on the larger discursive and social contexts in which inarticulate speech could come to mean something to a larger community.

Another approach would foreground treatments of the rift, in both classical and biblical contexts, between eloquence and wisdom—the ultimate threat to idealizations of rhetoric as a vehicle for intellectual inquiry, prudence, and civic advancement. Within these traditions, the inarticulate could be a mark of wisdom, particularly given the Socratic tradition of learned ignorance[40] and biblical precedents of stammering, incoherent, and prophetic speech.[41] The Neoplatonist Pico della Mirandola, for example, defends speeches "now harsh, now disconnected, [and] always inharmonious" as products of philosophical investigation: "The barbarians have had Mercury [god of eloquence] not on their tongue, but in their breast, and . . . even though they lacked eloquence, they have not been lacking in wisdom."[42] Prioritizing discovery over rhetorical craft, he writes, "We seek *what* to write, not *how*; or rather, we seek how to do so without the pomp and flowers of speech." In Pico's letter to Ermolao Barbaro, barbaric language (from the Greek for unintelligible language of foreign speakers) should sharpen the ears, compelling the listener to move "into the inner sanctuary of the spirit and the retreat of the mind."[43] The utility of inarticulate wisdom, expressly challenged in Cicero's *De inventione* and *De officiis* is recuperated by Pico, who tweaks Cicero's own words to emphasize the disjunction rather than the union of wisdom and eloquence: "The most inarticulate wisdom can be of use; witless [unwise] eloquence, like a sword in the hand of a madman, cannot help but threaten the greatest harm."[44] There is no small dose of humor in this encomium on barbarism composed for Barbaro, but such delight renders Pico's instruction all the more compelling, and his defense of the inarticulate resonates with Paul's emphasis on linguistic incoherence in the face of the divine (Corinthians 2:1–9).[45]

Pico's defense would find strong parallels in Erasmus's *Praise of Folly*, where the speakers who should be taken most seriously are not simply ineloquent but speak "non satis coherentia," or (as Thomas Chaloner rendered it in 1549) "speake certaine thyngis *not hangyng one with an other*, nor after any earthly facion, but rather dooe put foorth a voyce they wote neuer what, muche lesse to be vnderstode of others."[46] "I chose to offend rhetoric," Erasmus famously wrote of his *Folly*, "not to injure piety."[47] Erasmus's theological writings would be especially important were one to pursue this approach to the inarticulate, since in them we so often find the humanist most strongly associated with eloquence and rhetoric turning against his own eloquence and rhetoric in the name of accessing another kind of truth. When Erasmus asks, for example, "What is Philosophy?" in a treatise on reading scripture, the question is less rhetorical than antirhetorical: he goes on to emphasize the limits of rhetorical and logical method for approaching the less expressible "affectes of the minde" necessary for encountering Christ.[48] The profundity of scripture, he writes, "seameth aboue all capacitie" because it requires one to abandon the illusion of power in order to experience it, to "kysse" it, to "dye" in it.[49] Elsewhere, Erasmus lauded the "homely" and often incoherent writings of the Evangelists as well, so he did not simply detach eloquence from the domain of faith but attached ineloquence to it.[50]

One might also approach the inarticulate through recent work in philosophy and literary theory. In their own variant of the question, *What Is Philosophy?* (1991), for example, Gilles Deleuze and Félix Guattari ask, "What is the thought that can only stammer?"[51] Or in an alternate formulation, they position stammering as a prerequisite for thought: "What violence must be exerted on thought for us to be capable of thinking?"[52] For these two philosophers, thinking is predicated on at least a temporary lapse of linguistic coherence, through which even the most learned discourse (following Kleist and Artaud) "begins to exhibit snarls, squeals, stammers; it talks in tongues and screams, which leads it to create, or try to."[53] The dumbfounding dimensions of thought are similarly explored in Avital Ronell's *Stupidity*, which aims to dismantle post-Enlightenment polarizations of judgment and stupidity and follows Paul de Man in recuperating "the stress of not knowing," the "crucial dumbfoundedness" integral to any textual composition or encounter."[54] It is no coincidence that we find Ronell momentarily adopting Erasmus's "Folly" as her persona, as she plays the cannily "dumbfounded" theorist who turns confounded utterance into creative and poetic forms of thought.[55] In a heavily Erasmian formulation, she notes that "interpretation masters interference and the contingencies of textual disturbance. It does not allow for the stammers and stalls that reading . . . necessarily confronts."[56]

All of these alternative approaches, while promising, can easily lead to a transhistorical account of the inarticulate that forecloses certain kinds of inquiry. What might "interference" and the "contingencies of textual disturbance" that inform halted speech look like from a historical perspective? Such approaches can also lead us to neglect what "inarticulate wisdom" or "affectes of the minde" might have looked or sounded like when unhinged from a sacred sense of truth. Rather than turn to contemporary theory,[57] the medical diagnoses of Hippocrates, the Neoplatonism of Pico, the Christian humanism of Erasmus, or even the spiritualism of Augustine, for whom prayer "consists more in groaning than in speaking, in tears rather than in words,"[58] *The Inarticulate Renaissance* historicizes thwarted or indistinct speech in terms of particularly volatile moments within English history and the history of the English language, at a time when distinctions between articulate and inarticulate began to consolidate but faltered in the process. While I resist reifying the inarticulate by examining a *variety* of historical approaches to the problem of spoken language, I attend to the roots of reification in the pathologizing discourse of the period. I examine fictions of pathology, moreover, in order to examine how thoughts and feelings produced at the limit of speech could register larger cultural uncertainties and tensions. In doing so, I argue that Renaissance drama found novel ways to expose the limits of such reification and to approach aspects of the inarticulate in new ways. Finally, by using the term "Renaissance" rather than "early modern," I aim to signal that, in making the topic of the inarticulate "modern" before its time,[59] we risk slighting the specificities of particular contexts of language production and dissemination.[60] We risk missing out on moments in history when the inarticulate, the disjointed, the undistinguished, the incoherent, made a very peculiar kind of sense.

In short, this book aims to think historically about three questions asked by Ronell: "What is unintelligibility? Why does it provoke such (pre-) critical rage? . . . To what extent do we rely upon unintelligibility . . . [and] to what extent does it guarantee and underlie the very conditions of intelligibility?"[61] By examining specific instances within Renaissance religious, humanist, legal, print, medical, and antitheatrical culture that codified particular forms of speech as incoherent and ineffective, I show how such codifications managed to create fictions of internal coherence. Drama, by contrast, often thrived precisely by exposing fictions of coherence (and the fictions of incoherence that helped to define them), and by mobilizing apparently inarticulate and ineffectual forms of utterance in ways that opened up new forms of expression and audition.

At the same time, we might invert Ronell's formulation in order to ask ourselves, in the present day, "What is intelligibility? Why does it provoke such (pre-) critical rage? . . . . To what extent do we rely upon intelligibility . . . to what extent does it guarantee and underlie the very conditions of unintelligibility?" To close my Introduction in the present tense, or what Marjorie Garber has called the "tense present"—when the status of literary study is under pressure to define its methods and aims in new ways—I want to consider the forms of "rage" that might be embedded in our own resistance to forms of disciplinary *intelligibility*.[62] Within the literary and rhetorical history of the past three decades, cultural models of eloquence that purport to guarantee cultural authority and moral transformation have often been exposed as hopelessly idealistic. For Anthony Grafton and Lisa Jardine, Renaissance humanism's limits as a socially operative program leading to virtuous personhood, ethical citizenship, and political transformation gave rise to the humanities as they inform our institutions today.[63] So, too, the ideologies of power and privilege integral to social divisions based upon speech performance have come under fire in literary scholarship inspired by various strains of deconstruction, cultural materialism, feminism, historical epistemology, and the ethical and political criticism of postcolonialism. Rather than direct our rage against the intelligible toward, for example, an abstract ethos of indeterminacy, we might go back to moments in history in which the intelligible was set against other kinds of meanings.[64] For these meanings were not simply reducible to the collapse of determinacy or to the violent "transgression" of cultural norms but could, in the best of worlds, evoke a more inclusive and ethically capacious form of "humanism" than we might otherwise imagine.[65]

CHAPTER ONE

The Renaissance of Mumbling

Latinity, Reformation Polemic, and the Mother Tongue

Mum, mum, mum, mum.
    —Thomas Tomkis, *Lingua* (c. 1602)

WHILE PHENOMENA SUCH as slips of the tongue, aphasia, glossolalia, stutter-ing, stammering, and talking to oneself have all been integrated into a range of historical and theoretical approaches to language use and communication, mumbling has been largely neglected as a subject of investigation. In many ways, this is no surprise, given that mumbling itself typically resists "capture"; it involves a domain of linguistic and acoustical self-reference that is constitu-tionally resistant to context and clear reference. The epigraph above from a late Tudor play simply suggests how difficult it is to *represent* mumbling on stage in a way that suggests anything more than the absorption of speech into the speaker's own mouth. "Mum, mum, mum, mum" is absurdly onomatopo-etic, suggesting that mumbling lacks content even for the speaker. But the difficult question of "mumbling" became an important topic of religious con-troversy in Tudor England. The social and religious history of mumbling can help us understand the significance of indistinct utterance on stage. It can help us, more specifically, to respond to a central question of the next chap-ter: What is Madge Mumblecrust, a character named for her habits of speech, doing in the landmark drama, *Ralph Roister Doister* (c. 1550–53, printed 1566), composed by the humanist educator and religious reformer Nicholas Udall? In order to approach this question, let us examine the centrality of pronunciation in both humanist and Reformation contexts and the particular status of "mumbling" as a central keyword and concept in religious debate.

Mumbling: On Public-Private Utterance

What kind of speech is better than that which is open, clear, and distinct?
—John Jewel, *Oratio contra Rhetoricam* (c. 1548)[1]

The Protestant Reformation and the humanist revival of classical rhetoric in England had in common a vivid concern with bad pronunciation. Pronunciation was the fifth division of rhetoric, dealing with vocal and bodily modulation, and it was an important focus of reformers aiming to facilitate communicative clarity and social uniformity in liturgical practice. John Jewel, the classical humanist and Protestant reformer, seems to ask a rather simple question in the treatise on rhetoric cited above: "What kind of speech is better than that which is open, clear, and distinct?" But if the question is rhetorical, the implications in Tudor England involved a network of more difficult questions about theology, sociology, and the linguistic coordinates of selfhood and social participation. To begin, we might note just how capacious the category of "pronunciation" was. If we think about the idea of a "renaissance," or rebirth, of concerns about indistinct pronunciation, classical and biblical precedents abound. Demosthenes, for example, as Thomas Wilson put it in *The Arte of Rhetorique* (1553), who was "not able to pro-pronounce the first letter of that Arte whiche he professed, but would say, for, Rhethorique, Letolike," inspired would-be orators by overcoming a "tongue vnreadie and obscure," a voice "childishe and small," and a constitutional "bashfulnesse and shamefastnesse."[2] In sociolinguistic terms, we may recall Cicero, as adapted by Wilson and others in Tudor England, and his corrective attention to rustic, regional, and foreign "mispronunciation" in late republican Rome.[3] Or in Reformation theology that drew on early Latin Christianity, we find consistent attention to the importance of clear pronunciation in the transmission and reception of the Word.[4] In sixteenth-century approaches to the spoken Word, however, we also find an acute awareness of one form of flawed enunciation without classical or biblical precedent: the phenomenon of *mumbling*.

In his *Apologia Ecclesiae Anglicanae* (1562), Jewel reconfigured the question mentioned above as a direct challenge not to the limits of rhetorical pretense decried in the *Oratio* but to the limits of rhetorical pretense operative in the Catholic liturgy. For Jewel, the use of Latin by Catholic clergy, alongside the ritual of quietly uttering prayers over the Eucharist, was antithetical to "open, clear, and distinct" speech. As the 1564 translation reads: "The aucient Emperour Iustinian commaunded, that in the holy administration all thinges should be pronounced with a cleare, lowde, and tretable voyce, that ye people might receiue some fruite therby. These menn [Catholic priests] least the people shoulde vnderstande them, mumble vp all their seruice, not onlye with a drowned and hollowe voice, but also in a straunge and Barbarous tonge."[5] As glossed here, to "mumble vp" suggests acoustical submersion, tonal and affective emptiness, and estranging (ecclesiastical Latin) elocution: language swallowed at the moment of utterance, sound resisting transmission in the "holy administration" of the Word.

Unlike frequently diagnosed speech problems in the ancient and Renaissance medical traditions, mumbling in Reformation polemic was aligned less with involuntary disfluency than with presumptions of agency ("least the people should vnderstand them") and volitional obfuscation.[6] To the extent that Catholic priests were aligned with mumbling, it thus came to suggest a form of passive aggressivity on an institutional scale. Conversely, for parishioners repeating prayers in a language that they did not know, the mumbling that reformers cast as mere sounds suggested a form of mindless iteration or ignorant mimesis. At the same time, unlike the minimally audible but secretive "murmuring" (as in the famous "murmurings," or collective complaints, of the Israelites in Exodus 16:7–8), "mumbling" in Protestant invective often implied sound without coherent content, thus without the apparent power of a secret. The specific English phrase "mumble vp" was first used by William Tyndale in 1528 in reference to Catholic liturgical utterance, and it surfaces in the 1564 translation of Jewel's *Apologia*, cited above, to render the verb *mussitant*.[7] "Mussitant" (from *mussare* and the iterative *mussitare*, meaning to grumble or mutter) suggests a close enough equivalent or precursor to "mumble,"[8] but the translation created a heated debate about the stakes of the word.

In early English translations of the Bible, God's words never included "mumbling." Even if we consider possible equivalents, no translation from the Wycliffite Bible to the King James Bible renders variants of the Vulgate's *mussare, mussitare, murmurare* (to murmur), and *muttire* (to mutter), or variants from the Greek, as "mumble."[9] Nor is "mumble vp" as glossed in Jewel's text above *precisely* equivalent to these terms in classical rhetoric. But the Germanic "to mumble" (and the close French *marmonner*) gained unusual currency among reformers challenging the spoken language in Catholic liturgical practice, where the word carried a seemingly minor but, as we will see, potent charge in excess of the Latin terms above.[10] The fact that "mumbling" was never used in biblical translation made it all the more effective as a term to describe the linguistic practices of those who allegedly *departed* from scripture, from the meaning of God's Word, in the act of speech. Reformers as diverse as Zwingli, Luther, Calvin, Tyndale, Hugh Latimer, John Bale, Thomas Becon, Anne Bacon, and others aimed to develop and endorse practical theologies antithetical to what was called, with startling regularity, "mumbling." Seemingly a tiny word in the great flood of Reformation polemic, "mumbling," referencing that odd and often comically portrayed problem of unintelligible speech, became a key term in Reformation satire and delegitimation.

Combining inaudibility, incomprehensibility, and undistinguished syllable formation, mumbling suggested (at best) inaccessible content, (at worst) no content, and (either way) a passive or active resistance to norms of community and communicability. "To mumble" often implied a mind wandering in the process of speech, a species of selfhood not properly subject to the Word. While focusing on the comic potential of mumbling, this chapter will also ask how this form of incommunicative utterance implied, enabled, or—through polemic—disabled a variant of selfhood quite different from rhetorically eloquent or plain "Renaissance self-fashioning."[11] From this perspective, mumbling was part of the ever-expanding, ever-contested story about the "rise of the individual" in the Renaissance.[12] Also, given the inescapably oral inflection of "mumbling" that made the word so often a term of abuse within heavily literate communities, it was part of the story about how oral and textual cultures were understood, differentiated, and defined in Tudor theological and, ultimately, dramatic contexts.

But to start with a simple point: the Reformation idealization of vernacular plainness as a vehicle of scriptural and liturgical translation found its diabolical antitype in ecclesiastical Latin mumbling. Church mumbling, set apart from the classical Latin of humanism, became all the more evacuated as a "common" language of religion through Reformation polemic. As in Jewel's comment, mumbling was understood to involve vices of elocution (word choice) as well as pronunciation (delivery), thus easily absorbing charges of pre-Christian "barbarism" and what Hugh Latimer, bishop of Worcester, called anti-Christian "bybble bable."[13] Elocution was as important as pronunciation in the phenomenon of unintelligible and curiously public-private utterance, particularly given that the distinctly vernacular resonance of "mumbling," a homegrown, everyday, and clearly non-Latinate word, gave it all the more purchase in the Reformation word battle against the "mumbling masses"[14] of Catholic Latinity.

It is worth attending to this point at the outset, examining the volatility of the word itself in a debate over Jewel's *Apologia*, one of many texts that argued that reformed vernacular religion was not in fact new but on a continuum with the writings of early church fathers. The *Apologie* was published in both Latin and English in 1562,[15] thereby aiming to reach a broad readership throughout Europe and within England, and was quickly followed by a revised translation by Lady Anne Bacon (mother of Francis Bacon) in 1564. Bacon's 1564 translation occasioned a vigorous response by the Catholic apologist Thomas Harding, who, in the process of chastizing Jewel for misunderstanding Justinian, misreading scripture, and debasing the sacred languages of Greek, Latin, and Hebrew, raised the knotty issue of word choice: "The third lie is, in that they saie, we do whisper al our Seruice, *so is the Latine, albeit this good Lady liketh better the terme of mumblinge*."[16] This particular "terme" comes from a vernacular idiom that Harding sees as distant from the "mystical tongue" of church Latin and the learned tongue of Justinian's Latin. He associates it with the "common prophane tongue" "moste vsed of the vulgare sorte," perhaps implicitly (through the "good Lady" translator) the gendered mother tongue (515). Bacon's translation was fully sanctioned by Jewel, and thus Harding's pejorative "good Lady" aims at two birds with one stone: it challenges Bacon's lexicon but also Jewel's defense of the vernacular's authority over the Word. Harding, in other words, turns the non-Latinate "mumblinge" against itself to encapsulate the distance between Jewel's vernacular theology and early Christian precedents, emphasizing that mumbling is a matter of *English*, not "the Latine."

This signals the huge potential of a backfire of mumbling as a strictly anti-Catholic, anti-Latin term of abuse. For Reformation polemic doubled as a form of self-defense about the vulnerable status of the English tongue, which could itself, as Harding suggests, be said to mumble; it could pose problems of intelligibility in the formation and establishment of common prayer. Let us notice just how close a reader Harding was: he seems to have spotted *the* single substantive change made from the 1562 translation of the two sentences cited above, where the 1562 "whysper" ("so is the Latine," as it appears in Jewel's original "summissa uoce" and "mussitant") is revised to the 1564 "mumble vp."[17] But Bacon knew her Latin, and was one of the most learned women in England at the time; her liking "better the terme of mumblinge" was very much in line with Reformation polemic, not to mention the spirit of Jewel's invective.[18] Harding's quibble with this word provoked Jewel to respond in a marginal gloss: "*Vntruthe For M Hard. Owne Councelles express it by . . . *Murmurare*" (515). While *murmurare* is a biblical and fully classical Ciceronian term, meaning to murmur in a low-pitched voice,[19] it was not actually the original word translated from Jewel's text, and had neither quite the inflection of combining "a straunge and Barbarous tonge" with "a drowned and hollowe voice" nor the vernacular charge antithetical to Catholic Latin. The word "murmuring" was commonly deployed, as we will see in the next chapter, as a sign of conspiracy, implying consciously muted though internally comprehensible sedition. But the course of true translation never did run smooth, least of all in Tudor theology.[20] The big battle over small words for Harding and Jewel clearly indexes the struggle of both Catholic and Reformation theologians to ground authority in texts. Debates over theology were equally cast in terms of debates about philology and rhetoric; as early as the Middle Ages the "substitutive structure" of vernacular exegesis, as Rita Copeland has put it, represented "the mastery and appropriation of a privileged discourse."[21]

It is important, however, that Jewel's response to Harding redirects the charge by grounding Protestant invective not in the Cicero of his earlier training and teaching or in the scriptural "murmurers" of his preaching and study but in more recent Catholic Latinity: "*These woordes,* Whisperinge, and Mumblinge, *mislike you mutche, Yet your owne frendes, intreatinge hereof, haue often vsed the same woordes*" (516). Jewel again cites "murmurent" in "your late Councel of Colaine [Cologne]," then implicitly defends Bacon's translation by rendering the term as "mumble vp."[22] If, as Harding points out, these are not *exactly* the "same woordes," what is at stake is the much larger issue of English as a medium of translation, and the difficulty for Jewel of using Latin texts (as his many critics pointed out)[23] from early Christianity in that process of justification. *"Notwithstanding* . . . Whisperinge, or Mumblinge, *or by what so euer name els it shal please you to call it,"* writes Jewell, reestablishing the distance between Protestant English and Catholic Latin, *"ye shoulde so vtter al thinges in the Congregation, Distinctely and Plainely, with lowde, and Open Voice, that the people might vnderstande you, and answeare* Amen. . . . Blessed is the people, that vnderstandeth, what they singe" (516–17). Further raising the pitch by citing Ambrose on the importance of "lowde" volume, he adds: "The Singinge togeather of Menne, *Wemen,* Maides, and litle Children, the Churche [should] soundeth, as if it were the dasshinge of the Sea" (517). The italicized *"Wemen"* alongside the inclusion of "Maides" swiftly counters the exclusionary logic operative in both the offensive "this good Lady liketh better the terme of mumblinge" and, more broadly, the use of liturgical Latin so often said to be antithetical to the democratizing drive of Reformation vernacularism. If the mother tongue is "vulgar," so be it, Jewel implies, since it was crucial for a larger social project that aimed to level out social difference in matters of the Word.[24] "Doctrine," as he emphasizes again and again, should be *"knowen, not onely of them, that are the* Doctours *of the Churche, and the* Maisters *of the people, but also euen of the* Tailers, *and* Smithes, *and* Weauers, *and of al* Artificers: *Yea, and further also of* Weemen: *and that, not onely of them, that be Learned, but also of* Labouringe Weemen, *and* Sewsters, *and* Seruantes, *and* Handemaìdes. *Neither onely the* Citizens, *but also the* Countriefolkes *doo very wel vnderstande the same. Yee maie finde, yea, euen the very* Dichers, *and* Deluers, *and* Cowheardes, *and* Gardiners Disputinge of the Holy Trinitie, and of the Creation of al things" (507). Clearly echoing Erasmus's *Paraclesis* (1516),[25] which was appended to Tyndale's translation of the New Testament, while attributing the sentiment to the church father Bishop Theodoretus (c. 393–457), Jewel offers yet more Catholic precedents for vernacular theology.

The fuss over single "woordes" such as "mumbling" thus situates the question of devotional utterance within a nexus of tensions about precedent as well as gender, rank, philology, ideology, and the linguistic coordinates of a proper devotional community. Jewel's initial response alone, however, in which he grounds his anti-Catholic rhetoric in intra-Catholic debate, is important in another way. Jewel alludes not to classical or biblical precedents but to another prehistory of Reformation mumbling, namely, the mumbling in Catholic approaches to what it meant to be a good and proper liturgical subject. When Jewel writes that when St. Jerome *"forged the* Rule of Monkes . . .

[he] *chargeth them in any wise to pronounce euery woorde distinctely, and war-*
ily, leste by theire foolishe vtterance they shoulde make the Angelles to falle a
laughinge" (742), we see him co-opting Catholic approaches to the importance of diligent pronunciation in devotional utterance. As we begin to examine the seriocomic logic of mumbling, we might note that the production of
"laughinge" was no small side effect within such serious debates, not least because mumbling had an onomatopoetic (undistinguished noise-making)
function that emphasized the spiritually perilous but also ridiculous facet of
"copying" mere sounds.[26] Further, the semantic range of mumbling, which
long included the process of ineffectual eating as well as ineffectual speaking,[27] added to vividly embodied accounts of Catholics unable to digest the
Word through the Mass and unable to digest the Spirit through the Eucharis-
tic bread, or what Erasmus called the errant "dreame of corporall foode."[28] As
an extension of this, mumbling also figured in satires of Catholic parishioners
given only bread without wine to wash it down. Mumbling as a process of
pronunciation (again, involving vocal and bodily modulation) thus looked
rather grotesque: lips and tongue detached from mind and heart, sound production at odds with the experience or expression of thought and feeling.
Nicholas Udall's Madge Mumblecrust—a character who utters Latin prayers
to God, eats dry bread and speaks at the same time, compromising effective
chewing and speaking at once, and whose speech leads a character in the play
to say, "What?"—may seem, at least on first glance, an incarnation of strictly
anti-Catholic polemic.

But Udall moves beyond such polarizing polemic, granting Madge Mumblecrust a good bit more agency in the process. Thus we might consider the
more complex processes involving the use of non- or quasi-representational
terms in spoken utterance. Focusing on the process of mumbling is difficult,
particularly given the longstanding cultural bias toward the articulate and rationalized subject. Such a bias is implicit, for example, in eighteenth-century
guides to religious rhetoric and devotional pronunciation,[29] in a nineteenth-
century psychiatric treatise entitled *Classification, Training, and Education of the*
Feeble-Minded, Imbecile, & Idiotic, where "Mumbling, stuttering, hesitating and
low speaking should be guarded against,"[30] and even in a late twentieth-century
critical approach to *King Lear,* where the king's impassioned speech is reduced
to "demented mumbling."[31] Nor is Robert Burton's 1621 *Anatomy of Melancholy*
much help, with the "mumbling of [rosary] beads" aligned with "bables" and
"gibberish" antithetical to mature, plain-speaking, heartfelt devotion.[32] But if

approached as more than a bodily or infantile process, mumbling may be seen to open up potential for accessing tacit as well as culturally marginalized forms of knowledge otherwise occluded by the articulate speech of the "self-fashioned" sociolinguistic subject. As the Russian Formalist Viktor Shklovsky once noted in emphasizing the power of the "trans-sense" impact of sonorous transmission, what may seem to be ecclesiastical nonsense can translate directly into overpowering sensation and individualized comprehension: "I have seen how simple people can be moved to tears by holy books in Church Slavonic although they understand nothing."[33] Shklovsky, here citing a contemporary writer, adds that "sensations of the sound aspect of words" can evoke "particular feeling and a particular understanding of these words independent of the words' objective meaning" (12). The doubly emphasized "particular" and "independent" suggest important keywords for aiming to apprehend individualized involvement in what may otherwise seem a form of institutional dependence and noncommunication. At the same time, Shklovsky, a central reference point for twentieth-century experimental language poetry, may eventually help us shed light on the sonorous dimensions of words that operated quite differently from semantic sense-making in the formation of much earlier, and not only Latin but also distinctly English, communities of sound.

More recently, drawing on Michael Polanyi's conception of tacit knowledge, two scholars of heuristics have pointed out that the activities of "staring, moving, mumbling, doodling, and noise prove to be highly generative because they bridge the gap between tacit ways of knowing and verbal, articulate knowledge."[34] Turning the tables on twentieth-century pedagogical theory, Toby Fulwiler and Bruce Petersen argue that signs of incomplete participation or even nonparticipation in discursive communities have the potential for approaching problems in innovative and original ways. "The activity of mumbling," for example, "prolongs word-search and increases the chances for original solutions," signaling a form of cognition with an extended temporal duration.[35] Despite the difficulty of subjecting "mumbling" to "articulate knowledge," examining how the very idea of mumbling *others* could bolster, by opposition, fantasies of "articulate knowledge" can help us to explore tensions within competing language practices and ideologies as they led, on the one hand, to vigorous polemic and, on the other, to dramatic innovation in Tudor England, where mumbling took on relatively productive, expressive, residually (and not simply anti-) Catholic dimensions.[36]

Syllable Thieves: Catholic Latin and the Protestant Humanist

Mumbling, now often read as a mark of shyness, preoccupation, shame, or even passive aggressivity,[37] had, as has already been suggested, more charged meanings in the devotional contexts of medieval and Renaissance England. In late medieval England, mumbling could imperil the soul. In medieval folklore and drama, a character named Titivillus was said to collect mumbles in a bag: unspoken *fragmina verborum*. These were scraps of syllables and words "ouer-skyp[ed]" by preachers and parishioners who mumbled sacred language and angered God.[38] We are told in the early fifteenth-century devotional guide, *Jacob's Well*, of a "holy man" standing in a church choir, who saw this "feend beryyng a gret sachett full of thyng."[39] Asking after the contents of the bag, the fiend responds, " 'I bere in my sacche sylablys & worrdys, ourskypped and synkopyd, and verse & psalmys the which these clerkys han stolyn in the queere [choir], & haue fayled in here seruyse' " (114). The criminalized theft of syllables here draws from an earlier account in Jacques de Vitry's *Sermones Vulgares* (c. 1220), where the mumble-catcher adds explicitly that these sounds are "stolen from God: you can be sure I am keeping these diligently for their accusation."[40] Similar diligence embodied in this figure of acoustical copy-editing is recorded in another early fifteenth-century devotional text, *The Myrroure of Oure Lady*, where "Tytyuyllus" gathers up "a thousande pokes full of faylynges" each day "of neglygences in syllables and wordes / that ar done . . . in redynge and in syngynge," that, whether produced through haste, ignorance, or distraction, become "proof" for his master, the devil, of spiritual negligence to be reckoned with in the afterlife.[41]

In these cases, with evidence of criminality wedded to the "ouerskypped," the omitted, and the unspoken, we have a vivid fantasy of transmission exactly where transmission is most compromised. As John of Wales wrote earlier in his *Tractatus de Poenitentia* (c. 1285), "Fragmina verborum Titivillus colligit horum / Quibus die mille vicibus se sarcinat ille."[42] Collecting a thousand sackfulls of verbal scraps a day suggests Titivillus had his hands full, both encouraging and preserving all manner of linguistic negligence, sins of syllabic and lexical omission, to reproduce for "moterers and mumlers,"[43] or imperfect speakers, on Judgment Day. In some accounts, such as the Towneley Judgment play, Titivillus collected not only mumbled or skipped units but also evidence of "church chatter," including gossip, slander, lies, and idle talk.[44] It is no surprise that in one account his sack tore and burst, sending him tumbling in the middle of a sermon. Titivillus's relationship to idle church gossip has been the subject of recent medieval scholarship, but the equally powerful and in many ways antithetical idea he represents about *nontransmitted* speech deserves further consideration.[45] What is striking about Titivillus is not simply the material heft of sound he lugs about but the fact that what he collects is not limited to the said but includes, in the case of sacred mumbling, *the unsaid*. The weight of the "unsaid," that category of discourse that has become so central to contemporary philosophy, psychoanalysis, and cultural studies, finds a striking early incarnation in Titivillian mythology. In this case, however, the unsaid is subject to vivid capture, and preserved for release at a future moment.[46]

The image of the freshly dead confronted with a massive heap of disarticulated sounds that they *should* have said on earth vies with the well-known Rabelaisian fantasy of spoken language freezing in winter and thawing in spring, melting into sounds such as "hin, hin, hin, hin, his, tick, tock, crack, brededin, brededac, frr, frrr, frrr, bou, bou, bou, bou, bou, bou, bou, track, track, trrr, trrr, trrr, trrrrrr," and so on, in the absence of speakers and the presence of new listeners.[47] While Rabelais' sonic thaw here indexes the temporal effect of words spoken coming back to haunt speakers in contexts beyond their control, the fantasy of Titivillus expands the temporality of speech well beyond the seasonal calendar, with the twist of capturing those "syllables and wordes" lost in the moment of speech. The spectacular return of the unsaid in the domain of final judgment not only codes uncareful textual selection ("ouerrskypp[ing]") as morally perilous but also makes "bad" pronunciation a species of sin. This eschatology of mumbles was enough to haunt even, or especially, the most earnest of speakers, who in this early context would have been priests, nuns, and largely illiterate parishioners relying on the difficult medium of liturgical (or church) Latin. While for some the sheer velocity of speeding through psalms in a habitual manner could be taken to imply a failure of deliberation, thoughtfulness, and devotional respect, for others, who had minimal or no facility with Latin, mispronunciation or misunderstanding could lead straight into the clutches of Titivillus. *The Myrroure of Oure Lady* was a guide to Latin liturgical practice composed for nuns at Syon Abbey, with English translations to help them comprehend the significance of Latin texts. This text, as Rebecca Krug puts it, insists on "verbal accuracy" as a prerequisite for full "spiritual understanding."[48] Or as the *Myrroure* puts it, the Lord's Prayer must be "cut in gobbetts / for all the wordes and syllables oughte to be sayd dystynctely from the begynnynge vnto the ende": if speakers wittingly or unwittingly "clyppe away . . . eny wordes or letters or syllables / & so false yt from the trew sentence / or from the trewe maner of saynge therof deserue to be greuously punysshed agenste god" (F2r).

Following Krug and others, we might note here the disciplinary attention focused on regulating female speech, down to the syllable, within the institution of the church.[49] At the same time, however, the emphasis here on precise and heartfelt enunciation, so often understood as a hallmark of Reformation devotional practice, is equally significant in this earlier Catholic context. A Tudor book of Protestant devotional commonplaces reads: "We may become like vnto God, as farforth as the weake nature of man can beare. But the likenesse cannot be without knowledge, neither is knowledge without doctrine, and the beginnyng of doctrine is speache: and the partes of speache, be wordes and sillables."[50] This Protestant commonplace was once a Catholic commonplace drawn from St. Basil, and both were relevant for men as well as women. The author of *Jacob's Well* addresses his readers as "syres" and "freendys" and writes of the clergy as well as the (nongendered) "peple," or parishioners, in the account of the demon of mumbles filling up his sack;[51] and when Thomas Betson, a brother at Syon, helped bring the *Myrroure* into print in London in 1530, the text was issued not simply for nuns but "*for all relygyous persons*," including lay readers. The broadened stakes of enunciation from nuns to "all" churchgoers were already emphasized by Betson, whose own *Ryght Profytable Treatyse* (1500), an English/Latin guide to devotion for "men" universally, not only urges all worshipers to "Remembre also yf yu hast ouerskypped in the seruyce of god ony wordes / verses / or ony Inclynacyons" (A5v) but also offers a prayer designed to redeem the souls of those who "vnderstande not theyr seruyce in latyne" yet speak it anyway.[52] In this respect, Titivillus exemplified an imperative for linguistic accuracy and comprehension that, in the context of an unlearned laity, was deemed constantly to reach its limit: hence his thousand trips a day, and an afterworld packed with fragmina verborum.

But such a figure within Catholic tradition poses a further question about the said: What are we to make of a kind of language use that manages to "unsay" the thing said, that signifies "vndeuocyon" if uttered improperly or without understanding?[53] And if God is as concerned with the unsaid as the said, in what language should one speak to say it "all," and to say it well? There's little more daunting than the prospect of speaking with the best of intentions to a God who does not hear or understand; thus the specter of mumbling became a potent tool for emphasizing the dangers of the nonreciprocal, and thus nondevotional, devotional utterance. Indeed, the eschatological stakes of pronunciation in these opening examples are highlighted, in part, simply to spark curiosity into the conceptual potential of one species of lapsed articulation:[54] mumbled words as they may have circulated within communal as well as individualized scenes of worship. But sacred eschatology is one thing, social etiology another: for how would one even go about historicizing, or thinking about, the mumble? The fact that Titivillus typically wrote down his verbal errors on a *scroll* adds to the impossible fantasy of capturing verbal indistinction in writing. (In several accounts, his scroll is simply too narrow for the diligent recording of sonic error, and he attempts to stretch the scroll with his teeth with such an effort that he bangs his own head against a wall.)[55] Mumbling is, in other words, difficult to historicize, never mind record, without eschatological perspective as a guide. Like other aspects of the "inarticulate" examined in this book, mumbling is interesting, Titivillus shows, because, unlike silence, it registers a form of spoken language resistant to established communal or communicative contexts. If to keep mum is to be silent, to mumble is to perform a spoken resistance (witting or no) to being heard: one typically mumbles to oneself, not to others, thus becoming the object and subject of one's speech.[56]

To complicate further the idea that mumbling primarily served to code and control speech within Reformation as well as Catholic contexts, we might turn to another moment in Rabelais that demonstrates the broader cultural and eschatological resonance of the term, as well as the comedic potential of mumbling ("marmorrent") while speaking to another—especially when that other is God. Monks, in Thomas Urquhart's translation of *Gargantua*, "mumble out great store of Legends and Psalmes, by them not at all understood: they say many *patenotres,* interlarded with *ave-maries,* without thinking upon, or apprehending the meaning of what it is they say, which truly I call mocking of God, and not prayers."[57] In addition to Titivillus's focus on mispronounced Latin, here Latin prayer itself equips monks only to mock the God they speak to, leaving devotional sincerity outside the scope of the said. This is quickly elaborated on as Friar John, defending himself against charges of idle and ineffectual prayer, says that while "dispatching our matines and anniversaries [for the dead] in the quire; I make withal some crossebowe-strings, polish glasse-bottles and boults; I twist lines and weave purse-nets, wherein to catch coneys; I am never idle; but now hither come, some drink, some drink"

(181–82). So much for Latin prayers for the dead. Adding insult to idleness, a sonic equivalent of "blockish mumbling" (93) emerges as flatulence: wine and chestnuts are sure to make one (says John) an admirably "fine cracker and composer of bumsonnets" (182).

If in the beginning there was nonsense, such an end is no surprise. From eschatology to scatology, the ends of ecclesiastical Latin backfire in one way or another. "A monk in Rabelais," Bakhtin once wrote, "is first and foremost a glutton and a drunkard."[58] But beyond the Rabelaisian carnivalesque, the reduction of Catholic persons to unbecoming, ill-defined bodies and sounds became commonplace in prose and dramatic satire composed by reformers attempting to wrest the Word from the clutches of ecclesiastical Latin. In order to demonstrate the excesses of anti-Catholic polemic, the Counter-Reformation apologist Friedrich Staphylus cites Luther, who wrote of "a certain priest being wel tipled, saieng his complet in his bead, and spetting, as he praied, letted also a greate farte: well quôd he, Diuell such praier, such frankensence. The like maye be saide of all their mumbling in churches and monasterys. For they can not praie nor wil not praie, nor know not what to praie, nor how to praie."[59] Staphylus was not pleased with Luther's story: his marginal gloss, "on the ciuility of Luthers Spirit," offers rhetorical understatement to counter Luther's style. But what we see in these small moments from Rabelais and Luther is the Titivillian capture of "unsaid" scraps at the interstices of utterance and belief being converted to wholesale culture capture: the "unsaid" accomplished precisely through the saying of it, proper pronunciation or no. Church Latin, that is, encodes multiple forms of theft: words and syllables stolen from God and, in Reformation contexts, stolen also from parishioners, who "can not praie nor wil not praie, nor know not what to praie, nor how to praie."

The initially Catholic concern with ecclesiastical Latin pronunciation and heartfelt utterance became, in Reformation contexts, integral to inter-Christian warfare. The mumble, that index of a fracture at the heart of God's "imagined community," emerged as a ubiquitous feature of sixteenth-century invective, with Latin in the mouths of Catholic priests, monks, and parishioners consistently reduced to what the influential reformer Thomas Becon called "mumbling masses."[60] The stakes were not small, since the ultimate imagined auditor was God. In Thomas Chaloner's 1549 translation of Erasmus's *Moriae Encomium*, Folly remarks on the liturgical mumbling and buzzing that separates language from the "hert": "Howe priestes muste be free from all worldlinesse, to passe on nothyng els, sauyng heauenly treasure. But sooner at these daies my *Iolie sir Iohns* doe take it for a sufficient furniture of their roomes, as longe as they mumble ouer theyr *portes seruice*, thei care not how rasshely, whiche (on my faith) I wonder what god heareth, or vnderstandeth? seeyng they them selues dooe almost neither heare, nor wote [know] what they saie, whan only with theyr lippes thei make a certaine buszyng, no whitte procedyng from the hert" (P3v). Coming close to Titivillus's concern with the eschatology of the mumble, the Englished Erasmus collects incomprehensible mumbles (his verb, *permurmurarint*)[61] in a book if not a bag for a kind of final judgment: "I wonder what god heareth, or vnderstandeth?" With less wonder and more directness, Calvin would inhabit the place of that imagined auditor; it is "not to delite God with singing and wyth mumbling not vnderstanded."[62]

When Thomas Key, a Tudor cleric and translator of Erasmus's paraphrase on Mark, composed a preface to Mark that attributes the Catholic practice of "mumbling of psalms not underst[oo]d" to a "doctrine of Antichristes inuencion, and not of god," he typified Reformation complaints about Catholic rituals and the use of Latin prayer.[63] But "inuention" is, of course, always mediated by languages, practices, and interpretive frameworks, and what is at stake here is no less than the proper language through which to discover, apprehend, and disseminate the secrets of God. Erasmus's Englished *Paraphrase* on the Gospels (1548), patronized by Katherine Parr and edited by Nicholas Udall, was ordered by injunctions of both Edward VI and Elizabeth to be purchased and present in all parishes in England.[64] Here we find the earlier concerns of Titivillus now a weapon in the hands of reformers, who absorb the imperative to notice and "capture" in print the vices of "unsaying" or "mumbling" integral to ecclesiastical Latin usage. In a text published five years earlier, *Yet a course at the Romyshe foxe* (1543), the Protestant polemicist and anti-Catholic playwright John Bale upbraids "mattens mongers, masse momblers, holy water swyngers, and euensong clatterers" who "exyle the gospel" and damn those duped into believing "without vnderstandynge."[65] Ecclesiastical Latin becomes "latyne wawlynge" (3r), "Romyshe rablementes" (9r), "latyne jabberynge" (43v) and "moche bablynge, and lyppe labour," for it is "madnesse to vtter a processe in an vnknowne language amonge the peple . . . makynge Gods commaundements of non effecte" (24v). The power of "non effecte," or of ineffectual speech to undo divine effects, which gets at the heart of Reformation concerns about the Latin Mass, turns comic for Bale as Catholic priests, consecrating the bread and wine, convert a common and symbolic experience into a "brekefast of [their] owne deuysynge": with "arses to the peple," they speak with literal indirection, "to the walles, wyndowes, aulter clothes, and Ydols in a foren language whych the more part of yow vnderstaundeth not" (61r).

Positioned in light of the famously postulated "rise of the individual" in early modern England and Europe, mumbling certainly stands as a humbling variant, suggesting less a rise than a *fall* of the individual into minimally communicable, even heretical selfhood.[66] Anxieties about mumbling can thus be understood to mark a range of cultural concerns about individuals operating within communal contexts. The process of praying in a foreign or "mystical tongue," though defended by Catholics as enabling spiritual agency, individualized expression, *and* communal participation, could easily be reduced by Rabelais' Friar John, Erasmus's "sir Iohns," Becon's "mumbling masses," and Bale's "masse momblers" to mere bodily emissions, dissociated from the heart. In this form, they are comically ineffectual products of misguided devotion. While mumbling in public can be peculiarly embarrassing, leaving, as it does, a speaker alone in the midst of potential communication, its historical alignment in Reformation England with collective Catholic expression suggested a more shared embarrassment and shame, where the specter of errant mimesis seemed antithetical to both heartfelt and communal prayer. As we will see in the next section, which focuses on excess rhyme as a potential form of errant mimesis and noise-making, English reformers themselves often made an awful lot of noise in the name of battling against it. By doing so, they unwittingly implicated themselves and their mother tongue in the very departures from direct and referential speech with which they took issue. Attending to problems of plain and scripturally based speech within Protestant contexts will bring us closer to the logic of disavowal informing anti-Catholic polemic in the first place.

On Rhyme and Protestant Bibliocentricity

This specter of ineffectual Catholic mumbling, implying not only linguistic opacity but also tonal exclusivity (that is, failures of both elocution and pronunciation), clearly bolsters Protestant self-definition, implicitly valorizing plain speech as an index of devotional sincerity and uplifting English translation as a key to providing communal access to God's "inuention." Hugh Latimer, comparing "hypocriticall babblyng, speakyng many wordes to littel purpose" to the convoluted language of dishonest lawyers, emphasizes the use of simple speech in prayer to avoid false advocacy of the self in the eyes of God: "It is better to say [the Lord's Prayer] sententiously one time than to runne it over an hundreth tymes with humblynge and mumbling."[67] Here we have an ideal of spoken language that hinges on "sententious" representation, on the capacity of words to signify particular and purposive mental concepts. But the ritual function of repetition and rhyme in Latin prayer was crucial to establishing a form of communion that often hinged on something quite different from "sententious" brevity or semantic accuracy. As Ann Moss has written of liturgical Latin, as opposed to humanist Latin: "[Ecclesiastical] Latin functions as a semiological as much as a semantic system, a system in which words are signs to be matched not solely to the mental concepts of the things they signify, but also to each other, as markers to interlace elements of composition and create sound patterns. It was this use of Latin that produced the complicated language games involved in the distinctions and divisions and the rhyming prose of the late medieval sermon and much liturgical material."[68] This semiology of sound, an early variant of Shklovsky's "sonorous" transmission, is clearly mocked by Latimer's rhyming and repetitive "humblynge and mumbling." For when viewed from a strictly semantic perspective, liturgical Latin was easy to empty out by positioning repetition and rhyming as estranging, defamiliarizing, and divorcing form from content and context. "Mumbling" was often paired in the period with "humblyng," "stumblyng," "tumblyng," "bumblynge," and the like, as if the word itself called out for rhyme to make it intelligible, if all the more wedded to sonorous silliness.

From the discussion of invectives against Catholic mumbling, humbling, repetition, and rhyming, a question emerges: What do we make of Protestant polemic as a series of noise-making strategies designed precisely to reform noise? Aside from well-known concerns about the idolatrous potential of Catholic music, how did Protestants attempt to quiet the sounds of the enemy, reproducing those sounds without disquieting themselves? As a species of sonority that could establish coordinates of meaning across, rather than in direct relationship to, single words, rhyme proved a conceptually dense form of expression as Protestants attempted to reform liturgical practice with an emphasis on instruction rather than sensual, self-referential, or mystical delight. Interestingly, while Thomas Wilson lauded the moderate use of rhyme in English writing, he counterbalanced his own criticism of immoderate vernacular rhyme (which "werieth mens eares") with the allegedly more serious vice of "rymed sentences vsed without measure" in the Catholic Mass: "I thynke the Popes heretofore (seeyng the people[s'] folie to be suche) made al our Hymnes & Anthemes in rime, that with the singyng of men, plaiyng of organnes, ringyng of belles, & rinyng of Hymnes, & Sequencies the poore ignoraunt might thinke the Harmonie to be heauenly, & verely beleue that the Angels of God made not a better noise in heauen" (*Rhetorique*, 108v).

That Wilson grants Catholic "rime" and "noise" a powerful if deceptive efficacy is notable, particularly given that sound games and verbal repetition often animated the very polemic directed against excess rhyming and repetition. Not long before Tyndale attempted to banish railing rhymes from religious protest—"Wyth Gods word ought a man to rebuke wikednes and false doctrine and not wyth raylyng rimes"[69]—John Skelton wrote more than a few such "rimes" against the Catholic clergy. Though later called, by George Puttenham, a "rude rayling rhymer" whose excessive verbal echoes "glut the ear" and please "only the popular ear," Skelton used rhyme to protest ecclesiastical corruption effectively enough to be lauded, by Bale, for having "waged war on certain babbling friars" and on "evil deeds being carried out among the clergy."[70] While Bale himself would pray to God to quiet the sounds of Catholic protest (as well as worship)—"Let not the vncircumcised papists & carnal epicures triumphe ouer vs. Let them not giest vpon vs, with mockes & tauntes, in rimes and balades for their pastime"[71]—he composed a number of Protestant dramas that turned "rymed sentences vsed without measure" against the church.[72] Further, while challenging "raylinge rymes" in print, Bale lets loose more than a few r's of his own: "RIallye styll ruffleth this rutter in his ragged rymes of rustycall rudenesse."[73] Parodying sonic repetition while marshalling its power (here using that "*Dog's letter*," as Ben Jonson put it, of R, which "hurreth in the sound," with "the tongue . . . trembling about the teeth"),[74] Bale counters acoustical excess with a bark as big as his bite. While no one had a monopoly over "rime," its alignment with the "popular ear" and with Catholic liturgical practice and protest added, in the early years of the Reformation, to the Protestant arsenal of undesirable, defamiliarizing, and idolatrous sounds to be exposed and expunged even while being appropriated. What is interesting is the extent to which even parodies of sonic excess manifested an investment in the very language games so fiercely disavowed.[75]

Although Tyndale himself emphasized a scripturally based, plain-speaking style of religious protest without "rayling rimes," his own polemic against Catholic mumbling offers a notable, if relatively subtle, infraction of this rule. Using the Catholics' tools to parody them, he writes of curates: "Nether care they but even to only mumble vp so moch every *daye* (as the pye & *popyngay* speake *the[y]* wote not what). . . . Yf they will not lat the lay man have the worde of God in his mother tonge / yet let the prestes have it / which for a greate part of them doo vnderstonde no latine at all: but *synge & saye* and *patter all day*, with lyppes only, that which the herte vnderstondeth not."[76] With the stressed "day," "popyngay," "the[y]," and especially "synge & saye and patter all day," the "patter" of sound patterns implies mindless mimesis among members of the clergy, who apparently "vnderstonde no latine at all." If Tyndale's observation smacks of commonplace polemic, it raises a more complex question about the reification of Catholic *orality* in Reformation invective. In contrast to early Catholicism, Protestantism has long been cast as a religion of the book and ear; the Reformation calling card, *sola scriptura*, enabled the unprecedented development of literacy, and the development of vernacular preaching offered an expanded model of liturgical participation.[77] The Protestant elevation of ear over eye, and of book and Word over less intelligible forms of Latin utterance, is familiar to contemporary scholars of Tudor England. Tyndale's part as a translator and controversial reformer in that process was remarkable,[78] and he was followed by Foxe's famous panegyric to the printing press as an agent of divine change. Together, these efforts clinched for many what Alexandra Walsham has called "Protestant bibliocentricity."[79]

But the defining of Protestant bibliocentricity depended in large part on the exaggeration of Catholic bibliomarginality. Indeed, we might note, in the passage above, just how strenuously "the book" is taken from the hands, ears, and eyes of Catholic priests: liturgical authority is rendered as so much oral gibber jabber detached from what was, at least for some, the scriptural foundation of the Mass. The "pye & popyngay," not those prophetic birds of the psalms such as the owl, sparrow, and pelican, incarnate species sounds that resist abstraction or recuperative signification. As Bale imagined it, if ever the pope were to "haue home agayn the fedder he hath putt" out, he would see "a verye naked monstre not all unlyke vnto . . . [the] Jacke Dawe" (87r). Or in canine rather than avian terms, Udall's epistle to King Edward prefacing the *Paraphrase* notes, "What thyng hath the whelpes of Romishe Antichriste so fierceley alwaies barked against, as at the translatyng of Scripture and other bookes concerning matiers of religion into the vulgare tongue for the vse of the people."[80] This common trope of aggressive, antihumanist barking could not be more antithetical to the productive endeavor of "translatyng" books for the "vse of the people." Calvin (whose own *sola scriptura* was endlessly repeated) codes Catholic textual scholarship itself, or in his terms the overzealous philological diligence of "syllable catchers," as "the heretikes barke" (*Institution*, 30v). The religion of the book and ear thus defined itself, in part, by reformers configuring that earlier religion as one of the less-than-human mouth. From the sonic idolatry implied by mumbling, excess rhyming, or "sound patterned" semiology, in liturgical practice to the less apparently congruous barks of philological investigation and printed debate, diverse Catholic relations to the Word easily devolved through polemic into so much noncommunicative noise. The endlessly articulated split between heart and tongue (or worse, "lyppes"), while a very real concern for reformers, nonetheless hollowed out the potentially humanizing scriptural or even quietly mystical dimensions of the Latin Mass, evacuating content from liturgical Latin as an otherwise potent (or in the words of Thomas Drant) "couert toung."[81]

A response to such anti-Catholic polemic emerged, curiously enough, in a lengthy debate composed by the Protestant warden of Winchester, Thomas Bilson, which features "Theophilvs the Christian" sparring with "Philander the Iesuite" over the stakes of conducting Mass in Latin as opposed to English.[82] Here we find Philander arguing, "It is not necessarie to vnderstand our praiers" (605). This suggests that Latin for the unlearned cultivates a more individualized relation both to prayer and God and lets them "*not be parrets*" by simply repeating recognizable vernacular prayers uttered by priests (605, emphasis added). "In our prayers wee speake to God and not to men," Philander adds, for the "speciall vse" of prayer "is to offer our heartes, desires and wants to God and this euery catholike doeth for his condition, whether hee vnderstande the woordes of his prayers or no" (627). While Philander's position is countered at every step in both text and margins (here the marginal gloss reads, "The voice of the hart is vnderstanding"), he nonetheless articulates an alternative framework of belief that might be fostered by semiotically sustained mysteries of the Word. Against charges of mere parroting, in other words, Philander argues for a radically individualized and heartfelt "vnderstanding" detached from institutionalized linguistic authority. We need to hear the undertone of the Catholic position even in its polemical form.

The same sentiment is expressed more moderately by the Catholic apologist Harding, who writes that "we thinke it not conuenient, in a common prophane tongue, to vtter high mysteries," and "Some fruit is alwaies had euen by secrete praier, and more fruit sometime, then by lowde praier" (515). At the same time, Harding takes pains to emphasize not only the private "mysteries" and personal efficacy of "secrete praier" but also the nexus of common, shared meanings through which the Mass encouraged active and collective participation. He goes so far as to express the aspiration that the entire laity learn Latin to have full access to the Word (515).[83] Beyond the personified "Philander," that is, we see in Harding an attention to both the "secret" and the common, to both the oral and the textual dimensions of Catholic devotion. John Rastell, joining the chorus of protest against John Jewel, would similarly defend Catholicism on textual and communally instructive grounds: "For the Publike Seruice consisteth chiefly of the Scriptures, as the proper bookes of Christians (whiche are to be, either instructed, Or furthered, Or perfited in the lawe of God) and as mooste proper for that place, where all Prophane thinges sette a syde, the Diuine Hystoryes, Psalmes, Gospels and Lessons are to be rehersed & considered."[84] In arguing against Catholic bibliomarginality, I do not mean to champion Harding and Rastell but rather to unsettle the postulate of "Protestant bibliocentricity" and the comparative "inwardness" of devotion it was said to enable.

This allows us to complicate recent challenges to the once dominant formulation in the cultural history of religion that aligned the developing Reformation emphasis on the "inward" life of devotional subjects with the disintegration of the corporate model of Catholicism. The Protestant Reformation, as Ramie Targoff argues, in fact emphasized if not invented standardized group participation through the corporate and unified model of "common prayer," while Catholicism privileged individuation through the lack of a "common" language of devotional practice.[85] This observation was also made by John Bossy, who noted that "in the practice of the vernacular hymn the Reformers did surely achieve something of the immediate and unproblematic unity at which they aimed: a congregational homophony for which Luther himself, and for European civilization in general, did not entirely exorcize nostalgia for the polyphonic mysteries of the mass."[86] For Bossy, however, "the medieval mass was a composite of two ritual traditions inherited from early Christianity and through it from the ritual corpus of antiquity: the tradition of the public worship practised by whole communities, and that of the private, family, domestic cult" (51). This nuanced approach to the blend of public and private aspects of "the Mass as a social institution" emerges precisely because Bossy aimed to examine medieval Catholicism on its own terms, as it combined mystery and shared meanings, without the distorting lens of Reformation polemic. Indeed, the clearest roots of the skewed religious history that Targoff challenges are to be found in strategies of Reformation polemic. Historiographic distortion was a necessary component of Protestant self-definition, in which common and participatory dimensions of Catholicism were reduced through caricatures of institutionally mediated mimesis (copies made not even of public but of unintelligibly "private Massing").[87] In these caricatures, the potentially affective and individuating dimensions of Catholic devotional utterance were reduced to superstition, or belief fostered by illiteracy and ignorance. Charges of "humblynge and mumblynge" were an important part of that distortion, implying a fully compromised "inwardness" (rather than a powerful, and at times extradiscursive, affinity with an individualized God), and a compromised form of communal iteration, leading to heresies and embarrassments of public culture.

Reformation common prayer and spiritual inwardness would of course be of benefit as self-defined "correctives" to both forms of misguided devotional practice.[88] The Reformation concern with restricted public access to Latin (though it overlooked vernacular guides and forms of instruction) was certainly valid, as were concerns about the extrascriptural defenses of confession, purgatory, and indulgences. But the heavy emphasis on unredemptive *orality* in liturgical practice, clerical learning, and even scrupulous philology undermined the scriptural bases of Catholicism, which many a Catholic apologist understood as very much a religion of the book.[89] (Philologically speaking, we might recall that Harding compared the Latin, Greek, and Hebrew scriptures, as Zwingli did early on, even as he continued to defend extrascriptural practices as well.) As far as the laity was concerned, to suggest that Catholicism was devoid of either heartfelt devotion or a sense of common, scripturally based communion would be to underestimate the power of the Mass and of repeated Latin prayers, rhymes, and phrases as conduits for *both* participation and individuation. If the Reformation led to new forms of devotional aggregation and a model of individuated reading through which the Word could be encountered anew, polemical distortions that overstated the case of Catholic incoherence, orality, and unintelligibility remain open to critique.

Overstating the case was the job of polemic, as anti-Catholic plays, satires, and countless treatises authorized by the Crown demonstrate. But hyperbole is most interesting when understood in terms of disavowed forms of conflict within, in this case Reformation technologies of the Word; the majority of the laity could not *read* English, many Englishmen and women remained deeply wedded to the Catholic tradition,[90] and the standardized English liturgy and Book of Common Prayer came under fire for being anything but uniformly comprehensible within Britain. The archbishop of Canterbury Thomas Cranmer's own concern with what we might, inverting Walsham's phrase, call "Protestant biblio*marginality*," is most evident in his articles of 1549, largely designed to protect The Book of Common Prayer from various oral transgressions that threatened to unsettle it. Cranmer's articles aim to legislate not only against Latin mumbling (against any who "praie in a tunge not knowen, then in englyshe") but also against "any that doo *preache, declare or speake any thyng* in the derogation or deprauyng of the said boke of common praier, or seruice of this Churche of Englande, or against any thyng therin conteyned, or of any part therof," as well as "any person or persons, what soeuer they be, do in any *enterludes, plaies, songes, rimes, or by any other open wordes, declare or speake any thyng* in the derogation, deprauyng, or despysynge the sayd booke of Seruice."[91] No less concerned with church chatter, he prohibits "any iangle, talke, walke or otherwyse trouble," "whether in the communion, preachyng, or diuine seruice tyme" (A4r). We can see here Cranmer working to create something like the "fixity of print" *avant la lettre*, not by attending to the materiality of the book but by outlawing forms of oral (and predominantly vernacular) interference that just might unfix it. Aiming to secure what we saw earlier (through the myth of Titivillus) as a juridical fantasy about the possibility of protecting the written Word from all too human mouths, Cranmer mobilizes his juridical power to foster a regime of bibliocentric and uniform speech. Cranmer's text thus betrays a deep nervousness about oral departures from the printed Word *within* the Church of England, not simply from Catholic clergy and worshipers without.

The making of noise through polyphonic performances of "interludes, plaies, *songes, rimes*," and "*other open wordes*" became a central metaphor for Protestants aiming to emphasize either the comically ineffectual or dangerously effective dimensions of speech neither plain nor clearly communicative. Given the relative inaccessibility of Latin, the semiology of repetition and recitation discussed above, and the charges that Catholicism was a deceptively unified public culture, it is no surprise that Reformation writers typically

reduced Catholic "humblynge and mumblyng" to a species of that other suspect form of public oral exchange, drama. As Jonas Barish points out, anti-
Catholicism and antitheatricality became twin tools for Protestants aiming to
dismantle the Latin Mass.[92] More recent scholars, such as Jeffrey Knapp, Kent
Cartwright, and John King, following David Bevington, have complicated
Barish's study, mining the Protestant and late medieval morality drama that
flourished in the midst of the "antitheatrical tradition," which could recuperate the visual when properly mediated through the ethical and comprehensible word.[93] But it is important to note how the communal dimensions of
mystical or "secret" prayer were both highlighted and recoded by reformers
through antitheatrical rhetoric, where undistinguished noise-making became
explicitly aligned with dangerously unifying, collective theatrical *spectacle*. Indeed, mumbling, though oral and acoustical, was part and parcel of iconophobia, implying an overreliance on vision as a vehicle of collective
perception. As a species of what Bruce Smith has called "logomarginality"
(meaning extralinguistic sound production), mumbling implied by extension
image centrality.[94] For John Foxe, "Masse mumbling," the incomprehensible
"droanes of Monkes, Friers, and Massemongers," is but a "pageant to the
full," a performance of "counterfeit sinceritie of vnspotted life, yea outwarde
resemblance of true religion, thereby to dazel more easily the eyes and heartes
of the vnlettered."[95] While "dazel[ed]" eyes and hearts emphasize blinding visual mediation, a congregation, as he puts it, "busied busily in fasting, almes
giuing, in Psalms singing, in prayers and Masse mumbling" (11), summarily
eclipses the potential for heartfelt experience. But to complicate the story, it
is to the comic potential not only of Latin but also of *English* speech and pronunciation that I will now turn.

Vernacularism and the Making of Comedy

We couldn't be much further at this point from Fulwiler and Petersen's claim,
introduced at the outset of this chapter, that activities such as "staring, moving, mumbling . . . and noise prove to be highly generative because they
bridge the gap between tacit ways of knowing and verbal, articulate knowledge." If Cranmer tried to burn that bridge in order to stabilize the newly
printed logos of the English Church, Tyndale did no less in anti-Catholic contexts, at one point putting the stakes of speaking church Latin in explicitly

dramatic terms: "Antychristes Bisshopes preach not and their sacrementes speake not / but as the disgysed Bisshopes mum / so are their supersticious sacramenets doume [dumb]."[96] While "mum" and "dumb" offer yet another aggressive rhyme, the communicative potential of sacrament and sound are altogether evacuated. This is further developed by Tyndale who, in a discussion of baptism, reduces the Latin "mum" to theatrical "mummynge": "The prest ought to teach the people and Christen them in the english tonge / and not to playe the popengay with Credo saye ye / volo saye ye and baptis mum saye ye / for there ought to be no mummynge in soch a mater" (Mɪr–v).[97] The conflation of mumbling, mumming, and theatrically silent liturgical practices (or "dumb" shows) of course obscures rather than illuminates meaning, reifying the inarticulate to avoid confronting the power and significance of linguistic alterity and the performance of the Mass. The link between liturgical mumming and mumbling,[98] which cast potentially high mystery as base manipulation, owes something to the etymology of mumbling, which suggests visual as well as sonic forms of concealment. The Dutch verb *mommen*, "to speak indistinctly," and the German *mummen*, "to mumble," combine with the Middle Dutch and Middle Low German verbs *mommen* ("to go about in a mask or disguise") and *mummen* ("to go about in a carnival mask"), an etymological coincidence indexed in the common association of "mumbling" with theatrical incarnations of concealed truth.[99] Because of this linguistic chain, mumbling becomes aligned with the concept of performative concealment or hiding, and in the terms above, hiding from God. The exposure of persons "hiding" what turns out to be *nothing* was often negotiated through Reformation satire, which featured many a character caught speaking only to himself or herself, less with heart and brain than (as in Tyndale's grotesque of "lip service") "with lyppes only." The mispronunciation of Latin by priests and monks occasioned a range of mid-sixteenth-century satires, drawn from a much older Catholic tradition of church satire,[100] of breaches of linguistic decorum amplified by breaches of social and bodily decorum. Luke Shepherd's *Doctour Doubble ale* (1548) features a drunken priest who mumbles incoherent Latin in a tavern, a scene paralleled in Anthony Scoloker's 1548 translation of Hans Sachs's Lutheran dialogue in which a popish parson wanders out of church, mumbling prayers to himself.[101] In both cases, the speaker moves out of the contexts of a church or congregation, emphasizing Latin's relation to self-talk, which in Shepherd's case is matched by the slur of intoxicated speech.

What is notable in the works of Shepherd and Sachs, as in those by Erasmus and Rabelais, is the easy comedic potential of liturgical Latin for the representation of social indecorum and self-talk, which, I argue, registers a residual if caricatured awareness of mumbling's power to articulate a species of selfhood operating *without* regard to official social networks of exchange. In Henri Bergson's theory of comedy, laughter is understood to emerge from the sudden confrontation with a specter of "mechanical inelasticity *just where* one would expect to find the wide-awake adaptability and living pliableness of a human being."[102] If we take this to be true, mumbling may be a perfect proof: not because mumbling is in itself mechanical or inelastic but because it is not; not (to complicate Bergson's formulation) because mumbling betrays the senselessness of sleeptalk but because it can suggest a process of thought unmoored from conscious communication and regulated interactivity. Few of course want to be caught sleeptalking in a public context defined by articulate exchange. When situated within norms of public interaction, the formation of unintelligible or self-referential sounds can quickly be taken for utterance emptied of content, detached from the humanizing dimensions of sociolinguistic decorum. Yet mumbling can be funny *because* of its thwarted potential to suggest the opposite of a "mechanized," "inelastic" self; comedy emerges "*just where*" something altogether more interesting might be happening. It is the no laughing matter of devotion that Jewel is confronting when he notes that even "the Angelles . . . falle a laughinge" at the indistinct or "foolishe vtterance," and further that "God him self . . . doth from heauen laugh at their enterprises."[103] Such claims to divine hilarity by Protestants of course animate linguistic indistinction to disempower persons and collectives that operate outside emergent norms of communicability.

But the operative term here is *emergent*, since early and mid-sixteenth-century English Reformation attacks on Latin mumbling arguably doubled as a form of self-defense, an often explicit redirection of concerns about vernacular barbarity (as well as of the kinds of bibliomarginal interference prohibited by Cranmer). The famously "barbarous" vernacular that reformers had to contend with, particularly given its necessity for biblical translation, seems comparatively civilized when viewed in the light of Catholic mumbling. The charge of mumbling thus becomes double-edged. Thomas Key, in the same preface to Mark cited above, challenges Latin "mumbling" but also takes pains to excuse his own vernacular ineloquence compared with Erasmus's Latin: "It is not possible for a person . . . to set out euery thing specially in our English tongue being very barrain of wordes and phrases (I will not saye barbarous withall) so lyuelye, & with like grace as he wrote it fyrst in the Latine" (2r). The idea of the vernacular "barrain of wordes and phrases" for concepts and things was a common concern of the time.[104] Indeed, compared to Latin, English left a lot "unsaid." Returning for a moment to the preface to the 1530 edition of the *Myrroure* (which featured, as we have seen, Titivillus on the lookout for unsaid syllables and words), the author emphasizes that "YT is not lyght for euery man to drawe eny longe thyng from latyn in to oure Englyshe tongue. For there ys many wordes in Latyn that we haue no propre englyssh accordynge therto"; therefore "some tyme I folowe the sentence and not the wordes as the mater asketh" (A5v). The use of English thus lent *itself* to the perils of "ouerskipping," the sins of omission in the Latin liturgy captured by Titivillus in the same text. Further, the author notes, "Oure language is also so dyuerse in yt selfe / that the commen maner of spekyng in Englysshe of some contre / can skante be vnderstondid in some other contre of the same londe" (B1v). With this formulation, he apologizes for his "feoblenes" in coining words where there are none and for using a language that might "skante be vndersondid" (B1v). Where sometimes there are no vernacular words for concepts and things in Latin, other times, as the author points out, English words have such a density of implication that they could be easily misconstrued as meaning something else altogether. These realities combine to make the translator, in the logic of the text, rather vulnerable to the clutches of a Titivillus. For comparing English with Latin (or with Latin, Greek, and Hebrew) might well make what Janel Mueller has called Tudor "scripturalism," the "commitment to vernacular expression and to a view of 'wordes' as profoundly and mutually efficacious for author and reader on the model of God's Word," smack of those perilous *fragmina verborum* so infuriating to God.[105]

"This I dare auouche," wrote Nicholas Udall in the preface to his translation of Erasmus's Paraphrase on Luke, "that yf any interpretour shoulde in sum places bee as breefe in the English translacion as the autour is in the latine: he should make thereof but a darke piece of worke."[106] Brevity for this Protestant humanist is not, apparently, the soul of wit. At the same time, the emphasis on copious vernacular exposition is, as Udall emphasizes, a product of avowedly imprecise *and* figural translation: "Though I haue not been hable in all behalfes and pointes requisite, fully to discharge yᵉ office of a good translatour, yet I haue expressed yᵉ sence & meaning of the autour," and importantly: "I haue not so precisely bound my self to euery woord and sillable of the letter, but . . . I haue taken more respect to the explanacion and declaring of the sence, then to the noumbre of the latine syllables" (5v). The deficit of "latine syllables" and words is counterbalanced, in other words, by an excess of vernacular "sence" and "sentence" making. The elevation of the figural over the literal interpretation in English Reformation theology is no surprise,[107] but noting just how suitable this theological principle was for negotiating the vernacular as an inadequate vehicle for translation can help us consider the linguistic subtexts of ideological justification. For what of a dropped Latin "woord" or "sillable of the letter" here or there when what matters is "the sence"?

As William Fulke put it plainly in the matter of the transubstantiation (or Christ's words, "This is my body"): "We quarell not as those heretiques did, and M. Rastel a Popish heritique doth, of letters, syllables, words, and sounds, but we stand vpon the sense, meaning, vnderstanding, & doctrine which we affirme to be perfectly contained in scripture, what so euer is necessarie to saluation."[108] Cranmer, like many other reformers, earlier grounded his reading of the figural dimensions of Christ's body in Paul, "*least we might stande stiffely in the letters and syllables, and erre in mistaking of Christes wordes*" when Christ said, "This is my body."[109] Cranmer, Fulke, and Udall bring us to a curious situation in which a rather specific species of syllabic "overskipping" in Reformation theology, not in pronunciation but in translation, is now not the infraction but the law. As Jewel put it, "The question bitweene vs this daie, is not of the Letters, or Syllables of Christes Woordes . . . but onely of the Sense, and Meaninge of his woordes: which, as S. Hierome saith, is the very pith and substance of the Scriptures. And the Lawe itselfe saith, . . . *He committeth fraude against the Lawes, that, sauinge the woordes of the Lawe, ouerthroweth the meaninge.*"[110] As Udall writes here and elsewhere, the vernacular's limit as a mimetic medium becomes productively animated for the benefit of figural translation. As for the "barrain" vernacular, Udall transfers responsibility from the mother tongue to the humanist scholar: "I see no man is so barrain, but he is able with sum woorde or other to helpe garnishe his mother tongue, with other like saiynges proceding from humanitie and fauour to encourage suche as are studious" (6v). While the idea of the "barrain" vernacular was at times compatible with the Reformation search for naked or plain language with which to approach the truth, it could also imply a lack of fertility with which to match the creativity of the maker. When Key evinces a devotion to humanist Latin, for instance, that highlights the barren and (unsayable but nonetheless said) "barbarous" dimensions of English, we see a tension between the agendas of the restrained Protestant reformer and the copious classical humanist, negotiating between the "civilizing agency"[111] of humanist Latinity and the reputed barbarism of English. At the same time, Key's attack on Catholic "mumbling" (echoed by Udall)[112] helps to shore up the vagaries of the vernacular, which was to be aligned with transparency rather than opacity of meaning.

But in another twist to the story of mumbling, English itself as a model for biblical translation was associated not simply with barbarism but, not so long before Key and Udall, with mumbling. We might recall now the attention paid to the proto-Reformation Lollards. The Lollards were associated with John Wycliff, who produced the first complete vernacular English Bible (known as the Lollard Bible).[113] Their name, through a false etymology, seems to have separated from the German Walter Lolhardus and taken on a life of its own, becoming associated through the German *lollen*, "to mumble," and the derogative Dutch *lollaerd*, "a mumbler," with the English word "mumblers." "I smelle a Lollere in the wynd," the famous quip by the Host in Chaucer's *Canterbury Tales* (who imagines a sermonizing tale to come), is quickly followed by the Shipman's fret, "He [the Lollard] wolde sowen some difficulte, / Or springen cokkel in our clene corn," a comment that pokes fun at the often difficult and Latinate diction of early biblical translators, as well as their heretical status.[114] But Protestants often heralded a Lollard-friendly Chaucer as a protoreformer: Simon Birckbek draws on these very lines in Chaucer as "evidence" of "a company of true and godly professours," "the faithfull in *England* . . . called Lollards," who helped to found the Church of England.[115] Because Birckbek lauds Lollards as reformers, that there is no mention of mumbling is no surprise. But of those "callyd 'lolleres,'" writes William Langland in an earlier and imaginative etymology, "as by enclische of our elders of alde menne techynge. He that lolleth is lame . . . his leg oute of joynte, [or] meymed in som member, for to meschief hit [it] souneth."[116] If the pun is lame, the logic is telling, aligning bodily (and implicitly syntactic)[117] with sonic "meschief" in matters of the vernacular Word. A bit of mischief surfaces in the Towneley Judgment play as well, where Titivillus, demon of mumbles, calls himself a "master lollar."[118] In this context, with a figure capturing errant speech by the sackful, Lollardy *might* be said to offer an alternative framework for recuperating the necessary relation between the tongue and the heart, between devotion and comprehensible pronunciation in devotional practice. But this is more likely a joke about Titivillus's bag of mumbles (or "lolls"), an anti-Lollard joke about what were often said to be the "jangling" translators, as well as a possible allusion to English spoken among inattentive parishioners in church.[119] Either way, the connection between Titivillus and the Lollards or vernacular "mumblers" is compelling. If Titivillus the *Lollard* seems a stretch, this possibility was nonetheless registered in William Dunbar and Walter Kennedy's hilarious poem "The flyting of Dunbar and Kennedy" (printed in 1508). In this contest of insults, Kenney hurls an abusive term at Dunbar, calling him "Tutiuillus," "monstir of all men," and, seconds later, "lollard laureate," an enemy to the faith, a Lollard demon of mumbles.[120]

This early transfer of Titivillus from the Latin homiletic to the anti-Lollard, antivernacular scriptural tradition suggests the adaptability of such a mythic figure with his bagful of indistinct speech. But in both Catholic and anti-Lollard contexts, the bias is as much against vernacular as bad Latin speakers. A Latin poem in John of Bromyard's *Summa Praedicantium*, an influential compendium of moral and theological examples, captures formally the disruptions of the vernacular operative in poor Latin pronunciation: "Hii sunt qui psalmos corrumpunt nequiter almos, / Dangler, cum jasper, lepar, galper quoque draggar / Momeler, forskypper, forereynner, sic et overleper/ Fragmina verborum Tutivillus colligit horum."[121] English words encroach upon the Latin verse to emphasize multiple forms of corrupt pronunciation. The wicked speakers accused—the dangler, the grasper, the leaper, the galloper, the dragger, the mumbler, the foreskipper, the forerunner, the overleaper—are all given in English, keeping Titivillus busy collecting sonic errors aligned with vernacular speech. Although the poem focuses on the Latin psalms and follows a tradition of church satire against those who speak poor Latin, the panoply of bad pronouncers given in English mirrors another Latin poem, where "Tres sunt qui psalmos corrumpunt nequiter almos, / Quo sacra scriptura dampnat, vetant quoque iura: 'Momelers, foreskippers, and ouerskippers' sunt tria mala."[122]

It is not a far leap from this explicitly vernacular trifecta to the question of English itself as a "foreskipper," "ouerskipper," and possibly even "momeler" of sorts in comparison to Latin. This anticipates the problem addressed by Udall above on English's relation to the Latin language, even as he and others found ways to compensate for the missing words and "latine syllables" in translation. Calling for innovative vernacular enrichment to compensate for such a comparative deficit, Udall nonetheless betrays nervousness about being mocked for doing just that: "Sum others would ampliate and enrich their natiue language with mo vocables whiche I also commend, if it be aptly and wittily assaied. So that if any other doe innouate and bryng vp a woorde to me afore not vsed or not heard, I would not disprasse it: and that I do attempt to bryng to vse, another man should not cauayle at. For an easy thyng it is to depraue, and a small glory for one man, in matters of nothing, to laboure to deface an other" (Udall, Preface to Erasmus's Paraphrase on Luke, A6r). While Udall, in this same preface, follows the polemical line in deriding Catholic Latin "mumblers" (A3v), he is himself worried about being criticized for using "mo vocables" (and words not before "heard," thus outside common comprehension). As seen earlier, he was also concerned about over-skipping more than a few "latin syllables" in translation.

   In short, what is fascinating is how the "mumbler," that intra- and ulti-mately anti-Catholic buzzword, could speak to problems of English as well as Latin, to the perils of vernacular translation and Catholic Latinity. Accusations of mumbling by Catholics and Protestants alike thus elucidate the function of focusing on the enunciative and lexical indistinction of others as a means of establishing *internal* coherence, especially when, practically speaking, such coherence was impossible to enact. As we now begin to move toward Udall's drama and other works, I want to emphasize how this logic of the demonized misspeaking other as a means of self-definition was both exposed and complicated through challenges to the idea of common prayer. In *The Arte of Rhetorique* of Thomas Wilson, a devoted student of Udall's from Eton,[123] we read two simple sentences: "I knew a Priest that was as nice as a Nonnes Henne, when he would saie Masse, he woulde neuer saie *Dominus vobiscum*, but *Dominus vobicum*. In like maner as some now wil say, the Commendementes of God, blacke *vellet*, for Commaundementes and blacke *veluet*" (Gg1v–2r). With demands of Latin and English pronunciation drawn together in one fell swoop, we find that pronunciation in both tongues requires a regime of syllabic precision, without which speakers lose credibility as participants in communities of learned speech and common prayer. The swift redirection of the common anti-Catholic charge of mispronounced Latin toward vernacular reform ("in like manner") is particularly notable, where now a dropped *English* syllable here or there becomes close to heretical in the realm of common prayer. Even this small citation from Wilson might lead us to ask a larger question: Just how common was common prayer?

Might charges of anti-Catholic mumbling have masked challenges to commonality and communicability made possible by the newly standardized vernacular liturgy?

As Targoff argues, "the wide availability of the Prayer Book as a material text; the audibility of the priest's words to all listeners; the emphasis upon the laity's comprehension of and engagement with the service" in Protestant England all "reconceived the relations between the language of personal and liturgical prayer" (18). Catholics certainly challenged this logic, as did the Prayer Book riots of 1549, with inhabitants of Cornwall, now vigorously wedded to Rome, writing in protest, "And so we Cornishmen (whereof certen of us understand no English) utterly refuse this new English" (169).[124] And well after the establishment of The Book of Common Prayer, others such as Rastell fully unsettled the ideal of "common prayer." In *Beware of M. Iewel* (1566), Rastell writes: "When your felfe doe preache, M. Iewell, some, I beleue, vnderstande you not, and some vnderstand you: (for many stand a far of & some nerer vnto you) & some vnderstand not all fyne English, yet some vnderstand it well inough" (46r). Although Paula Blank suggests that "the earliest recorded use of the word 'dialect,' referring to a manner of speaking," occurs in 1577,[125] some eleven years earlier than that date Rastell writes: "Though the Tounge of Saxonie, Flanders, England and Scotland be one: yet because of a peculiar Property and Dialect whiche is in them, the Vulgar Saxons are not only Strangers to Englishe men, but allso to the Flemminges their neighbors: and the Vulgare Scottesman not only vnderstandeth not the Flemming, but of the Sowtherland so nigh vnto him, he knoweth not the wordes and meaning" (64v). Given such diversity, it is no less than "a miracle," writes Rastell (in a delicious use of Catholic rhetoric to undermine the idea of common prayer), when "English men of diuers Sheers . . . when they, Englishe men borne, vnderstand the self same tounge in an English Preacher" (65v).[126] The treatise, life-threatening to Rastell, was published in Antwerp, and such an unmuffled criticism from abroad is perhaps no surprise.

But Wilson, an avowed Protestant, expressed more than a few concerns about what we might call "uncommon prayer" in the vernacular service. Other than competing dialects and lexicons operative in England that he famously frets about (including "outlandishe Englishe" newly cluttered with Latin, French, and Italian terms antithetical to common understanding [P2r]), he emphasizes the more basic problem of liturgical inattention. In contrast to the Protestant emphasis on a plain, audible, effectively communicative liturgy, Wilson notes how little preachers are actually listened to: "Preachers [are] not so diligently heard as common Plaiers," and while "menne commonly tary the ende of a merie plaie," they "cannot abide the halfe hearyng of a . . . Sermon" (A2v). In a nice complication of antitheatrical rhetoric, "common plaiers" now trump "common prayer" in the cultivation of communal attention.[127] For not only is loud and clear pronunciation needed at the pulpit, so is a bit of theatrical mirth to keep ears, hearts, and minds from wandering: "Preachers, must now and then plaie the fooles in the pulpite, to serue the tickle eares of their fleetyng audience," or they will continue (like the Catholic priests earlier derided by Bale and others) to "preache to the bare walles" (A2v). Unlike Cranmer who aims to outlaw sonic interference with the preached and printed Word, Wilson suggests that tiresome and ineffectual preaching is the problem, leading to daydreams, sleep, or other forms of compromised inwardness. To keep audiences from fleeing into sleep or dream, Wilson himself practices what he preaches about the instructive efficacy of "plaie" in the third edition of his logic textbook, *The rule of Reason* (1553), where he entertains the reader by incorporating a scene of disastrous pronunciation from Udall's *Ralph Roister Doister*.[128]

But beyond the auditory trials confronted by preachers, lawyers, and scholars in Wilson's texts, we find that everyday "common" habits of utterance in England pose problems for the establishment of both sacred and secular community. On "Faultes in pronunciation" in the *Rhetorique*, Wilson begins a seemingly endless catalogue of "euill voices & suche lacke of vtteraunce" among his countrymen that "muche defaceth all their doynges": "One," he writes,

> pipes out his woordes so small through defaulte of his wynde pype, that ye woulde thinke he whisteled. An other is so hource in his throte, that a man woulde thynke he came lately from scouryng of harnesse. An other speakes, as though he had Plummes in his mouthe. . . . An other speakes in his throte, as though a good Ale crume stacke fast. An other ratles his wordes. An other choppes his wordes. An other speakes, as though his wordes had neede to be heaued out with leauers. An other speakes as though his wordes shoulde be weyed in a ballaunce. An other gapes to fetch wynde at euery thirde woorde. This man barkes out his Englishe Northrenlike with *Isay*, and *thou ladde*. An other speakes so finely, as though he were brought vp in a Ladies Chamber. As I knew a

Priest that was as nice as a Nonnes Henne, when he would saie Masse, he woulde neuer saie *Dominus vobiscum*, but *Dominus vobicum*. In like maner as some now wil say, the Commendementes of God, blacke *vellet*, for Commaundementes and blacke *veluet*. Some blowes at their noistrelles. Some sighes out their wordes. Some synges their sentencies. Some laughes altogether, when they speake to any bodie. Some gruntes lyke a Hogge. Some cackels lyke a Henne, or a Iack Dawe. Some speakes as thoughe they shoulde tel a tale in their sleeue. Some cries out so loude, that they would make a mans eares ake to heare them. Some coughes at euery worde. Some hemes it out. Some spittes fier, they talke so hotely. Some makes a wrie mouthe, and so they wreste out their wordes. Some whynes lyke a Pig. Some suppes their wordes vp as a poore man doth his porage. . . . There are a thousand suche faultes emong menne bothe for their speache, and also for their gesture, the whiche if in their young yeres they be not remedied, they will hartely be forgotte when they come to mans state. (Gg1v–Gg2r)

Capturing "a thousand suche faultes emong menne," Wilson becomes a kind of neo-Titivillus, preserving "euil" sounds through onomatopoeia (barkes, gruntes, cackels, hems, spittes, whynes, and the like) for a much printed afterlife (the book went through eight editions by 1585).[129] Wilson is having his own fun with sound games here. But in continuity with the use of Titivillus in the 1530 *Myrroure*, the focus on ineffectual sound production attempts to manage less tractable forms of resistance to the linguistic consolidation of group identity (most evident in the Prayer Book riots, where thousands lost their lives in a fight against the "liberatory" Reformation ideology that was experienced by them as linguistic colonialism and restriction of religious liberty). We might notice that while establishing the sonic coordinates of "our common speach and language,"[130] Wilson draws differences of region (Northern and Southern dialects), religion (Catholic Latin and mispronounced English), gender (the effeminizing "Ladies Chamber"), and rank (eating words "as a poore man doth his porage"), as he puts it, "al into one plumpe" (S2v), invalidating alternative beliefs, practices, and cultural allegiances.

Wilson's language ideology is thus antithetical to the liberatory Reformation theological principles that he stands for, principles he articulates even more powerfully in *The three Orations of Demosthenes* (1570).[131] Despite what has often been described (following the early editor G. H. Mair) as Wilson's commitment to plain and "pure speech of the common people,"[132] what is curious is that the offending aggregate above so threatening to "pure speech" is no less than the "common people" themselves. Accordingly, the over-the-top logomarginality in the passage can be seen as helping to define, by opposition, the idealized logocentricity of what Wilson calls "our Countrie speech."[133] As late as 1570 Wilson would bemoan the inadequacy of English translation for leaving out essential components of classical texts, not only in Latin but also in Greek: "For that there are hydde in [Demosthenes] many secrete ornamentes, the which at the very first, doe not appeare, and are hardly to be vttered by me I confesse, in our Englysh tongue."[134] "And manye times I haue bene ashamed of my selfe, when I compared his Greeke and my English togither."[135] If, as we have already seen, Protestant self-definition was bolstered by anti-Catholic mumbling, in Wilson we see an internalized extension of this, now with the vices of everyday English "lacke[s]" in pronunciation making the dream of a common language, as it were, all the more pronounced.

But at the same time, something else is clearly happening in Wilson's text. The use of comic exaggeration produces a form of polemic that laughs at polemic, a self-reflexive variant of a potentially unreflexive mode. Wilson here follows his own recommendation for rhetoricians not simply to "heap" examples to "appere more vehement" (S2v) but also to deploy "mirth" to keep people from falling "a slepe" from "right wholsome matter" (T3r). The lengthy passage above is only a *section* of what he gathers together in a kind of monstrous list, demonstrating how quickly lists can become comic and, indeed, literary, hyperbole suggesting something more complex than polemical vehemence. Drawing on commonplaces and associational logics ("like," "as if," "as though"), Wilson moves from fact to counterfact, list to literary satire, invention (finding) to invention (creating). As in any endless list (where "An other" follows "An other" and the word "some" is repeated some twenty-four times in the full passage), hilarity ensues: words become unhinged from apparent reference and begin to refer to each other, and by extension to the writer, who makes "raids on the inarticulate" for dramatic effect.[136] As Wilson mines and hyperbolizes problems of pronunciation in order to help establish an emergent norm of "our common speech and language," he also reflects upon the comic potential of polemic as it records and indeed relies upon the very vices it aims to squash.

While we can clearly see how Wilson's rhetoric draws energy from rhetorical disability, how failures of expression enable expression, and how the absence of speech inspiring *pathos* enables the elaborate production of speech pathology, what it nonetheless produces is a variant of what we might call (reformulating Benedict Anderson's famous phrase) an "underimagined community" subtending the emergence of imagined ones in Tudor England.[137] This is not to say that Wilson was not deeply serious about reforming the vernacular or that his underimagined community is really given a voice, but that his attempt at "mirth" through the creation of a kind of anticommunity of sound gives us at least a glimmer of all of those "voices" that many proponents of "vulgar eloquence" would become so willfully deaf to.[138] Wilson, to be sure, gives us only a series of caricatured effects; we imagine only one who "speakes in his throte, as though a good Ale crume stacke fast."[139] Others, such as Nicholas Udall, went much further when they placed those very "euill voices" and bodies on stage, as, for example, in the form of one Madge Mumblecrust. On stage, when such "effects" are situated within specific networks of exchange, located within religious and socioeconomic circumstances, space is often opened up for reflection about cause-effect relations that complicates, even as it draws upon, polemical "vehemence" with regard to the indistinct utterance.

This very principle has come into view in contemporary heuristics, with Fulwiler and Peterson, for example, observing that "low-level articulation"—when dislodged from a longstanding rational bias through which only articulate speech counts as thought—can be seen to index a mind at work that "seeks, explores, and discovers," and that is thus able to access tacit forms of knowledge precisely disabled by articulate speech: "Since language as an agent in problem solving is well documented," they write, "it is time to take low-level articulation (prewording) seriously."[140] The same can be said about critical approaches to Renaissance drama, for "low-level articulation" was indeed taken seriously by a number of Renaissance playwrights, leading to forms of "problem solving" that high-level articulation failed to access. Well before Shakespeare's *King Lear* featured such a strange concatenation of sounds as "Alow: alow, loo, loo," "O, do, de, do, de, do de," "sayes suum, mun, nonny," "fie, foh, and fume," "fie, fie; pah, pah," and "sa, sa, sa, sa"[141]—and indeed well before Thomas Kyd's *Spanish Tragedy* featured an inset playlet marked by "mere confusion" at the level of the word[142]—Udall investigated the social and seemingly subliterate, subliterary logic of the mumble; the indistinct utterance, the nongrammatical repetition, and the nonsense rhyme. When used strategically as a means for moving beyond the often restrictive methods of humanist and Reformation fault-finding, the apparently ineffectual utterance could direct attention to the fault lines of articulate speech so that new constellations of meaning, and communities of interaction, might emerge into view. In *Ralph Roister Doister*, mumbling became aligned with a curious form of problem solving even—or especially—as it was antithetical to both classically rhetorical and English Protestant self-fashioning.

CHAPTER TWO

From Fault to Figure

The Case of Madge Mumblecrust in *Ralph Roister Doister*

THE INARTICULATE UTTERANCE, when represented as something to be heard and not simply dismissed as a comedy of error or a marginalized sociolect, could generate a halting effect in the process of reception as well as transmission, a halting that could make space for alternative temporalities and directions of thought otherwise eclipsed by the flow of verbal fluency. Departures from communicative "norms," such as mumbling, mispronunciation, defamiliarizing repetition, and rhyming beyond reason, which operated within a network of competing traditions and driving commitments, provided drama with an almost ready-made form of tensional error: occasions for laughter, doubtless, but also for investigating the psychological, sociological, and theological stakes of indistinct speech. On stage "euil voices" speak, but they speak to and within imagined dramatic and auditory communities, at times complicating the influential argument by Margreta de Grazia that in Tudor English drama, "when language fails, the fault is with the speaker, not with speech itself," since "linguistic deterioration was seen as a sign of moral corruption, not of inherent inadequacies in language itself."[1] Sometimes this is true, sometimes it is not: the pressure here is on what "fails" and "fault" might mean, and how "faults" might prove productive for something other than a corrective to moral norms. When unhinged from dominant cultural and religious blame games, apparent errors of speech and language could lead to a different understanding of the bounds of linguistic community and the structure of lexical and textual authority. The pathologizing discourses through which Catholic but also various country speakers were excised from the "common" authorized speech of Reformation England gave more than a little food for thought to dramatists, especially those, such as Udall, who aimed to move beyond errant and corrective "types" of the morality tradition toward a more complex representation of both "error" and character.

I now turn to the interplay of sacred and secular speech in Udall's prose writing and particularly his drama *Ralph Roister Doister* (c. 1550–53, printed 1566),[2] featuring none other than one Margorie Mumblecrust, or as she is called most often in the play, Madge Mumblecrust. Debates about "mumbling" in both humanist and Reformation contexts inform the use and abuse of language in this play, but in no simple way. Udall was a devotee of classical Latinity also invested in Protestant projects of translation, and his allegiances ranged from Katherine Parr and King Edward to Catholic Queen Mary (who honored him, despite his staunchly Protestant writings and translations, for bringing "Dialogues and Enterludes" before her).[3] He was thus in a rather curious position between competing language ideologies and practices. As an admirer of Erasmus, that Catholic reformer and humanist rhetorician who nonetheless confronted the limits of rhetoric,[4] Udall seems to have learned a trick or two about finding a middle way between political and theological extremes. He could be polemical to be sure, but the form of drama for Udall helps to pave a middle way, where his own dramatic "praise of folly" at once debunks delusions of authority that prove harmful to socially marginalized speakers and recuperates agency for some who might seem mere fools. If Udall plays the fool with an interlude in conspicuously "doggerel" rhyme and alliterative play (the name Nichol Neuerthrives, for instance, recalls the author himself), it is in the name of establishing a form of acoustical community that polemical extremism with regard to language use and religious affiliation disable. Attending to the vexed linguistic texture within and around *Ralph Roister Doister* helps us to understand the ways in which English comedy could reformulate theological as well as humanist problems of mumbled, mispronounced, or indistinct words. In Udall's hands, such a reformulation inaugurates a sociologically complex drama about the power as well as the limits of "self-talk," where even mumbling and other forms of lapsed pronunciation, syllable skipping, and rhyming are recuperated, refashioned, and understood anew. Who, Udall encourages us to ask, plays Titivillus now? And how are *fragmina verborum* caught, and caught up in, innovations in Tudor English drama?

The Reformation of Error

> *What?*
> —Nicholas Udall, *Ralph Roister Doister*[5]

Nicholas Udall's preface to Erasmus's Paraphrase on Luke offers a slight corrective to Tyndale on "disgysed" Catholics who "mum,"[6] emphasizing that priests "swarmed among vs like disguised maskers & not mummers, but mumblers" (A3v). The correction positions acoustical indistinction as no less damning than idolatry in the mire of "Romyshe Babilon."[7] Sanctioning Henry's mandate that the "Bible should be set forth in our owne vulgar language," Udall aligns ecclesiastical Latin with the commonplace of spiritual muck: "Muddie lakes, & puddles purposely infected with ye filthy dregges of our Philistines the papistes, who had stopped our springes to driue vs to their poysoned muddy gutters" (A4r). Vernacular translation, in contrast, also in a commonplace formulation, could express "the synceritie of Christes doctryne" through a "clere fountain and spring of the ghospell" (A3v). This may well index Janel Mueller's understanding of Tudor Protestant "scripturalism."[8] But in the same preface, Udall also positions English as woefully digressive and lexically insufficient as a vehicle of translation. Much like Thomas Key's preface to Erasmus's Paraphrase on Mark, Udall's qualification reads: "As for the grace of the latine tonge I thinke vnpossible to be liuely expressed, as [Erasmus] doth it in the latine by reason of sundry allusions, diuerse prouerbes, many figures, and exornacions retoricall, with Metaphores innumerable, whiche cannot with ye lyke grace be rendred in any other language then in the latine, or greke, besydes that an infinite sorte of wordes there be, whose full importyng cannot with one mere Englishe worde equiualently be interpreted" (5v).

The gap between classical languages and the less than graceful English language might be said to have occasioned conditions of uncomfortable and unfashionable self-fashioning for the Protestant humanist, even as concerns about "mere Englishe" as a language of devotion were counterbalanced, as we have begun to see, by the demonization of Roman Catholic Latin.[9] Udall's anxiety about his departure from humanist ideals in the process of English translation is palpable in his lengthy elaboration on the styles of Demosthenes, Ovid, Cicero, Sallust, and others: "This I speake, rather in commendaioun of eloquence, of copie, of elegancie of style where it is, then to

claime [that] there is any such here" (6r). He also defends vernacular enrichment even in the composition of a "playne" text where there are simply no
English words to match those of classical languages. "No man of our tyme
and in our Englishe tounge," he notes, "writeth so ornately, but that he hat in
sundry woordes & phrases sum smatch of his natiue country phrases, that he
was born in" (6r). While making space for some "smatch of his natiue country phrases," Udall nonetheless apologizes for the distance between English
and humanist Latin, challenging "Romyshe Iuggling" and Catholic idolatry
while coming close to idolizing Erasmian Latinity. His preface to the full volume emphasizes two justifications for the English plain style:

> The translatours haue of purpose studied rather to write a plain stile,
> then to vse their elegancie of speche, partly because there cannot in al
> pointes be expressed in the English tong the grace that is in the laten,
> much lesse (of my self I speake) the plesauntnesse that is in the stile of
> Erasmus, a man of moste excellent learnyng and exquisite eloquence in
> this kinde (thoughe in dede not altogether a Ciceronian, but yet feact,
> pleasaunt, swete, elegaunt, & sensible) & partly because there was a
> special regarde to be had to the rude and vnlettred people, who
> perchaunce through default of atteigning to the high stile, should also
> thereby haue been defrauded of the profit and fruict of vnderstanding
> the sence, which thing that they might doe, was the onely pourpose
> why it was first translated, and now by the kinges most excellent
> Maiestie willed to be read.[10]

The "special regarde to be had to the rude and vnlettred people" sanctions a
departure from humanist eloquence, providing an ethical correlative to the
problem of English as an inadequately "graceful" medium. In line with our
discussion of Udall's relation to "latine syllables," here the doubly emphasized
"purpose" reconfigures problems of translational accuracy in the name of civic
purpose, transforming linguistically and mimetically based deficits into a
moral strength.

Still, the tensional triad of humanist Latinity, Catholic Latinity, and the
still barren, partially expressive, and regionally inflected English marks Udall's
approach to translation. While English is wanting in Udall's prefatory remarks, Latinity is complicated by its double status as the vehicle for
"Romyshe Babilon," on the one hand, and the "grace" of Roman models, on

the other. As Ann Moss has noted, with the rise of humanism in the sixteenth century, well before the century's end, "Humanist Latin use has become the norm, and medieval [liturgical] Latin variously deemed to be deviant, grotesque, quaint, and finally, incomprehensible."[11] The battleground for competing domains of Latinity in the early and mid-sixteenth century was, in Moss's framework, predominantly theological, and entered into educational contexts of grammar instruction:

> In many schools round about 1500, boys would be taught at a quite elementary level to correct [ecclesiastical] Latin, for example to emend liturgical hymns in false meters. The sense that the language of religion could be "wrong" was inculcated at a very impressionable age. At the very least, pupils emerged from the grammar class convinced that the late medieval Latin of the Church and the late medieval Latin of the logic curriculum and of the other disciplines to which they were to transfer was incorrect by the standards of "authentic" Latinity, that it was represented by "bad" as opposed to "good" authors, that it was arid (*siccus*) and meagre (*ieiunus*) by contrast with the rich vocabulary resources of the classical language, and that it was inflexible and culturally void. (246–47)

Such a linguistic battleground, but with English now in the mix, brings us directly to the dramatic world of *Ralph Roister Doister*, a play composed for grammar school students. If Latin proves exemplary to imitate for classically derived acts and scenes and characters drawn from Plautus and Terence, medieval Latin proves anti-exemplary. At the same time, English, with more than a few "smatches" of country rusticity, becomes a locus of verbal mishap alongside, and as a partner to, liturgical Latin, both deviating from the standards and ideals of classical Latinity and ideals of plain speech.

Such a vivid nexus of linguistic tension in a play designed for school boys may well underlie Madge Mumblecrust's triply marginalized relationship, as a woman, an "olde" nurse, and a country rustic, to humanist languages and spheres of learning. But she is not alone or the central target of attack, and she comes to seem comparatively ethical in relation to other characters such as Mathewe Merrygreek and Ralph Roister Doister, who have access to privileged domains of learning and culture. As we will see, there is "a special regarde to be had to the rude and vnlettred people," since the play renders suspect not only Catholic practices, languages, and ideologies but also the misuses, abuses, and potential *inefficacy* of humanist, aristocratic, and even plain-speaking self-fashioning.

The play, often labeled "secular" in contrast to the morality tradition,[12] has long been singled out for its innovative engagement with Plautus and Terence, its revival of Roman "types" (the parasite and *miles gloriosus*, or braggart warrior), and, more recently, its reflection of homosocial pedagogical practice in Tudor England, the play having been composed for grammar school boys by an accused "bugger."[13] But Udall, a translator of Terence's dramas and of Erasmus's *Apophthegmes* (1542), also edited Erasmus's *Paraphrases* (1548), translated the Continental reformer Piermartire Vermigli's (Peter Martyr's) *Lordes Supper* in 1550[14] (a treatise devoted to challenging the Real Presence), and composed a response to the Cornish Prayer Book rebellion of 1549 in a *comparatively* nuanced defense of The Book of Common Prayer. Udall's play negotiates problems of speech and pronunciation in the classical comic tradition, the late medieval homiletic tradition, and the Reformation anti-Catholic tradition, while using techniques of secular allusion, vernacular sound games, and socioeconomic ethics to configure such problems anew.

Udall's prefatory poem draws on Plautus and Terence as exemplary playwrights to sanction his comedy: "The wyse Poets long time heretofore, / Under merrie Comedies secretes did declare / Wherein was contained very vertuous lore, / With mysteries and forewarnings very rare" (1r). But the preface, closing "by Gods leaue and grace," signals a faith distinct from that of classical antiquity to match Udall's vernacular drama, suggesting divine "mysteries and forewarnings" now hidden in English "myrth" (1r). What "secretes" are hidden or buried in the play? What is the relation between humanist eloquence, English comedy, and Christian virtue and rare "forewarnings"? And how might the "not said" and "unsaid" come more clearly into view? Mathewe Merrygreek's speech at the outset of the play, where he aligns himself with an expansive cohort, will help us attend to these questions. Discussing "where I dine" with not a little anaphoristic enthusiasm, Merrygreek reveals his relation to both the classical "parasite" (Terence's Gnatho) and the morality tradition:

My lyuing lieth heere and there, of Gods grace,
Sometime wyth this good man, sometyme in that place,

Sometime Lewis Loytrer biddeth me come néere,
Somewhyles Watkin Waster maketh vs good chéere,
Sometime Dauy Diceplayer when he hath well cast
Kéepeth reuell route as long as it will last.
Sometime *Tom Titiuile* maketh vs a feast,
Sometime with sir Hugh Pye I am a bidden gueast,
Sometime at Nichol Neuerthriues I get a soppe,
Sometime I am feasted with Bryan Blinkinsoppe,
Sometime I hang on Hankyn Hoddydodies sléeue. (iv, emphasis
   added)

We have here but the first of a series of intersections between humanist and
Reformation impulses. Not only does the classically derived parasite speak
"of Gods grace" while feeding off a range of personified and morally suspect
hosts, but in the middle of the list we find Tom Titiuile, the mumble col-
lector from the homiletic tradition, who "sometime . . . maketh vs a feast."
This calls our attention to the entertainment value but also the potential
theological stakes of the many *fragmina verborum* yet to come in the play.
The name Titiuile arguably anticipates many a dropped syllable and
dropped silences in pronunciation, and also the excessive gossip and vernacular noise-making (which our earlier Titivillus both fostered and bagged)
that will be especially prevalent in the latter half of the play. Thriving as one
of Merrygreek's companions alongside Blinkinsoppe, Hoddydodie, Loytrer,
Waster, Diceplayer, and Neuerthrives, Titivillus seems both part of and
counterpart to the feast of lapsed habits of morals, minds, and speech that
surface in the play.

But no sooner is this list of dramatis personae announced than it is dismissed: Merrygreek will focus "thys day" only on his "chiefe banker / Both
for meate and money," Royster Doyster (iv). This suggests a narrowed focus
on the classical parasite and miles gloriosus, and on idolatrous love (since
Ralph falls head over heels for any smile or wink that might come his way).
The plot of the play centers on Ralph's fruitless pursuit of an engaged widow,
Christian Custance, whose fiancé, Gawain Goodluck, is away at sea until the
very end of the play. It clearly thematizes, as scholars have observed, problems of unwanted courtship, and the vulnerable position of a woman who is
both widow and newly engaged but on her own to defend herself from unwanted advances.[15] It also suggests the limits of aristocratic privilege, as

Ralph is an aristocrat in love with, and rejected by, a woman engaged to a merchant. Since Custance, vulnerable to gossip and slander as a woman on her own, has to defend her reputation, female credibility is the deliberative issue of the play, as Joel Altman and Lorna Hutson have argued.[16] To add to Altman and Hutson's observations, but to explore in different terms the play's attention to rank as well as gender, I want to suggest that the deliberative issue of the play centers on the credibility of diverse vernacular language practices, practices that, even as they seem to err or fall on deaf ears, in many ways define Udall's own investment in developing vernacular drama in England. If we listen closely to the language of the play and consider that language in terms of Udall's other writings, we can see how the play both mobilizes and complicates not simply patriarchal but also humanist and Reformation evaluative mechanisms for the discernment of "error." To begin, following the hint provided by the allusion to Titiuile, we can attend to the play's reflection on the sound of its own words, to the sound of a vernacular drama in the making.

The very title of the play announces its interest in a rather silly species of vernacular sound-making: the *sound* of "Ralph Royster Doyster" cannot be missed. Unlike Dauy Diceplayer, Watkin Waster, and the other, almost exclusively alliterative, names in the play, Ralph's name announces the potential silliness of rhyme as well as alliteration. The nonsense "doyster" simply echoes "royster"; this is an appropriate enough name for a character who consistently refers to himself, even in the process of addressing others. In Ralph, the only character with a rhymed as well as alliterated name, we find a characterological antitype of Udall's dramatic form, which is of course in English (Ralph speaks no Latin, though three other characters do) and is structured in rhymed couplets (except for some of the songs and the prologue in rhyme royal), providing much self-reflexive to-do about vernacular sound-making ("royster" means a typically vacuous, riotous noise maker).[17] If Donatus called the subject matter of comic drama "impetus periculorum," or petty disturbances,[18] Udall takes small sonic disturbances to the highest of pitches, emphasizing how "roysting" can get in the way of real listening.

Ralph pursues Christian Custance, a rich widow whom he claims to love but whose (rather unforgettable) name he forgets, though he's heard it two or three times before (3v). Even after recalling her name, in a conspicuous example of his insensitivity to the *sound* of language, he sings in a form of rhyme that is merely repetition:

I Mun be maried a Sunday
I mun be *marieb* a Sunday,
Who soeuer shall come that way,
I mun be maried a Sunday.

Royster Doyster is my name,
Royster Doyster is my name,
A lustie brute I am the same,
I mun be maried a Sunday.

Christian Custance haue I founde,
Christian Custance haue I founde,
A Wydowe worthe a thousande pounde,
I mun be maried a Sunday. . . . (32v–33r, emphasis added)

"Mun be" for "must be" offers at least an internal rhyme with "Sunday" and implies a mind on the money, but "*marieb*"? "Marieb" recurs soon again in the song, so it seems to be not a typographical error but an enunciative anticipation of Ralph's ultimate exclusion from that speech act and comic unifier, marriage, that promises to bring the play to a close.[19] (That Ralph later replaces syllables when alluding to God in "by gosse," "gogs armes," and "pashe" (for the Passion of Christ), further thematizes his compromised relation to a spiritual community.) The triplet "name," "name," "same" offers a redundancy atypical of the verse in the play (where couplets and occasional triplets typically unite unlike things), and the song's six repetitions of "Sunday" may at least hint at the association of immoderate rhyme we earlier saw linked to the Catholic liturgy.

Udall himself, writing on the topic of rhyme in a gloss to Erasmus's *Apophthegmes,* referred to "merrie songs and rymes for makyng laughter and sporte at marryages . . . and other feastynges" as a "ragmans rewe, or a bible."[20] "Bible" is a variant of "babble" (as in "bybble bable"), but a curious one in this context, since Udall's single example of such rhymes is of one "now . . . used to syng songes of the Frere and the Nunne" (245r). If rhymes and songs are invoked for Udall in "merrie" anti-Catholicism (or for Wilson and others in not so merry anti-Catholicism),[21] we might ask how a comedy structured by acoustical coincidence, excessive rhyming, and more than a few syllabic missteps might have enabled vernacular innovation and sonic uniformity at a time when English rhyme, though used by poets such as Chaucer and Skelton (both echoed in the play), remained to be fully theorized and validated.[22] In 1555 Richard Sherry would note that poets often skipped or added syllables for the sake of meter and rhyme ("as Chaucer sometyme calleth hym Nerown, whose name in dede is Nero," or where in the phrase "whan Boreas gan . . . is taken awaye a syllable from the begyunyng, gan beyng put for began").[23] What may seem errant pronunciation in one context (Nerown for Nero) is fruitful in another, when "because of the Metre, in stede of fault it is called a figure" (B5r). Apparent mistranscription and mispronunciation, in other words, is sanctioned in poetic verse: "Who will saye, and say truely, *porge dexsram,* for, *porrige dex eram*: and yet so sayeth Uirgill," writes Sherry, while encouraging such experiments in English verse (B4r–5r). Here we find, now in a poetic rather than a theological context, another recuperation of syllabic "ourskipping" or adding in English as well as in Latin verse, where what is otherwise a fault proves a figure. And so "Titiuile." Udall, we have already seen, sanctioned experiments with "mo vocables" in English writing and translation, discouraging critics from finding fault with what he saw as necessary innovations. Linguistic "faults," when unhinged from blame, could thus signify "mo vocables" available for communal aggregation and social participation. Certainly, following Plautus, Terence, and Donatus (in his commentaries on Terence) as well as medieval moralities, Udall knew well of the importance of "error" as constitutive of comic effect. Ralph, however, bears the structural brunt of this in the play, in part freeing many others from what might otherwise be simply coded as errant anti-exemplarity.

Udall, we might say, encourages acoustical "error" in a number of contexts, not least through the very name Ralph Roister Doister, which takes us from alliterative to rhymed sound. If we drop or "ourskyppe" a consonant or two (as the mention of "Titiuile" might compel an attentive auditor to do), we hear "oyster, oyster." Silly as this sounds, Udall often rhymed with a reason, and here we have not one but three: the iconography of the oyster, so central to merrymaking, was a common symbol for eros, aligned with Aphrodite, and signals Ralph's weakened constitution when it comes to the ladies.[24] It also suggested matter with little commercial and symbolic value, neatly encapsulating the content-challenged brags of the boasting warrior who couldn't "kéepe the Quéenes peace" if he tried (2r). More interestingly, the oyster was also aligned, as early as 1499, with stifled speech: "a choking oyster" was "a reply which silences someone."[25] (Udall registers a "stoppyng oystre" in the *Apophthegmes* as a form of speech that stops the mouth of the auditor or interlocutor, as if stuffing food into his or her mouth [55v].)

The *love* that is also implied by oyster is itself entwined with problems of pronunciation from the first, leading Ralph, according to Merrygreek, to mispronounce "love" as "lubbe" (4v), nicely echoed later in "marieb." Here Udall situates an early syllabic mishap in terms of a condition of erotic idolatry that doubles as religious idolatry, with Ralph swearing moments before "by swéete Sainct Anne" (4r). Ralph's idolatry seems to know no bounds (even after death: "In fayth Custance if euer ye come in hell, / Maister Roister Doister shall serue you as well" [16r]). In humanist as well as religious terms, Ralph, who has fallen for an engaged widow yet must "haue hir to my Wife [or] I shall runne madde" (3v), evinces twinned departures from the mean emphasized in emotional and vocal terms in Udall's *Flovres for Latine Spekynge* (1534), translations from Terence composed as a student textbook. There we see that a man lacking restraint in "affections, passions, or desyres of his mynd" is "so ferre out of reson, beyonde hym selfe, or so outragious, that he shulde labour and goo a boute to haue hir to his wyfe, ageynste the vsage and custome of al honest men in the citie."[26] This demeanor is manifest in his speech: "Thy stumblynge or tryppynge in thy wordes, speking one thyng for an other, thy stretching or puttyng forth of thy necke, thy syghyng, spyttyng, cowghyng, & laughyng or gyggelyng" (144r–v).

The student of Udall's textbook on eloquence is of course directed to "forbere" (144v) such "stumblyng or tryppynge," to internalize a logic of clear speech, composed bodily comportment, and moderate passion, all of which Ralph fails to do (as is the case with a number of characters in Terence's plays). When Ralph first speaks to Merrygreek, his love-struck "heart" renders him minimally audible: "But vp with that heart, and speake out like a ramme," says Merrygreek, "Ye speake like a Capon that had the cough now" (3r). Ralph gives it another go, and Merrygreek affirms him: "So loe, that is a breast to blowe out a candle" (3r). Muffled speech proves to be the least of Ralph's problems: Merrygreek's lessons in the art of delivery only elevate this minimally audible lover to disruptive royster. As Ralph puts it later, "I will speake out aloude best, that she may heare it" (22r), yet he brings such a sonic boom to Custance's home that it penetrates her domestic space: "What caitifes are those," she says, "that so shake my house wall?" (28r). Ralph's inability to modulate, or find a middle way between extremes ("Is there no meane your extreme wrath to slake?" asks Tristram Trusty [27v]), proves antithetical to the integrating coordinates of moderated "myrth" mapped out in Udall's prologue (1r). So, with a blindingly idolatrous and immoderate speaker in Ralph (also called a "bibbler" [21r]), and with Tom Titiuile invoked at the outset, the audience is called on to consider the "stumblynge or tryppynge" of vernacular noise-making in humanist and religious, in English and Latin contexts—not least by considering the potentially anti-exemplary dimensions of Madge Mumblecrust herself.

In the play, Madge, missing some teeth, mumbles with food in her mouth (hence "mumblecrust"), embodying a concept of mumble-chewing (talking with food in one's mouth) that puts commonplaces of undigested textual material into vivid culinary terms. In contrast to Udall's elaboration of the nourishing "substanciall meate" of vernacular scripture and commentary (opposed to indigestible Latin mumbling) in his preface to Erasmus's Paraphrase on Luke (A3v), Udall's Madge emerges with a crusty bite, and more than a "smatch" of "natiue country phrases." Curiously, she speaks a number of dialects, variations of country rusticity. Her "God yelde you sir, chad not so much ichotte not whan, / Nere since chwas bore chwine, of such a gay gentleman" (7v) invokes a manifestly southern dialect, alongside the southern *z* in "William zee law, dyd he zo law?" (8v). Here Udall aligns the personified "Mumblecrust" with dialectical and cultural difference. In an anticipation of the "mumbling" nurse in *Romeo and Juliet*,[27] Madge delivers a love letter and is said to talk more than she works. Although Mumblecrust challenges Tibet Talk Apace for acting too much like her name ("Ye were not for nought named Tyb Talke apace") and asks her to sit down and work at her sewing "like a good girle," Tibet responds: "Though your teeth be gone, both so sharpe & so fine / Yet your tongue can renne on patins as well as mine," and "So would I [work], if you coulde your clattering ceasse / But the deuill can not make the olde trotte holde hir tong" (5v–6r). Given such onomastic self-reflexiveness, as well as the emphasis on rapid speech, female talkativeness, and the male lover-warrior's disfluency—all invoking specters of idleness rather than industry—we can easily imagine an extraliturgical Titiuile behind the scenes, gathering sound bites aplenty for his mythic sack. But we can also glimpse him before the scenes, in the figure of Udall himself, scribbling down variegated sounds in a world so distinct from the Rome of a Terence or a Plautus.

Most interestingly for approaching religious as well as secular forms of discursive errancy in the play, Madge Mumblecrust is alone in mumbling the

Latin *Nomine patris* (8r) and *Iesus, nomine, patris* (9v) a number of times, uttering words to "God" at almost every step. Here the Latin "mumblers" so derided in Udall's preface to Erasmus's Paraphrase on Luke, there referring to
male priests, emerge as a gendered, focalized, and extraliturgical form of talk.
Further, the very idea of "mumblecrust" (as the play puts it, "Olde browne
bread crustes must haue much good mumblyng" [6r]) positions "mumbling"
as a sign not only of verbal but also of hermeneutic indistinction, alluding to
the confusion between symbol and substance in the Catholic doctrine of transubstantiation.[28] God's "bread," reads Erasmus's Paraphrase on John in
Udall's edition, "is not receiued by gapyng of the mouthe, but through beliefe
of the soule," nor is it "chewed with teeth, and whiche beeyng conueied
throughe the throte into the stomake, swageth bodilye hungre for a season,
but of heauenly bread, whiche is the woord, of God."[29] If "bread crustes must
haue much good mumblyng" (5v), Madge Mumblecrust may seem to epito-
mize the literalized "dreame of corporall foode" banished in Erasmus's paraphrase and replaced with the incorporeal "woord, of God." Udall's translation
of Thomas Gemmius's 1445 anatomical text, *Compendiosa totius anatomie delineatio,* is also worth noting here, where "yf the teathe be lackynge oure woordes maye not playnelye nor well be pronunced."[30] Mumblecrust's name and
missing teeth thus function as internal stage directions, and call attention to
the intersections between speech, bodies, food, and, particularly, bread.

The play begins and ends with references to eating, from the parasite
looking to "dine," Ralph's gluttonous appetite, and the servants' much discussed desire for food and drink, to the final promised feast at the play's close,
which combine to suggest festivity and also to thematize the question of food,
and indeed bread, as a symbolic unifier. In Udall's translation of Peter Martyr's *Lordes Supper,* the Real Presence is vividly debunked by taking "carnal
eating" to extremes: if Christ literally meant, for example, "this is my body"
at the Last Supper, "it should folowe that Christ didde eate hymselfe" (F3v).
It would not be much of a stretch to imagine such extremes to subtend the
anti-Catholic strain in Udall's play. Udall, who writes in the preface of being
"woondrefully rauished" by Martyr's text, fully sanctions the subjection of the
whore of Babylon's "foule stynking puddle of idolatrie and supersticyon to en-
delesse damnacyon," and offers his translation for "good persones & curates"
with minimal Latin better to instruct their flock (*A2r, *A3r). In addition to
the *Paraphrases,* we might consider Martyr's *Lordes Supper* as a gloss on
"Mumblecrust," particularly as this text twins the Catholic mystification of

the bread with the mystification of the Word, both enabled by a variant of enunciative "ourskipping" once captured by Titivillus. That priest is marked as "euill," for example, who "myght passe ouer those woordes of *consecracion* and recite neuer a one of theim, or might chaunge theim, or els might turne them a contrarie waye" (D4v). The distinctly *figural* dimensions of God's bread, Martyr emphasizes, would be revealed with a scripture "perfeictlye pronounced euen to the last syllable," not overskipping, for example, Paul's reading of Christ's body as spiritual food (a point emphasized by countless reformers [E2v].)[31] Nothing should "bee ommitted or leaste vndoen" in liturgical pronunciation (D4v), nor should any "gappe" be opened by the use of exegetical "fansie" unsanctioned by "Goddes worde expressely . . . leste we open a gappe, and minister occasion to Heretiques" (D2v). Such a "gappe" might lead to unwelcome fancies such as the Real Presence, the worship of saints, or the turn to "a litteral sense which killeth" (H3r).

All this adds up to quite a mouthful for a mumbling character who invokes saints, who utters Latin devotional phrases in inappropriate contexts, who turns words, as we will see, "a contrarie waye," and whose toothlessness (following the Wife of Bath's "gap") suggests lack of disciplinary and discursive restraint.[32] But the story is not so simple. While Martyr's simultaneous demystification of bread and spoken word offers a potential gloss on Mumblecrust, Madge takes on more compelling significance as she is understood to inhabit a world where "gappes" exist not simply within individual bodies and discursive habits but, centrally, *between* social persons separated by rank and gender, something that Udall foregrounds even in the midst of a heavy-handed anti-Catholic and, as some have suggested but I will dispute, ultimately misogynist comedy.[33] As Custance puts it after being slandered for simply being seen in the presence of Ralph and Merrygreek, "O Lorde, how necessarie it is nowe of dayes, / That eche bodie liue vprightly all manner wayes, / For lette neuer so little a gappe be open, / And be sure of this, the worst shall be spoken" (34r). With her fiancé at sea, Custance has been more than "vpright" in her sexual comportment—though she seems to have internalized a logic much challenged by Udall in the play, since her only flaw in the domain of sexual openness was not being able to stop Ralph and Merrygreek from coming to her door (in fact "entering" acoustically with talk and sound from without), and for that involuntary and structural "gappe" she suffers from slanderous gossip. Kent Cartwright and David Bevington rightly argue for Udall's sympathy with Custance as a much abused widow, though

Bevington goes further, in an argument I will soon complicate, to suggest that her exemplary "courage" and "charity" are a mirror for Mary Tudor herself, and that the play itself is a "courtesy book for young women rather than scholars."[34]

But what of Madge Mumblecrust, in whom we have a body that is itself curiously marked by a "gappe," a mouth missing teeth and mumbling on crust, and who, as an unmarried "old" nurse, seems in a precarious position in a play so heavily focused on courtship and marriage? Importantly, Mumblecrust becomes legible within a broader socioeconomic rather than strictly religious economy, or even within the coordinates of "courtesy book" decorum. Dry "bread" that lingers in the mouth awaiting liquid to wash it down (hence producing mumbled speech) recalls the much criticized Catholic practice of withholding wine from parishioners (the servants in fact sing about their wish for drink: "Olde browne bread crustes must haue much good mumblyng, / But good ale downe your throte hath good easie tumbling" [5v]). More interestingly, "old" and crusty bread is explicitly distinguished in the play from the longed-for and more palatable "white bread" of *aristocratic* consumption (5r). This signals Madge's rank-specific diet of old crust and links "mumbling" to conditions of secular impoverishment, not simply Catholic incoherence. As we will soon see, the attention to socioeconomic disparity in the play will trump its anti-Catholic inclinations.

Emphasizing the social dimensions of poverty and material want was often integral to Reformation strategies of demystifying the doctrine of the Real Presence. When Martyr, like Erasmus, foregrounds the relation of bread to conditions of "bodilye hungre," he both places literalized "common bread" at a far remove from the figural, spiritual dimensions of nourishment and enmeshes it in social contexts of hunger and "common" food. On the impossible paradox of "how so great a body maye possibly be conteyned in suche a litle piece of breade" ("not onely in a litell cake of breade, but also in the very least piece therof" [A2v–A3r]), Martyr emphasizes the scriptural attention to bread as a matter of material, not spiritual ingestion, pertaining to the passions of hunger, "the vulgar and common foode of people" (B4v). To literalize the bread would thus be to treat Christ like common food needed for basic bodily needs of infants and the hungry. "In the fiftie ninth chapitur of the prophet Esai," notes Martyr, "Breake thy bread vnto the houngry: and in the fowerth chapitur of the Lamentacions of Hieremie. Their litel babes craued breade & there was none to breake it" (B4v). As the wafer becomes thinner in

Reformation theology, we might say, the plot thickens for Udall's comic drama, adding a curious imperative to consider "Mumblecrust" in terms of the domain of basic food distribution; the "vulgar and common foode" in this play is aligned with her, even as she is separated from the spiritual food of the Word. Similarly, the concept of the morally challenged "parasite," emphasized at the outset in Merrygreek, becomes the occasion for examining broader conditions of social dependence of those who eat on those who provide mere crumbs.

Nursing Wounds: Gender, Humanism, Religion

So what do we make of mumbling explicitly associated with a woman? Do we have in Mumblecrust a commonplace strategy for gendering and displacing a much broader cultural nexus of linguistic and theological tensions? Yet another instance that equates female verbal and bodily license, a convenient form of blame and abuse not recognized as such?[35] Or yet another "nurse" emerging from the tradition that led Thomas Elyot, in *The boke named the Gouernour* (1531), to call "nourises" and "folisshe women" those who omit "lettre[s] or sillables" in verbal "wantonnesse," fostering "corrupte and foule pronuntiation" among young boys in their care (L3v), an antithesis of what Walter Ong long ago called the distinctly male "puberty rite" of Latin language acquisition?[36] As tempting and historically relevant as such perspectives are, particularly given the play's place in the environment of the grammar school, the drama situates Madge as only one part, and by no means the worst part, of a broad sociolinguistic community of lapsed pronunciation and rhetorical mayhem. Within the logic of the play, she along with other servant-mispronouncers comes to stand apart from the dangers of linguistic and behavioral "wantonnesse" marked by the undiscriminating idolatry and vacuous sound-making of the aristocratic Ralph, and the rhetorical machinations of his learned and Vice-like sidekick, Merrygreek.

To examine the question of gender and humanist rhetorical self-fashioning before turning to the question of rank, let us return to Merrygreek's inaugural correction of Ralph's pronunciation ("But vp with that heart, and speake out like a ramme. . . . Ye speake like a Capon that had the cough now"). Here Udall tweaks one of his classical sources to reformulate what was understood as the problem of women as sources for lapsed pronunciation. A "capon" suggests at once a castrated cock and, as illustrated by Udall's translation of Erasmus's *Apophthegmes,* an ineloquent babbler who lacks wisdom: "Metellus was so shuttlebrained that euen in the middes of his tribuneship he left his office in Roome, and sailled to Popeius into Syria, and . . . came flyngyng home to Roome again as wyse as a capon."[37] Metellus, "wyse as a capon," an antiexample of humanist eloquence, is contrasted here with Cicero: "So carefull was *Marcus Tullius* to tell his tale after a good & perfecte sorte, and would bestowe so thoughtful study on such a matier [that] no woord might bee placed out of square" (or as Udall's gloss reads, "out of frame" [312r]). Lacking skills in "oratory" while claiming to have "more trueth" than "eloquence to persuade" (307r), the neutered Metellus falls far from the tree of "the father of all eloquence" (303v), and is rather said to have inherited his promiscuous *mother's* mutability, following every "pangue that shotte in his brain" (307r). Further, his undisciplined mother seems to have infected him with species mutability, as Metellus is likened to the capon but also the crow, "a byrde that hathe none other musik, nor can none other songe ne tune but ka, ka" (307v). This already potent insult is intensified by Udall's Ralph, a capon "with the cough," suggesting a lovesick self-interruption antithetical to humanist, manly self-assertion (implicit in the "syghying" and "cowghyng" of the *Flovres* cited above). Ralph emerges as the schoolboy's nightmare, one who lacks the oratorical "meanes to moue," who makes a fool of himself, loving "singyng out of measure" (without hearing the double sense of his own words), yet believing his "matter frameth well" (3v, 5r).

But Udall also importantly complicates the distinct gendering of ineloquence in the *Apophthegmes.* Ralph is never aligned with suspect maternal influence but seems rather to orbit in his own sphere: his wild, promiscuous falling in love with women while forgetting their names suggests that he operates without any knowledge of women at all. He is himself an aging bachelor, and the fact that he is likened to more than a few farm animals (from "dawes" to a "kite," "calfe," "sheep," a "horse," a "dogge," and a "brute beast"), along with the fact that he vacillates between amorous and homicidal passions (both signs of idolatry as well as grandiosity), make his counterpart, the aging, unmarried, though God-fearing Madge Mumblecrust, look comparatively decorous. Christian Custance, a chaste widow who takes the place of the classical courtesans of Plautus and Terence, rejects out of hand this "sottish dolt" with "as much brain as a burbolt," and echoes words spoken earlier by Merrygreek, noting, "If he come abroad he shall cough me a mome" (meaning, if he comes near me he will prove himself a poor-spoken blockhead [14v]). As we consider gender and speech in the play, we should note that Custance speaks with a clarity and concision of speech that directly contrasts with Merrygreek's later account of it to Ralph. She does give Merrygreek license to improvise her account of saying no to Ralph's relentless courting, to "adde what so euer thou canst" (while aware of the need for hyperbole for Ralph to "hear" her "no," she has no interest in elaborating further [14v]). But when recounting her rejection to Ralph, Merygreek fabricates an unbounded insult allegedly from Custance's "mouth" with a conspicuous hurl of terms, including "Ye are such a calfe, such an asse, such a blocke, / Such a lilburne . . . such a lobcocke / . . . the veriest dolte that euer was borne, / And veriest lubber, flouen and beast."

This unrestrained stream is capped off with Merrygreek's "But I coulde not stoppe hir mouth" (15v). Ralph is thus surprised when he meets Custance moments later. "Hir talke," he notes (struck by her wittiness, brevity of repartee, and what Merrygreek calls her "Rhetorik"), is as if "she had learned in schooles" (17r). Here Udall clearly stages female mouthiness, unbounded speech, or what Lauren Berlant has called the backfiring "female complaint,"[38] as a fiction designed for male-male exchange and bolstered masculinities. As Merrygreek puts it before delivering the fictive heap, "I shall paint out our wower in colours of the best. / And all that I say shall be on Custances mouth" (15r). But Custance's mouth, as if "learned in schools," has little problem "stopp[ing]," exposing Merrygreek's misogyny and, more subtly, calling attention to Udall's deployment of the talkative female servants earlier in the play, who only momentarily deflect attention from the predominantly male forms of discursive and ideological errancy in a drama for schoolboys. If Custance sounds "learned in schools," what of Ralph, who speaks out of school and (alternating between loving women and wanting to kill them) lacks the moral consciousness of mumbling Madge, who at least evinces concern with what it means to act like a "good girle" (5v) and later prays to God to guide her conduct?

While Custance and Mumblecrust both find ways to uphold variants of the "good," Ralph and Merrygreek continue to decline for the benefit of the comedy. Returning to the question of Madge's association with Latin mumbling, though her name suggests a distinctly female focalization of ecclesiastical ritual, we soon hear the protean Merrygreek deploying Latin more extensively in a mock-eulogy for Ralph (who claims he has died of love).

When Ralph says, "The pangs of death my hearte do breake," Merrygreek responds with a performance of Catholic ritual: "Holde your peace for shame sir, a dead man may not speake. / *Nequando:* What mourners and what torches shall we haue? . . . He will go darklyng to his graue, / *Neque lux, neque crux, neque* mourners, *neque* clinke, / He will steale to heauen , vnknowing to God I thinke. / *A porta inferi,* who shall your goodes possesse?" (15v). Attending to candles, crosses, mourners, prayers, bells and property in what one scholar has called a "jumbled parody of the Roman ritual for the Dead,"[39] Merrygreek calls on the "parish Clarke":

> Now Iesus Christ be your spéede.
> Good night Roger olde knaue, farewell Roger olde knaue,
> Good night Roger olde knaue, knaue knap. *vt infra.*
> Pray for the late maister Roister Doisters soule,
> And come forth parish Clarke, let the passing bell toll.
> Pray for your mayster sirs, and for hym ring a peale. (16r)

With no less than *five* bell sounds to follow, and with Catholic apparati in full gear, we have a clear send-up of what Hugh Latimer would deride as "halowed belles, palmes, candelles, asshes, and what not" that take "awaye some parte of Christes sanctificacion," for "the deuill taught vs holy belles."[40] Udall's noisy drama for the dead, an appropriate enough farewell to a roisterer, is especially effective, since Ralph is, of course, not dead. Merrygreek's elegiac apostrophe is designed, no less than his many other performances of social subordination (he variously plays a woman devoted to Ralph, a slave tending on his every need, and now a Catholic worshipper mourning his lost friend), to mirror Ralph's overstated affect in order to get him back in the game of mischief making.

But the loud homiletic strain has its own function for the dramatic economy, as it enables Merrygreek at least momentarily to silence, or symbolically kill off, the blubbering Ralph, in order to reshape him as a "man" ready for more action. Merrygreek pretends to revive him in a mock-resurrection by rubbing his temples, and then gives him not a Catholic but a humanist lesson on how to fashion himself anew:

> Vp man with your head and chin,
> Up with that snoute man: so loe, nowe ye begin,

So, that is somewhat like, but prankie cote, nay whan,
That is a lustie brute, handes vnder your side man:
So loe, now is it euen as it shoulde bée,
That is somewhat like, for a man of your degrée.
Then must ye stately goe, ietting vp and downe,
Tut, can ye no better shake the taile of your gowne? (16v)

Here we have another lesson in "pronunciation," that part of rhetoric concerned with bodily as well as vocal modulation. Can humanist pedagogy correct such bumbling idolatry? Might an anti-Catholic play based on Plautus and Terence suggest as much? Apparently not, for what is interesting is how inefficacious such pedagogy proves to be. Ralph, believing himself a man reformed, only goes headlong into further disasters of self-fashioning. Humanist learning, through which Merrygreek aligns Ralph with classical examples ranging from Cato and Hercules to Hector and the nine worthies (4r–v), proves only to bolster his delusions of grandeur, his "facing and craking / Of his great actes in fighting and fraymaking," that prevent him from seeing himself as others do, and from seeing others as they are. Though Merrygreek counterposes his classical examples with those of popular literary consumption (he claims to have overheard many a lady comparing Ralph to heroes of romance), his use of classical learning encourages no less "error" than was commonly associated with the distinctly female reading of vernacular romance.[41]

Lest we think Udall unequivocal about Terence, that classroom staple for cultivating rhetorical and analytic skill, what he essentially stages is a microcosm of what Anthony Grafton and Lisa Jardine have understood as the disjunction between humanist training and ethical social participation.[42] While Merrygreek's classical learning renders him the capable antithesis of *vir bonus dicendi peritus* (the good man skilled in speech), conversely, a servant of Ralph's errs in the pronunciation of a Latin phrase (7v) yet proves ever more canny and sympathetic than his master. But in a useful enough ambiguity for Udall—the Protestant convert who survived comfortably under Catholic Queen Mary (and very likely penned her coronation play, *Respublica* [1553]) and translator who sanctioned "special regarde" for the "rude and vnlettred" of England yet wrote a response condemning the Cornish Prayer Book rebellion—we find that it is not entirely clear, in the domain of language "abuse," just what historical communities or language practices (humanist or religious, textual or oral) are subject to "blame." Potentially anti-Catholic rhyme and sound-making add to the comic festivity, contributing to a comedy of sonic error that manages, somehow, to unite *most* of the "commontie" in the end.

As far as the status of sound in relation to the written or printed text is concerned, other than the Latin texts and vernacular Romances already alluded to, we have two central texts worth noting at this point. One is an amorous epistle that backfires through mispronunciation when read aloud; this speaks to the instability of the text as a reliable guide to spoken utterance.[43] The other is "the Gospell," which emerges in the printed play's afterword as a text under the protection of a "renowed Queen" who aimes for "learning and vertue to aduaunce, and vice to correct," in the country (32r–v). This queen has variously been deemed by scholars to be Mary Tudor, Elizabeth I, or even Edward VI (since "king" might have been altered in the printing),[44] but she could equally be Katherine Parr (particularly given Udall's elaborate panegyric, in his preface to Erasmus's Paraphrase on Luke, to her well-known efforts to spread learning and virtue).[45] But the fact that scholars differ over the identity of this imagined auditor speaks to the "middling" status of the play with regard to religious polemic. For despite the roistering, bells, rhymes, songs, and whistles that might be glossed as anti-Catholic, the closing words to the queen about the Gospels are sung, and sung collectively, in that "ragman's rewe or bible" of rhymed couplets. Why not have a single plain-speaking Christian Custance offer the final tribute? It seems that Udall wants to keep the tension alive between that printed Gospel protected from "error" and the potentially logomarginal sound-making that can challenge it or bring it to life in another way. The closing song in fact follows Ralph's final words: "Sing on, & no mo words make" (32r). This privileges musical harmony (or perhaps polyphony) over the play's verbal and textual division.

Udall claims, in conventional form, to have composed a comedy "auoiding such mirth wherin is abuse" and "auoidyng all blame" in the "mirth we intende to vse" (1r). Hence it is unsurprising to find the cultural logic of blame so integral to Reformation theology becoming, in and through the play, ambiguated. If, as a character puts it, "with turnyng of a hand, our mirth lieth in the mire" (11r), Udall lightened what we have elsewhere seen as his heavy hand—not the least with playful rhyme consistently counterbalancing polemical potential with sonic "mirth." "For Myrth prolongeth lyfe, and causeth health. / Mirth recreates our spirites and voydeth pensiuenesse, / Mirth increaseth amitie, not hindring our wealth, / Mirth is to be vsed both of more and lesse, / Being mixed with vertue in decent comlynesse" (1r). Mirth has its own uses, and it enabled Udall to approach a tension integral to Reformation approaches to "common" language explored above, which aimed to liberate "*the* Tailers, *and* Smithes, *and* Weauers, *and of al* Artificers: *Yea, and further also of* Weemen: *and . . . of* Labouringe Weemen, *and* Sewsters, *and* Seruantes, *and* Handemaìdes" (as Jewel puts it in *A Defence of the Apologie of the Churche of Englande* [507]), yet would establish a "common speach" of prayer that would in fact do injustice to the language of many a common folk and country people. This tension was equally central to developments in vernacular verse: Richard Tottell prefaced the *Songes and sonettes* of 1557 by defining "English eloquence" against "swinelike grosseness," "the rude skill of common eares."[46] In Udall's play, just what are the coordinates of justice when it comes to linguistic liberty?

From one perspective, Udall's concerns about his own departure in the *Paraphrase* from the standards of classical Latinity, where the vernacular limits his capacity to fashion language with equal elegance and grace, might be understood to find a vigorous outlet in this play, where discursive self-fractioning is pushed *outward*, located in terms of *various* social roles and codes of rhetorical and behavioral decorum. This would be analogous with Thomas Wilson's comedy of collective mispronunciation in a text that aimed to transmit classical rhetoric into "common" English. Udall's vernacular play is, as we have now begun to see, rife with characters animated by linguistic indistinction: Tibet Talk Apace named for discursive speed (5v), Mumblecrust incarnating what Udall elsewhere calls "mumblers," and Dobinet Doughtie mingle-mangling the Latin "*Nobs nicebecetur Miserere*" (7v) all lead to comic confusion (Merrygreek mistakes Madge for the object of Ralph's amorous passion).[47] But beyond laboring servants, Merrygreek chastises Ralph for "blubber[ing]" (18v), three times mockingly mispronounces "love" as "lub" and "lubbe" (4v, 19r), and deploys Catholic Latin in a mock-requiem. And Ralph himself sends Custance such an ambiguously backfiring love letter that Wilson adopted it under "Ambiguity" in *The rule of Reason* (1553) as "an example of soche doubtful writing, whiche by reason of poincting maie haue *double sense*, and contrarie meaning."[48]

Udall's whole play, however, exemplifies an ambiguous "double sense," where abuses of language, particularly of the English language, come head to head with anti-Catholic and anti-Catholic Latin satire. The play is less a single than a double anamorph, where, on the one hand, the Reformation

concern with liberating the "rude" laity from conditions of religious subjection is positioned alongside an acute awareness of broader forms of socioeconomic disparity, and, on the other hand, a humanist drama that sends up
rhetorical misuse manages to recuperate such misuse in the name of a more
equitable species of humanism. In a play that helped to set the stage for the
development of (Roman) English comedy in (Catholic) Protestant England,
this doubly anamorphic structure enabled Udall to maximize his resources: to
activate Protestant and humanist dogma while expanding the sense, or double sense, of both.

The Truths of Bad Pronunciation: Rank, Complaint, and Acoustical Grandiosity

If we listen closely, as Udall encourages us to do if only to dis-identify with
Ralph, we can even begin to hear forms of bad or mispronunciation operating with this double sense. For if humanist lessons in pronunciation prove futile for Ralph, we find other moments in the play where lapses of
pronunciation are not only conspicuously *performed* but also curiously *efficacious*, turning ideals of both plain speech and vernacular eloquence on their
head. Returning to the fact that, as W. W. Greg once pointed out, Madge
Mumblecrust, "for no apparent reason, lapses into dialect,"[49] I now want to
tend to the canny dimensions of mis-performance by servant-laborers in the
play. The servants are typically petrified at being evaluated by their social superiors, and they live in fear of being chastised and "beaten" (6r). Since Udall
is famed for his harsh pedagogical beatings, we might leap to the assumption
that servants are stand-ins for the potentially unruly students who were playing parts in his play.[50] The plain-speaking Christian Custance's heavy handed
rule may strengthen this reading, while expanding the specter of corrective
severity from humanist classroom to theologically ordered household. But
this does not do justice to the unusual attention Udall pays to the bodily and
vocal vulnerability of the servants in the play, not to mention in his nondra-
matic writing. As Udall writes in a gloss to Terence, drawing on Cicero to il-
lustrate the accusative case, "Meminerimus autem et aduersus infimos
iusticiam esse seruandā for seruandum esse iusticiam, *And we must remember
to kepe Iustice, that is, to dele iustly and truely also with the poorest and lowest
persons that be*" (*Flovres*, 121v, emphasis added). In one of Udall's many glosses

to Terence that exceed the demands of textual clarification, he explains "pistrinum" but goes on to emphasize injurious conditions of labor for those who make bread: "*Pistrinum* was a place where the corne was grounde and bredde made: and it is deriuied of *pinso, sis, sui, situm, uel pistum*, whiche is either to grynd with mylstones or to bete to meale with a pestle in a morter, as (for lacke of mylles) men in olde tyme dyd: and bycause it was a verye peynefull thynge, and full of labour, many vsed for punyshement of their seruantes to put them to that office, whiche was to them a sore and greuous punishement and enprisonment" (16v).

Servant work turns out, in Udall's play, to be a "verye peynefull thing, and full of labour" often aligned by servants with "punishement," "enprison-ment," and physical pain. In the play, Udall has three female servants (in the company of Ralph, Tibet Talk Apace, Madge Mumblecrust, and Annot Ale-face) sing a song of four verses with repeated logomarginalia, such as "Trilla, Trilla, Trillarie" (6v–r). But Udall encourages us to hear complaint within what may seem mere festive noise: the verses that begin as a song to speed in-dustry end as a song where complaints of hunger, thirst, fatigue, and the pain of menial drudgery lead this triplet to imagine abandoning work. Despite the festive sounds and noises, the content of the song is worth noting, as it sug-gests that noise might well conceal something important. The opening verse, "Pipe mery Annot. &c. / Trilla, Trilla, Trillarie. / Worke Tibet, worke Annot, worke Margerie. / Sewe Tibet, knitte Annot, spinne Margerie / Let vs see who shall winne the victorie," is followed by: "Trilla. Trilla. Trillarie. / What Tibet, what Annot, what Margerie. / Ye sléepe, but we doe not, that shall we trie. / Your fingers be nombde, our worke will not lie. . . . / Pipe Mery Annot. &c. / Trilla. Trilla. Trillarie. / Nowe Tibbet, now Annot, nowe Margerie. / Nowe whippet apace for the maystrie / But it will not be, our mouth is so drie. . . . / Pipe Mery Annot. &c. / Trilla. Trilla. Trillarie. / When Tibet, when Annot, when Margerie. / I will not, I can not, no more can I. / Then giue we all ouer, and there let it lye" (6v–r). Interestingly, at the song's end, Madge suddenly realizes that one man (who turns out to be Merrygreek) has heard her singing in the presence of another (Ralph), something she frets about as bespeaking impropriety: "Yond stode a man al this space / And hath hearde all that euer we spake togyther" (6r). While Tibet Talk Apace could not care less (calling the man a "loute" who would care to "listen to maidens talke"), Mumblecrust is more concerned and wants to find out who caught her in an act of unre-strained vocality (6r). This fits with the concern articulated moments earlier that she *not* be seen as a complainer for simply urging Tibet to work: "I dyd neyther chyde, nor complaine, nor threaten. . . . I dyd nothing but dyd hir worke and holde hir peace" (6r).[51]

It is at the moment that Madge becomes self-conscious about *complaining* and singing in the presence of Ralph and now Merrygreek, the former a presumptuous man of "degree" who gives her a kiss, that she lapses into dialect, just after attending to the dirt on her body that makes her an unsuitable object for a kiss (6v). "God yelde you sir, chad not so much ichotte not whan, / Nere since chwas bore chwine, of such a gay gentleman" (6v). While she apparently thanks and compliments him for the kiss (God repay you, sir; I have not had so much since I don't know when, / Never since I was born, I think, from such a merry gentleman), why the dialect? After being caught in acts of singing and complaining, and after being chastised by Tibet (who wishes Custance present to demonstrate proper indignation in the face of such a kiss), Madge arguably *performs* dialect to quickly reestablish her proper "place" in a discursive sphere, reasserting gender decorum and reestablishing social distance by inhabiting rusticity.[52] While Madge "will not stick for a kosse [kiss] with such a man as yow" (7r), we also find her performing sociolinguistic marginality in order to establish distance from one who, we hear soon enough, makes her feel frustrated and sad rather than "gay." Tibet Talk Apace, true to her name, wields her tongue more explicitly.[53]

While Tibet Talk Apace says directly, "No forsoth, by your leaue ye shall not kisse me," Mumblecrust is *indirect,* calling attention again to Ralph's elevated status by responding to his "Ah good sweet nurse," with "Ah, good sweet gentleman" (7r). Interestingly, her comment here is apparently mumbled (perhaps without conviction or said inaudibly in turning away from another attempted kiss), since Ralph responds, for no other apparent reason, "What?" (7r). What follows is a staccato-like dialogue in which Madge (who has suggested that Custance is interested in him, distracting him with another object) offers minimal responses to his eager queries for more information with no fewer than six consecutive utterances of "Een so sir" (7r–v). The rustic southern dropped *u,* which differs from her fully pronounced *u*'s elsewhere, is so conspicuous as to lead one to wonder if she is playing a variant of Tituile herself, capturing syllables on purpose. It is as if Madge is trying to escape into the margins of the encounter through the sparsest of words. She at once mirrors Ralph's grandiosity and "self-unfashions" to resist his jurisdictional presumptions: "What ayleth thys fellowe?" she says in the very next scene. "He driueth me to wéeping" (7v). For Madge, consonant and vowel manipulation instantiate a dialect that implies a subaltern form of female agency and performative self-awareness. Even as her sudden lapses of speech may seem to validate assumptions implicit in the humanism that Elyot invokes in his description of nurses mispronouncing words in the presence of young boys, or in problems that dialect poses to the ideal of "common speech," or even in the relation between discursive and ethical lapses, here we have a form of unfashionable self-fashioning that manages to "do" something without appearing to be direct complaint; and so, she is promised money for new clothes by Ralph to deliver a letter to Custance.

If Madge's relative indirectness speaks to the *problem* of speaking one's mind directly in the play, a problem for women much abused by presumptuous men, it also smacks of a form of indirect negotiation associated with her socially disempowered status. Indeed, rather than simply seeing Madge as an ignorant, rustic, and unwitting co-conspirator in the comedy of roistering, we might recall that earlier, when Madge says, "I dyd neyther chyde, nor complaine, nor threaten," Ralph interrupts her: "It would grieve my heart to see one of them [the servants] beaten" (6r). The costs of speaking out are part of what creates distortions of language akin to mumbling. When Madge is alone (later realizing her error in transmitting the letter to Custance), we see a plain-speaking variant of her language above: "I Was nere so shoke vp afore since I was borne. . . . And I pray God I die if I ment any harme."[54] For it is only in the presence of male social superiors that her dialectical difference and dropped syllables conspicuously emerge, emphasizing linguistic distance just where social decorum is being breached. Unlike the aristocratic female complainer we will see in a moment, Madge has more freedom to move about in both language and the world. (We might also note that it is only in the company of Ralph and Merrygreek that Madge utters Latin, rather than plain-spoken, devotional phrases.) In some ways we have come full circle, from Titivillus's capture of the "unsaid" within the mumble to the use of mumbling in order *not* to have to speak directly but to *do* something else.[55]

This brings us to a consistent concern of the play, one possibly obscured by the critical focus on the inept or merely comic *miles gloriosus*: under so much noise-making Udall calls attention to the difficulty of verbal negotiation under the regime of a hearing-impaired and jurisdictionally grandiose title character. As Ralph puts it when waging war, with the encouragement of Merrygreek, on the house of Custance, "I mine owne selfe will in this present cause, / Be Sheriffe, and Iustice, and whole Iudge of the lawes, / This matter to amende, all officers be I shall, Constable, Bailiffe, Sergeant," and "I will take the lawe on her withouten grace" (28v). The dramatic pattern of challenged militarism turned juridical grandiosity turned domestic tragedy may well resonate for many a Renaissance scholar: some fifty years later these juridical roles would be played by Othello, who is manipulated by his own parasite, Iago, in the suffocation of Desdemona.[56] In Udall's world, though we are far from domestic tragedy, we are nonetheless asked to consider what it means to inhabit a sphere of single-minded authority that remains deaf to other voices, deaf in particular to the sound of complaint, which becomes paradoxically diminished when rendered excessive.

This issue surfaces in another play, *Respublica*, composed for Queen Mary in 1553, convincingly attributed by W. W. Greg to Udall.[57] To take a single detail: the character "People," sympathetically portrayed as a canny yet abused collective ("Representing the poor Commontie"), who suffers under a corrupt governmental and erstwhile unjust Protestant regime, speaks with the southern dialect used by Madge.[58] On the matter of direct complaint and the tricky situation of any voice of possible protest in the Republic, however, People's complaints of mistreatment are quickly recoded by (corrupt) counselors "Insolence, all*ias Authoritie*" and "Oppression, all*ias Reformation*," who say they "crow against your betters!" and "murmoure against the Lawe!" (4.4.1143–46).

In light of the accusation of "murmuring" hurled against the justly concerned rustic People, and Madge Mumblecrust's circumvention of direct "complaint" through her canny performance of lexical and dialectical subordination, it is suggestive that Udall attempted—in his written response to the demands of the real Catholic people of England, who protested against the "new English" of common prayer in 1549—to forge a middle way between direct and indirect complaint. While many of Udall's contemporaries responded to the demands of the Cornishmen with unequivocal hostility, Udall took a more multifaceted tack. When the rebels refused the "common" vernacular so different from the Celtic traditions operative in Cornwall, they also demanded to preserve the traditional Latin Mass, and to have all vernacular translations of the Bible recalled. One of their articles reads: "Item, we will not receive the new service because it is but like a Christmas game, but we will have our old service of matins, mass, evensong, and procession in Latin, not in English, as it was before. And so we Cornishmen (whereof certen of us un-

derstand no English) utterly refuse this new English" (169). Udall's first response was very much in line with Reformation polemic. Challenging the
rebels for demanding a service in Latin, he wrote in response to their *written*
articles: "Have ye now so little fear of god and so evil consciences that ye dare
with such rebellious mouths openly repel that all the royalme besides do justice good and godly?" (171). Udall defended the Book of Common Prayer as
having been produced by "the King's Majesty's Council, the wisest men, the
best learned bishops and doctors of the realme, [who] so long sitten together
in conferring, writing, and framing it. . . . The whole Convocation and parliament upon mature examination thereof allowed it for service most godly
and most mete to be uniformly used throughout all the King's dominions and
so admitted it by a law, and make ye thereof a Christmas game?" (169). Further, he challenged the logic of the articles: "Good neighbours, ye Cornishmen, do ye not understand English as well as Latin? Yes (I dare say) both more
of you in number and also better do ye understand the English than the
Latin." In what should now seem a familiar maneuver, incomprehensible
Latin was used here to validate ideally "uniform" English.

But what is perhaps most interesting of all, Udall provided an alternative
form of political representation through which the rebels might in fact suc-
ceed in having a service in their own language. "If ye had understand no English," he wrote, "and for that consideration had by the way of petition made
humble request to the King's Majesty and his Council in this or some other
like fourme," then their concerns would likely have been heard. What follows
is an epistle, composed in their name:

> Where it hath pleased your most excellent Majesty by the authority of
> your high court of Parliament to sette forth unto your most loving and
> obedient subjects in the English tongue one uniform way of divine
> service to be used in all churches within this your highness' realme of
> Englande, So it is, most gracious sovereign, that we the Cornishmen,
> being a portion of your most loving faithful and true obedient subjects,
> being also as much desireous to take thereby such ghostly consolation
> and edifying as others of your majesty's subjects do, and being no less
> hungry, prompt, glad, and ready to receive the light and truth of God's
> most holy word and ghospel than any part of your Majesty's realm,
> most humbly beseech your Majesty that with such convenient speed as
> to your most excellent highness shall seem good we may by your grace's

provision have the same fourme of divine service and communion derived and turned into our Cornish speech that goeth abroad among the rest of your most loving and obedient subjects in the other parts of this your realm of England, etc. (171–72)

Udall, ever the playwright, composed words of protest, modulating the inefficacy of direct complaint with an *appearance* not of self-fashioning but of other-fashioning. Udall's sample epistle emphasizes the power of rhetorical self-subordination, of linguistically elevating God's anointed sovereign and of establishing the appearance of consent to the "uniform" tongue, in order to validate the regional speech excluded by the newly nationalized "English tongue." "If ye had (I say) made such an humble and godly request as this I doubt not but the King, our sovereign lord's Majesty, would have tendered your request, and provided for the accomplishments of your desires" (172). Udall thus called for a deliberate muting to temper the tone of resistance so explicit in the articles, offering this letter that, though apparently self-abasing, suggests a middle way through which "Cornish speech" might be acknowledged without threatening the concept of a "uniform" kingdom.

Udall certainly knew whereof he wrote, for he seems to have been the master of rhetorical abjection and self-unfashioning.[59] His career, as one scholar puts it, was "one vast contradiction: apparently from early youth an ardent Lutheran Protestant, his highest distinction was attained at the hand of the Catholic Queen Mary; a Puritan, yet at one time master of the Court revels; writer of pious treatises on religion, a priest of the Established Church, and yet, dismissed from his high office at Eton under serious charges of robbery and gross immorality with two of his students; dismissed from Eton under a cloud, and created Headmaster of Westminster only about ten years later."[60] Udall wrote the response to the rebels under, or in the name of, "the King's Majesty and his Council," yet found a way to articulate a double sense that could at once condemn the rebels on behalf of the state and acknowledge their exclusion from "common" English. This double sense is encapsulated in the epistle, which fully sanctions royal authority while articulating some the limits to that authority when it comes to linguistic uniformity.

The call for diplomatic muting is worth noting in a text that consistently deploys the word "murmuring" (the word hurled against People in *Respublica*) to describe the seditious rebels (used no fewer than twelve times in this short tract). The term recurs with its full biblical import: "Ye play now like as the

Jews, when they murmured against God and against their governour Moses in the wilderness" (166). We find no mumbling here; the complaints in the written articles are too direct for that. Yet, "Ye must be brideled of your unreasonable requests" (180), wrote Udall, aiming to find a way to tame the rhetoric of conspiratorial resistance *and* to tame his own polemic in the process. Udall's emphasis on performativity, "Ye play now like as the Jews," is part of that taming, anticipating the performative adaptation enacted in the epistle above. With flatteries, self-abasements, and interrogatives in the place of direct "complaint," Udall imagined a position for the Cornishmen similar to the linguistically deferential position Mumblecrust takes in her encounter with the jurisdictionally grandiose Ralph, who disrespects moral and social boundaries of decorum, aims to possess what is not his, and, in a totalizing if comic vision of conquest, feels it his right to kiss (or later to kill) anyone he pleases.

It is, to be sure, a leap from a political tract to a comic drama, but the tract gives us a powerful sense of Udall aiming to find ways *between* positions divided by polemic, or tactically speaking, between ineffectual directness and effectual indirectness: between the urgently "said" and the "fourme" of address that might leave a great deal unsaid but still manages to get something done. In contrast to the tension that we saw in Wilson's *Rhetorique* between liberatory Reformation theology and the more restrictive imperatives of national language formation, Udall postulated a middle way that both sanctioned the king's complete sovereignty and opened the way for an alternative model of a communally constructed sense of the "uniform" or authoritative whole. The emphasis on Udall's treatment of the linguistically marginalized Cornishmen and on Madge's performance of linguistic subordination in the play calls attention to the ways in which apparent lapses of utterance on stage can be *strategic*: they are not simply a mirror, for example, of deficient regional speech deployed for comic or normativizing effect but also a way to index particular frames of mind that, if imperceptible to aristocratic or scholarly listeners within the play, may be perceptible to an attentive audience. Udall's response to the Cornishmen consistently positioned itself on the side of the innocent, the "simple people," and the laboring masses, whom he believed to be duped by Catholic ringleaders or "rank papists."[61] Early on he addressed the composers of the articles as "we," thereby integrating a space of common ground in order to be heard. "You" gains frequency as Udall's rhetoric and outrage intensify, but he still attempts, in his epistle, to find another "fourme" through which to arrive at a more diverse constellation of "we." Such a postulate of "we" is implicit in *Ralph Roister Doister* in the evident sympathy with much abused laborers, whose relationship to language is often challenged most conspicuously in the presence of their "betters."

Two of these laborers are "manual" workers of a different sort: Dobinet, Ralph's servant, who says he is anything but a "pen man," and finally the penman himself, the Scrivener, hired to write Ralph's epistolary plea. When Dobinet mangles the Latin phrase I quoted above, this too is in the presence of his superiors. It comes, in fact, just after Dobinet acknowledges that servants "douke" in fear and deference in the presence of superiors and "crouche at euery worde / . . . whether our maister speake earnest or borde [jest]" (7v). For this cowering self-abasement Dobinet is rewarded: "For this lieth vpon his preferment in deed" (7v). Linguistic and gestural cowering has its own paradoxical "capital," which leads to "preferment in deed" by maintaining the illusion of social difference. But despite Dobinet's gestural deference and mispronounced Latin, he is *also* given the longest soliloquy in the play, where he proves more canny than his "maister." For what he says when alone is just as telling as what he says, or mis-says, in the presence of his social superiors. Having been sent as yet another go-between (to deliver a ring from Ralph to Custance), Dobinet says:

> Where is the house I goe to, before or behinde?
> I know not where nor when nor how I shal it finde.
> If I had ten mens bodies and legs and strength,
> This trotting that I haue must néedes lame me at length.
> And nowe that my maister is new set on wowyng,
> I trust there shall none of vs finde lacke of doyng:
> Two paire of shoes a day will nowe be too litle
> To serue me, I must trotte to and fro so mickle.
> Go beare me thys token, carrie me this letter,
> Nowe this is the best way, nowe that way is better.
> Up before day sirs, I charge you, an houre or twaine,
> Trudge, do me thys message, and bring worde quicke againe,
> If one misse but a minute, then his armes and woundes,
> I woulde not haue slacked for ten thousand poundes. . . .
> I trowe neuer was any creature liuyng,
> With euery woman is he in some loues pang,

Then vp to our lute at midnight, twangled our twang,
Then twang with our sonets, and twang with our dumps,
And beyhough from our heart, as heauie as lead lumpes:
Then to our recorder with toodleloodle poope
As the howlet out of an yuie . . . should hoope.
Anon to our gitterne, thromple dum thrumpledum thrum,
Thrumpledum, thrumpledum, thrumpledum, thrupledum thrum.
Of Songs and Balades also he is a maker,
And that can he as finely doe as Iacke Raker,
Yea and *extempore* will he dities compose,
Foolishe *Marsias* nere made the like I suppose,
Yet must we sing them, as good stuffe I vndertake,
As for such a pen man is well sittyng to make.
But then, from his heart to put away sorowe,
He is as farre in with some newe loue next morowe.
But in the meane season we trudge and we trot
From dayspring to midnyght, I sit not, nor rest not. (10r)

Three things are notable here: Dobinet's clarity and self-awareness of speech, the recurrent emphasis on the pains of physical labor, and the explicit situation of sonic foolery (from ill-composed sonnets to "thromple dum thrumple dum" and "twangled . . . dumps") as a coerced ventriloquization of the master, Ralph. The lexicon of slow-motion labor—trotting, trudging, and carrying, which "lame" the body—and the image of acoustical "dumps" (sad songs) and "lead lumps" mirror Tibet Talk Apace's self-image of her own physical motion: she moves "lumperdée sumperdée like our spaniell Rig," whereas if she had money of her own, she imagines, the world might "sée hir glide" (11v). Similarly, Madge, the "old trotte," when asked to deliver the love letter from Ralph to her mistress Custance, remarks, "I trude wt your letter" (9r). So too there is much ado later in the play about the "slow goer" Tristram Trusty, who seems to take forever to come to Custance's home to do her a favor (though this also thematizes the long process of establishing communal trust and female credibility in the world of the play [24v]).[62]

Udall slows the pace of the drama through Dobinet's soliloquy in order to attend to conditions of social subordination that undergird compromised speech and bodily comportment. Dobinet, who fears "wounds" more than he desires "pounds," has clearly not been given directions by Ralph but must fill in the gaps in communication with bodily work. In the cases of both Madge and Dobinet, we find verbal and behavioral indistinction linked to conditions of uncomfortable subordination. If Madge shifts her dialectical and acoustical register, or "mumbles" to preserve her integrity, Dobinet, in a sign of learning (though he be not a "pen man"), locates the real source of acoustical mayhem in the foolish Marsayas. Marsayas, the Phrygian satyr who challenged Apollo to a contest, wielding his *aulos* (double reed pipe) against Apollo's lyre, found himself out of his depth. Having lost the contest, Marsayas was flayed alive for his presumptuous pride; his skin was later nailed to a tree, as Ovid recounts, and his blood flowed along with tears to create the river Marsayas.[63] Dobinet's allusion renders Ralph a wind instrument bound to fail, yet before Ralph gets his comeuppance, the "woundes" are borne only by the servant, and the lover's "pang" becomes the servant's "twang."[64]

Ralph, competing with Custance's fiancé by sending an amorous epistle in rhymed couplets, is clearly out of his depth as well: while he is not exactly flayed alive, he is mortified when the letter is read *aloud* to Custance by Merrygreek, who—playing the part of Ralph's servant—mispronounces the letter, disregarding punctuation (or "pointing") in favor of stressed rhyme, so that it suggests hate instead of love. Rather than reed pipe against lyre, we have speech against text. Instead of "Swéete mistresse, where as I loue you, nothing at all / Regarding your richesse and substance," when the writing "doth speak" we hear:

> Swéete mistresse where as I loue you nothing at all,
> Regarding your substance and richesse chiefe of all,
> For your personage, beautie, demeanour and wit,
> I commende me vnto you neuer a whit.
> Sorie to heare report of your good welfare.
> For (as I heare say) suche your conditions are,
> That ye be worthie fauour of no liuing man,
> To be abhorred of euery honest man.
> To be taken for a woman enclined to vice.
> Nothing at all to Uertue gyuing hir due price. . . .
> If ye mynde to bée my wyfe,
> Ye shall be assured for the tyme of my lyfe,
> I will kéepe ye ryght well, from good rayment and fare,
> Ye shall not be kepte but in sorowe and care.

Ye shall in no wyse lyue at your owne libertie,
Doe and say what ye lust, ye shall neuer please me,
But when ye are mery, I will be all sadde,
When ye are sory, I will be very gladde.
When ye séeke your heartes ease, I will be vnkinde,
At no tyme, in me shall ye muche gentlenesse finde.
But all things contrary to your will and minde,
Shall be done: otherwise I wyll not be behinde
To speake. And as for all them that woulde do you wrong
I will so helpe and mainteyne, ye shall not lyue long. (17v–18r)

If "mispronunciation" at the outset of this study could constitute a sin, here
the "bad" pronunciation by Merrygreek, who "ourskippes" and inserts stops
to accommodate metrics and rhyme,[65] speaks truth: he betrays Ralph's interest in the widow's "richness," his capacity to be "vnkinde" and to "loue . . .
nothing at all." The letter, with "correct" punctuation marks, is later recited
in full, and to opposite if insincere effect, giving rhyming with a reason a
whole new meaning, since rhyme exposes reason in this case.

We might further situate this performance by turning to Udall's *Flovres*,
where he glosses a phrase from Terence: "*Inuerto, tis, inuerti, inuersum*, is to
tourne the contrary side outwarde, as of a furre, or of a cappe, or of any other
thynge, and therof *inuertere uerba, est praeposterè aliquid efferre*, to pronounce
wordes, and brynge them out, so that we speake one thynge for an other, as
they vse to do, whose tongues commenly speake that thynge, vppon whiche
their mynde runneth moste" (144r–v). In Merrygreek's pronunciation, we
come tantalizingly close to a (metrically orchestrated) "slip of the tongue" in
which speakers just might say, to their dismay, what "their mynde runneth
[to] moste."[66] The letter, mispronounced so as to "speake one thynge for an
other," converts love to hate in a way that exposes Ralph's hatred of his beloved
object. For Ralph soon recovers from abjection only to vow that he "wyll
vtterly destroy hir, and house and all." This proves the veracity of the mispronounced utterance that his erstwhile love "shall not lyue long" and that he will
"kéepe [her] ryght well, from good rayment and fare." Unlike the carefully
constructed epistle for the Cornishmen, Ralph's epistle is less than careful, for
he is unaware of its double sense: he does not seem to "hear" the words on the
page. The paradoxically "errant" economy of oral and rhymed pronunciation
trumps a written economy of speech. Reforms in vernacular orthography and

spelling were just beginning at this point in Tudor England, but Udall capitalizes on the potential errors of reading aloud to lead to a different species of reformation. Though this is a love letter and not the Gospel, we find here a nice contrast to Cranmer's attempts to outlaw all manner of oral transgression in the matter of the Book of Common Prayer; where we saw Cranmer trying to establish a textually based "fixity," Udall renders unfixity productive for the communal recognition of truth.

This brings us, last but not least, to the figure of the writer in the play, who is a possible stand-in for Udall and a counterpart to Tituile: the Scrivener, who finds himself in danger for his life. The Scrivener was paid to write the original love letter, which was then copied by Ralph in his own hand, so that he could claim, "I wrote it myself" (9v). After hearing the catastrophic sound of the letter, Ralph imagines that it was the Scrivener who botched the punctuation: "I woulde be auenged in the meane space, / On that vile scribler, that did my wowyng disgrace. . . . I wyll hewe hym all to pieces by the Masse" (19r–v). Purposely pronouncing "scrivener" as "scribler" (Merrygreek notes the insult), Ralph seems to want to find a way to appropriate the very mispronunciation that led to his public humiliation. He denies any error on his part and intends to blame the writer. He turns out to be wrong. The "fault" is said by the Scrivener to lie not in the writing but in the reading: "In reading and pointyng there was made some faulte" that made "this letter . . . sonnded so nought" (19v–20r). And indeed Merrygreek eventually confesses to misreading the letter by reading it aloud. But even if Ralph were right to blame the Scrivener or Merrygreek, he still would be in the wrong, since the letter he himself "wrote" was a copy of the original: Could he not have spotted such errant punctuation in the process? As the Scrivener puts it, "He disgraced hym selfe, his loutishnesse is suche" (19v). Appropriately responding to Ralph's twice-uttered "scribler," the Scrivener calls Ralph a "bibbler" (21r), a rhetorical double punch since it implies a babbler who can't even babble right and a "*bibler*." This subtly calls attention to the theological stakes of a Catholic Ralph improperly versed in the vernacular word. Importantly, the word "bibbler" (recalling Udall's noun for rhyme) suggests that the Scrivener at least *heard* the letter in the reading, whereas Ralph only experienced it in the writing. An iconophile to the last, Ralph becomes humiliated precisely by his inability to hear what he sees and, in particular, by his insensitivity to the (truth-) telling sounds of English verse in rhymed couplets, as these couplets were embedded in the letter in the first place.

In Udall's own brand of Erasmian folly it is the potentially nonsensical "ragmans rewe" of vernacular versifying that, through communal attention, participation, and continual adaptation, ultimately establishes the coordinates of community in the play. Udall has created a community of sound that Ralph does not *hear*.[67] Mumblecrust (who, appropriately enough, transmits the love letter, just as her name anticipates the botched pronunciation to come) says plainly: "Open the writing, and see what it doth *speake*" (9v). If the figure of Titiuile bodies forth through the Scrivener, stretching his medium for the daunting task of recording sonic error, Udall stretched his medium as well. While using the morally corrective tradition of comic drama to expose "error," and what we have seen as the Catholic and anti-Catholic forms of rhyme, songs, mumbling, and dialect so wedded to the "popular ear," he also found ways to convert apparent "faults" into "figures." He found a way, in other words, not simply to expose but also to preserve apparent errors for those who might hear more than the devil in the details, who might (as grammar school boys) learn not just to read closely but also to listen more closely and to listen for possible figures, be they in dialect, in English or Latin, in servants' and women's voices, or in something as basic as that "ragman's rewe," vernacular rhyme. Through the sonic coordinates of meaning in the play—from "mumblyng" and "tymbling" to "freet and rage" and "your owne marriage"—rhyme, however humbly, however foolishly, finds its own middle way, where sense becomes doubled and faults are figured anew.

Ralph Roister Doister incarnates not simply a "dolt" but a portrait of dysfunctional authority grounded in the failure to acknowledge internal limitations in speech, writing, and social jurisdiction, as well as the failure to acknowledge the diversity of sounds and the meaning they convey in the worlds around him. Yet, why is he forgiven and welcomed into the marriage feast in the end? Is this an optimistic sign that society can best operate through generous interpellation, through the collective suspension of judgment and the recognition of error as part and parcel of what it means to be human? If ludic "play," as Johan Huizinga once pointed out, operates according to a logic through which distinctions between wisdom and folly prove too rigid, and in which "blame" proves inoperative for the broader aim of integration and collective participation, it is important to point out that Udall warns against this idea in the end.[68] While the play opens by emphasizing the medicinal spirit of comedy, the necessary "health" of good laughter and good sport, thereby suggesting a relief from gravitas in the name of harmonic recalibration, what are we to make of the fact that Goodluck, who has "hearde no melodie all this yeare long" (32r), essentially joins up with Ralph in order to enjoy the pleasures of feasting and song, turning a conspicuously deaf ear to Custance's much deserved complaint? Though Custance alone continues to loathe Ralph as a "vsurer" to the end (32r), in a disconcerting departure from the strength of women's will, she agrees to submit to her husband's will (the triumvirate of chastity, silence, and obedience looming large). Despite her palpable resistance, Ralph is told that he is forgiven by *all*, "euen in one voice" (31v). Sonic uniformity clearly has a cost. If we are to hear beyond or within the noise, we see that with Custance's voice drowned out we have an extended situation, though now within marriage, in which a woman's no is simply not heard. This complicates the concept of social cohesion and comic unification at the end. The demands of comedy just may have a grandiosity of their own, which suppresses complaint for the sake of apparent unity.

Ironically, Madge Mumblecrust, alternately entertaining and serious, rhetorically as well as morally adaptive, and free from marriage in her later years, provides a counterpart to the confines of comic closure. If we are promised at the outset that "Tom Titiuile" might "maketh us a feast," it is Udall who has "been at a great feast of languages, and stol'n the scraps,"[69] the *fragmina verborum* through which even mumbling would have its day. In the process, Udall offers no less than a soundscape of those "unimagined communities" otherwise rendered less than audibly complex by jurisdictionally grandiose and "somedele deaf" forms of courtship, humanism, nationalism, and reformation of the Word. If that grandiosity remains, in the figures of Ralph and his new friend Goodluck, it remains to be checked, corrected, and subjected to a more collective conception of authority. For it is in the communal observation and experience of the unsettling said, or the said but unheard, that the unsaid just might come into view. Here the *limits* of humanist eloquence, Protestant plain speaking, and even noise for noise's sake become the occasion for more serious thought.

As the philosopher Jacques Rancière once put it of "political interlocution": "The problem is knowing whether the subjects who count in the interlocution 'are' or 'are not,' whether they are speaking or just making noise."[70] But the problem investigated here lies in that very distinction, through which speaking and noise-making, articulate and inarticulate, and by extension literate and oral became differentiated; it was because of this distinction that "mumbling" was relegated to the category of the "not." If Udall begins to untie this knot, giving mumbling—an otherwise powerful vehicle of sociolinguistic negation—a peculiar agency and affirmative complexity of its own, he demonstrates how approaching verbal indistinction as something other than "noise" could lead to a form of problem solving that could involve a range of participants in a diverse commonwealth. Some kinds of "noise" drown others out, other kinds draw others in, at least a bit closer in, to hear what the ruckus is about. Thus the answer to the question I quoted near the beginning of Chapter 1—"What kind of speech is better than that which is clear, open and distinct?"—might be that the unclear, the less than accessible, distinct, or even audible, when examined as a process rather than a product, was the key to transforming tragedies of cultural deafness into a comedy of another kind. Conversely, the resistance of individuals and collectives to acknowledging the potential content and power of the indistinct utterance could lead to something more like tragedy, or to something, in the dramatic, political, and protonationalist contexts of later Tudor England, called *The Spanish Tragedy*.

CHAPTER THREE

Disarticulating Community

Nation, Law, History, and *The Spanish Tragedy*

Growing Pains: National Sentiment and the Tragic Vernacular

IN CONTRAST TO low-level articulation that reached new heights and expanded the bounds of community in Nicholas Udall's *Ralph Roister Doister*, in Thomas Kyd's *The Spanish Tragedy* high-level articulation plummets into chaos and thwarts community altogether. In this revenge drama, which contains the first play-within-a-play in any extant English drama, language itself comes to the foreground of the theatrical agon in a way that took the concept of mutual unintelligibility into a whole new dimension. As Hieronimo, the play's central figure, himself a playwright and revenger, tells the actors who will perform *Soliman and Perseda*, his "stately-written" tragedy, at court:[1]

> Each of us must act his part
> In unknown languages,
> That it may breed the more variety.
> As you, my lord, in Latin, I in Greek,
> You in Italian; and for because I know
> That Bel-imperia hath practised the French,
> In courtly French shall all her phrases be.
>   (4.1.172–78)

"But this will be a mere confusion," protests Balthazar, "And hardly shall we all be understood" (180–81). Since Hieronimo insists upon staging the tragedy in an amalgam of Greek, Latin, French, and Italian, *The Spanish Tragedy's* play-within-a-play stands as an inarticulate Renaissance in the extreme, with classical and vernacular languages coexisting but refusing to cohere. Language is, of course, not the only casualty of *Soliman and Perseda*. As viewers of the play will know and never forget, Hieronimo uses the playlet to kill his son's murderers, who seem to be merely playing the parts of murder victims themselves until it is time for them to stand for applause, which, alas, they cannot do. Because the use of tragic drama as a killing machine *alone* would have produced an astonishing theatrical effect, why, we need to ask, did Kyd choose to fuse *Soliman and Perseda* with such a radical departure from ordinary language—from ordinary speech that could have exposed the tragic, in language as well as action, as all too real?

In psychological terms, such an inarticulate, or even incomprehensible, piece of theater fused with revenge marks a drama of truncated mourning, a furious disavowal wedded to a revenge upon *oratio* itself, the Latin word for "speech" that is the root of the dead son's name, Horatio. With language functioning less *as* language than as "mere confusion," we have a clear relocation of Hieronimo's verbal impotence—his "unfruitful words" and his futile if "ceaseless plaints for [his] deceased son" (3.7.67, 4)—to the resoundingly inarticulate space of the theater. With a theatrical instantiation and amplification of the very "noise," "shrieks," and "dismal outcry echo[ing] in the air" that drew Hieronimo from sleep during the murder itself (4.4.108–10), it is as if the *rant* of the revenger that might, to borrow Hamlet's words, "split the ears" of an auditor, "tear a passion to tatters," and even out-Herod Herod is here dispersed across a whole community of speakers.[2] Given that this is the first play-within-a-play of the period, and a playlet staged in a chaos of classical and vernacular tongues, the staging of tragic affect at the limits of representation suggests as well another mark of disavowal; it is as if Hieronimo becomes, for the budding playwright Thomas Kyd, an internal antitype, a dramatist who fails to fully synthesize classical and contemporary materials in his own experiment in the tragic genre.

The strategic placement of a troubled and indeed incoherent oratio onto a whole community of speakers could evince, in broadly historical as well as psychological and generic terms, powerful forms of disavowal. Indeed, given the contemporary "art" of Tudor Protestant polemic, it should not be hard to hear in the sound of *Soliman and Perseda* a kind of large-scale, anti-Catholic "mumble," only now situated well beyond the borders of "little England" (1.4.160). Drawing upon the writings of that other "Hierome," St. Jerome, in order to denounce Catholicism as a merely unintelligible "stage plaie," John Jewel wrote that "*S.* Hierome *saithe of your Fathers . . . Of the House of God they haue made a stage plaie of the people. And speaking of the Valentinian Here-tiques he saith . . . With a Barbarous vnknowen sounde of wordes they feare the simple, that, what so euer thei vnderstand not, thei maie the more esteme, and haue in reuerence.*"[3] This may seem, at least upon first glance, a particularly fitting gloss to *Soliman and Perseda*, bolstering the influential argument by S. F. Jonson that Kyd's Hieronimo, by engineering the fall of Roman Catholic Iberia, stands as a "confirmed Anglophile" in an avowedly Protestant drama.[4] For Jonson, as for many critics of *The Spanish Tragedy*, what *Soliman and Perseda* signaled was the sociolinguistic fall of "Babylon-Spain,"[5] thus en-abling an English audience to experience, by contrast, a great deal of pride in its own national language on the rise. The profound "national sentiment" through which literature in England, especially during the years of anti-Spanish sentiment, began to find its own voice, has been taken as the dominant historical context informing both the playlet and the play. "The national lan-guage, symbol of new-emerging national sentiment," explains M. C. Brad-brook, "replaced Latin when the King replaced the Pope as supreme Head of the Church; its great literary flowering coincided with the great upsurge of pa-triotic fervor in the decade of the Armada."[6] Because English identity began to consolidate in the 1580s in particular opposition to Catholic Spain, it is no surprise that Kyd is often understood as having catered to his audience's hos-tility to Spain and its "jingoistic faith in England's national superiority."[7] Even Seneca, whose "natiue soyle" (as the first English translator of *Thyestes* emphasized in 1560) was not Rome but "Spayne,"[8] might well emerge as a cultural ancestor of Spanish bombast and confusion in Kyd's pro-English play.

Yet *The Spanish Tragedy* exposes what can be seen as the less than articu-late underside of imperial ambition and Protestant protonationalism in Tudor England. The extent of this underside has not been visible, because the im-portant but overstated focus on "Babylon-Spain" has eclipsed attention to other historical models of discourse through which "confusion" was said to be produced in England in the years surrounding the production of Kyd's play. If we shift our angle of vision, as we will do several times in this chapter, we can see the various tragedies of the inarticulate staged by Kyd as reflections upon language in England, not Spain. For the first popular revenge tragedy is as much about conditions of linguistic incoherence and "confusion" at home as it is about the triumph of England, and English, over classical and other vernacular languages and literary-cultural traditions. To start with an extremely simple point, *Soliman and Perseda* registers clear questions about the problem of creating *art* at the intersection of various linguistic and cultural traditions. Given that after reading from a book of Seneca's Latin tragedies on stage Hieronimo produces a "fruitless" (4.1.72) tragic drama marked precisely by the resistance of words to be translated into "our vulgar tongue" (4.4.75), we may wonder if Kyd was registering something about the elusive status of tragic drama in England in the years that led up to the production of his play.[9] After all, it was in England that translations of Seneca, produced between 1559 and 1582, featured extended laments about the insufficiency of English to do justice to Seneca's Latin.

Describing his translation of *Thyestes* (1560) as "a barrayne booke . . . throughout all full fruteles," and his translation of *Troades* (1559) as having "swerved from the true sence, or not kept the roialty of speach, meete for a Tragedie," Jasper Heywood was merely the first to point out the limits of English as a medium for this classical genre.[10] For "our English toung . . . is farre vnable to compare with the Latten," and some of Seneca's words "haue no grace in the Englishe tounge, but bee a straunge and vnpleasaunt thinge to the Readers."[11] The "straunge" and "vnpleasaunt" sound of tragic Seneca in English led Heywood—in the preface to *Thyestes*—to feature a ghost of Seneca that haunts him and demands: "Make me speake in straunger speeche and sette my woorks to sight" (*6r). Similarly, John Studley's *Agamemnon* (1566) begins with a disclaimer: "Although it be but groslye, & after a rude maner translated, contemne it not for the basenes of the phrase, but embrace it for the excellencie of the matter therin conteyned."[12] When Hieronimo stages a tragedy "containing matter" (4.1.161) but little manner, he seems to be following in the wake not of the Latin Seneca but of the English Seneca. Alexander Neville's preface to his translation of *Oedipus* (1563), the first designed for "showe vpon Stage," similarly apologizes for removing Seneca "from his naturall and loftye Style to our corrupt & base, or as al men affyrme it: most barbarous Language."[13] Moreover, when Neville urges the reader, "Wondre not at the grosenes of the Style" but "Marke thou rather what is ment by the whole course of the

Historie" (A5r–v), we see not only a correlative to similar questions raised with regard to Biblical translation[14] but also an early English translator-dramatist splitting off two technologies of dramatic construction; he separates the power of words from the power of framed action. Kyd's Hieronimo does the same, for he divorces the "matter" of the action, distributed in the form of a "plot" and "argument" (4.1.51, 107), from the "manner" of the playlet's speech.

Since, in the sixteenth century, tragic drama emerged in English along-side a rhetoric of vernacular barbarity, and since Kyd was the first in England to compose a full-blown neo-Senecan revenge play, we might imagine Hieronimo as an ironized embodiment of barbarous English Senecanism. At the very least, Hieronimo "swerve[s] from the true sence" and "roialty of speech, meete for a Tragedie." The frustrations of spoken communication that mark early revenge tragedies such as Kyd's had a historical parallel—if not an outright "motive and a cue for passion"[15]—in the difficult process of translating classical tragedy into the comparatively inarticulate English tongue. By the time Kyd composed *The Spanish Tragedy*, moreover, translating Latin tragedy into English was not the only linguistic problem. Writers were focusing on the resistance of the ever-changing vernacular to cultural intelligibility even as such intelligibility appeared to be on the "rise." As William Fullwood put it in *The Enemie of Idlenesse,* a text printed five times between 1571 and 1593, "Most part of our English termes are very farre different from our vulgare and maternail speache, in such sort, that those who so fully vnderstandeth not the Latin tongue, yea and also the Greek, can scarse vnderstand them."[16]

Such concerns were not lost on Richard Mulcaster, famed proponent of the enriched English tongue who headed the Merchant Taylors School where Kyd was a pupil. Mulcaster stressed the "extreme confusion" and "despare" felt by many of his contemporaries who believed "that the [English] tung was vncapable of anie direction."[17] His 1582 *Elementarie* addressed the problem of vernacular language that "boroweth daielie from foren tungs," from "the *Latin* and *Greke* . . . but mostwhat thorough the *Italian, French*, and *Spanish*" (80). This common observation from the period may help us begin to see *Soliman and Perseda*—which staged the chaotic interaction of these very languages in a manner at once confused and "most passing strange" (4.1.84)—in a new way. The languages listed by Mulcaster, listed too in Hieronimo's playlet, were of course central to humanism, biblical scholarship, and literary cosmopolitanism. But some were also drawn from Roman Catholic countries and traditions, thus creating the potential for a radical departure in England from the ideal of plain style. Despite "our religion . . . which half repines at eloquence," wrote Mulcaster, and "liketh rather the naked truth," an elevated English that might compare to Cicero's Latin necessitated a confrontation with words that seemed anything but plain (257). While Mulcaster hoped, through the importation of foreign words, to transform the vernacular into a medium capable of transmitting what he called "the articulate voice" (103), he also emphasized that such a process required tolerance for the apparently unnatural, inarticulate, and incomprehensible sounds that emerged from a tongue that—through the efforts of various writers and speakers—"brought furth new words" through the "strange deuises" and "strange deliueries" (154). For "why do we persuade our peple to sound *Latin* thus, *Greke* thus, *Hebrew* thus, *Italian* thus, if it be not a thing to be made of acquaintance, by customarie vse?" (90).

Yet those "both vnkinde, and vnnaturall to our owne natiue language in disguising or forging strange or vnvsuall wordes," wrote Samuel Daniel, "make our verse seeme an other kind of speach out of the course of our vsuall practise, displacing our wordes, or inuesting new."[18] What we might call growing pains of lexical expansion that could seem or feel "vnkind" or "vnnatural," and even violent in "displacing our wordes," formed a nexus of sociolinguistic tensions through which individual and communal forms of verbal alienation could be set to the stage. For well before Hieronimo urged his actors to speak in "unknown languages," Sir John Cheke urged his countrymen to resist the bold "venture of vnknowen wordes." Excess borrowing, Cheke stressed, could "bankrupt" the English language.[19] The radical breech of linguistic custom and decorum in *Soliman and Perseda* indexed not simply the fall of Catholicism into so much unintellibible bible-babble but also the perils of vernacularism at a time when the English tongue was, and was not, its own.[20]

For many writers of the period, attempts to enrich the language could seriously compromise natural bonds integral to both communal intelligibility and national coherence. "Some men seek so far for outlandish English, that they forget altogether their mothers language, so that if some of their mothers were aliue, they were not able to tell, or vnderstand what they say." This sentence, familiar to many from the third book of Thomas Wilson's *Arte of Rhetorique* (1553), was placed at the very outset of Robert Cawdrey's dictionary of English words in 1604.[21] Such a vision of a native speaker alienated from his own "mother," as it moved from text to preface, underlines a common and increasing nervousness about the seemingly unnatural and elusive status of the vernacular. Indeed, the unprecedented influx of thousands of new words into English from Latin, Greek, French, and Italian in the latter half of the sixteenth century led to extensive debates about the presence of foreign elements within the national vocabulary. While some writers argued that enrichment was civilizing and others that it was barbarizing, everyone recognized the essential "otherness" of the new terms that seemed to be invading the English language.

"Farre fette words," wrote Sir Philip Sidney, "may seeme Monsters: but must seeme straungers to any poore English man."[22] And "some people," wrote Edward Phillips, "if they spy but a hard word, are as much amazed, as if they had met with a Hobgoblin."[23] Whether representations of vernacular expansion were fused with images of monsters, hobgoblins, or uncomprehending mothers, the range of responses to new words in England dramatizes concerns about cultural and national coherence.[24] Even English preachers, as William Perkins emphasized, had to think twice about their own choice of words so as not to seem incoherent and thus confuse an otherwise attentive audience: to "intermingle" native terms with "words of arts . . . Greeke and Latin phrases and quirks" would only "disturbe the mindes of the auditours, [so] that they cannot fit those things which went afore with those that follow."[25] A single "strange word," Perkins stressed in his phenomenology of distraction, "hindreth the vnderstanding of those things that are spoken. . . . It drawes the mind away from the purpose to some other matter" (K1v). Perkins followed others such as Wilson, who earlier complained about the use of "English" in church, where "we see that poore simple men are muche troubled, and talke oftentymes, thei knowe not what, for lacke of wit and want to Latine & Frenche wherof many of our straunge woordes full often are deriued."[26] So too, Wilson remarked on problems of communal comprehension posed by linguistic formations drawn from "Greke as Latine" and "Angleso Italiano" as well as French (Y3v, Y2r). Wilson's vigorous call for Protestant plain style exposed what was, within England, a model for the otherwise apparently foreign "Catholic" confusion that Kyd's play seems to stage.

It is easy to forget how such "quirks" of an expanding language could, as Perkins put it, "disturbe the mindes of the auditours" in theatrical as well as devotional contexts. This is particularly so given the influential arguments about the late Tudor "triumph" of vernacularism, the cultivation of "vulgar eloquence," and the surge of national sentiment in an increasingly "plain-speaking" England.[27] Such amnesia is due not simply to contemporary but also to historical arguments, fostered by the likes of Thomas Heywood, for example, who defended the theater itself as a vehicle through which the English language became "most perfect and composed." English, as he famously put it, "which hath ben the most harsh, vneuen, and broken language of the world, part *Dutch*, part *Irish, Saxon, Scotch, Welsh*, and indeed a gallimaffry of many, but perfect in none, is now by this secondary meanes of playing, continually refined, euery writer striuing in himselfe to adde a new florish vnto it; so that in processe, from the most rude and vnpolisht tongue, it is growne to a most perfect and composed language, and many excellent workers, and elaborate Poems writ in the same, that many Nations grow inamored of our tongue (before despised)."[28]

Yet what Heywood forgot to mention here was the central place of classical and other vernacular languages in the composition of a national language. John Greene was quick to point out Heywood's oversight. The very "Play-poets" championed by Heywood, for refining the language and strengthening the nation, for Greene only exacerbated confusion and attenuated social bonds in England: "[Heywood] sheweth (and to the disgrace of his mother-tongue) that our English was the rudest language in the world, a Gallymafry of Dutch, *French*, Irish, Saxon, Scotch, and Welsh, but by Play-Poets it hath beene refined. *But doth he not forget, that whiles they adde Greeke, Lattine, and Italian, they make a great mingle-mangle . . . ['our English tongue'] is become more obscure, and used amongst few; for the simple vulgar people cannot understand it: And a plaine man can scarce utter his mind, for want of Phrases (as I may say) according to the fashion"* (emphasis added).[29] Words derived from Greek, Latin, French, and Italian, that is, managed to "obscure" an otherwise "refined" tongue distinct to England. This knotty issue of enrichment, in which the "plaine"-speaking "vulgar people" could be precluded from understanding and full participation, marked for Greene a theatrically exacerbated form of antinationalism. It is as if what even Mulcaster called a national tongue that seemed to have no fewer than "two heds, the one homeborn, the other a stranger" (153) could prove an impediment not simply to ideals of "plaine" speech but also to both theatrical and national consolidation.[30]

Given the place of the theater for the display and transformation of local and national linguistic "fashion," the vexed condition of representation in *The Spanish Tragedy* can be seen as complicating the "new-emerging national sentiment" that the play seems otherwise to celebrate. Calling for a tongue expanded by nonnative words, "fetcht from thence" to be used "copiouslye for varietie," George Pettie, like Mulcaster and other defenders of enrichment, emphasized the process of *eventual* naturalization through which strange and variegated words would seem plain and homegrown.[31] Kyd, conversely, encouraged an audience to reflect upon the denaturalization of a communal language enhanced precisely for the sake of "variety." The playlet's implicit engagement with contemporary debates about language is signaled by Hieronimo himself, who stages the play in "unknown languages" so that it will "breed the more variety." While critics have called this motive a "lame and queer explanation"[32] or seemingly insignificant,[33] its importance in terms of the play as a whole cannot be overstated. The logic for staging the play as a theater of linguistic difference is articulated in terms commonly deployed in arguments about the status of English.[34] Eloquence necessitated a fusion of *copia* and *varietas*, and it was in the effort to "breed the more variety" that much linguistic borrowing took place.[35] That "extreme confusion" and internal alienation were often said to result—and that enrichment was often aligned with crime and corruption[36]—can help us to see Hieronimo as complicit in the process of vernacular corruption.

Hieronimo, moreover, manipulates the stage in order to breed representational "variety" that is at once verbal and visual. By combining polyglot with polygarb, he generates a visual spectacle of international clichés:

> You must provide a Turkish cap,
> A black mustachio and a fauchion.
> You with a cross like to a knight of Rhodes.
> And madame, you must attire yourself
> Like Phoebe, Flora, or the Huntresse. (4.1.144–48)

The disjunction between the verbal and the visual breeds further confusion. The *English* actor who plays *Spanish* Bel-Imperia plays *Italian* Perseda who speaks "courtly French." The *English* actor who plays *Portuguese* Balthazar plays *Turkish* Soliman who speaks *Latin*. The *English* actor who plays the *Castilian* Lorenzo plays a knight of *Rhodes* who speaks *Italian*. And finally, the *English* actor who plays the *Spanish* Hieronimo plays the *Bashaw* who speaks *Greek*. The mixing of linguistic, cultural, and national identities is meant, at the very least, to signify "confusion."

Yet the spectacle of clashing words and garments conjures up the image of gross heterogeneity that was central to satires of "Englishness" in the late Tudor period. William Harrison's 1587 comment about the unsettling morphologies of English sartorial splendors provides, for example, a particularly fitting gloss for *Soliman and Perseda*: "Such is our mutabilitie, that to daie there is none to the *Spanish guise,* to morrow the *French toies* are most fine and delectable, yer long no such apparell as that which is after the high *Alman fashion,* by and by the *Turkish maner* is generallie best liked of. . . . you shall not sée anie so disguised, as are my countrie men of England."[37] In an age of the unprecedented consumption of foreign goods and foreign manners, the "countrie men of England" could seem so mutable as to constitute, for Harrison, "men transformed into monsters."[38] So too the "confuse mingle mangle of apparell," as Philip Stubbes wrote in *The Anatomie of Abuses* (1583), made it "verie hard to knowe, who is noble, who is worshipfull, who is a gentleman, who is not."[39] And with some dressed after the "Spanish, French, & Dutch fashion," a "perfect Anatomie of that Nation in Apparell" was but a "cursed Anatomy" of a nation in textural shreds (C6v, D6v).[40] Or finally, as Joseph Hall would later comment, exposing the confounding "variety" among the English, "Suppose here were a Colledge of *Italians, Spanish, French, Danes, Dutch* and *Polacques*? doe you think to find more variety of dispositions in this company of Students, then you may doe amongst your owne *English*?"[41]

Such a historical surround of more and more variety should make it more difficult, now, to see *Soliman and Perseda* as a triumph of national sentiment and easier to see it as a species of nationalism undone. For the ambivalence about forms of cultural fusion and confusion inherent in the establishment of a national tongue and the sculpting of a national self are all too conspicuously displaced onto Iberian, and indeed Turkish, confusion in the playlet. Kyd can be seen, moreover, as exposing fantasies of linguistic imperialism implicit, for example, in Mulcaster's *Elementarie*, where a foreign word "is a metaphor, a learned translation, remoued from where it is proper, into som such place where it is more properlie vsed. . . . And when the foren word hath yeilded it self, & is receiued into fauor, it is no more foren, tho of foren race, the propertie being altered" (268–69). While strange words are just "metaphors," they are still "of foren race" and need to be fundamentally "altered."[42] "Is it a stranger? but no Turk," wrote Mulcaster of alien terms newly peopling the English lexicon, "& tho it were an enemies word, yet good is worth the getting, . . . as well by speche of writers, as by spoill of soldiers" (269). This equation of military and linguistic "spoill," and the allusion to spoils that might smack even of the "Turk," is itself suggestive given the Turkish setting as well as the displaced militarism of *Soliman and Perseda.*

Over the course of *The Spanish Tragedy,* the anxiety that war poses as a threat to cultural integrity—the very sound of which "gapes to swallow neighbour-bounding lands" and results in corporeal "scattering" (1.2.51, 62)—is relocated to language itself, which becomes a spectacular war zone for the interplay of difference. Hieronimo's playlet, precisely because it conflates the "speche of writers" with the "spoill of soldiers," foregrounds the cost of imperialist ambitions in the domain of language as well as that of war. Hieronimo's "variety" is of course madly cacophonous, and the "breeding" thereof profoundly unnatural; barbaric language and barbarism converge in the copious spillage of blood and words.[43] This linguistic battlefield, even as it raises arms against the enemy, backfires as a species of "mere confusion," marking a theater of internal as well as external conquest. Even the "confirmed Anglophile['s]" sole conspirator in staging the fall of Iberia, Bel–Imperia (whose symbolic name cannot be missed), dies in the playlet along with the others.

Contemporary concerns about language and nation could hardly have escaped Kyd, a translator of French and Italian texts, a poet, a dramatist, and a student under Mulcaster. The structure of *The Spanish Tragedy* itself suggests the extent to which Kyd was concerned with the relationship between language, society, and nation. The first of Hieronimo's theatrical productions, the historical masque in act 1 that stages England's triple conquest of Spain and Portugal, signals the play's engagement with popular forms of nation-making and historical representation.[44] Hieronimo himself is repeatedly associated with questions of translation, linguistic diversity, and the "vulgar tongue." He plots his revenge with materials he "wrote as a student," quotes writers ranging from Claudian to Alan of Lille, cites and translates Seneca, and speaks English, Latin, Spanish, and Greek over the course of the play. The polyglot structure of Hieronimo's *Soliman and Perseda,* moreover, is anticipated by the linguistic texture of *The Spanish Tragedy,* which itself combines the "vulgar tongue" with fragments of Latin (1.2.12–14, 56–57; 1.3.15–17; 2.5.67–80; 3.11.102–3; 3.13.1, 6, 12–13, 35), Spanish (3.14.118), and Italian (3.4.87–88, 3.14.168–69). Hieronimo's playlet is thus positioned as a kind of grotesque variant of the fusion and confusion of cultural differences that pervade the play.

While the geographical location of the play is Spain, for example, "the characters in *The Spanish Tragedy* bear predominantly Italian names, save Don Cyprian, the duke of Castile."[45] And while the play begins with a conventional structure of antitheses (soul/flesh, past/present, freedom/confinement, summer/winter, life/death, love/war, and true/false), a series of rhetorical and thematic moves soon call into question the very logic of difference; we even hear the King of Spain say, "Spain is Portugal, / And Portugal is Spain" (1.4.132–33).[46] While this statement makes sense because it is uttered by a character who has just conquered Portugal, it also has uncomfortable implications. These implications are theatricalized by Hieronimo's first masque, as it stages the vulnerability of both Spain and Portugal in the face of English power.[47] This seemingly mild form of theatrical subversion (later paralleled by Hieronimo's destruction of the court) certainly establishes the Spanish Hieronimo as being complicit with the conquering powers of "little England."

But given this, we should wonder just what kind of "Anglophile" he represents, particularly given his elitist understanding of what might constitute the "common" or the "vulgar." When Balthazar suggests that "a comedy were better," Hieronimo argues,

> A Comedy?
> Fie, comedies are fit for common wits:
> But to present a kingly troop withal,
> Give me a stately-written tragedy,
> *Tragedia cothurnata*, fitting kings,
> Containing matter, and not common things. (4.1.157–61)

Hieronimo's invocation of the truism—"comedies are fit for common wits"—echoes the earlier contrast he draws between his own murderous cunning and "the vulgar wits of men, / With open, but inevitable ills" (3.13.21–22). Hieronimo repeatedly emphasizes the boundary between the stately spectacle and the common world, between the aristocratic and the vulgar. This distinction would have been compounded for the members of an early audience who literally could not understand the "unknown languages" invoked in the playlet.

At the same time, while the alienating effect of language in *Soliman and Perseda* accentuates social distinctions in the play and in English drama, it also signifies their dissolution. It is through the playlet, after all, that Hieronimo (the Knight Marshall) asserts his power over the court and (as he deprives both rulers of successors) his political destiny. As "life" bursts through the art of Hieronimo's final masque and leaves three fathers standing over their dead children—"Speak, Portuguese," says Hieronimo to the stunned Viceroy, "whose loss resembles mine" (4.4.114)—we see an attempt to dissolve the very differences so wildly enacted in the sundry tongued spectacle. "As dear to me was my Horatio / As yours, or yours, or yours, my lord, to you" (169–70). The King's earlier rhetorical statement—"Spain is Portugal, /And Portugal is Spain"—has been rendered devastatingly real by Hieronimo.

As Hieronimo suddenly transforms what seem to be mere theatrical signs into horrifyingly literal referents (dead bodies, not only of the actors but also of his son, revealed behind a curtain), it may seem that what he ultimately stands for is a more coherent relationship between signs and things. The use of deictic in his epilogue may seem to suggest just this:

> See here my show, look on this spectacle.
> Here lay my hope, and here my hope hath end;
> Here lay my heart, and here my heart was slain;
> Here lay my treasure, here my treasure lost;
> Here lay my bliss, and here my bliss bereft;
> But hope, heart, treasure, joy and bliss,
> All fled, failed, died, yea, all decayed with this. (4.4.89–95)

Hieronimo's first and last words ("See . . . this") and his reiteration of the word "here" signify his desperate urge to signify linguistically the presence of his dead son. His apparently plain speech and simple anaphoristic repetitions, while contrasting dramatically with the sundry-tongued playlet, parallels the description of the battle in act 1: "Here falls a body scinder'd from his head, / There legs and arms lie bleeding on the grass" (1.2.57–58). In the play, Kyd emphasizes "here" and "there," simple word pointers that signify material presence, we might say, in highly charged emotional moments.

Yet if, as many critics have suggested, Hieronimo's return to the "plain" speech of "our vulgar tongue" was a means by which Kyd aligned Hieronimo with a plain-speaking England, we should notice how Hieronimo's plainness, here and elsewhere, begins to dissolve and become defamiliarized. The word "here" itself—which is repeated eight times in four consecutive lines—borders on losing its referential ground.[48] These repetitions are anticipated, one scene earlier, by Hieronimo's use of the word "revenge": "Hieronimo, to be revenged. / The plot is laid of dire revenge: / On then,

Hieronimo, pursue revenge, / For nothing wants but acting of revenge" (4.3.27–30).[49] Even as verbs of action dominate, "style" is consumed in the quest for the "acting of revenge," with repetition at line ends replacing rhyme and linguistic diversity. Indeed, if Protestant plain speech seems to offer a welcome alternative to so much "Catholic" confusion in the play, we should recall that the one character who explicitly recommends the use of "plain terms" is the wholly corrupt Lorenzo (1.4.92). "Every word to the purpose," Lukas Erne observes of Lorenzo's speech, which "is pragmatic and devoid of flourishes."[50] Yet with "plain terms" embraced and performed by the all "too politic" Machiavellian "orator" (3.10.83–85), Kyd makes plain the susceptibility of plainness to both moral corruption and foreign influence.

Foreign influence—as Kyd would have known through his knowledge of Latin, French, and Italian—was itself part and parcel of a range of sixteenth-century "plain terms." What could seem utterly "plain" and "common" in English, as Pettie stressed in 1581, was often drawn from other languages—as in the case of these two Protestant keywords themselves, derived from Latin through Anglo-Norman and Middle French words: "What woord can be more plaine then this word *plaine*, & yet what can come more neere to the Latine? What more manifest, then *manifest*? and yet in a manner Latine: What more commune then *rare*, or lesse rare then commune, and yet both of them comming of the Latine."[51] This might simply sharpen our attention to the sociolinguistic complexity and internal discord of even "plain" or "common" speech in *The Spanish Tragedy*. Particular words for speech in the play, including the verb "plain" and the nouns "plaints" and "complaints," and indeed Hieronimo's word for his epilogue above, "oration," index failures of being heard at the same time that they encode a pathos of a language that is, and is not, its own.[52]

When Hieronimo attempts, in act 3, to bring his "ceaseless plaints" to court and "plain me to my lord the king" (3.7.4, 67), although he fails as a plaintiff, for he remains unheard, his speech begins to take on another life of its own. We hear the dead son's name itself repeated four times in four lines, "Horatio . . . Horatio . . . Horatio . . . Horatio" (3.12.59–62), and followed immediately by Hieronimo's five calls for "justice" in the three lines to follow (63–65). Precisely because Hieronimo speaks to no effect, we can hear a kind of cry for a judicial oratio that both eludes and precludes him, underscoring the fact that his tongue is not entirely his own.[53] "Horatio— / Oh let me dwell a little on that name," says Hieronimo in the counterpart to Kyd's tragedy, *The First Part of Hieronimo* (itself recorded by Philip Henslowe as the "*spanes comodye donne oracioe*").[54] If the "closer the look one takes at a word," as Karl Krauss famously put it, "the greater the distance from which it looks back,"[55] such is the case in *The Spanish Tragedy* with the simple word and common name "Horatio" (whose "lamentable death" is announced on the first printed title page of the play).

For when we begin to see the Latin *oratio* within "Horatio," we can see how often, when Hieronimo speaks of the loss of Horatio, he also unwittingly speaks to the fact that he has lost not only a son but also a tongue that he might call his own.[56] Consider, for example, Hieronimo's unwitting pun when he responds to a question asked by the Senex in the next scene— "whence springs this *troubled speech*?"—with "But let me look on *my Horatio* . . . how art thou changed in death's black shade!" (3.13.144–46, emphasis added). What Hieronimo is literally saying is itself a product of fantasy: he believes the "old man" that he encounters, who has lost his own son, to be a ghost of Horatio. But he also comments upon the fact that his own speech has begun to falter in light of "death's black shade." Looking this "Horatio" in the face, he soon realizes he sees a mirror of himself, indeed of his troubled *oratio*: a "lively image of my grief" with "muttering lips / Murmur[ing] sad words abruptly broken off / By force of windy sighs thy spirit breathes" (165–67). The image of "sad words abruptly broken off" could not be a more perfect description of *Soliman and Perseda*, which becomes most visible as a play about the loss of *oratio* as well as Horatio. Hieronimo's comment to the rulers of Portugal and Spain after the playlet, "Oh good words! / As dear to me was my Horatio / As yours, or yours, or yours" (4.4.168–70), becomes visible as a moment of linguistic as well as emotional self-reference.

But let us look more closely at the logic of Hieronimo's *oratio* well before the playlet, when he imagines a form of aesthetic dissonance through which to express his grief. Aiming to comfort himself and the old man, he says:

> Come in old man, thou shalt to Isabel;
> Lean on my arm: I thee, thou me shalt stay,
> And thou, and I, and she, will sing a song,
> Three parts in one but all *of discords framed*—
> Talk not of *cords* . . .
> For with a *cord* Horatio was slain.
> (3.13.170–75, emphasis added)

Hieronimo, suddenly talking to himself—"Talk not of cords"—is startled with the dissonance of the tripartite "cord," which accrues "three parts in one" and seems to strike out at him even as he aims to express dissonance through song. In the black shade of death, Hieronimo's own *oratio* produces homophonic ghosts, as it were, of its own accord. His speech, "troubled" even when it is at its most plain, confronts him with the sound and image of the "cord" that hung Horatio even, or especially, as he seeks discordant consolation. The eerie alienation of words from themselves here, while psychologically pointed, is not unrelated to the "discords framed" in *Soliman and Perseda*. For if Hieronimo suddenly finds the word "discord" to be "of discords framed," his knowledge of other tongues might well encourage us to recall that the "English" word "cord" was anticipated by earlier Greek, Latin, and French terms (including the Latin *chorda* and the French *corde*).

This is simply to stress how even apparently "plain terms" become complicit with frustrations of communication that become, by the same token, engines of dramatic affect. Hieronimo's inability to represent a "loss," as he puts it, that "resembles" his own (4.4.114) leads him to a revenge upon representation itself. This feature of *The Spanish Tragedy* was further highlighted by the 1602 additions to the play. Before he plots an actual revenge, Hieronimo asks a painter to reproduce the spectacle of his murdered son: "Paint me this tree, this very tree. Canst paint a doleful cry? . . . paint me a youth run through and through with villain's swords, hanging upon this tree. Canst thou draw a murderer? . . . let them be worse, worse: *stretch thine art*, and let their eyebrows jutty over. . . . Then, sir, after some violent noise, bring me forth in my shirt, and my gown under mine arm, with my torch in my hand, and my sword rear'd up thus. . . . Make me curse, make me rave, make me cry, make me mad, make me well again. . . . At last, sir, bring me to one of the murderers, were he as strong as Hector, thus would I tear and drag him up and down."[57] The desire to have pain painted in the plainest of terms—but in doing so to "stretch" the form of visual art to encompass acoustics, physical movement, and temporal sequence—prefigures Hieronimo's use of the theater to do the work of bloody revenge. Indeed, his desire to reproduce (and in a way revenge) the murder in the bloodless and contained spheres of painting and narration only leads him to a feverishly confused and actively destructive state. When asked how the painting should "end," Hieronimo proceeds—in perfect anticipation of his revenge on the world of representation—to beat the painter, ultimately declaiming, "*Vindicta mihi.*"

The failure of mimetic representation is central to any revenge drama, since revengers exceed the crime they strive to imitate. But the revenge that Hieronimo takes is a revenge upon mediation, or upon the inability of the tools of the artist and the lawyer alike to make things matter. Indeed, his reference to the importance of a "stately-written" tragedy "containing *matter*" eerily anticipates the bloodying of an otherwise "fabulously counterfeit" world (4.4.77). His psychological state intensifies into an extreme reaction to the disjunction between sign and referent that constitutes the fabric of the play. In his imagination ontological boundaries collapse, word and thing congeal, the discursive becomes physical and the physical, discursive. When the citizen-petitioners approach him in search of justice in act 3, Hieronimo imagines the legal petitions to be the bodies of his enemies and tries to "rent and tear them thus and thus / Shivering their limbs in pieces with [his] teeth" (3.13.122–23). When blamed for tearing the documents, he replies, "That cannot be, I gave it never a wound; / Show me one drop of blood fall from the same: / How is it possible that I should slay it then?" (129–31). Hieronimo's confusion here between the corporeal and the textual, between the scattering of representation and the scattering of bodies, indexes his drive to make *matter* out of textual materials, and prefigures the allegorical significance of his grotesque self-mutilation.[58]

In one of the most unforgettable acts of violence on the Renaissance stage, Hieronimo "bites out his tongue" (4.4.191). Although he has confessed everything, he defies the authority of his questioners by excising the instrument of speech from his body. Hieronimo believes that he bites off his tongue to protect a secret, but the secret is that there is no secret. For Hieronimo has no further information to disclose.[59] While critics have often noted the sheer sensationalism of the act, the additions to the 1602 edition of the play accentuate its thematic significance by inserting "Now to express the rupture of my part" before "First take my tongue, and afterward my heart."[60] Hieronimo's metonymic self-representation clearly dramatizes his sense of the partiality, fragmentation, and impotence that fracture established discursive systems. But "the rupture of part[s]," a metaphor for Hieronimo's fragmented state, also becomes a metaphor for the relation of words and things in the play as a whole. As language fragments, so do bodies, psyches, and nations. A contemporary of Kyd's seems to have recognized the symbolic import of Hieronimo's self-mutilation when he equated him with "Ruffinus," whose grotesquely dismembered body is described at length in Claudian's *In Rufinum*.[61] John

Weever wrote a comic and punning response to the staged dismemberment in *Epigrammes in the Oldest Cut, and Newest Fashion* (1599): "Ruffinus lost his tongue on stage, And wot ye how he made it knowne? He spittes it out in bloudy rage, And told the people he had none: The fond spectators said, he acted wrong, The dumbest man may say, he hath no tongue."[62] While the foolish spectators thought "he acted wrong," Weever saw Hieronimo's "bloudy rage" as a way of "making known" the fact that he had already "lost his tongue."

The stakes of Hieronimo's staged autoglossotomy are further dramatized by the implicit association of Hieronimo with Zeno of Elea (c. 490–c. 430 B.C.E.). Zeno, a Stoic philosopher, bit out his tongue in an act of political resistance that was universally interpreted as heroic.[63] In Plutarch's *De garrulitate*, Zeno becomes an emblem of lingual continence: "Zeno, the philosopher, in order that even against his will no secret should be betrayed by his body when under torture, bit his tongue through and spat it at the despot."[64] In most versions of this story, Zeno's self-mutilation functions to dramatize a solidarity of spirit that contrasts with the fragmenting and fragmentable material world.[65] While these representations of Zeno cast self-mutilation as an act of stoic heroism, a literalized spitting in the face of tyranny, for Kyd it signaled a profoundly antiheroic surrender to (and complicity with) a world of fragments and self-alienation.[66]

Zeno bit out his tongue to express his sense of internal wholeness; Hieronimo does so "to express the rupture of [his] part." The powerful contrast between the two figures thematizes the anxieties about the relations between part and whole that Kyd dramatized in *The Spanish Tragedy*. Zeno of Elea was as famous for his logical paradoxes about the relations between part and whole as for his autoglossotomy. In an argument against plurality, he posited that if parts existed, they had to be "so small as to have no size" and "so large as to be infinite."[67] In many ways, Kyd's spectacle of heterogeneous horrors can be seen as expressing a kind of "Zenophobia," a deadly anxiety about the possibility that there might be no end to the parts that make individuals and nations who they are. For if, in Willy Maley's words, "the nation . . . is always a metonymy of one sort or another, a privileged part made to stand in for an imaginary whole," then the metonymy in Kyd's play announces the representational power of a nation unable to negotiate its own parts—or perhaps more aptly, unable to find, to locate, or ultimately to use its own voice.[68]

Thus if there is a "national sentiment" at play in *The Spanish Tragedy*, it is that sentiment itself, meaning the experience of powerful feeling, comes to the fore when the nation, or the nation's "vulgar tongue," cannot speak for itself. This pathos of a language undergoing growing pains extends to the realm of legal representation in the play: for if Hieronimo embodies the drama of the voiceless-voice of the people, he also embodies, in the more specialized context to be examined next, the drama of the voiceless-voice of the law. Since Hieronimo is not simply a playmaker but the play's central legal figure, both lawyer and judge, and indeed the play's central plaintiff, it is important for us now to consider how the law in the late Tudor period—like the estranged vernacular that we have already examined—could seem no less strange, variegated, and alienating. As the law existed in no fewer than "three seuerall tonges, to wytte, in the English tongue, ye french tongue, & ye latine tongue,"[69] it could be seen to pose serious problems not simply for plain speech but also for equitable as well as intelligible representation. To shift our angle of vision once again now to examine another aspect of linguistic sparagmos that hit home in *The Spanish Tragedy*, let us consider the question of legal language as it could disrupt protocols of humanist eloquence, plain speech, and indeed just communal formation. Much like my analysis of the exclusionary principles operative in the formation of English "common" prayer and speech in my earlier chapters, Kyd arguably makes visible the ideologies of an uncommon-common law as well as an uncommon-common tongue, as they could exclude the *vox populi*, the voice of the people, that they purportedly represented.

Action and Humanism in the Mouth of Law

> The Magistrate . . . is the mouth of the law.
> —Miles Mosse, *The Arraignment and Conuiction of Vsurie*
> (1595)[70]

"Each of us must act his part / In unknown languages." These are words that Kyd put in the mouth of a scholar and legal advocate renowned "for learning and for law" (3.13.52). The explicit alignment of Hieronimo with humanism and law, we might say, grants certain validity to his polyglot "invention." The playlet, after all, was originally composed for "gentlemen and scholars" while he was a student at university, presumably studying law, and rediscovered in his "study so well furnished" (4.1.102, 63). This learned context of the playlet is important because it raises questions about how the multilingual dimensions of humanism and the law may have impacted popular dramatic innovation.

The cognitive and imaginative potential of thinking *between* languages has been powerfully emphasized by Ann Moss, who observes that even basic Latin "ideally enabled [the schoolboy] to move imaginatively between cultures, to enter other minds and appropriate other worlds."[71] Indeed, scholars have long established the extent to which exercises in rhetoric and translation at grammar schools and universities, including the Inns of Court, sparked developments in imaginative fiction, particularly in vernacular drama.[72] The rhetorical-legal exercise of *argumentum in utramque partem* (arguing persuasively on both sides of a question), the practice of eloquence through moots and academic performances, and the power of *translatio imperii et studii* through which "other minds" and "other worlds" could be appropriated, have all been aligned with Tudor dramatic development. The enormous success of *The Spanish Tragedy*, as Jordi Coral Escolà observes, has commonly been understood to be a "product, in the public theatre, of the received values of conventional academic drama."[73] These values include, as Thomas McAlindon puts it, "the humanist idea of language as the primary instrument for social unity and civilized patterns of behavior, making the abuse, obstruction, and final abandonment of speech a major symptom of violent confusion."[74]

Soliman and Perseda, however, pushes us to think in more complex terms about how ideals and practices of learning may have translated or failed to translate into the world of popular dramatic entertainment. Hieronimo in fact pitches the performance of sundry tongues as an exercise in copious elocution (or word choice) designed to try the "wit" and "cunning" of his actor-speakers through cultivated "variety" (4.1.164, 179, 174). But rather than uphold or transmit "the received values of conventional academic drama," which include, among other things, the cultivation of conversation, debate, and civic humanism, it of course does the precise opposite. With various characters made to speak at odds, we have but a parody of *argumentum in utramque partem* transferred to the stage. If the actors on stage are "hardly . . . understood," we have no and all sides of a question bodying forth in and through the very medium that emerged out of the *ars rhetorica*.[75] And if the performance is imagined by Hieronimo as an opportunity for the "practise" of elocution (171), and is aligned with courtly drama in Augustan Rome (87–88), what is produced is an anti-Ciceronian and anti-Horatian word monster that resists unity for the sake of variety. When Hieronimo says that the playlet "profit[s] the professor naught," yet may be "passing pleasing to the world" (73–74), he identifies himself as a playwright at once fleeing the university but also tethered to it as he encounters "the world."

It is not simply that Hieronimo embodies the antithesis of the Ciceronian orator who uses rhetoric for the good, or that he is simply a lawyer turned lawless or a scholar-poet turned mad. He also calls attention to problems implicit in the practices of both humanist eloquence and legal argument as they were, at times, confronted with less than coherent tools and forms of public speech. Although in the Tudor period troubles with speech could index moral waywardness, for the humanist educator Roger Ascham this formula could work the other way around. Observing that the practice of elocution should be central to the training of young scholars, Ascham wrote: "But, now, commonlie, in the best Scholes in England, for wordes, right choice is smallie regarded, true proprietie whollie neglected, confusion is brought in, barbariousnesse is bred vp so in yong wittes, as afterward they be, not onelie marde for speaking, but also corrupted in iudgement: as with moch adoe, or neuer at all, they be brought to right frame againe."[76] Here "confusion," "barbariousness," and "marde . . . speaking" derive not from the moral laxity of particular students but from institutional neglect of proper elocutionary training, leading to "yong wittes" out of discursive as well as judicial "frame." The difficulty of making the "right choice" of words in order to constitute and express "iudgement," moreover, was a particular problem for those dealing with language at the crossroads of classical and vernacular speech at law.

Indeed, Ascham's worst fears emerge in a Cambridge University drama by Thomas Tomkis, *Lingua* (c. 1602), which featured an elaborate send-up of elocutionary "confusion" and "variety" at law. In this microcosmic allegory about language in and around the human body, Lingua, the personified tongue, goes to trial bearing several legal "actions" in order to plead, as both lawyer and plaintiff, for the right simply to be heard and incorporated as a legitimate member of the "common-wealth."[77] Although the tongue attempts to perform the power of judicial oratory and speak on behalf of the "common," it only manages to baffle auditors by mingling—in a *single* sentence— Greek, Latin, French, Italian, and English: "Especially so *aspremente spurd con gli sproni di necessita mia pungente*, I will without the helpe of Orators, commit the *totam salutem* of my action to the *Volutabilitati* [*ton gynaikion logon*] which (*avec votre bonne playseur*) I will finish with more then *Laconica brevi-tate*" (F2r). Given that this is only one *half* of the sentence, perhaps Lingua should have pleaded the fifth. With a pleader presenting such a nonsensical legal "action" we have a send-up of "so many Retoricians, Logitians [and] Lawyers" who rely upon this polyglot tongue for the establishment of author-ity (F2r). That this organ-advocate presents an "action" *without* "the helpe of Orators," however, signals a particular rift between the tongue's otherwise elo-quent moments in the play and its manifest departure from humanist elo-quence, judgment, and coherence in matters of law. Just what it might take to bring this polyglot tongue, to borrow Ascham's phrase, to "right frame again," is a central concern of the play. What is at stake is no less than the co-herence of the commonwealth. It is no surprise to hear Lingua say, "*The common-wealth of* Microcosme at this instant suffers the pangs of death, 'tis gasping for breath" (E1r). Nor is it surprising to find the litigious Lingua ul-timately imprisoned within the mouth, guarded by the personified teeth who threaten to bite down should it dare to range abroad again.[78]

Tomkis's send-up of polyglot confusion and lingual exile might well be seen as a comic variant of Hieronimo's "unknown languages" in *Soliman and Perseda*, as well as his later extraordinary act of biting out his own tongue.[79] In more general terms, however, *Lingua* made light of what was for many in the Tudor period a serious and seriously vexing problem of judicial oratory. The difficulties of persuasion and appropriation entailed in what the legal scholar Abraham Fraunce, Kyd's contemporary, called the "framing of an English tongue to vnknowen languages"[80] were due, in part, to the need for lawyers to negotiate between classical and medieval Latin, Norman French, and English, as well as, at times, Greek and Italian.[81] When Sir Thomas Smith approaches the concept of legal "actions" themselves in his *De Repvblica Anglorvm The maner of Gouernement or policie of the Realme of England* (written 1565, pub-lished 1583), he is confronted, Lingua-like, with the task of sorting through Greek, "barbarous" Latin, French, and English variants: "All pursuites and ac-tions (we call them in our English tongue pleas) and in barbarous (but now vsuall) latine *placita*, taking·that name *abusiue* of the definitiue sentence, which may well be called *placitum* or αρεστον [*areston*]. The French vseth the same calling in their language, the sentence of their iudges *areste* or *arest*: in which wordes nothwithstanding after their custome they do not sounde the s. but we call *placitum* the action not the sentence, and *placitare* barbarouslie, or to pleade in english, *agere* or *litigare*."[82] Elsewhere Italian, Dutch, and Old

English emerge alongside Greek, Latin, and French verbiage in the mix of legal languages and traditions.[83] Such a condensed field of legal language, though clearly set forth by the Greek-speaking, enormously learned, and explicitly Protestant Smith,[84] could create—in Protestant England and not simply elsewhere—an appearance of what Kyd's Balthazar calls "mere confusion" at law.

This was the case not simply for the unlearned but also for those deeply engaged with legal theory and practice. Fraunce, for example, took issue with "confused" forms of speech and writing that, as he stressed, posed cognitive, moral, and professional challenges to English lawyers. English legal practice, "mangled and confused," he stressed, lacked logical method through which to establish coherence and consensus in public speech (B4r).[85] Fraunce's 1588 *The Lawiers Logike* addressed the Sisyphean pains of lawyers attempting to "frame" their thoughts and speech using lexical and textual materials that resisted clear abstraction. These pains ranged from wading through "barbarous" Latinisms and the "Dunsicalitie" of "Hotchpot French, stufft vp with such variety of borrowed words, wherein our law is written" (3r–v) to dealing with the "many particularities" of common law that—"being subiect to such continuall change and alteration"—raised the difficult question as to whether law "can bée made an art" (119v).

This is to emphasize—as we move toward situating Kyd's Hieronimo within his designated profession of law—the antithesis of the classically based commonplace that the "law is an art of persuasion and has always availed itself of those means of persuasion discovered through rhetoric,"[86] and of the related conception that the law in the Renaissance was a highly "*articulate* as well as learned profession."[87] For in the late Tudor period the law could seem both inarticulate and unpersuasive. One of the professional embarrassments of neglecting rational reform at law was, for Fraunce, a continued public specter of improperly digested and incoherent speech. The legal advocate and the public rhetorician in this "age of ours," he stressed, can neither "well vnderstand his vniointed discourse, nor the hearers conceaue his vncohaerent iangling" (4r). Such jangling incoherence resulted from common practices of merely "tasting" without properly digesting and rationalizing legal texts, as well as from the polyglot texture of the law (3v–4r). Indeed, emphasizing the material condition of law, "in vaste volumes confusedly scattered and vtterly vndigested," Fraunce called for lawyers to attend to the fact that "vniointed" legal rhetoric and a dispersed and ineffectual textual culture combined to disable judicial oratory (3v). Legal inarticulacy, in other words, signaled, for

Fraunce, the status of English law at the crossroads of various linguistic as well as of oral and increasingly textual modes of reception and transmission.[88]

For Richard Mulcaster, too, legal language—as it indexed an as yet unrationalized and heterogeneous mix of legal languages and traditions—could produce what he called "distraction" in English law: the "three seuerall professions in lawe bewraye a three headed state, one *English* & *French*, an other, Romish Imperiall, the third Romish ecclesiasticall, where meere *English* were simply our best."[89] The professional and political hazards of judicial oratory surface as well in a range of Tudor texts. In his "Exposicion of Wordes," William Fleetwood, for example, observed that when "Certain old Terms or Words" were used for argumentation in a particular legal case, "the Court did not vnderstande what the Meaning of the words were."[90] And as Thomas Egerton, the jurist and adviser to Elizabeth, said to Parliament in 1597, the laws in England contain "superfluity," "defect," and "ambiguity" that prove "burthensome . . . to the Common-wealth"; with "many of them so full of difficulties to be understood that they cause many controversies and much trouble amongst the Subjects."[91]

As the son of a legal scrivener and a probable scrivener himself,[92] Thomas Kyd would have been exposed to the concerns addressed above, variants of what even Sir Edward Coke—the English Jurist, common law proponent, and apologist for legal language—"confesse[d]" to be "a writing or a scribbling world" of law, rife with forms of "obscuritie, ambiguitie, ieperdie, noueltie, and prolixity."[93] This motley picture of the law, with material conditions of speech at odds with ideals of communal comprehension and civic cohesion, can help us bring *The Spanish Tragedy*—a play of course preoccupied with questions of justice, law, and revenge—into focus as a sustained reflection not only upon vernacular estrangement but also upon the law itself as an anti-art of persuasion. For *Soliman and Perseda* is itself a recreation of a criminal action, composed by a legal advocate and judge, in which the speech "community" produced is "hardly . . . understood." While *The Spanish Tragedy* deals with problems of justice on a grand scale, the problems that a polyglot and often "vncoherent" law could pose for legal advocates inform the play in ways that scholars have not yet recognized.[94]

This is, in part, because critics of the play typically presume a clear split within Hieronimo in act 3, where we see an otherwise laudable "lawyer-poet" "become his own opposite";[95] a judge "abjure legal justice," a lawful advocate turn "lawless."[96] In light of the context of legal language in the period, however, such a clear dichotomy begins to seem, while psychologically intuitive, historically anachronistic. Recalling now the complicated status of the legal "action" in both Tomkis and Smith, it is suggestive that when Hieronimo is told that a group of citizen-petitioners want him to "plead their cases," he asks not once but twice, "That I should plead their several actions?" (3.13.48–49, and again, "That I should plead your several actions?" 64). This repeated question emphasizes what is, for the already distracted Hieronimo, a daunting task ahead. After he asks the petitioners, "what's the matter?" he is given not one or two but "several actions": an "action . . . of debt," an "action of the case," an "*ejectione firmae*" or a violated "lease," and a "supplication," or formal petition for a murder case (59–79). If scholars have quibbled over the nonsensical "*ejectione firmae* by a Lease" (a variant of *ejectio firmae*),[97] we should remember that this botched English-Latin legalism is uttered by a citizen turning to a legal official for assistance and assurance.[98] But rather than correct or speak for, in, or on behalf of such legal language, Hieronimo shoves the "actions" into his mouth and tears them to pieces with his teeth (122–23).

If, as Miles Mosse put it in a treatise on legal and theological principles of exchange value, "the Magistrate . . . is the mouth of the law,"[99] Kyd's Hieronimo throws open the question of what it might have meant to have the law, literally, inside one's own mouth. If we consider, that is, the extent to which late Tudor legal language was understood to pose serious problems for judicial pleading, legal consensus, and the administration of justice, Hieronimo—whose mouth destroys the very actions it paradoxically "represents"—becomes a vivid incarnation of common concerns about law not only in the hands but also in the mouths of men. Hieronimo in many ways expresses the law's difficulty in establishing justice through a coherent model of speech and unified body of law. On the one hand, if the citizen-petitioners evince a marginalized relationship to legal language, Hieronimo destroys the documents as if emphasizing that he is now no longer a lawyer or judge but a disempowered petitioner himself. Without doubt, this moment clearly dramatizes the torment of a father seeking justice for the murder of his son that the law cannot seem to offer. But on the other hand, this scene also, importantly, provides us with an image of a legal "advocate" (52) confounded by the materials of his own trade.

Hieronimo puts such phrases as "*ejectione firmae*" and "action of the case" into his own mouth, as if attempting at once to ingest and expel what the legal-dictionary compiler John Rastell described as the "certeyn obscur and derke termys consernyng the lawis of thys realme and ye nature of certeyne wrytts."[100] A single glance at Rastell's multiply reprinted and expanded glossary of legal terms in English, Latin, and French suggests how "difficult" the language of the law could be, even for students of the law, for whom he wrote the book. There we find the word "action" to be anything but a simple matter, divided into various terms, including "Accion," "Actions personals," "Actions populer," "Actions reals," "chose en action," "circuit de action," "actyon of dette," and so on.[101] Smith, as we have already seen, further glossed "actions" in Greek, Latin, and French. When Hieronimo later turns to drama to perform what he calls an "action" in these very languages, we have not simply a movement away from the law but also, as I have been suggesting, a movement into the thick of it (4.1.166). Indeed, if, in the plainest of terms, "accion is a suit geuen by the lawe to recouer a thing" (Rastell, 7r), to "suit the action to the word, the word to the action"[102] was no easy feat in matters of law.

The complex filter for the legal comprehension of action in Rastell and Smith provides a nice gloss on Hieronimo's despair at having to plead "*several* actions," and on the fact that "action" is itself repeated four times at the opening of the scene alone. It is here that legal language enters most explicitly into the domain of dramatic "action," leading to tragic sparagmos in the domain of text; legal mediation is now all too vividly (to remember Fraunce) "vndigested" and "confusedly scattered." If, moreover, we consider this scene not as an isolated incident of a "lawyer-poet" becoming his "opposite" but rather as an extension of a central issue at stake in the play, we find that Hieronimo's treatment of the documented "actions" of others expresses a rupture in the fabric of judicial discourses introduced at the outset of the play. For the problem of discerning even a *single* action is posed in the play's opening scene. There, the audience is given a multiplicity of frameworks for comprehending and judging the action—documented "in graven leaves of lottery" and drawn from a pot (1.1.36–36)[103]—that led to the death of Andrea in the prehistory of the play. The judges of the underworld, Minos, Aeacus, and Rhadamanth, are unable to come to a consensus about how to interpret the document explaining Andrea's case.

To this problem of consensus we can add the host of competing narratives provided by witnesses to the act, including the ghost of Andrea himself, the military General, Horatio, Balthazar, and Villuppo. The first half of the play centers on the extent to which even a single action can be unmoored from narrative consensus.[104] Hieronimo's paper rage can thus be seen not simply to depart from but also to dramatically incarnate a problem of judicial oratory as it might obscure or splinter, rather than clearly index, an action. When the Senex, Hieronimo's double in the play, is asked to "tell" his own "suit," or to speak of his "action," he is unable to suit the action to the spoken word: "No sir, could my woes / Give way unto my most distressful words, / Then should I not in paper, as you see / With ink bewray what blood began in me" (3.13. 73–77). That the legal writ, however impoverished as a substitute for unutterable pathos, is so quickly undone in the advocate's own mouth, signals a double crisis of iterability; writing as well as speech become subject to the mouth of a law that consumes its subjects.

Shakespeare's *Hamlet* would famously highlight the convoluted language of the law as a medium through which to ascertain the significance of "action."[105] But in this earlier revenge, legal language and textuality disrupt orality even as it enters and exits an advocate's and an actor's mouth. In a striking variant of Exodus 1:9, "The Lord's law may be in thy mouth," the mouth as an instrument of delivery now bites, chews, and spits out a dish of indigestibles. Again, lest we think this a mere departure from the law, the question of digestion and indigestion in matters of legal learning and oratory was a common motif in the period. Like Fraunce's concern with undigested textual matter, though with more moderation, Coke urged the reader of his own *Reports*: "In reading these and other of my Reports, I desire the Reader, that hee would not reade (and as it were swallow) too much at once; for greedie appetites are not of the best digestion: the whole is to be attained to by parts, and Nature (which is the best guide) maketh no leap . . . a cursarie and tumultuarie reading doth euer make a confused memorie, a troubled vtterance, and an incertaine Iudgement."[106] These commonplaces of textual indigestion, mnemonic confusion, and troubled speech and judgment—linked elsewhere by Coke to the ineffectual status of legal material culture—converge in the figure "renowned for learning and for law" as he confronts legal documents.

For Fraunce, the problem of consensus at law was a feature of rhetoric unmoored from logic. Those who "break and dismember things" through legal rhetoric, he wrote, following Plato, are like "bungling Cookes" producing so much indigestible matter (Q1r). "This is a lamentable want in our law, I meane exact diuisions, in place whereof wee haue nothing els, but eyther *A B C* methode without coherence, or *primo notandum, 2. not. 3. not. 4. not.* & so on till hée come to *decimotertiò notandum,* like dunses in schooles, and séelly bablers in pulpits: that a man were farre better make a new spéech, than remember their waste and confused *Schediasmata* [off-the-cuff rambling]."[107] Alphabetical ordering and enumerative notation, "method[s] without coherence," only exacerbate "confused" speech. In a suggestive corollary to Kyd's "graven leaves of lottery"—where the central actions of Andrea's life and death are first inscribed—Fraunce imagines how entire epistemological "lotteries" could possibly be brought to order. Citing Ramus, he encourages his reader to "imagine . . . that all definitions, diuisions, and rules of any art . . . and euery rule were written in a seuerall schrole, euery schrole béeing put into an earthen pitcher, as they vse in lottaries, and there shuffled together: what part of Logike now must order these confused rules and scattered schroles?" (116r). "I will séeke in this pot," he continues, "Not Inuention, for they bée found out already: not axiomaticall Iudgement, for they bée iudged and allowed as true," but rather "method" to sort out the shuffle of distinctions otherwise lost to both individual and collective memory: "Methode and order is the chiefest helpe of memory" (116v).

The specific question of logical "method" as a means for sorting through confusion in the specific case of Kyd is one to which we will return, but it is worth now observing that no such method is offered in the case of Andrea. Rather, in the opening act of the play, a single text, read aloud, leads immediately to disagreement about how to interpret it: through axiomatical judgment, Aeacus reads it one way, Rhadamanth another (1.1.41–50). Thus Minos throws the case into the court of Pluto, who allocates judgment to his lover, Proserpine. Proserpine's judgment is then expressed only as a whisper "in th'ear" of Revenge, one that the audience does not hear but that is cast as the drama to unfold in *The Spanish Tragedy* itself (81). Whereas a single action splinters into multiple narrative possibilities in the drama that follows, the multiple legal actions brought before Hieronimo are chewed up so as paradoxically to unify a diverse collection of legitimate complaints representing the citizenry.

As Hieronimo obliterates "several actions" in his single-minded quest for what he calls the "acting of revenge," we see revenge functioning to narrow the sphere of action as well as speech—and obliterating a collective process of juridical negotiation through which "equity" might be established in the process. When Hieronimo says to the petitioners, "*all as one* are our extremities" (3.13. 92, emphasis added), only to swiftly "rent and tear" their costly documents ("it cost me ten pound!" exclaims a citizen, 127), we see a dangerous form of "common" law that disregards those that it purports to represent.[108] Hieronimo's impulse to unify diverse forms of action and injury—effected by a form of acting through and against text—reduces the heterogeneity of the law to "mere confusion": reifies it, that is, into a ruptured totality. At the same time, the *vox populi* is suppressed even as it is represented in the form of "all as one." Revenge, even in this early instance, can be understood to be a product of and not simply a departure from the law. For the "commonality of common law," as Peter Goodrich has observed, was "not resident in any literal expression of *vox populi*, popular will, sentiment, custom or voice, but rather in a considerably older theology of royal power whereby the people and their law were stored in the Emperor's breast. . . . That which belonged to or was expressed by the crown was law and such law was common to his or her people."[109] Since Hieronimo himself has been prevented from accessing the King with his own plea for justice, we see him in act 3 at once resisting and reenacting, as a servant of the state, an exclusionary principle of legal justice.

Given Hieronimo's "acting out" both in and through legal documents, we might imagine Kyd exacting his own species of revenge on the very legal texts that his father—and quite probably he—as a scrivener, would have had to reproduce. More to the point, we see how Kyd drew on a problem of legal language, a specialized form of discourse that did not mesh well with vernacular language or "common" representation, and converted it into a visceral and conceptually productive dramatic moment. We witness the limits of professional speech converted into a conduit for affective intensity and dramatic action otherwise occluded by the technical and often exclusive language of injury, loss, and compensation. Hieronimo's oral relationship to legal "instruments" of paper and ink involved in the production and transmission of "actions" speaks to a larger cultural drama about the limits of humanism in matters of legal language and textuality. His representational sparagmos, moreover, anticipates his decision to disjoin languages in *Soliman and Perseda*. In both cases, the inarticulate becomes an aggressive means of mobilizing while also exposing a form of constitutive disjointure; the *vox populi* is all but devoured by the mouth of the law.

Catastrophes of language in *The Spanish Tragedy* thus concern more than a shift from law to lawlessness. They suggest the extent to which the contemporary sprawl of legal discourse, as well as that of vernacularism more generally, could provide models of inarticulate ("unjoined") speech through which tragic drama in England found a new "voice." Given the context of the formation of English national identity at the time, Kyd stages the limits not simply of humanism at law but also of a form of legal nationalism that, as Goodrich has argued, defined itself by displacing internal forms of intolerance and confusion onto cultural others, both at home and abroad.[110] While scholars of the play, as we have seen, have often understood *Soliman and Perseda* to evince a form of Protestant self-definition based upon the denunciation of barbaric others, this very strategy, as Goodrich has taught us, was integral to the formation of the common law: "The foundational texts of the common law tradition borrow their argumentative (dialectical) structure and oratorical form from the theological genre of *antirrhetici,* namely discourses of denunciation directed at outsiders, heretics, iconoclasts and more anciently still against those who have harmed their kin."[111] If this antirrhetic stance functioned to define the common law as *antithetical* to a "theater of cruelty associated with the heathen, the Roman and the barbarian, the excluded, the stranger and the beast" (214), it did so, in part, in order to fend off the presence of those very properties within the law. "The unity and identity of law" was established by marking "an outside or externality which is both heteroclite and dispersed, confused and dissembling" (219).

But Kyd deconstructs this model of legal unity so that, in fact, the central legal official and Anglophile in the play actively produces the "heteroclite and dispersed," the "confused and dissembling," in order to define himself. That Hieronimo kills off the actors in the playlet, along with an innocent bystander soon after, pushes an audience to consider just how a "theater of cruelty" might define a brand of English legal as well as Protestant nationalism as at once appealing and appalling. The antirrhetic stance of *Soliman and Perseda* of course backfires, so that Hieronimo becomes subsumed by the theater of cruelty he attempts to stage, ultimately exiling himself in a symbolic because otherwise senseless act of biting out his own tongue. "The antirrhetic established," in Goodrich's terms, "an imaginary—or indeed a bestiary—of lost objects, exiled subjects, illicit images and condemned words" (219). It peopled the legal text "with the orthodoxies, the *iuris vincula,* of dogma and faith while establishing an unconscious lexicon of the voiceless, the silent, the exiled and the excommunicated. . . . Yet a speech which has lost its subject, a speech which represses its 'other scene' or unconscious bonds cannot mourn its losses and so cannot recognize either the death of the subject or the antirrhetic of the text implicit in the violence which legal discourse does to things"

(219). This "unconscious lexicon" of legal self-definition emerges into view in Kyd's drama because the one most wedded to the law demonstrates, through his treatment of the petitioner's "actions" and through his polyglot charade, the "violence which legal discourse does to things," particularly when that which is "lost" is not "mourned." This haunts the advocate, who establishes himself as both agent and victim of a law at odds with the popular voice within itself.

Hieronimo, however, stands as a legal figure who demonstrates another kind of "violence" done to things, not through the arts of rhetoric but rather through the arts of logic. The central thesis driving Fraunce's *Lawiers Logike*—written at a time when the arts of logic began to flourish in England—was that the law could be consolidated in and through the art of logic.[112] This seemed to Fraunce all the more crucial at a time when dominant practices of legal rhetoric seemed to be tearing the very profession apart. Following Ramus, who famously separated logic from rhetoric (placing invention and disposition in the former category, elocution and delivery in the latter), Fraunce turned to logic as a means of establishing forms of "coherence" that rhetoric alone could not. The cultivation of logic—above and beyond rhetoric—was for Fraunce the key to reforming legal practice; freeing it, that is, from the vicissitudes of spoken language. He in fact emphasized the power of logic to trump communal speech: "The whole force and vertue of Logike consisteth in reasoning, *not in talking*," and "because reasoning *may be without talking*, as in solitary meditations and deliberations with a mans self, some hold the first . . . most significant" (1r, emphasis added). In contrast to the "vnionted discourse" of legal rhetoric, the use of logic could lend coherence by providing a means through which to discern "the finall cause, the end, purpose, intent, drift, marke, or scope, as it were of *the whole action*" (25r, emphasis added). Logic, that is, could establish "exactly the order and due coherence" of any whole action relevant to a criminal case, or what Thomas Wilson earlier called "the whole course, & order of the thing," "the whole course of the matter" at law, otherwise obscured by so many "patches and pieces."[113]

This brings us to one form of *coherence* or representational integrity in *The Spanish Tragedy* that we have not addressed, one mobilized as an explicit alternative to the incoherence of spoken dialogue. I am alluding to the clearly structured and indeed "whole action" of *Soliman and Perseda*. While incoherent as speech, the playlet is entirely coherent as plot. Plot, that is, surfaces as *the* technology of intelligibility in an otherwise chaotic verbal universe. Hieronimo, in fact, repeatedly calls attention to the playlet's overarching structure: he gives what he calls the "plot" or "argument" of it to the actors (and offstage audience) in advance and to the onstage audience in paper form before the performance begins, and he rehearses it once again in the playlet's epilogue (4.1.51, 107). Whereas the playlet's language is disorganized and multidirectional, its action is marked by a tight structural economy, designed to move swiftly from beginning to middle to end, where it "shall be concluded in one scene / For there's no pleasure ta'en in tediousness" (4.1.188–89). When Hieronimo says to his actors, "The conclusion / shall prove the invention" (4.1.181–82), he underscores the power of logical method as a vehicle for organizing tragic dramatic action. Although the 1602 additions to the play added the line by Hieronimo that "there is no end: the end is death and madness," if Hieronimo is mad in Kyd's play, his madness takes the form of a deliberative and methodical approach to the composition of a unified action.[114] For he will present a tragedy *"containing* matter."

Hieronimo's drive toward unified action, before *Soliman and Perseda*, in the case of so many legal "actions," becomes focused upon the single "action" of the revenge "plot," a plot that he begins to formulate, moreover, in a soliloquy *directly* before he encounters the petitioners. For Hieronimo, the legal figure, the playmaker, and indeed the playwright of what he calls historical "chronicles" (4.1.108), the logically produced plot becomes a mechanism through which he can make his way, methodically, through a world that is in so much rhetorical confusion. Although scholars have often noted that Hieronimo logically pieces together events leading to the death of his son,[115] as the play progresses he converts a *retrospective* logic of legal inquiry into a *prospective* pattern for the creation of a "whole action": a revenge plot that doubles as a theatrical plot.

The peculiar coherence of Hieronimo's tragic drama raises broader questions about the place of logic in the making of coherent tragic as well as historical drama. Hieronimo, after all, turns not to a textbook of logic or law but rather to tragic and historical materials in order to construct *Soliman and Perseda*. As we will now see, his concerns went hand in hand with contemporary questions of the concept of the coherent plot—in both tragic and historiographic contexts—as a mechanism through which coherence might be attained in the face of incoherent language practices. In both of those contexts, language itself was said to be unwieldy, but for some Tudor scholars, tragic and historiographic materials could be rationalized by the application of logic, and in particular, by the logic of the plot.

Revenging the Plot: The Structure of Coherence

For why, the plot's already in mine head.
            —Hieronimo, *The Spanish Tragedy* (3.74.)

Amid all the scattering of rhetoric in *The Spanish Tragedy*, it is significant that Hieronimo attempts to deploy a peculiar form of *logic* precisely as a means to resist plurality and establish coherence. In all his fury, he aims to import logical method into the art of tragic playwriting. We see this, first, when he turns to the plays of Seneca. For he closes the scene of reading by invoking those central topics of logical reasoning, "when, where, and how" (3.13.44), so that it becomes clear that he has taken from Seneca an inspiration to derive a coherent plan for the plotting of an action. This particular use of Seneca should seem odd; not simply because a character mines the plays of Seneca for models of retributive action but also because we see a character using Seneca to construct a coherent plot. The Latin Seneca was of course valued *not* for the logic of his plots but precisely for the power of his words. As Ascham put it, while "the *Grecians*, *Sophocles* and *Euripides* far ouer match our *Seneca* in *Latin*, namely in [*oikonomia*] *et Decor*"—meaning the organization and decorous presentation of subject matter—"*Senecaes* elocution and verse be verie commendable for his tyme."[116] That Seneca's words held sway when his plots were found wanting is no surprise, since Senecan tragedy, as Martin Mueller has argued, was "a rhetorical genre," with "almost total indifference to the Aristotelian ideal of a plot constructed in accordance with the demands of probability and necessity."[117] "Humanist writers inherited from antiquity," moreover, "the concept of the tragic style as the '*non plus ultra*' of rhetorical dignity" (182). So, then, why does Kyd's Hieronimo take from his reading of Seneca an inspiration to construct a tragedy in which a reasoned plot utterly usurps the function of speech, "rhetorical dignity," and "tragic style"?

This question can be addressed by considering the status not of the Latin but of the English Seneca in the years leading up to the production of Kyd's play. As we saw at the outset of this chapter, translators of Seneca demonstrated a characteristic lack of faith in their own "vulgar tongue" to capture

Senecan eloquence. But more important for the present analysis of the chiasmus of speech in decline and plot on the rise in Kyd's play, the translators also demonstrated a new faith in the compensatory powers of logical patterning, making Senecan drama intelligible as a mechanism for the discernment of the logic of action. In the preface to Thomas Newton's collection *Seneca: His Tenne Tragedies* (1581), for example, we see Newton describing his own translation of *Thebais*—which drew from "so meane a stoare" of vernacular words—as "an unflidge nestling, unable to fly: an unnatural abortion, and an unperfect Embryon."[118] Yet he also lauds Seneca for providing coherently framed action, so that "of each one of his Tragedies" cohered around a "whole issve" (A4r). Newton attended to various actions in Seneca's plays that, though appearing repeatedly in the plays, did not constitute a unified action for Seneca. In Newton's account, however, the following actions—"sinne, loose lyfe, dissolvte dealynge, and vnbrydled sensvality . . . filthy lvst, cloaked dissimulation, & odious treachery"—did. They constituted the "dryft, wherevnto he leueleth the whole issve of each one of his Tragedies" (A4r). Further, to counter critics such as Stephen Gosson who felt Senecan tragedy a "school of abuse" for the teaching of sin, Newton emphasized that such a reading could only be produced by those who refused to draw on the topics of logical reasoning—"to marke and consider the circvmstaunces, why, where, & by what maner"—to understand the overarching moral logic of Senecan tragedy."[119]

The emphasis by Newton and others on the coherence of Seneca's unified plots can help us further understand Kyd's playlet and also, in a broader context, further understand the gradual development of tragic plots in England. The development of tragic plots has long been wedded not to the tragedies of Seneca but to the comedies of Plautus and Terence.[120] But this genealogy can lead us to overlook the ways in which the translators of Seneca aimed to rationalize tragedies that—to Ascham and others—seemed wanting in the organization of matter. Indeed, while bemoaning a "most barbarous" vernacular,[121] Senecan translators often made changes to the Latin texts in order to rationalize them and to laud what one translator, John Studley, called the "perfect paterne, as it at large [is] shewed in the Tragedie itself," or what another, Alexander Neville, called "the generall Proces of the whole Historie."[122] Studley rewrote parts of Seneca's *Medea* precisely to foreground the "perfect paterne." He replaced Seneca's prologue, for example, with a plotline, "The Argument to the Tragedie by the Translatour," which added the double homicide that marks the tragedy's end (*4v), and also "chaunged the fyrste Chorus, because in it I sawe nothyng but an heape of prophane storyes" (*3r–v). Jasper Heywood composed a new conclusion to *Thyestes* (1560), thereby redefining the structural coordinates of the play. He also added many new elements to *Troades* (entitled *Troas*, 1559), including a ghost of Achilles (who enters as a character rather than through Tathybius's narrative) as a lover-warrior bent on revenge. Since this ghost of Achilles calls for revenge for specific injuries, "rysing from hell to requyre the sacrifice of Polyxena" (A4r), putting him within the frame of the play's action stands as an attempt both to sensationalize and to rationalize the play; it adds the supernatural while extruding the logic of cause and effect that informs the action. Seneca's other dramas of course featured ghosts, three in fact, but I simply want to point out here that Heywood made such changes, including the new conclusion to *Thyestes* and the addition of the lover-warrior ghost in *Troas*, in order to correct Seneca, as he puts it, who is "in some places vnperfyte" (*Troas*, A4r).

Thomas Nashe famously derided Kyd for his alleged reliance on the "English Seneca," which marked the "homeborn mediocrity" of a playwright whose inferior text so mangled the original as to let Seneca shed "bloud line by line and page by page," only to "die to our stage."[123] But while Kyd engaged with the "English Seneca," he did so not simply to imitate these translations but also to mount a critical response to the process of turning away from a shared language deemed to be barbarous and toward a grandiose logic of plot, and of turning Seneca himself into a dramatist of patterned action as opposed to powerful words. Kyd's insertion of the ghostly lover-warrior Andrea at the outset of *The Spanish Tragedy*, for example, may seem to be indebted to Heywood's insertion of the ghostly lover-warrior Achilles in *Troas*. Kyd's ghost, however, arguably sends up such an artificial mechanism through which to emphasize plot coherence.

Kyd's lover-warrior, a contemporary figure who finds himself newly lodged in a classical underworld, does not seem to belong in a neo-Senecan revenge play at all. In fact, his death is clearly defined, from the first, as a *military* casualty (1.1.15–17, 40, 46–47). The entire focus of Andrea's opening narrative is on the problem of eschatology in an underworld that cannot accommodate him as *both* a lover and a warrior; for in this underworld lovers and warriors are separated, "either sort contained within his bounds" (1.1.62). Yet Revenge steps in to provide a clear plot: "Andrea . . . / . . . shalt see the author of thy death, Don Balthazar, the prince of Portingale, / Deprived of life by Bel-Imperia" (87–89). The *inappropriateness* of this plot to the situation at hand can help us to see that Kyd was interested, from the first, in unsettling the logic of action through which a tragic drama might be framed. The over-simplistic plotline leads to Andrea's anxious frets along the way—as he stands alongside Revenge to observe the play and encounters situations that exceed that plotline.

This opening scene of *The Spanish Tragedy* is worth reconsidering, more-over, because it raises issues about the relationship between forms of speech that seem to lead nowhere and the emergence of a plot that promises coher-ence of another kind. Of the classical underworld in which Andrea finds him-self newly situated, he says, "I saw more sights than thousand tongues can tell, / Or pens can write, or mortal hearts can think" (1.1.57–58). With so many tongues and pens and hearts overwhelmed by the riches of the classical past, this inarticulacy topos at the intersection of classical and contemporary intro-duces questions of vernacular imitation that preoccupy the play. The particu-lar problem of spoken language is further developed as Andrea moves on to describe himself in a scene of ineffectual juridical rhetoric where Aeacus and Rhadamanth, judges of the underworld, debate fruitlessly about where to lodge him for eternity. This rich field of inquiry produced at the outset—about the ability of speech to do justice to, and in relation to, the classical past—is abruptly supplanted by the telos of the revenge plot.

We have here writ small a tension, dramatized elsewhere in the play, be-tween the potential of speech at the crossroads of languages and cultures to disrupt the telos of action and foster reflection, and the power of plotted ac-tion to override that potential. This tension anticipates the uneasy confronta-tion of classical and vernacular languages in *Soliman and Perseda*, which are pitched against—and subordinated to—the coherence and driving telos of the "plot." It also anticipates the scene of Senecan "reading" alluded to above, where Hieronimo spends time reading and then translating the Latin Seneca, only to derive a suddenly false "conclusion" and plot his way to revenge.[124] For it is important to note that this scene stands out in the play as scene of *translation*. No other Latin passages in *The Spanish Tragedy*, including Hieron-imo's fourteen-line dirge (2.1.66–80), Castille's prayer in thanks for military victory (1.2.12–15), the Viceroy's dejected submission to fortune (1.3.15–17), or Lorenzo's Latin tag (2.2.106), are translated or glossed in this way, nor are shorter statements that are uttered in Italian or Spanish. Rather than under-stand the Latin Seneca onstage as a means by which Kyd, the nonuniversity playwright, hoped to "increase his respectability," as Lukas Erne has suggested, "by proclaiming his debts to Seneca" in Latin, we might wonder why Kyd has Hieronimo "English" that Latin text.[125]

By calling attention to Hieronimo's negotiation between Latin and English, this scene of translation slows the pace of the play. It develops upon questions about the relationship between the classical past and the vernacular present, and about English as a medium through which to render that past. For in the translation scene there is a curious decline of Hieronimo's own verbal skill—in comparison with his verbal fluency earlier in the same act. As he says earlier,

> With broken sighs and restless passions,
> That winged mount, and hovering in the air,
> Beat at the windows of the brightest heavens,
> Soliciting for justice and revenge;
> But they are placed in those empyreal heights,
> Where, counter-mured with walls of diamond,
> I find the place impregnable; and they
> Resist my woes, and give my words no way. (3.7.11–18)

Such poetry of the inarticulate, of "broken sighs" and unheard words, transforms in the scene of Senecan translation into a less elevated, far less eloquent language. In Hieronimo's "*Per scelus semper tutum est sceleribus iter*" (3.13.6), we have a slight alteration of Clytemnestra's "*Per scelera semper sceleribus tutum est iter*" in *Agamemnon* (I.115).[126] Hieronimo follows the Latin quotation in a manner that captures the Latin sense, "For evils unto ills conductors be," but in a way that departs from the kind of eloquent style that he has proven capable of earlier. As he elaborates, "For evils unto ills conductors be, / And death's the worst resolution. / For he that thinks with patience to contend / To quiet life, his life shall easily end" (8–11). Although aligning Hieronimo with Seneca the playwright rather than Seneca the philosopher of "patience" and quiet, Kyd pitches Hieronimo's rhetoric at a far remove from the verbal fire of Clytemnestra's own words following the line cited above: "*Tecum ipsa nunc evolve femineos dolos, / quot ulla coniunx perfida atque impos sui / amore caeco, quot novercales manus / ausae, quod ardens impia virgo face / Phasiaca fugiens regna Thessalica trabe*" (I.116–20).[127] Hieronimo's language in this scene is rigid and formulaic, especially when compared to his rhetoric in the scene just *before* he enters with Seneca in hand: "I'll rip the bowels of the earth, / And ferry over to th'Elysian plains, / And bring my son to show me his deadly wounds. / Stand from about me! / I'll make a pickaxe of my poniard . . . / To be avenged on you all for this" (3.12.71–78). This is simply to point out that sudden decline of Hieronimo's rhetorical skill occurs within a scene of both reading and "Englishing" Seneca aloud.[128]

The slowed process of linguistic and cultural negotiation, however, contrasts with the mounting tension, evident in the middle of the translation scene, in which Hieronimo declares, "I will revenge his death!" (3.13.20) and then plots the way to do it. Like Revenge himself, Hieronimo turns away from a scene of complicated linguistic negotiation and toward a coherent conclusion. Here again we see the machinery of plot functioning to bypass, rather than compass, problems of speech and action, for Hieronimo barely seems to "hear" the very words that he reads and translates. That his "dire plot" is coincident with diverse but unintelligible speech, and that the plot itself is ultimately realized, so that he kills off his enemies who believe they are only acting the parts of murder victims, suggests a profound skepticism about the power of plot to evacuate, as opposed simply to organize, content. The fact that the "argument" of *Soliman and Perseda* is given to the King (and audience) in advance clearly foregrounds the dominance of plot over dialogue. But the fact that Hieronimo's distributed theatrical plot is *incomplete*, without the crucial detail that murder will substitute for mimesis, foregrounds the problem of what it might mean to rely on plots to comprehend what is unfolding before one's eyes and ears.

Indeed, it would be a mistake to conflate Kyd as playwright with Revenge, with Hieronimo, or with other characters who turn away from scenes of failed interlocution to ones of plotted action.[129] R. L. Kesler, however, does just this in arguing that "the plot structure of *The Spanish Tragedy* is founded in the causal logic of revenge."[130] Kesler interprets the conspicuous attention to "plot" within the play as Kyd's *own* attempt to provide audiences a new "pedagogy" for the comprehension of dramatic action, for the apprehension of "the basic form of the play's representational structure"(485–86). But by so conspicuously divorcing linear and unified plots from the complications of spoken language—in *Soliman and Perseda* but also well before it—Kyd radically unsettles the logic of the plot, rendering it suspect both as dramatic technology and as a guide for comprehending events. Indeed, although Hieronimo tells Bel-Imperia, "For why, the plot's already in mine head"

(4.1.51), such a heady plot leads to an occlusion of otherwise crucial details about the world around him. He seems to forget to tell Bel-Imperia not to kill herself in the playlet: "For though the story saith she should have died," Hieronimo "otherwise determine[d] of her end" (4.4.140–42). Hieronimo's plot not only stages problems of communication but is informed by it: his own wife kills herself out of despair while he is engineering a plot in private. Like Revenge's plot, the unified plot of *Soliman and Perseda* (itself designed for a *wedding* celebration) comes—within *The Spanish Tragedy*—to violate decorum on a grand scale.

"The end is crown of every work well done" (2.6.8), says Revenge to settle the unsettled Andrea; and so Hieronimo asks his own actors to trust that the "conclusion" to *Soliman and Perseda* will make an otherwise confusing playlet make sense. But these are far from consoling promises for the establishment of a dramatic coherence or unity based on a clear "end."[131] The sense of an ending that would enable us to understand *The Spanish Tragedy* in terms of plot structure, moreover, is unsettled precisely by the reestablishment of the unrationalized order of Senecan misery. Promising to bring Andrea's "foes" to "deepest hell" for "just and sharp revenge" (4.5.16, 27), Revenge declares, in the final line of the play, "For here, though death hath end their misery, / I'll there begin their endless tragedy" (47–48). A reader might see here—in the shift of both mortal and dramatic ends to an alternative teleology of action in the afterlife—a promise of a total and just retribution against those who have injured others. As Thomas Heywood would later write, "If we present a Tragedy, we include the fatall and abortiue ends of such as commit notorious murders, which is aggrauated and acted with all the Art that may be, to terrifie men from the like abhorred practises."[132] But included in the list of Andrea's "foes" we find "Don Cyprian" (Castille), who will take Tityus's place so that the vultures will feed daily on his ever-renewing entrails (31–32). Since Castille is apparently innocent in the play, we have an image of an end that is hard to recuperate within any logical order, moral or dramatic.

Kyd's process of unsettling plotlines with clear beginnings, middles, and ends is emphasized, moreover, by the fact that the play ends exactly where it begins, with Andrea and Revenge plotting a revenge. What is notable at the play's close, however, is a shift of judgment, a kind of final delegation in the administration of justice. Whereas Revenge stepped in to plot an "end" on Andrea's behalf, now it is Andrea who wants to plot the "end":

Let me be judge, and doome them to unrest:
Let loose poor Tityus from the vulture's gripe,
And let Don Cyprian supply his room;
Place Don Lorenzo on Ixion's wheel,
And let the lover's endless pains surcease—
Juno forgets old wrath, and grants him ease;
Hang Balthazar about Chimaera's neck,
And let him there bewail his bloody love,
Repining at our joys that are above;
Let Serberine go roll the fatal stone,
And take from Sisyphus his endless moan;
False Pedringano for his treachery,
Let him be dragged through boiling Acheron,
And there live, dying still in endless flames,
Blaspheming gods and all their holy names. (4.5.31–44)

Here we have a list rather than a plot informing the "endless tragedy" of the imaginary afterlife of the play. As Andrea invokes the prerogative of judge and dramatist, his rhetorical style recalls the Fury of Seneca's *Thyestes,* whose accumulation of "Let. . . . Let. . . . Let" in the opening scene of Heywood's translation marks the onset of the tragedy and the dramatist's art in making things happen. "Let mightie fall to miserie, and myser clyme to myght. . . . Let them to mischiefe fall a freshe: as hatefull then to all," and so on; this culminates in twenty-two "Let"s in this opening speech alone (A2r–A3r). "Let" is a keyword that indexes both the list of events to unfold and the dramatist's art in letting things happen. At the outset of this scene, Andrea's retrospective description of *The Spanish Tragedy* entirely centered on action, offering a reductive account of the play just witnessed.[133] Indeed, anything but a plot of what J. R. Mulryne calls "dramatically coherent action,"[134] Andrea crams nine deaths into nine lines, offering a list of horrors rather than a whole action. So too his prospective description of the ensuing "endless tragedy" centers predominantly on spectacles of repetitive action, peppered by inarticulate wails and moans, with one blasphemer in the mix.[135] The play returns us to its own beginning, the "endless" punishments of the underworld described by Andrea at the play's outset (1.1.65–71), which promise a whole new drama that will "let" loose the "endless pain," "endless moan[s]," and "endless flames" that constitute Revenge's "endless tragedy."

As a space marked by unendingly repetitive action, hell certainly seems like a convenient paradigm by which Kyd can expose the limits of the revenge plot, but also, and more interestingly (given that Andrea now appropriates a classical "hell"), a good way to expose the limits of a playwright turning to models from the classical past to reconfigure them in and for the present. Again, whereas the classically situated Revenge engineered the initial plot, it is now the contemporary Andrea who emerges as the final playwright and "judge" directing Revenge. Andrea imagines this position as a form of writing his way into the classical past—indeed, of imitating it. Andrea aims both to emulate and to empty out the classical past, thereby relieving various sinners from the torture of repetitive action (with even Juno easing up on Ixion) in order to put contemporary figures in their place. Andrea's imagined conclusion, which shows a desire to appropriate the classical past—to "cast" characters within the play into the underworld where they can play the parts of erstwhile inhabitants—betrays limited judgment in imitation as well as juridical administration.

This "conclusion" should remind us of a curious parallel in Heywood's translation of *Thyestes*. Indeed, Andrea's desire to appropriate the classical past while imagining acts of substitution might be glossed by Heywood's version of the same: taking liberty to compose a new ending to Seneca's *Thyestes*, Heywood inserts himself into the act of final judgment as well as playwriting. In the process, Heywood implied that Seneca's "end" was simply "vnperfyte." Heywood's ending is strikingly similar to Andrea's in that it also features a character (Thyestes) who calls for hell to open up and swallow substitutes for Tityus, then Ixion, and then a figure burnt in endless flames of Phlegethon: "O filthy fowles and gnawyng gripes, that Tityus bosome reut / Beholde a fitter pray for you, to fill your selues vppone. / . . . Or whirlyng wheeles, with swynge of whiche / Ixion still is rolde, Your hookes vppon this glutted gorge, woulde catche a surer holde. / . . . thou ferfull freate of fyre, / Spue out thy flames O Phlegethon: and ouer shed the grounde. / With vomite of thy fyrye streame, let me and earth be drownde" (E4v). With his image of a Thyestes now "fitter" than Tityus or Ixion for eternal punishment in the underworld, Heywood creates a conclusion not merited by Seneca's drama.[136] This contemporary adaptation of classical materials is critically mirrored by Kyd's Andrea, a contemporary figure who appropriates the engine of revenge and attempts to compose a whole new end to a tragedy that, in dramatic terms, has already ended.[137]

Kyd's approach to the *accretion* of revenge plotting, within and then beyond the play, moreover, stands as both a reflection upon and an aggressive
act of competitive emulation. In Seneca's *Thyestes*, we find the playwright, via
Atreus, already aiming to outdo precedents in the domain of tragic plot construction. In that play, Thyestes's only sons are tragically murdered, leaving a
father tortured and bereft after he inadvertently eats them in a dinner cooked
by his brother, Atreus. Atreus positions himself not simply as an eye-for-an-
eye revenger but as a competitive emulator: "*Scelera non ulcisceris, nisi vincis,*"
"You do not avenge crimes unless you surpass them."[138] The revenge plot,
"Thracium fiat nefas maiore numero," a "Thracian tragedy, but in more numbers" (or in Heywood's translation, "Let myschiefe done in Thracia onse,
there lyght More manyfolde"), becomes a means to to out-Ovid Ovid. And
that is exactly what Atreus, and by extension Seneca, does: Ovid's Procne
cooking and feeding her one son to her husband, Tereus, becomes Atreus' dinner of (two named) sons, fed to their father, with a tortuously drawn out
recognition scene. As Atreus's servant puts it in Heywood's translation, "The
Thracian house did se / Suche wicked tables once: I graunt . . . the mischiefe
great to be, / But done ere this: some greater gilt and mischiefe more, let yre
/ Fynde out" (B2r). Ire, that topic of such deep interest to the Stoical Seneca,
becomes a vehicle for dramatic invention, which enables, in *Thyestes,* revenge
to double as literary competition, and which in turn informs Heywood's own
attempt to best Seneca, for at the outset of his translation he calls upon the
furies, not Seneca, to inspire his own "pen" (**8v).

In his own vernacular revenge, Kyd further doubles the casualties in the
domain of offspring: the corpses of *four* children (including Horatio, exposed
behind the curtain) now mark the bloodied stage. He also quadruples the
tragedy of sonless fathers: he leaves the sonless Hieronimo and Castille dead
and the heirless King and Viceroy "consumed" with grief. As the King of
Spain exclaims, "What age hath ever heard such monstrous deeds?" (4.4.202).
This comment recalls various attempts by characters within the play to outdo
what has come before in the invention of punishment. The Viceroy, for example, upon catching Villuppo at a treacherous lie, speaks of a punishment
that he will devise, "not so mean a torment as we here / Devised for him who
thou said'st slew our son" (meaning the plan to set Alexandro aflame, based
on the classical precedent of those thrust into the "unquenched fires of
Phlegethon" [3.3.58–59]), "but with the bitterest torments and extremes / That
may be yet invented for thine end" (3.1.100–101). So too, the King of Spain

says of Hieronimo, "We will devise th'extremest kind of death / That ever was invented for a wretch" (4.4.197–98). We might well see the quest to outdo classically based tortures as well as "ends" as a parody of competitive emulation that enhances plot through tragic accretion. Kyd, in other words, takes revenge on revenge as a double for besting one's forebears.

The Spanish Tragedy thus becomes comprehensible—not as the first revenge drama in England that playwrights such as Shakespeare would complicate—but as an anti-revenge drama on its own terms. By staging the potential for plots to accumulate, backfire, and complicate clear trajectories with beginnings, middles, and ends, Kyd produced a vividly "inarticulate" drama in structural as well as linguistic terms. The fact that Kyd drew on no single plot for the composition of *The Spanish Tragedy* is significant in this respect. For he demonstrates the productive dimensions of methodological as well as rhetorical "confusion." And the cultivation of confusion is something Kyd calls attention to as part of the playwright's art. Balthazar's statement about *Soliman and Perseda*, "This will breed mere confusion . . . and hardly shall be understood," while an accurate description, also begs the question of why theatrics should be designed to stage confusion. It is not just language but costumes and props as well that refuse to cohere: Bel-Imperia plays an Italian dame but speaks courtly French, and she is dressed up like "Phoebe, Flora, or the huntresse" from Greek and Roman mythology. She—fusing elements of the classical and the contemporary—is like a play unto herself within the play within the play. For in *Soliman and Perseda* we have a piece of theater jam-packed with competing forms of cultural reference, as if it were crying out for the very kind of complexity that is missing from Hieronimo's brutal and linear "plot."

In the final playlet, confusion, a "mixture in which the distinction of the elements is lost by fusion, blending, or intimate intermingling,"[139] is a hyperbolic instance of imitative pastiche, which alludes to the very thickness of *The Spanish Tragedy*, which features no fewer than seven languages,[140] draws on the Petrarchan love lyric, pastoral elegy, Senecan tragedy, commedia dell'arte, academic drama, court masque, and the history play, and juxtaposes fragments from a range of classical and contemporary texts in what F. S. Boas called "Kyd's singular fashion": "pastiche."[141] Kyd's play wants to maximize resources, not minimize them for the sake of the plot. Hieronimo's plot-driven playlet, however, reifies pastiche into so much "vncohaerent iangling"; it represents a fallen model of hybridity that is at once coincident with and conditioned by the rise of the "dire plot." Thinking about or experiencing *The Spanish Tragedy* as a whole in terms of a "causal logic" of plot threatens to eclipse everything that the play does beyond, beneath, and within the plot.[142] Even Hieronimo's status as a hybrid character, an official of the Spanish state who nonetheless stages the triple conquest of England over Iberia, suggests Kyd's interest in creating characters outside the clear plotlines provided by geography and drama. The wild confusion of Hieronimo's playlet can be seen as staging the costs attendant on a form of reductive mimesis, or "plot," that reduces so much difference to jarring forms of incoherence. For confusion, too, has a history, and to reify complex forms of textual and cultural interactions as "mere confusion" belies that history.

What Hieronimo kills off, and what Kyd attempts to save, is not only a process of drama but also a process of history in the making. It is evident in Hieronimo's statement that he has drawn the plot of *Soliman and Perseda* from the historical "chronicles." The detail stands out and provides a generic framework through which to view his tragedy. Hieronimo's eerily unified "history play," moreover, stands as a notable departure from the forms of historical narration in *The Spanish Tragedy* more generally. In the opening acts of Kyd's play—as many have critics observed—there are no fewer than *five* accounts of what happened during the battle between Portugal and Spain. Kyd thus exposes the *limits* of any single historical narrative. Conversely, Hieronimo's extraction of a single "plot" from the "chronicles" suggests a comparatively focalized, and therefore simplified use of historical narrative by a playwright. Whereas Kyd complicates historical representation, Hieronimo radically simplifies it; in fact, he epitomizes it in order to mobilize dramatic action.

English playwrights would of course turn to chronicle history in late Tudor England, and for many this constituted a rationalization of the chronicles. As Heywood put it:

> Playes haue made the ignorant more apprehensiue, taught the
> vnlearned the knowledge of many famous histories, instructed such as
> cannot reade in the discouery of all our *English* Chronicles: & what
> man haue you now of that weake capacity, that cannot discourse of any
> notable thing recorded euen from *William* the *Conquerour*, nay from
> the landing of *Brute*, vntill this day, beeing possest of their true vse, For,
> or because Playes are writ with this ayme, and carryed with this
> methode, to teach the subiects obedience to their King, to shew the

people the vntimely ends of such as haue moued tumults, commotions, and insurrections, to present them with the flourishing estate of such as liue in obedience, exhorting them to allegeance, dehorting them from all trayterous and fellonious stratagems. (F1r–v)

The idea that English drama would provide a "methode" by which to rationalize historical materials would be developed at length by J. R. Levy in his seminal *Tudor Historical Thought*, which anticipated Quentin Skinner's challenge to "the mythology of coherence" in historical method.[143] Levy granted to late Tudor and early Stuart drama the very "coherence" he found wanting in chronicle history, elevating playwrights such as Shakespeare because they transformed history as "agglomeration" into "history as the operation of ideas."[144] Rendering English chronicles accumulative rather than analytic, confused rather than coherent, Levy argued against the "conception of [Tudor] history writing as selective. . . . The criterion by which a historian was judged was the quantity of information he managed to cram between the covers of his book" (168).[145] This view has been challenged by scholars who discern "structural protocols" in chronicle history in order to reinstate "the idea of shared understandings and common practices."[146] But many humanists fretted about the mess of chronicle historiography because it was both verbally and organizationally incoherent. Ascham's *Scholemaster*, for example, took aim at Edward Hall's English chronicles (chronicles printed in 1542, 1448, and 1550), where "good matter is quite marde"; "wordes be vainlie heaped vpon one vpon another," and sentences "so clowted vp together, as though M. Hall had bene, not writing the storie of England, but varying a sentence in Hitching schole" (43v).[147] Curiously, whereas Ascham took pains to criticize published "epitomes," which, by oversimplifying material through abstraction, "hath hurt generallie learning it selfe, very moche," when it comes to chronicles such as Hall's, epitome seemed just the remedy needed to counterbalance the pitfalls of "Englishe":

Neuertheles, some kinde of *Epitome* may be vsed, by men of skilful iudgement, to the great proffet also of others. As if a wise man would take *Halles* Cronicle, where moch good matter is quite marde with Indenture Englishe, and first change, strange and inkhorne tearmes into proper, and commonlie vsed wordes: next, specially to wede out that, that is superfluous and idle, not onelie where wordes be vainlie heaped one vpon an other, but also where many sentences, of one meaning, be so clowted vp . . . surelie a wise learned man, by this way of *Epitome*, in cutting away wordes and sentences, and diminishing nothing at all of the matter, shold leaue to mens vse, a storie, halfe as moch as it was in quantitie, but twise as good as it was, both for pleasure and also commoditie. (43v)

Ascham mobilizes epitomes, which he defined as "belonging, rather to matter, than to wordes: to memorie, than to vtterance" (43v), as a vehicle to silence history in the making, "cutting away wordes and sentences," leaving "matter" intact for "mens vse" as "a storie," trimmed to the bones, "for both pleasure and also commoditie."

Following Ascham, "epitomes" might well be added to the prehistory of the dramatic plot. Certainly Hieronimo trims his chosen portion of the "chronicles" to skin and bone so that it contains "matter and not common things." He also calls the play both an "argument" and a "story" (4.4.141). But rather than take this as a sign of Kyd's own method as a playwright, we can see it as his antimethod. For Hieronimo's rationalization of the "chronicles," and his own transmission of the epitome to the King beforehand, so reifies a historical source as to bring history itself (the future of political succession) to a screeching halt. By contrast, the expansive, accumulative, and necessarily unfinished structure of chronicle histories might well be integral to something like the history of plot confusion in Renaissance drama.[148] This seems especially true of heuristic confusion—where playwrights left ends unsettled and plotlines incoherent—that instantiated an accretive and ongoing model of action and information. The potentially disorienting particularities of chronicle histories could be drawn on even as they were mocked in dramas. A character in Tomkis's drama observes that "now euery trifle must be wrapped vp in the volume of eternitie. . . . A dog cannot pisse in a Noblemans shoe, but it must be sprinkled into the Chronicles, so that I neuer could remember my Treasure more full, & neuer emptier of honorable, and true heroycall actions" (D4r). The fact that this character is Memory, who forgets things, like his glasses and his own memoranda, and who remembers only partial details (like the specific page number of Hall's chronicles where he left his glasses behind), shows a playwright experimenting with disorganized, rhetorically wayward, and accumulative materials in order to represent the complexity of the mind at work with a rich, because variegated and nonrationalized, textual culture.[149]

To think "particularlie," as Raphael Holinshed put it in his own

Chronicles in 1587, might be to resist the "vaine affection of eloquence" in order to enable new forms of thought and discovery.[150] Holinshed inaugurates his *Chronicles* with a rationalized resistance to both rhetorical elegance and logical method: "*I neuer made any choise of stile, or wordes*, neither regarded to handle this Treatise in such *precise order and method* as manie other would haue done, thinking it sufficient, truelie and plainelie to set foorth such things as I minded to intreat of, rather than with vaine affection of eloquence to paint out a rotton sepulchre" (A1v, emphasis added). The operative word here is "choise": more gatherer than hunter, Holinshed refuses to kill off the history of the living and the dead with the weapons of eloquence or logical method. Rather than treating chronicles, as Levy once did, as confused tissues of fiction and fact that are structurally incompatible with humanist principles of selection and imitation, we might rather consider, with Holinshed, the irrelevance as well as the potential violence of style, word choice, methodical arrangement, and distinction to "things" encountered and "set foorth." The resistance to method might, as Annabelle Patterson has suggested, have led to a democratizing of judgment, so that history could be subject to radically opposed interpretations,[151] but it could also have informed the open-ended *structure* of Renaissance dramas, which aimed to do the same.

We can now reflect back on Kyd's engagement not only with problems of rhetorical coherence in the Tudor period but also with cultural spheres of vernacularism, law, and historiography, in which the pitfalls of rhetoric gave rise, for some, to calls for methodical plotting. *The Spanish Tragedy* expresses the costs of moving too hastily from the acknowledgment that communication has been thwarted to an "acting out" through plot. To recall Erving Goffman's observation I cited in my Introduction, the most productive moments for understanding how communication works are those in which communication fails. "Disenchantment with an interaction," writes Goffman, "may take the form of preoccupation, self-consciousness, other-consciousness, and interaction consciousness."[152] Kyd's drama calls for a heightened awareness of social processes that comes to the surface when interactions fail and of the deep structure of feeling that can be lost if "interaction consciousness"—interactions between persons and themselves, other people, other languages, other histories, texts and contexts—is subsumed by a privatized solution, an acting out, a plotting forward that takes the place of enduring and understanding the moment. This explains why the play had such a curious reception, for it looked a lot like comedy.

The 1615 title page (reproduced in 1618, 1623, and 1633), *The Spanish*

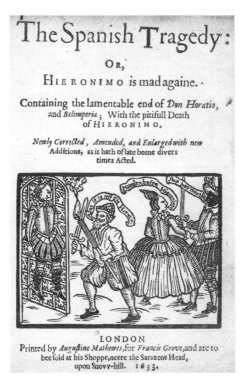

Figure 2. Title page, Thomas Kyd, *The Spanish Tragedy* (London, 1633). STC 15094. Courtesy of the Houghton Library, Harvard College Library.

tragedie, or, Hieronimo is mad againe. Containing the lamentable end of Don Horatio, and Belimperia; with the pitifull Death of Hieronimo, added "Hieronimo is mad again," as if the printer wanted to present Hieronimo's affect not as petition but as repetition (Figure 2).[153] This would not have been a misreading of Kyd's play (Kyd died in 1594) or necessarily a sign that tragic drama had developed so rapidly that it left Kyd outmoded: for Kyd took revenge on the ability of revenge to represent the real tragedy of what loss might look like.[154]

Shakespeare, too, would soon dig deeper into the origins of loss that could come into view when utterance failed to have a desired effect. In *Love's Labour's Lost*, the focus of the next chapter, we will revisit the question of methodical arrangement as it impacted the language of passion, but in terms of developments of love lyrics and pedagogical manuals in print culture that led to a curious form of acting in the passive voice, or what I call "the melancholy of print."

CHAPTER FOUR

Acting in the Passive Voice

Love's Labour's Lost and the Melancholy of Print

> *True loue lacketh a tongue.*
> —John Lyly, *Euphues and his England* (1580)

Sighs and Groans: The Voice in Print

WHEN WE THINK about the inarticulate in relationship to emotion in the Renaissance, there is perhaps no greater paradox than that of love. Unlike the seriocomic utterances of the mumbler or the furious rants of the revenger, where alternatives to eloquence gained audibility and visibility on stage and page, the inarticulate sighs, stammers, and groans of lovers could lead, through the tradition of Petrarchism and its classical and medieval forebears, to extraordinary forms of eloquence.[1] Cupid, "th'anointed sovereign of sighs and groans," as Berowne puts it in *Love's Labour's Lost*, could mobilize pen and ink even, and especially, as he made speech unable: "Never durst poet touch a pen to write / Until his ink were tempered with Love's sighs."[2] But the phenomenon of the inarticulate lover can be investigated as part of what I have called the "inarticulate Renaissance"—precisely because what so often came to the fore in early discourses of love was the alienation of a speaker from his own tongue, and indeed his own breath.

In the medical and poetic discourses of Renaissance England, for example, loving was often a matter of having one's breath literally taken away. Physiologically, love melancholy was diagnosed in terms of a kind of romantic arrhythmia or cardiac arrest, irregular or neglected breathing producing sighs, stutters, broken speech, and silence. Lovers, wrote Robert Burton in *The Anatomy of Melancholy*, not only suffer "palpitation of the heart," but *"cor proximumori . . .* their heart is at their mouth."[3] Indeed, cardiac, respiratory, and vocal motions were interdependent in a range of early texts, and broken hearts and broken speech went hand in hand. The ardent lover, according to Hoby's 1561 translation of Castiglione's *Il cortegiano*, has "a burninge hart . . . a colde tunge, with broken talke and sodeine silence."[4] In love lyrics of the period, hearts bleed, pens weep, and eyes speak volumes, while language seems in many ways disassociated from the human voice, somehow stuck in the throat or on the tip of the tongue. The beloved, urged to "hear with the eyes" "what silent love hath writ" (Sonnet 23), is asked again and again to animate the voice of the lover. Although many critics have found in the sixteenth-century love lyric "the deeply felt utterances of a self expressive speaking voice," it is striking how often the ultimate sign of love was precisely the failure of voice.[5]

"True loue lacketh a tongue," wrote John Lyly in a sentiment that, interestingly enough, seems to have become all the more popular just as discourses of love were becoming more and more available through the medium of print. Indeed, to begin to place tropes of amorous inarticulacy in a broader cultural context, I want to argue that the vocal insufficiencies of the melancholy lover in late sixteenth-century England were in many ways conditioned by the shifting status of the voice in print.[6] In what may be the genesis of the title of Shakespeare's *Love's Labour's Lost*, for example, John Florio suggested in *Florio His firste Fruites* (1578) that love need not be spoken of because it was already written and printed in excess: "We need not speak so much of loue, all books are ful of loue, with so many authours, that it were labour lost to speake of Loue."[7] The "loss" Florio imagines here is not so much the lost labor of love as the lost labor of speech in a world where passion and interiority are already located in printed books, which themselves seem almost to possess an interior, to be "full of love." The extent to which the sheer proliferation of amatory discourses in printed texts of the period could be imagined to result in a loss of voice is staged in *Love's Labour's Lost*, a play where texts themselves are "full of love" (4.2.769) and lovers full of text, and where the melancholy of love articulates a melancholy of speech in

Figure 3. "Melancholia," Henry Peacham, *Minerva Britanna* (London, 1612). STC 19511. Courtesy of the Houghton Library, Harvard College Library.

a world dominated by technologies of writing and print. That is, love melancholy, the most prominent disease in the play, is at once a dramatic realization of well-known Petrarchan conceits (where eye and text mediate or utterly replace tongue and voice) and a historically specific social ailment, articulating the oral and psychic self-estrangement of speakers living in a culture in transition to print.

In an analysis of the vocal dimensions of melancholy, Juliana Schiesari has distinguished between male melancholia, which is marked by a "topos of expressibility," and female depression, which is marked by "inexpressive babble."[8] Yet what is striking in a range of sixteenth- and seventeenth-century English texts is how often *male* melancholia encodes a cultural condition of vocal vulnerability, a marked failure of oral expression linked specifically to an overdependence on books. The prototypical melancholic in Henry Peacham's

Minerva Britanna (Figure 3), whose "mouth, in signe of silence, vp is bound," as the accompanying text reads, is identified by a gag over his mouth and a book in his hand.[9] While Schiesari, revisiting Freud, reads the "excessive verbalism" of Hamlet as a quintessential sign of the male melancholic, what is often at stake for the melancholic is not so much "excessive verbalism" as what might rather be called an "excessive textualism," a dramatically alienated form of orality that tends to foreground the distinctly bookish origins and dimensions of speech.[10] Hamlet may well be a case in point. As Margreta de Grazia has noted, in the 1603 Quarto Hamlet is said to enter, "poring uppon a booke" just before launching into "To be or not to be." "Is it possible," she asks, "that Hamlet's, Shakespeare's, the culture's most celebrated soliloquy, is read from a book?"[11] To extend the question to consider forms of melancholy more generally, what if melancholia is itself primarily a symptom of reading or, in the case of early modern drama, of reading aloud?

In *Love's Labour's Lost*, symptoms of love melancholy—the brokenness of speech, the stammering of voice, the sense of one's breath being taken away— are all staged as problems of reading aloud. Lovers onstage embody a veritable physiology of reading marked by a conspicuous dominance of eye, heart, and book over tongue.[12] The heart of love-struck and inarticulate Navarre is "with print impress'd," and "his tongue, all impatient to speak and not to see, / Did stumble with haste in his eyesight to be; / All senses to that sense did make their repair. . . . / . . . all his senses were lock'd in his eye" (2.1.234, 237–41). Similarly, in *Much Ado About Nothing*, Benedict imagines the power of love over Claudio as a shift from hearing to seeing or reading words; Claudio has "turned orthography, his words are a very fantastical banquet. . . . May I be so converted to see with these eyes?" (2.3.18–22).[13] The heightened visual sensations of love are here aligned with the distinctly ocular and graphic dimensions of speech: the inarticulate lover here and elsewhere becomes shorthand for speakers who speak as if they were reading and writing, and the distinctly bookish speech of the lover becomes a kind of mouthpiece for broader issues of linguistic self-estrangement.[14]

Indeed, it might be said that in representations of lovesickness in sixteenth-century England, the "melancholic ego" is itself conditioned by the "bibliographic ego"[15] as lovers and texts entwine in a discourse that conflates love melancholy with the conspicuous proliferation of text in the social world. According to Freud, "If one listens patiently to a melancholic's many and various self-accusations, one cannot in the end avoid the impression that often the most violent of them are hardly at all applicable to the patient himself, but that with insignificant modifications they do fit someone else, someone whom the patient loves or should love."[16] What can often be discerned in Renaissance discourses of love melancholy is the systematic introjection not so much of qualities of the beloved as of qualities of textuality more generally. "Sorrow," reads George Whetstone's 1582 *Heptameron*, is "The Great Impression."[17] And if "impression" in the post-Gutenberg era was a stamp of print as well as thought, the melancholic, that most impressionable of types, may be seen as a kind of walking pathology of print.[18] According to André Du Laurens's *A Discourse of the Preseruation of the Sight* (1599), not only does the melancholic "loue silence out of measure, and oftentimes cannot speake," his emotional habits result in the production of "impressions" that are always the same: "There is difference in the maner of their impressions . . . in melancho-like persons, the braine may seeme to haue gotten a habit, and therewithall the humour which is drie and earthie, hauing set his stampe in a bodie that is hard, suffereth not itselfe easily to be blotted out."[19] Similarly, as Jacques Ferrand wrote in his later *Erotomania, Or A Treatise Discoursing of the Essence, Causes, Symptomes, Prognosticks, and Cure of Love, or Erotiqve Melancholy* (1640), "For all Passions, that are of any long continuance, doe imprint ill Habits in the Mind; which by length of time growing stronger, are very hard to be removed. . . . he that hath contracted such an Amorous Disposition, is in love with every one he sees."[20] Interestingly, here it is the mechanical reproducibility of emotional life itself that constitutes the melancholic disposition. The "Amorous Disposition," like a printing press or a compulsive habit, reproduces versions of itself regardless of the context.[21]

In *Love's Labour's Lost* melancholy emerges as a form of textual reproduction, and vocal expressions of woe are themselves "lost" precisely because they are taken directly from printed books: "How canst thou part sadness and melancholy" (1.2.7–8), asks Armado, in a conversation that seems almost to emerge from the opening line and chapter of Timothy Bright's 1586 *A Treatise of Melancholy*, which focuses entirely on "*Howe diverslie the word Melancholie is taken.*"[22] Indeed, throughout the play, the persistent sense that *love* has overthrown oratorical power is entwined with the fact that books have overthrown the power of the tongue as "conceit's expositor" (2.1.72). Performances of speech are repeatedly imagined as forms of reading and writing; voices and passions are driven by a distinctly visual and spatial logic linked to the structure of the material book. While the "bookish" nature of the *Love's Labour's*

Lost has often been taken to be its ultimate failing, it is precisely the thematized failure of theatrical mimesis and oral performance that makes the play such a powerful commentary on the intersecting logics of inarticulate love melancholy and expanding literacy.

Love itself is staged as a kind of drama of public reading: the play foregrounds not performance but performance *texts*—from sonnet to playtext to schoolbook to dictionary—and most characters rely on conspicuously public texts for the expression of selves. As such, the play (always negotiating between text and staged voice) positions its own medium as an analogue to what might be seen as the increasingly scripted performances of identity, and the increasingly estranged conditions of orality, in the early age of print.[23] The relationship between the ineffectual speech of the lover and the unprecedented publication of love in both poetic and educational texts of the late sixteenth century is worth exploring in this respect; it can help us to understand the melancholy of love—in the play and in the period—not only as a product of print but also as a nostalgia for speech. Dramas of love, in this respect, can be seen as a kind of elaborate exercise in catching one's breath at the very moment it's being taken away.

Romance Languages: Loving by the Book

> *In short, love is an affliction, and by the same token it is a word or letter.*
> —Julia Kristeva, *Tales of Love* (1987)[24]

> *O Amo, thou euer hast too many wordes.*
> —Andrea Guarna, *Bellum Grammaticale* (1511)[25]

"*Honorificabilitudinitatibus,*" ONE OF the many bookish words in *Love's Labour's Lost,* is a word that literally takes one's breath away (5.1.40). The respiratory and vocal demands of wrapping one's mouth around hard words in the play are linked again and again with the conditions of loving so much that speech becomes difficult. Indeed, lovers in the play are as much love-struck as what Montaigne would call *lettreferits,* or "word-struck," the mark of pedants who speak "as though their reading has given them, so to speak, a whack with a hammer."[26] The absurdity of "loving by the book" is a recurrent trope in

Shakespearean comedy, where humanist and courtly models of engagement meet, clash, and generally result in the lost labor of love. The bookish lover tends to fail as a speaker, and love melancholy expresses as much a general problem of translating books into conversations as it does an inability to speak of, or to, a specific emotional condition.

The use of love lyric in printed textbooks about conversation can help us to consider the pedagogical context of just this problem. A range of educational manuals, newly available in the late sixteenth century, drew on the structures, vocabularies, and thematics of love and can be seen as a powerful instance in Renaissance culture of where love became a matter of learning (but not quite knowing) how to speak. *Love's Labour's Lost* engages with a number of these textbooks, which feature elaborate exercises drawing on the lexicon of love, the love letter, the poetic blazon, the sonnet, the ballad, and the rhyme itself. Turning first to a series of language manuals and then to the play itself, we can begin to understand the sociotextual as well as emotional-dramatic fusion and confusion of love and learning, lyric and argument, heart and tongue, in and around the play.

The first words one learns in a foreign language are often words of love (*amo, amas, amat; je vous aime, je t'aime; te amo*), and in many early language textbooks, grammatical "moods" and constructs of active and passive voice were taught through a lexicon of love. John Brinsly's *Ludus Literarius: Or, The Grammar Schoole* (1612), prescribes the following fairly typical dialogue for student and teacher:

> Q. I doe loue, or I loue?
> A. *Amo*
> Q. Grant I loue.
> A. *Vtinam amen.*
> Q. I may or can loue.
> A. *Amem.*
> Q. When I loue?
> A. *Cum amem.*[27]

Early pronunciation manuals frequently drew attention to language learning as a kind of loving: William Salesbury's 1550 guide to the pronunciation of letters opened with an appeal to the "philoglottous" or "Langage Louers," and George Delamothe's *The French Alphabeth* (1592) opened with an extended discussion of the "mutuall loue and agreement, betweene him that dooth teach, and him that dooth learne."[28] But in addition to prefatory commonplaces about the love of wisdom and the use of "love" as a paradigmatic verb, textual and pedagogical dimensions of love in practices of language acquisition and rhetorical facility were marked in a range of sixteenth-century textbooks. Erasmus's *De copia* (1512), for example, mobilizes the language of love to teach young students the art of writing and speech, listing "*desperdita amore* (Suetonius): madly in love," "*tui cupientissimus*: longing eagerly for you," and "*sic omnia tua exosculatur*: he so kisses all that is yours" among twenty-three possible expressions of love, all part of an exercise designed to help students develop eloquent and varied habits of speech and writing.[29] Similarly, in *Bellum Grammaticale*, an academic grammar play performed for Elizabeth at Oxford in 1592, Amo, the king of verbs, presides over Grammarland along with Poeta, the vividly melancholic king of nouns.[30] In this play, as in the hugely popular prose text upon which it was based (Andrea Guarna's *Bellum Grammaticale*, printed *seventy-five* times in the sixteenth century alone), the anatomy of love is an anatomy of grammar: a conflict between Amo (as verb and love) and Poeta (as noun and poet) leads to a civil war between parts of speech; towns such as A and V and E, I, and O are "taken" and "irregular" grammatical factions are created, and although Amo triumphs and reconciles with Poeta, the triumph of love and of "love-poetry" is essentially an intellectual one of letters and learning.[31]

The power of love as a vehicle for expanding literacy, as a basis of not so much intimate as social and even international relations, might be gleaned by considering the uses of love letters and love poetry in manuals on rhetoric, grammar, and foreign languages. At the end of Jacques Bellot's *Le maistre d'escole Anglois . . . The Englishe Scholemaister* (London, 1580), one of the first English grammars for Frenchmen, is a twenty four page text entitled, *The Poesy or Nosegay of Loue. Conteyning the Posies of sondrye Flowers, Hearbes, and Plantes. That are put commonlye in Nosegays. Directed to the true Louers.* This text, with English and French in parallel columns, contains extended lists of flowers ("*Bouquet d'Amours*"), foods ("*La Salade d'amours*"), and colors ("*La deuise des couleurs*") of love:

Le Geneure auec	The Junyper with
ses fleurs, se	his flowers, is
prend pour, Vous	taken for, You
desrobez mon coeur.	steal away my heart. . . .

La Plumersoe, ou	The Primerose,
Primerose, signifie,	signifieth,
le commence a	I beginne to
vous aimer.	loue you. . . .
La Saule, se prend	The Willow tree,
pour, Espargnez moy.	is taken for, Spare me . . .
L'incarnat,	The fleshe colour,
se prend pour,	is taken for,
Desespoir, ou	Desperation, or
Torment en	Torment in
amours.	loue. . . .[32]

Here the elements of love lyric and language lesson meet: tropes of love melancholy and isolated units of the poetic blazon are transformed into an elaborate list of adjectives, nouns, and verbs. What is striking here is the way in which the very discourse of love and poetic emblazoning is itself emblazoned (in every sense of the word "blazon," which meant to describe, to partition or catalogue, and to publish) and aligned along the visual coordinates of the page.[33] Like the main text of the *Scholemaister*, which begins by listing letters of the alphabet and ends by listing the seasons, *The Poesy* is structured as an extended list, concluding with a ballad and a series of sonnets. While the manual mimics poetic language and courtly lyric, in many ways it radically decontextualizes the language of love, not only from interpersonal contexts and continuous narrative sequences but also from the elite contexts of traditional lyric composition. As with so many early vernacular language manuals, which were largely designed for use outside the classroom, poetic modes are here essentially a vehicle for public education: the poetic blazon is a pedagogical tool, and the closing sonnets exhibit first and foremost a wealth of accumulated learning.

Similar uses of love poetry, love letters, and poetic emblazoning surface in the language manuals of John Florio and John Eliot.[34] In these texts, Petrarchism and pedagogy converge: acts of discursive and imagistic partitioning so integral to amorous epideictic become part of a broader program of learning and linguistic mastery. While Nancy Vickers has emphasized the psychic valence of the anatomical blazon, which "almost literalizes the logic whereby the self is collected, defined, and displayed *through* the process of splitting and exhibiting the other,"[35] it might also be observed that in the most practical sense the blazon as a mode of erotic description was compatible with the needs of foreign language manuals in print. For these manuals, which sought to teach basic nouns such as parts of the body and adjectives such as sizes, were structured according to loosely organized lists of isolated particulars and were themselves "collected, defined, and displayed through the process of splitting and exhibiting the other."[36]

It is no coincidence in this respect that the first words the pedant Holofernes speaks in *Love's Labour's Lost* fuse the language of the translation dictionary with that of the poetic blazon: "The deer was, as you know, *sanguis*, in blood; ripe as the pomewater, who now hangeth like a jewel in the ear of *coelo*, the sky, the welkin, the heaven; and anon falleth like a crab on the face of *terra*, the soil, the land, the earth" (4.2.3–7). The ultimate failure of the blazon as a method of organizing speech is here underscored by the subtle allusion to Actaeon, that prototype of amorous emblazoning who was ultimately transformed into a deer, deprived of voice, and torn to bloody bits by his own hounds. But more generally, the pedagogical uses and abuses of love poetry are highlighted throughout this scene, as Holofernes teaches a text that is itself a "canzonet": "Let me hear a staff, a stanze, a verse" (4.2.100), he says of Berowne's love sonnet to Rosaline, transforming the very lexicon of poetic form into a word list. While this may add weight to arguments equating Holofernes with Florio, what is on display here and throughout the play, in broader terms, is the use of distinctly literary and textually based discursive forms for the practice of speech: "You find not the apostrophus, and so miss the accent: Let me supervise the canzonet," says Holofernes to Nathanial (4.2.115–16), chiding him for reading the sonnet improperly.[37]

Throughout *Love's Labour's Lost*, love becomes a pre-text in the most literal sense, serving as a vehicle for the transmission of conspicuous book learning, entailing the articulation of rudiments of language, letters, and knowledge. If love in the play seems comic because of its detachment from specific persons and contexts, this may be seen to reflect the many public uses and articulations of love in the period, which often seemed defamiliarized— indeed less than articulate or skillfully "jointed"—through structures of listing, repetition, and mechanical reproduction. The language of love melancholy and poetic emblazoning in the play is not only referentially remote from actual beloveds, it is also entwined with a range of distinctly bookish and public discourses of woe. At one point lovesickness is presented as a rudimentary exercise for the use of prepositions: after pointing out that Armado has forgotten his love, Moth says: "Negligent student! learn her by heart."

> *Arm.* By heart, and in heart, boy.
> *Moth.* And out of heart, master: all those three I will prove.
> *Arm.* What wilt thou prove?
> *Moth.* A man, if I live; and this, by, in, and without, upon the instant: by heart you love her, because your heart cannot come by her; in heart you love her, because your heart is in love with her; and out of heart you love her, being out of heart that you cannot enjoy her.
> *Arm.* I am all these three.
> *Moth.* And three times as much more, and yet nothing at all. (3.1.33–46)

The question of whether the heart is "in" love or whether one is "out of heart" or loving "by" heart, while epistemologically and psychosomatically complex, reduces the anatomy of heartbreak to an anatomy of grammar.[38]

The grammar of the heart, or rather, the accumulation of prepositions and synonyms in oral expressions of love, amounts to what Erasmus terms "battologia," the vice of using words "more suitable for exercises than real speeches": "I observe that some public speakers of otherwise distinguished reputation, especially among the Italians, actually set out to waste time with strings of synonyms like this, as if that were some splendid achievement. It is just like someone expounding the verse from the psalm, 'Create in me a clean heart, O God' by saying 'Create in me a clean heart, a pure heart, an unsullied heart, a spotless heart, a heart free from stain, a heart unstained by sin, a purified heart, a heart that is washed, a heart white as snow,' and so on, right through the psalm. 'Richness' of this sort is practically battologia."[39] But the specter of lexical accumulation (or listing in public) in *Love's Labour's Lost* speaks less to the vice of a particular speaker than to the expanding literacies of the period, where new dictionaries, conversation manuals, and vernacular textbooks were creating whole new possibilities and problems for oral exchange.[40]

In Armado's case, listing is a kind of speech exercise learned from printed books *about* speech. Although praising the good god of "extemporal" rhyme, his soliloquy about "turn[ing] sonnet" in the first act of the play reads much like the strings of commonplaces in Florio's language manuals. "Love is a familiar; Love is a devil: there is no evil angel but Love" (1.2.162–63) might be juxtaposed to a speech in Florio's *First Fruits* that reads, "Loue is a delectable despite, and a spitefull delight. Honest loue is ordeyned of God: dishonest loue is forbydden of God. . . . Loue maketh it easie: that hardest thing that is" (S4r). Interestingly, this particular "dialogue" includes the lines "We neede not speak so much of loue, al books are ful of loue, with so many authours, that it were labour lost to speake of Loue" (S4r). Sidney, in fact wishing to separate "diction" from dictionaries, notes in an *An Apologie for Poetrie* that some Englishmen speak "as if they were bound to followe the method of a Dictionary."[41] So too, in *Astrophel and Stella*, "You that doe dictionary method bring / Into your rymes, running in ratling rowes, / You that old Petrarchs long deceased woes / With new borne sighes, and wit disguised sing; / You take wrong wayes, those far-fet helps be such, / As doe bewray a want of inward tutch."[42] Given the proliferation of translation dictionaries themselves, the making of dictionaries or word lists was itself, as Peter Levens put it in *Manipvlvs Vocabvlorvm. A Dictionarie of English and Latine wordes* (1570), "counted but as lost labour."[43] The culture of "lost laboure" in Shakespeare's play is not simply a matter of loving or simply a matter of listing but really a matter of loving to list.

Early language textbooks were generally incremental in structure (moving from lists of letters to lists of sentences and finally to categorically organized clusters of poetry and dialogue) and may well be seen to have created a kind of phenomenology of the list in the increasingly literate cultures of early modern England. "By, in, and without . . . I am all three of these": the structure of the list organizes the discourse of love here and in all of Armado's speeches and letters, where synonyms, numbers, and parts of speech abound in ways that comically disrupt a continuous narrative flow. Indeed, falling in love is for Armado a kind of fall into *lists*, that structural feature of discourse that theorists of literacy such as Jack Goody have linked specifically with communities of writing and print.[44] While it may well be an overstatement to say with Goody that there is no "oral equivalent" to the list as a form of discursive organization, the distinctly visual, graphic, and spatial dimensions of lists (which are in general more amenable to eye than ear) repeatedly surface in the mouths of characters in *Love's Labour's Lost* in ways that register the influence of printed textbooks.[45]

The logic of the list might well be seen as a dominant principle of the play, which begins, for example, with the reading of "*Items*" on a contract, and which foregrounds letters of the alphabet, parts of the body, seasons of the year, basic numbers and forms of measure, figures of speech, and words in the dictionary. Similarly, word lists in Bellot's *Le maistre d'escole Anglois* are categorized in terms of numbers, the days of the week, the months of the year, the four winds, the seven planets, twelve astrological signs, and finally, the four seasons. Like Bellot's *Poesy*, which closes with a sonnet entitled "De faire tout en saison," the anonymous early French textbook *A very necessarye boke bothe in Englyshe & in Frenche* (1550) comes to a close with a rehearsal of the seasons and the "names of the yere."[46] Colors, flowers, and seasons, parts of the visible and temporal world, were as integral to discourses of love as they were to popular language textbooks, a fact that informs the melancholic dimensions of speech in *Love's Labour's Lost*.[47]

The catalogical, indexical, and visual structures of love and learning in the play may well be a send-up of Bellot in particular, whose textbooks on speech were in circulation in the final decades of the sixteenth century. His *Familiar Dialogues* (1586), another manual with French and English dialogues printed in parallel columns, features a whole series of conversations that consist entirely of lists (exciting questions such as "What collor haue ye?" are answered with a list of colors, enhancing the reader's vocabulary and ability to converse at once).[48] Again, *The Poesy or Nosegay of Love* draws together the catalogical dimensions of love and learning by foregrounding the isolated discursive units of love, such as colors and flowers, and deploying sonnets and a ballad at the close of the text ("*Balade sur la devise des Couleurs*," about the colors of love, which concludes with an "envoy"). The list of colors in Bellot's *Familiar Dialogues*, but most especially in his *Poesy* (which reads, for example, "Le Roux, signifie, Petitesse, Humilite, ou melencolie en Amours / The russet coulour signifieth Lowelinesse, Humillitie, or mellancholye in Loue"), resonates with the textual colorphilia of *Love's Labour's Lost*. The first scene of the play foregrounds Armado's "sable-colored melancholy," in which he emblazons his own writing, the "snow-white pen" and "ebon-coloured ink" of his own text (1.1.238–39). Or, "Green indeed," says Armado at one moment in the play, "is the colour of lovers" (1.2.81). Although this statement has frequently been read as a reference to Shakespeare's contemporary Robert Greene,[49] it is also part of a conversation about the literal "colors of love" that culminates in Moth's own poem or "definition" of "white and red" (88–100). Even the play's closing songs about winter and spring, which many have read as an ultimate reconciliation of art and nature,[50] read at first like a rudimentary list of flowers and colors of love, a vocabulary list transformed into a song about the seasons: "When daises pied and violets blue / And lady-smocks all silver-white / And cuckoo-buds of yellow hue / Do paint the meadows with delight" (5.2.886–89).

The conspicuous textuality of listing as a quality of ineffectual speech is highlighted in the play's emphasis on love poetry as "numbers" (4.3.318), where lyric becomes detached from the acoustics of music and abstracted as a form of counting; "he came, one; saw, two; overcame, three," reads one amorous "ballad" (4.1.71). Interestingly, Bellot's final "pronunciation" guide, *The French Method* (1588), concludes with a chapter on versification, where the ballad, sonnet, envoy, and a range of French verse forms are defined and demonstrated, and where metrics are strung out in narrative form like so many numbers on a page. What "*the French men doe call* Enuoy," he writes, "Is made sometimes of seuen meeters, and sometimes of fiue: Being of seuen, it is formed of three colours, The first and second meeters being one colour, the third, fourth, and sixt, of an other, and the fift, and seuenth of another."[51] This vocabulary of the abstract poetic coordinate is taken rather literally by the speakers in *Love's Labour's Lost*. Indeed, the ado about "l'envoy" in the play (a French word used only here in the Shakespearean corpus and uttered a mind-numbing sixteen times within fifty-three lines, 3.1.66–119) arguably sends up the scholastic appropriation of lyric in Bellot. The word is formally defined (79–80), repeatedly demonstrated with a poem about counting (81–95), and translated and mistranslated at length (66–119). But more generally, the recurrent link between poetic forms and "numbers" (from Holofernes's treatment of *L* as a letter and a roman numeral to the arithmetic thematic of the "l'envoy" itself),[52] speaks to the insinuation of formal vocabularies of versification and number into spoken verse forms. It renders comic and absurd the movement of poetry from the domain of the ear to that of the eye (and vice versa).[53]

While the play is often said to have no single source, it takes pains to dramatize the many textual sources of melancholy utterance in printed books of the period, working to foreground what might be seen as a perilous textuality of voice. The ballad about King Cophetua that Armado decides, as he puts it, to "newly writ o'er" is a case in point (1.2.108). For what he creates while drawing on an "oral" tradition is ironically a text that—in addition to rehearsing fundamentals of grammar, vocabulary, and composition—features

Latinisms and demonstrates an expressed contempt for the vernacular ("O base and obscure vulgar!" [4.1.69–70]). And all for a woman who is, in fact, illiterate:

> By heaven, that thou art fair, is most infallible; true, that thou are most beauteous, truth itself, that thou art lovely. More fairer than fair, beautiful than beauteous, truer than truth itself, have commiseration on thy heroical vassal! The magnanimous and most illustrate king Cophetua set eye upon the pernicious and indubitate beggar Zenolophon, and he it was that might rightly say, *veni, vidi, vici;* which to annothanize in the vulgar (O base and obscure vulgar!) *videlicet,* he came, saw, and overcame: he came, one; saw, two; overcame, three. Who came? the king: why did he come? to see: why did he see? to overcome. To whom came he? to the beggar: what saw he? the beggar: who overcame he? the beggar. . . . Thus, expecting thy reply, I profane my lips on thy foot, my eyes on thy picture, and my heart on thy every part. (4.1.61–86).

This "ballad" is essentially a series of lists, moving from adjectives to numbers to prepositions to body parts. Emblazoning in this letter is just one of many forms of list making and is at once a symptom of reading and of love.[54]

Armado's creation of a literate "song" for the benefit of an illiterate, combined with his contempt for illiteracy, is perhaps a perfect metaphor for the pretensions and narcissism of the lover. But it also parodies the uses of love lyric in educational practice of the period, and reflects ironically upon the many claims made about the pedagogical value of love poems in print in the latter half of the sixteenth century. The first major book of vernacular love lyric published in England, *Songes and sonettes* (1557), for example, was justified by Richard Tottel on the grounds that "learned" lyrics might "profit . . . English Eloquence" and prove beneficial even to the "rude skill of common eares."[55] The emphasis on love lyrics and love letters as a kind of lingual and acoustical enhancement calls to mind John Eliot's satiric language guide *Ortho-epia Gallica* (1593). The following love letter (which Eliot claims to have reproduced from an original) might be juxtaposed to Armado's ballad:

> *Mistresse your beautie is so excellent, so singular, so celestiall, that I beleeue Nature hath bestowed it on you as a sampler to shew how much she can do*

when she will imploy her full power and best skill. All that is in your selfe is
but honie, is but sugar, is but heavenly ambrosia. It was to you whom Paris
should have iudged the golden apple, not Venus, no, nor to Iuno, nor to
Minerua, for neuer was there so great magnificence in Iuno, so great
wisdome in Minerua, so great beautie in Venus, as in you. O heavens, gods
and godesses, happie shall he be to whom you grant the fauour to col you, to
kisse you, and to lie with you. I cannot tell whether I am predestinated by
the Fairies, wherefore I commend me to your good grace, kissing your white
hands, humbly I take my leaue without Adieu.[56]

What is remarkable about this amorous epistle is that it is framed as part of a
lesson on speech and pronunciation: in the right-hand margin of the page
(and in the left-hand margin of the facing page in French) are guides to the
proper pronunciation of vowels and consonants. That is to say, this literary
letter in a printed manual on vocabulary and pronunciation finds its parallel
in *Love's Labour's Lost*, not only in Armado's silly ballad but also in the transformation of love letters into awkwardly *spoken* discourse both in the play and
in the domain of public theater. The clichés in Eliot's letter are themselves integrated into dialogue in the play, as Berowne says, for example, "White-
handed mistress, one sweet word with thee," to which the Princess responds,
"Honey, and milk, and sugar: there is three" (5.2.230–31). The awkward sound
of words such as the comically Latinate "*honorificabilitudititatubus,*" moreover, might be read in terms of Eliot's own satiric play with excessively inky
word formations in a text on proper pronunciation.

For Eliot himself comically claims to have "dezinkhornifistibulated a fantasticall Rapsody of dialogisme," while attending to the genuine difficulty of
transferring foreign words on the page to the domain of oral utterance; where
the phrase 'Prins en amour ardant embrassoit vn image" for example, should
be sounded as, "Preenzanamoorardantambrassoettewnneema^{z}ieh."[57] This
conglomerate "word," not unlike "dezinkhornifistibulated," constitutes a veritable feast for the eye in Eliot's printed text. Indeed, Eliot calls attention to
the visual appearance of words in his book precisely to emphasize what he
calls "the difficulties of the French pronounciation, which indeed is an intri-
cate thing, and for any English at the first or second sight irremarkeable." So
"that thou mayest haue a view thereof," he writes to his reader, "cast an eye
after the Table of my booke, looke a little, view, see what a dish of rare dainties there is for thee" (B2r). Given such highlighted difficulties in transferring

a visual world designed for the "eye" of the "reader" to an acoustical world designed for the ear of the listener and speaker in what Eliot calls his own "fantasticall Comedie" (B3r), it is no wonder that Eliot's portrait of the love melancholic embodies the dominance of eye over tongue. Indeed, the lover said to have composed the mock love letter above will *"neuer speake to any bodie," "always mumbling,"* as he is, *"or recording some thing in English verse, that he hath made to his sweet-heart and minion"* (V4r).[58] This "poore passionate is cruelly eclipsed," or rather his capacity for speech is eclipsed, for he seems only capable of making *"the aire eccho with his sighs, complaints, murmurings, rages, imprecations"* (V4v).

If the habitual assumption of London playgoers, as Andrew Gurr has suggested, was "that poetry was words for speech rather than the page," then a play such as *Love's Labour's Lost* becomes all the more interesting because it stages as comic spectacle the composition, circulation, and reception of love poetry; that is, it stages the pathologies of poetry configured as words for the page.[59] Throughout the play, the oral performance of poetry is disrupted precisely because it is imagined to be governed by acts of seeing, and ultimately acts of reading. Just after Holofernes chides Nathanial ("You find not the apostrophus, and so miss the accent: let me supervise the canzonet" [4.2.115–16]), he underscores the distinctly visual regime of both poetry reading and pedagogical practice by rephrasing his role as a "super-*visor*" as one who "overglance[s] the superscript" (4.2.126). The many poems within the play are not only "read aloud" but are also "supervised," "overglanced," "o'er-eye[ed]" (4.3.77), and "overview[ed]" (4.3.172). In the first letter read aloud in the play, the scopophilia of the lover translates into a form of graphic narcissism: a "most preposterous event, that draweth from my snow-white pen the ebon-coloured ink, which here thou viewest, beholdest, surveyest, or seeth" (1.1.233–35). Even in the first moments of the play, love melancholy is linked to variations on the word "to see."

The ocular thematics of the love sonnet have recently been seen to be compatible with the influence of print technologies, which, according to theorists such as Walter Ong and Marshall McLuhan, contributed to the predominantly visual orientation of Western culture.[60] As Wendy Wall writes, "In the sonnets, writers refocus this newly important visual force by rendering it frighteningly desirable and perverse."[61] But at the same time, it is precisely the visual dimensions of the love lyric that, when enacted on stage, become a vehicle for articulating the relatively *undesirable* situation of the son-

the publication of poetic and scholarly texts in the vernacular. In many sixteenth-century printed texts, the term "scholar" itself came to include anyone who could read; not only the "learneder sort," as Edmund Coote put it in the preface to *The English schoole-maister* (1596), but also foreigners and "unskilfull . . . men and women of trades (as Taylors, Weauers, Shop-keepers, Seamsters, and such other) as have undertaken the charge of teaching others."[69] Similarly, the textual culture in *Love's Labour's Lost* that emerges in act 1 as the exclusive province of the "little academe" quickly comes to include women, servants, foreigners, and even those who cannot read or write. Although Navarre opens the play by celebrating the elitism of the scholarly "academe" and the transcendence of the book (1.1.56), idealist conceptions of texts clash again and again with materialist conceptions of the physical book in the social world. Moth, himself a "page," literally follows Armado, imagining himself as a "sequel" (3.1.130). Holofernes, "man of letters," sets standards of learning even for members of the "little academe," deeming Berowne's own sonnet to be "very unlearned" (4.2.152).

The language of textbooks that informs Holofernes's and Armado's use of love poetry is paralleled by the aristocratic tropes of conversation as instruction, and the comedy of a quintessentially *educational* poetics is dramatically magnified through the very concept of Navarre's "little academe." Ironically, scholarship in this "little academe" produces anything but the powerful orator, that humanist ideal who speaks powerfully and well, who does things with words, and (perhaps most importantly) who speaks to others. What all of the lovers and scholars have in common in this play is a notable detachment from the audience they presume to know. Interestingly, this detachment had a corollary in Ramist rhetoric, which "virtually banished the audience by contemptuously considering them unnatural to the conditions of thought."[70] Ramus himself went to the College of Navarre, and it is at the very least suggestive, given the educational poetics at work in *Love's Labour's Lost*, that he believed poetry to be the ultimate pedagogical tool.[71] Indeed, Navarre's "little academe" may in many ways be read as a spoof on Ramist educational theory, which was marked by a prioritization of the written over the oral, by an "insistence that the elements of words and of all expression are not sound . . . but letters," and by "a devaluation of the classical rhetorical ideal in which the orator could incite passion by understanding the passion and the very soul of his listener(s)."[72] As Walter Ong puts it in a discussion of the compatible logics of Ramism and print culture, in Ramist rhetoric "the role of voice and per-

son-to-person relationships in communication is reduced to a new mini-
mum:"[73] "The Ramist arts of discourse are monologue arts. . . . In rhetoric,
obviously someone had to speak, but in the characteristic outlook, fostered by
the Ramist rhetoric, the speaking is directed to a world where even persons
respond only as objects—that is, say nothing back."[74] This dynamic is played
out in a number of ways by the members of Shakespeare's mock French academy, where sonnets are composed for people imagined not only as "objects"
but also as simple reflections of the academy itself. While the women are "the
books, the arts, the academes" (4.3.348), the scholars themselves, as Berowne
puts it, are "authors of these women" (4.3.355). Even as Berowne tries to distance himself from the constraints of academe in this famous speech, over the
course of it love seems to become more and more bookish (353–58). Interestingly, two versions of the speech itself were printed in the 1598 Quarto, marking signs of revision, so that even as Berowne rhetorically tries to abandon
"literal" books, the printed text calls attention to the ambiguous status of his
speech *in* a printed book. It is to the dramatic implications of speech in print
that I would now like to turn, considering aspects of the play and the 1598
Quarto that foreground the interanimation of oral/aural and visual/textual
technologies so marked in printed books about speech in the late sixteenth
century. The typographic dimensions of the Quarto highlight the relations
between reading, speaking, and loving in the play, and call attention to the
difficulty of wrapping one's mouth around a word.

"Dumbe Masters": Words Made Visible

> *Thou consonant.*
>   —Holofernes to Moth, *Love's Labour's Lost* (4.1.49)

In "Prickly Characters," an essay on Shakespeare and punctuation, Bruce
Smith writes: "Printhouse compositors, no less than William Shakespeare and
Richard Burbage, spoke, read, and wrote within an *episteme* that gave primacy
to voice and ear, not print and eye. They understood writing to be a transcription of voice, and they marked punctuation in accord with that understanding."[75] But at the same time, with the development of print and the
expansion of literacy, the marked visibility of typography, of punctuation, and
of alphabetic and lexical units was often seen to compete with that privileged

"*episteme* that gave primacy to voice and ear." As the orthographer John Hart plainly put it in his preface to *A Methode or comfortable beginning for all un-learned whereby they may be taught to read English* (1570), educational "books (which are dumbe masters) . . . often preuail more than the liuely voyce."[76] Indeed, in the latter half of the sixteenth century, the specular dimensions of language and sound were increasingly foregrounded with the proliferation of textbooks on language and pronunciation.

As the "dumb master" (the printed language textbook) became more and more dominant as a pedagogical vehicle in the sculpting of popular literacy, books began to compete with persons as repositories of knowledge.[77] So too, as printed texts began to "preuail more than the liuely voice" (precisely for teaching "the framing and sweete tuning of thy voyce"),[78] print and eye be-came increasingly central to the transmission and acquisition of knowledge

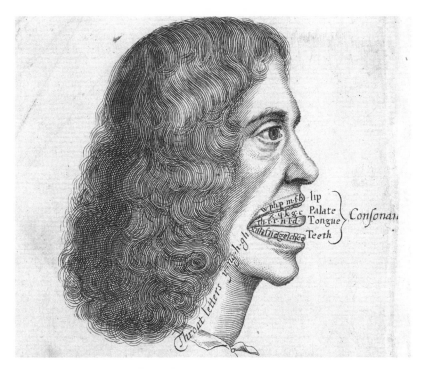

Figure 4. Speaker, Owen Price, *The Vocal Organ, or A new Art of teaching the English Orthographie* (London, 1665). EC65.P93165.665v. Courtesy of the Houghton Library, Harvard College Library.

about speech. On stage, the ascendancy of a predominantly visual linguistic episteme was perhaps most apparent in the tradition of academic drama, which included texts such as *Bellum Grammaticale* and *Heteroclitanomalonomia*, a grammar play written in English, featuring characters such as Parenthesis, who holds "semicircles in [his] hand" to represent himself.[79] In a later variant of this tradition, the dramatic tension of Samuel Shaw's *Words Made Visible* (1678) hinges precisely on the marked visibility of grammatical and social positions, with characters such as Mr. Article, the King's Attorney General, and a cast (or typecast) of those representing nouns, verbs, pronouns, participles, adverbs, conjunctions, prepositions, and interjections.[80]

Love's Labour's Lost stages the drama of the inarticulate in a world of shifting epistemes, where "dumb masters" not only inform but also consistently threaten to "prevail" over the "liuely voice."[81] Throughout the play, words are not so much spoken by as graphically relocated in the mouths of characters. Not unlike the speaker with a mouthful of consonants in Owen Price's orthographic treatise (Figure 4), Holofernes's mouth seems less an instrument of speech than a repository for letters. Not only does he rehearse a "script" that is not meant for, and is not suitable for, social interaction or dramatic performance: "a, e, i . . ." (5.1.52), but at one point he creates a panegyric to the letter *L*, and relates to other characters as if they were parts of speech. Speech becomes the dominant spectacle of the play, and the mouth itself a site to be seen. Mocking the scholars, Moth notes that "they have been at a great feast of languages and stolen the scraps," and Costard responds, "O, they have lived long on the alms-basket of words. I marvel thy master hath not eaten thee for a word; for thou art not so long by the head as *honorificabilitudinitatibus*" (5.1.35–40). This word, which would make even Lucian proud, is perhaps the most remarkable example of textual indigestion on the Shakespearean stage.

Even Moth, though he mocks the scholars, has "fed on the dainties that are bred in a book" (4.2.23), and his alignment with the scholars is implicit in his very name. Although Moth has been regularly glossed as an "Elizabethan and Shakespearean spelling" for *mot* or *mote*, meaning "word" or a "tiny particle,"[82] G. Blakemore Evans, editor of the Riverside Shakespeare, retains the spelling "Moth" because of the "possibility that Shakespeare was thinking primarily of the insect."[83] That this "page" may also be a "moth," that insect who was imagined as a consumer and a perpetual threat to books (Burton imagines neglected text, for example, "with moth & bookworms bit"), is teasingly apt in a play about "bookworms" who are said to consume texts.[84] Onomastically as well as thematically, Moth (whose very name suggests at once a word, a textual parasite, and, indeed, a "mouth") thematizes the satiric relocation of a textual world to the space of the embodied and the oral. While Rosaline longs for her powerful orator, at whose words "younger hearings are quite ravished, so sweet and voluble is his discourse" (3.1.70), this seductive relation of rhetor to body, of word to oral and aural, is contrasted with Berowne's distance from the phonic, signaled at one point by the fact that he actually *tells* his ear to listen: "Listen, ear" (4.3.42). While it has been argued that the play ultimately valorizes the "converse of breath," the immediacy of the embodied and the oral over the distanced and the written, the play goes far in undermining this dichotomy and instead thematizes the nostalgic dimensions of a culture that longs for a discourse that breathes, whispers, seduces, and ravishes.[85] Indeed, the oft-cited fantasy of an unmediated relation between—in Rosaline's words—the "ear" and the "fair tongue" (3.1.70–76, reiterated again at 5.2.833–61) is called into question by the structure of repetition and deferral at the close of the play. The ability of Berowne to shake the powers of books and become sensitized to the "sickly ears" of the "speechless sick," we are told, would take "too long for a play" (5.2.870). Theater itself falls short as a vehicle for the cultural work to be done here, and the deferral of comic integration is linked (particularly through Navarre's consolatory speech in which he still seems to have "all his senses . . . lock'd in his eye") with the persistent ocularity and textuality of spoken utterance.

The final song of the play, which has frequently been read as a kind of perfect conclusion (where the play "returns," as Kenneth Muir puts it, "to natural forms of speech and behavior"),[86] arguably repeats the central joke of the play by registering a textbook term that was used precisely to describe the failure of conclusions: the "cockoes song." In Thomas Wilson's *The rule of Reason*, this is a term for a conclusion that simply "repeat[s] what was spoken before": "the cuckowes song, that is, a repeting of that wholly in the conclusion, whiche before was onely spoken in the first proposition: or els by thynges doubtful, to proue thynges that are as doubtfull," and when the "conclusion is not well gathered, for it should not be vniuersall, but particular, & therefore seyng the same is repeted that was spoken before, with out any good probation: in my mynde it maie be called the cuckowes songe. Agayne, when an vnknowen thyng is proued by a thyng, that is as much vnknowen, as the other is."[87] Wilson's textbook is arguably parodied in the first moments of the play as well, as Costard repeats variations of "the manner and form following":[88]

"In manner and form following, sir; all those three: I was seen with her in the manor-house, sitting with her upon the form, and taken following her into the park; which, put together, is in manner and form following. Now, sir, for the manner,—it is the manner of a man to speak to a woman; for the form,—in some form" (1.1.202–8). If "it is the manner of a man to speak," that speech here is utterly confounded, a sign Costard may be drawing pearls of wisdom from Wilson, who uses this very language, interestingly enough, to extend his discussion of the "false conclusion(s)" of "the Cuckowes song": "The fault that is in the forme, or maner of makyng, as we call it, maie be dissolued, when we shewe that the conclusion, is not well proued by the former proposicions, and that the argument, is either not well made, in figure or in mode, or in both. . . . Thus we see a false conclusion, made of two vndoubted true proposicions. . . . the faulte is in the fourme, or maner of makyng and argument. . . . Some time the fault is onely in the matter, and not in the maner of makyng and argument, whereof there are diuerse examples aboue rehearsed. Sometimes the faulte is bothe in the matter, and in the maner of makyng an argument" (M5r–M6r). While Arden editor Richard David glosses Costard's speech as a "set expression of the time," perhaps the emphasis should be on "set," as the play's direct engagement with *The rule of Reason* calls attention to the influence of printed books *about* speech in this period, many of which were easier to read than to be spoken aloud.

The conclusion to *Love's Labour's Lost* and the conclusion to Eliot's *Ortho-Epia Gallica* are in fact strikingly similar; Eliot's conclusion focuses upon the language of love and ends with a "cockoes song" of its own. Eliot's final dialogue, by featuring "a yoong Academike" who (like the scholars in *Love's Labour's Lost*) aims to resist love in the name of book learning, sends up the ever-awkward relationship between the arts of learning and the arts of love. What is interesting is that the dialogue not only explores the jarring sounds of the "cookow" (a sound of springtime said to be pleasurable to the animal ear as opposed to the human)[89] but culminates in a send-up of its own ending, in which human words-sounds are reduced to the deflated status of the "cookow" and the "cuckhold" alike. Eliot's final words are as follows:

> *Truly one may hereafter take Lions by their crags, Horses by their maines:*
> *Beares by their nosthrils: Buffes by their mussels, Wolues by their tailes:*
> *Goates by their beardes:*

Birdes by their feete: Asses by their eares: men by their words.

And where will you take hold of Oxen and Cuckolds then?

By the hornes.

Tis pratled, chatted, & babbled inough. Lets go this way: lets go that way: Along, along.

This printed manual thus playfully reduces the "sounds" of its own many dialogues to but prattling, chatting, and babbling (or as the French has it, "C'est assez iasé, caqueté, & babillé. Allons de çà: allons de là: allons, allons"), and closes with a splitting up of a speech community ("Lets go this way: lets go that way") that parallels the famous final words of *Love's Labour's Lost,* "The words of Mercury are harsh after the songs of Apollo. You that way: we this way."[90] The "cuckold," that sign of ultimate vulnerability and dispossession, emerges in both texts as a sign of language, as well as love, not yet mastered and not yet rendered suitable for civil conversation or communal coherence. This is of course an appropriate end to Eliot's text, wonderfully entitled, within the text, ORTHO-EPIA GALLICA. *Or Le Parlement des Babillards: Id est: The Parlement of Pratlers,* in which "our English hybber-gybber" might possibly "iump iust with the Iargon of Fraunce" (B2v). But I also invoke the comparison in order simply to emphasize that if—as the King puts it in *Love's Labour's Lost*—"love is full of unbefitting strains, . . . / Form'd by the eye and therefore, like the eye, / Full of strange shapes, of habits and of forms," the language of love in Eliot's manual is rendered no less strange as it foregrounds the uneasy transmission of words on the page to words in the ear. The very phrase "Ortho-epia Gallica," comically compounded, is itself part of the extended joke about words that may resist communal coherence and communal intelligibility at the crossroads of oral and textual cultures as well as at the crossroades of languages.[91] The striking resemblance between Shakespeare's conclusion and Eliot's suggests the extent to which the play engaged with late-Tudor printed manuals on language learning that were fit for reading, but also for the often necessarily "unbefitting strains" of reading aloud.

The textual history of *Love's Labour's Lost* in fact foregrounds the difficulty in using the visual and largely decontextualized medium of print to *represent* an oral, theatrical, and contextually based medium, at least in the terms expected by many twentieth-century textual editors. G. R. Hibbard, for example, writes about the 1598 Quarto: "Q is *unactable* for a number of reasons. First it is plagued by a superfluity and confusion of names. Of its twenty characters, only six . . . have each a single consistent speech prefix for their parts. . . . Such variations in nomenclature as these are, of course, common enough in a dramatist's early drafts, *where he is naturally more concerned with a character's relation to others on stage than with that character's often arbitrary personal name,* and they strongly suggest that Q represents the play in a pre-performance state."[92] Hibbard here describes what he takes to be a confusing textual condition, but his words might well double as a reading of the plot. Within *Love's Labour's Lost*, "unactability," or bad theater, is itself imagined as a condition of expanding literacy and social life, a product of emergent forms of textuality that impede what might otherwise be seen as fluid performances of selves, communities, and cultures. As for the "confusion of names," most readers of the play will attest to the difficulty of keeping the names and identities of the characters straight, even when working with modernized editions with consistent speech prefixes. Many of the characters share such common linguistic traits stemming from linguistic habits of the sixteenth century that they are in many ways not only substitutes for each other but also substitutes for language itself. That is, the "characters' relation to others on stage," to adapt Hibbard's phrase, reflects a confusing textual condition linked to characters on the page. Within the play itself, it is precisely the logics of textual and representational "superfluity and confusion" that thwart the power of speech, recognition, theatricality, and coherent action. And given that *Love's Labour's Lost* is engaged with concerns about the implications of print and publication, it is only appropriate that the printed text of the play registers signs of the very "unactability" thematized by the play.[93]

Indeed, Richard David's description of the Quarto, in which "misprints abound, mostly 'literals'—one letter used for another," could not more perfectly describe the most basic plot element of the play: the mistaking of "one letter for another."[94] David's description of the printing of the Quarto continues: "The punctuation is chaotic: not even the most advanced theories of Elizabethan 'rhetorical punctuation' can make it consistent even with itself. Most significant of all, the compositor had not learnt to 'lock up' his type properly, so that when it was shaken, either in being carried to the press, on being dabbed with the inking balls, or under the stress of the actual impression, the letters tended to fall apart from each other or were jerked out altogether."[95]

The "stress of the actual impression," the lack of self-consistent punctuation, and the literal instability of the letter that led, in the printing of the Quarto, to the disintegration of verbal units and coherent systems all find a conceptual counterpart in the play of letters, identities, and emotions in *Love's Labour's Lost*.

Linda McJannet has challenged the binarism between stage and page, emphasizing the way printed plays could "suggest aspects of an audience's aural and visual experience in the theater."[96] "The design of printed plays . . . had mimetic qualities: it preserved or extended dramatic decorum onto the page by suggesting special vocal effects (such as reading aloud, dialects, or foreign languages), textual props (such as letters and proclamations), a cleared stage, and the movement of characters in and out of our field of vision."[97] But at the same time, it might also be said that the more self-consciously textual (or "unactable") drama was, the more it could translate mimetically onto the printed page. What is suggestive about the First Quarto of *Love's Labour's Lost* is the way in which font variations register the fundamental *writtenness* of the play. Indeed, it is the very writtenness of the play that disrupts mimesis on stage that most clearly translates, in true mimetic form, onto the printed page. The distinctly textual basis of Armado's melancholy, for example, is comically underscored by the fact that his first letter, "in ebon-coloured ink," is reproduced in the Quarto in italic font:

> *So it is besedged with sable coloured melancholie, I did commende the black opressing humour to the most holsome phisicke of thy health geuing ayre: And as I am a Gentleman, betooke my selfe to walke: the time When? about the sixth hour, When Beastes most grase, Birds best peck, and Men sit downe to that nourishment which is called Supper: So Much for the time When. Now for the ground Which? which I meane I walkt upon, it is ycliped Thy Park. Then for the place Where? where I meane, I did incounter that obscene & most propostrous euent that draweth fro my snowhite pen the ebon coloured Incke, which here thou viewest, beholdest, suruayest, or seest.* (1.1.233–47)[98]

While italics are used in the conventional manner throughout the Quarto to signify words that are not meant to be spoken, such as stage directions ("*He reads the Sonnet*") and speech prefixes ("*Arm.*"), they are also often used to signify words that are not *meant* to be spoken but are. The Quarto italicizes outrageous inkhornisms ("*posterior* of the day"), foreign words (Holofernes's speeches are littered with italics), much of the pageant of the Nine Worthies (which has the effect of foregrounding the relative "unworthiness" of the actors), the communal Petrarchan love lyric from the Muscovites to the ladies (which is itself read by a "*Page*"), marks of writing ("*Item*"), and all nationalities and names. While the italicization of characters' names is a common feature of printed plays, it nonetheless stands out in this particular text, as the typography aligns the very names of the characters within the play with other forms of distinctly written discourse. On the printed page, the speech prefix and the name exist in a typographic continuum; character meets character in a graphic enactment of the very "subject" of the play.

McJannet has further argued that the freestanding, left-hand speech prefix of Elizabethan page design visually "signals the autonomy and integrity of the character. He or she has a vocal and therefore 'existential' independence, appearing in the dramatic text without introduction or qualification of any other discernable voice" (61). But while page design may preserve an "independence of voices and . . . theatrical presence" (108), the integrity of voice can just as well be undermined by typographic features. In addition to the typographic correlation between speech prefix and explicitly *written* elements of spoken utterance in *Love's Labour's Lost*, for example, the vocal and "existential independence" of characters can be seen to be undermined by the very variation of prefixes, which alternate between individual names (Navarre, Holofernes, Jaquenetta) and social types (King, Pedant, Maid); as well as by the use of the same speech prefix for two different characters: "*Boy*" is a prefix used for both Moth and Boyet.[99] By and large, these and other seeming inconsistencies have been "corrected" in contemporary editions of the play. As such, a certain integrity of character and autonomy of voice has been edited into many modern editions by the standardization of speech prefixes, and by the preference for distinctive names over character types.

If, as Smith has suggested, recent editing practices influenced by the primacy of visuality and print often downplay the sonic and embodied dimensions of early modern typography, so too do these same editing practices (which standardize spelling and punctuation) often eclipse the striking textuality of many printed plays. Thematically as well as typographically, *Love's Labour's Lost* calls attention to the materiality of the text.[100] An edition of the play that retained many of the individuated letters in the Quarto, rather than spelling them out, would highlight many of the play's jokes *about* letters. A line uttered shortly after Holofernes's veritable panegyric to the letter L, for example, which reads in the 1598 Quarto as "Sir, I prayse the L. for you" becomes, in the 1623 Folio, "I praise the Lord for you," a transcription that (though logical, as L. was a common abbreviation for Lord) dilutes what seems to be a fairly straightforward joke about the deification of letters and learning (particularly as Nathanial follows this praising of *L* with the statement, "and so may my parishioners, for their Sonnes are well tuterd by you").[101]

In this play about "characters," divinity is embodied in a capital *L*, beauty is "Faire as a text B" (5.2.42), and the very sigh of the lover is reduced to a text "so full of O's" (45). Given the thematic emphasis on individuated letters, one can imagine a production of the play that, based on the Quarto, would *not* translate single letters into words and would, for example, highlight the graphic dimensions of the lover's vocabulary (riddled as it is with O's and I's). Particularly given the extent to which Rosaline foregrounds the silly literality of Berowne's "love letters," it is tempting to read the Quarto text of Berowne's solitary lament, "O and I forsooth in loue" as if the letters themselves were the mutually enchanted subjects of the sentence (3.1.175).[102] The entrances and exits (the very first of which reads, "*Enter Ferdinand K. of Nauar*") might well be incorporated into dramatic performance. Such a performance would of course dramatize the editorial decisions at work for any reader or listener of the play, but it would also emphasize the thematized relation between alphabetic units and exclamations of love, and highlight the drama of a play that essentially stages itself as a book.

Talking Cures

> So when love angred in thy bosome raves,
> And grief with love a double flame inspires,
> By silence thou mayst adde, but never lesse it:
> The way is by expressing to represse it.
> —Phineas Fletcher, *Poeticall Miscellanies* (1633)[103]

> The Italians *most part sleep away care & griefe* . . . Danes,
> Dutchmen, Polanders, *and* Bohemians *drinke it downe; our
> countrymen go to Plaies.*
> —Robert Burton, *The Anatomy of Melancholy* (1624)[104]

It is no coincidence that many of Shakespeare's dramas about love and lost love double as conspicuous performances of literacy. In *Romeo and Juliet*, Capulet, with typical sensitivity, gives his illiterate servant an invitation list to read. The servant, exclaiming, "I must to the learned" (1.2.44), brings the list to Romeo, who baldly states, "I can read," and proceeds to demonstrate, reading the lengthy list aloud (1.2.57–71).[105] The significance of this act as a performance of literacy is further suggested by the fact that the actual content of the list is relatively insignificant in terms of the plot of the play, most of the names never surfacing again. Like Armado's Latinate letter to an illiterate wench, what is thematized here is, on the one hand, the social distinctions between literate and illiterate, and, on the other, the rapid flow of information between literate and illiterate communities through the phenomenon of reading aloud. This flow of information through oral reading is a hallmark of sixteenth-century theater and discourses of love alike.

Indeed, it might well be said that the performativity of an increasingly literate social world finds its parallel on the early modern stage. The dramatic figure of the love melancholic is a particularly charged locus of performativity where experiences of interiority are frequently counterposed with distinctly textual domains of prescribed subjectivity. In *Love's Labour's Lost* the trauma of grief *is* the drama of literacy; tropes of woe drawn from Petrarchan lyric double as (and are doubled by) tropes of a specific form of representational loss: a melancholy of representation where books render strange voices of passion and intimacy. The relationship between literacy and failed love resurfaces in the final act of the play as books lead to thwarted communication between lover and beloved: "I understand you not: my griefs are double," says the grieving Princess after listening to Navarre's excessively technical and minimally intelligible consolatory speech (5.2.744). Here bookishness has the effect of literally "doubling" grief. Not only does the lover fail as a speaker, his failed speech leads to the production of sadness.

The position of the lover between script and speech, book and theater, is at once encapsulated and problematized in Shakespeare's Sonnet 23:

> As an unperfect actor on the stage,
> Who with his fear is put beside his part,
> Or some fierce thing replete with too much rage,
> Whose strength's abundance weakens his own heart;
> So I for fear of trust forget to say

The perfect ceremony of love's rite,
And in mine own love's strength seem to decay,
O'ercharged with burthen of my own love's might.
O let my books be then the eloquence,
And dumb presagers of my speaking breast,
Who plead for love, and look for recompense,
More than that tongue that more hath more expressed.
    O learn to read what silent love hath writ.
    To hear with eyes belongs to love's fine wit.[106]

Like the drama of desire in the play, where "contempt will kill the speaker's heart, / And quite divorce his memory from his part" (5.2.149–50), this sonnet imagines the silent and fearful lover in terms of an uncertain relation between actor and script. As in the play, "books" replace the voice of the lover and mediate the overwhelming passion of his "speaking breast." But what is represented here as a strength of love becomes a vulnerability on stage; the phenomenon of the silent and "imperfect actor," paired in the poem with a singular and unspeakable passion, translates on stage as a largely collective problem of emotional disengagement and vocal self-alienation. What is imagined in the sonnet as an erotics of synesthesia becomes on stage a comedy of disintegration, where "hearing with the eyes" what silent love hath writ foregrounds a distinctly alienated form of orality.

Love in an age of print may well have moved the rhetoric of intimacy further and further out of context, opening even wider the gap between lover and beloved already so integral to courtly love. But at the same time, for this poet-dramatist—for whom books became plays, for whom printed cultures were transformed into communities of speech—perhaps hearing with the *ears* what silent love hath writ opened up a whole new way, in the early age of print, of both loving and learning by the book. For it is in the space of the theater, where pages come alive and characters body forth, where voices are already alienated from themselves, where books both take the breath away and give it life again, that the lost labor of love may well be found.[107] Putting the "imperfect actor" on stage to act in the passive voice enabled the transferal of a form of pathetic textuality to another kind of loss, a more passive yet more communicative double, dramatic pathos, which combined the feeling of being lost with the wanting to be found.

To develop further our discussion of the inarticulate dimensions of affect, and the affective dimensions of the inarticulate, let us now turn to the experience of being moved by, but also beyond, words. For if drama itself had the power to touch, to move, to cultivate collective feeling, how did Shakespeare, among other playwrights, address the power of drama that was also, because it needed to be in order to work, beyond words?

CHAPTER FIVE

Feeling Inarticulate

On Communal Vulnerability and the Sense of Touch in *Lingua* and *Hamlet*

> *The history of criticism shows us too ready to indulge a not wholly
> inexplicable fancy that in* Hamlet *we behold the frustrated and
> inarticulate Shakespeare furiously wagging his tail in an effort to tell us
> something.*
> —Stephen Booth, "On the Value of Hamlet"

> Hamlet . . . *is full of some stuff that the writer could not drag to light,
> contemplate, or manipulate into art. And when we search for this
> feeling, we find it . . . very difficult to localize.*
> —T. S. Eliot, "Hamlet and His Problems"

Inarticulate Shakespeare?

T. S. ELIOT'S OBSERVATION that *Hamlet* was composed by an author who
could not find the words to express adequately a "feeling" through which his
drama might have otherwise cohered as "art" has long been easy to dismiss.
Stephen Booth's allusion to the "frustrated and inarticulate Shakespeare furi-
ously wagging his tail in an effort to tell us something" was a direct ironization

of the emphasis, by Eliot and others before him, on the concept of authorial un-intentionality and emotional inarticulacy that led, in Eliot's words, to the "artistic failure" that is *Hamlet*. Yet Eliot's observation is worth revisiting, not in order to recuperate an unknowing and thus "inarticulate Shakespeare" but in order to reconsider in a more productive way the relationship between aesthetics and the inarticulate in *Hamlet*—as well as in a number of other Renaissance dramas in which "feeling" proved "very difficult to localize."

What might be the relationship between the inarticulate and the aesthetic (from the Greek *aisthetikos*, "sensitive," from *aisthanesthai*, "to perceive, to feel"), particularly for the literary critical enterprise of elucidating the logic of affect in Renaissance drama? Such a question is, in light of Eliot's conception of aesthetics, somewhat counterintuitive, since the clear articulation of "feeling" is of course, for Eliot, a precondition of art. In his famous analysis, the theatrical expression of feeling requires an "objective correlative": "a set of objects, a situation, a chain of events which shall be the formula of [a] particular emotion; such that when the external facts, which must terminate in sensory experience, are given, the emotion is immediately evoked."[1] *Hamlet* thus constituted a bungling aesthetic failure because it provided no objective correlative for "feeling"—"Hamlet (the man) is dominated by an emotion which is inexpressible, because it is in *excess* of the facts as they appear"—and because the author himself put the audience members in a difficult position, since they "should have to understand things which Shakespeare did not understand himself."[2]

Eliot here raised an important issue about inarticulate feeling and the problem of objective correlation in *Hamlet* that has yet to be fully examined. Rather than simply dismiss his argument, I want to point out that it went both too far and not far enough. For it evinced a form of critical mastery defined by disavowing "the facts as they appear" in a drama that is, I believe, precisely *about* the aesthetic potential of the inarticulate. Hamlet, as both character and play, in fact foregrounds the inarticulate as a cultural construct, as a "problem" to be reckoned with, a locus of affect, and, ultimately, a means by which "feeling" could surface—through things unsaid, partially said, and even poorly said—as a principle of communal and communicable vulnerability.

To defamiliarize contemporary views of Hamlet as a "fastidious master of language,"[3] we might consider George Bernard Shaw's observation in 1903 that "Hamlet is inarticulate and unintelligible to himself, except in flashes of inspiration."[4] Shaw might be added to Eliot as an early critic who found

Shakespeare wanting in the construction of an "articulate" hero, though his focus was on Hamlet as an underdeveloped philosopher as well as speaker. "I have often felt tempted to rewrite Hamlet, making him philosophically conscious of the new dispensation which has descended on him, and taking a frightful revenge on his uncle by discussing the matter rationally with him (protected by his mother-aunt) until Claudius, worn out, abdicates and ends his life as a Charity Commissioner."[5] Intentionally hilarious as this revision may be, the extent to which Hamlet may evince forms of the "inarticulate" may have become lost to many contemporary readers through the massive editorial tradition of glossing, paraphrase, clarification, and emendation. The accrued cultural capital granted to Hamlet's many speeches, moreover, frequently elevates his seeming articulateness despite textual evidence to the contrary: as Walter Murdoch once phrased it, "The real difference between us and Hamlet is that we are inarticulate. We cannot express our deeper selves, and the reason why we are endlessly drawn to Hamlet is that he finds the words for us."[6]

Although it may seem paradoxical to imagine Hamlet himself, the master of "words, words, words," as inarticulate, when it comes to the public expression of "feeling," we see a number of instances in which he falters.[7] Perhaps most glaringly, his love letter to Ophelia at once professes and enacts a species of inarticulate love: "*I am ill at these numbers. I have not art to reckon my groans. But that I love thee best, O most best, believe it.*"[8] "O most best"? And elsewhere in the letter, "*To the celestial and my soul's idol, the most beautified Ophelia,*" is a poorly composed sentence that even Polonius comments upon: "—That's an ill phrase, a vile phrase, 'beautified' is a vile phrase" (2.2.109–11). Hamlet's superlatives, "most beautified," "best," "most best," alongside "the celestial," should recall the mock-epistle in that other Eliot's (John Eliot's) *Ortho-epia Gallica*, which we have already explored. Such a connection might easily encourage us to interpret the lover's style at this moment as a species of awkward and inept Petrarchism.

Yet doing so would be beside the point, since it would swiftly align us with Polonius, a character who, later in the same scene, says of the odd phrase, "*the mobbled queen,*" "that's good" (2.2.498–500). Indeed, Polonius's presence in this scene calls for a reassessment of any critical mechanism that might attend, first and foremost, to style as the arbiter of value in the expression of feeling, and for another kind of approach to forms of "feeling" that—here and elsewhere in the play—prove difficult to "localize" or "manipulate into art." This instance of Hamlet's emotional inarticulacy might well be seen as an epistolary performance of what had already become, by the late Tudor period, a cliché of passions so intense as to defy eloquent utterance. "Words cannot expresse the force of loue," wrote Sir John Davies, "What force it hath, is better felt then showne."[9] Is Hamlet merely performing the inarticulate as a guarantor of emotional authenticity? Is this yet another instance of role-playing through which direct expression is avoided? This may well be the case. But such an interpretation is, again, complicated by the dramatic context in which the shaming and censorious gaze of Polonius has the effect of making the feelings of the poor bloke, whose love letter was misdirected like so many others that we have seen in this book, suddenly seem to matter.[10] "There's matter in these sighs," we might say, to borrow Claudius's later formulation; " 'Tis fit we understand them" (4.1.1–2). What matters most in the scene of epistolary inarticulacy is that at the same time we witness Hamlet's "inarticulate feelings," we witness his expression of "feeling inarticulate," as if he has internalized, while alone in the composition of the letter, the very principles that Polonius stands for. This constitutes a doubled pathos of inarticulate expression that Eliot's (and indeed Shaw's and Murdoch's) analysis failed to acknowledge.

Being inarticulate, as I observed in the Introduction, is often conditioned by social contexts that, if undetected or unexamined, can lead to injurious forms of internalization, to the pathos of "feeling inarticulate" rather than a condition of fully understanding that one's thoughts and feelings have not been, or cannot be, acknowledged by, or interpolated into, the community of which one is a part. In this single scene in *Hamlet*, we see that process in action. The pathos is thus doubled. This is the case elsewhere in the play as well, where the sheer "force" of passions at the limits of articulation generate a number of highly successful aesthetic (again, from "sensitive" and "to perceive, to feel") moments. Ophelia's verbal "half sense," which nonetheless manages, within as well as beyond the play, to "move / The hearers to collection" (4.5.7–9) is a particularly striking example to which we will return.

This is simply to emphasize, at the outset of this final chapter, that dramatic exposures of forms of "feeling" that were, to borrow Eliot's phrase, "very difficult to localize" in both language and thought, could prove just as powerful for the invocation of dramatic *pathos* as the use of heartfelt, passionate speech. The strategic resistance to eloquent or clearly localized feeling in Renaissance dramas, moreover, could expose tacit forms of knowledge otherwise obscured by coherent, integrated, and indeed "articulate" (fully "jointed") expressions of feeling. Such is the case in one of the many plays to which *Hamlet* was indebted, Kyd's *The Spanish Tragedy*. When Hieronimo, who has no actual secret to protect, bites off his own tongue and stabs himself to death with a penknife—in the wake of having staged an unintelligible playlet—it is as if he has internalized conditions of larger social processes in which particular forms of expression have been exiled from a circuit of spoken and written communication. Here we see, in the simplest of terms, the pathos of inhabiting a community in which particular expressions of feeling cannot be fully acknowledged or taken in. Or in psychoanalytic terms, we see "incorporation" marking the failure of "introjection," where particular bodies and words bear cryptic but potentially legible signs of socially exiled feelings.[11] Introjection, as Anne-Marie Smith explains it, "is the metaphoric activity through which we acknowledge and symbolize loss; it characterizes normal mourning. . . . The fantasy of incorporation is anti-metaphoric, taking literally that which only has figurative meaning."[12] From this perspective, we can begin to understand the extent to which extraordinary forms of incorporation in Renaissance revenge dramas, including *Hamlet*, indexed in strategic form the limits of shared vocabularies of feeling though which communities could possibly cohere.

Certainly, to speak eloquently or articulately of feeling in the late Tudor period would be to confront what Michael Schoenfeldt has rightly called "the fecund incoherence with which early modern culture confronted the passions."[13] When Thomas Wright, in his 1601 *The Passions of the Minde*, observed that when "sometimes wee feele our selves, *we know not why*, moved to mirth, melancholy, or anger,"[14] he simply registered the difficulty of establishing causality with regard to the flux and effects of human feeling. Schoenfeldt cogently argues that "articulation of temperament," that is, the use of articulate speech through which to "give sorrow words" in medical and literary texts alike—including *Hamlet* and *The Winter's Tale*—was understood to be curative for the otherwise overwhelming and ever-intensifying passion of grief. In Chapter 4, I argued for an inversion of this "talking cure" operative in *Love's Labour's Lost*, one that involved the exposure of the strikingly passive and less than articulate voice on stage, which generated dramatic pathos by throwing the textual structures of affect into high relief.[15] This paradoxical "untalking cure," through which expressions of feeling became most visible, and communicable, at the limits of communication and intelligibility ("I understand you not: my griefs are double"), surfaces anew in this chapter.

We have already seen how theatrical incarnations of the inarticulate—while indexing rifts in the production of shared meanings in the various spheres of religion, humanism, law, vernacularism, historiography, and print culture—worked to expose and evoke forms of thought and feeling otherwise obscured by the relegation of the inarticulate to the domain of the senseless. All of the historical contexts examined thus far are in fact at issue in the two central plays examined in this chapter: Thomas Tomkis's allegory about language and sensory perception, *Lingua: or The combat of the Tongue, And the fiue Senses for Superiority* (c. 1602),[16] and Shakespeare's *Hamlet*, two plays recorded to have been performed at Cambridge University in the early 1600s.[17] Both plays interest me, however, for a comparatively simple reason: they both investigate, first in comic then in tragic form, the subarticulate dimensions of feeling. In each play, forms of affect are generated precisely when language seems most broken as a vehicle for communication, when language proves unable or unreliable as a vehicle for the establishment of "objective correlation" itself. Both plays thus push us to consider extralinguistic phenomena integral to the expression, and experience, of feeling.

Exploring the aesthetics of the inarticulate in and around Renaissance dramas can help us to see the "inarticulate Shakespeare," and indeed the "inarticulate" as a principle of dramatic composition, in a more positive light. To do so, however, we need to reconsider what might have constituted an aesthetics of feeling in the late Tudor period. The very phrase "aesthetics of feeling" may seem, to quote Polonius, an ill phrase, precisely because—given the etymology of aesthetics—it is redundant. Yet I invoke it to emphasize the extent to which modern aesthetic theories can fall short when it comes to grasping fully the extent of the "sensory experience" of feeling operative in texts such as *Hamlet* composed some four hundred years ago. Theories such as Eliot's can anesthetize us to the full constituents of "feeling" as it was understood as a physical as well as an emotional phenomenon, and thus to the full constituents of "feeling" that defied rational and logical articulation.

"To feel" was, in the Renaissance, a verb used interchangeably with "to touch," and both verbs implied physical as well as emotional sensation. Thomas Cooper's 1578 entry on the verb "to touch," precisely as it included "to mooue or grieue," can help us to see this.[18] But how might one even talk about, or find an "objective correlative" for, feeling as grounded in the sense of touch? To try to talk about this aspect of sensory perception and experience, as Eve Kosofsky Sedgwick observes in *Touching Feeling*, leads one away from objective correlation and into the domain of nonobjective, indeed non-dualistic thought. "Even more immediately than other perceptual systems," she writes, "the sense of touch makes nonsense out of any dualistic under-standing of agency and passivity; to touch is always already to reach out, to fondle, to heft, to tap, or to enfold, and always also to understand other peo-ple or natural forces as having effectually done so before oneself."[19] Sedgwick aims here to open up contemporary studies of affect by considering the nexus of "touch" as tactile and emotional, of "feeling" as a physiological and an af-fective sense. Such a conception of touch may well seem touchy-feely, but it aims to integrate the sense of touch into a tradition of aesthetics through which vision and hearing have long reigned dominant as vehicles for aesthetic experience and articulation.[20] Such a project is difficult because touch is a phenomenon that can prove resistant to clear and logical articulation, to the discernment of precise boundaries between the senses and language, between actions and passions, and between persons and other persons or indeed things.

Gesturing toward a similar way of integrating the "lower" senses more fully into the domain of aesthetic experience and critical vocabularies, Jean-Luc Nancy once suggested that "one has to understand reading as something other than decipherment. Rather, as touching, as being touched. Writing, reading: matters of tact."[21] Rather than "decipherment," or "close reading," Nancy aimed for a kind of reading for closeness, for a way of somehow *being* rather than simply reading between the lines, a way of bringing dead metaphors back to life. Such a concept may seem utopian, and even anachro-nistic for our present discussion; for how can we understand the status of af-fect in Renaissance dramas in terms of a "touching" and "being touched," particularly in a period well before the formalization of that category that we now call—and that Nancy called—"tact"? To have tact is to have just the right touch, a manifest sensitivity to one's social and linguistic surround. In this current sense of social sensitivity, "tact" may not have been fully spoken of or formulated in the Renaissance, but the need for it was expressed in the dra-mas we will consider, where the cost of a world without "tact" as an integra-tive social principle informed often intense and inarticulate forms of expression integral to revenge, madness, or tragic alienation.

Counterintuitive as it may seem to close a book on the inarticulate with a discussion of touch, I do so because Renaissance conceptions of touch so perfectly capture the paradox of the inarticulate that I have explored. What appears to be a form of "nonsense" could evoke meanings above, beyond, or indeed beneath dominant cultural conceptions of just what constituted sensible, articulate speech. Both like and *as* a form of inarticulateness, the sense of touch needs to be understood as a sense-making mode, one that could mark as well as surpass the limits of communal intelligibility to get at something more like communal vulnerability. For the very resistance of particular forms of "touch" and "feeling" to forms of meaning-making in Protestant, humanist, scholastic, and even early medical contexts could open up space, in drama, for a movement beyond the play of "words, words, words" toward something more like the feeling of the unsaid.

Hamlet is a case in point. But Shakespeare was by no means alone, so we will traverse a number of dramas before arriving at *Hamlet*, lingering at length on the lesser known play and microcosmic allegory, *Lingua*. *Lingua* is important for my concerns in this book because it, while dramatizing issues at stake in *Hamlet* in some fascinating ways, also takes place inside the often vividly inarticulate, yet highly emotional, human body, throwing various cultural conditions of the inarticulate into high relief. For in the play's opening moments, Lingua (the tongue and language) is said by Auditus (the ear and hearing) to be all too full of "tunes without sense, words inarticulate" (A3r). The personified tongue, unable to "make sense," or to be heard, understood, or fully recognized as a constituent of sense-making in the microcosm, focalizes its energies in a plot of "reuenge" against the body itself (A4v). Lingua's failure to simulate and stimulate "sensory experience" through words in order to make Auditus hear, "feel," and respond, that is, turns into a revenge upon the self: Lingua proceeds to set the senses themselves at odds, disintegrating them so that language may emerge victorious and be considered a "sense" in its own right.

Importantly, this drama indexes a phenomenology of the "inarticulate" lodged in an early variant of "sensory experience" that was itself, to recall Eliot, "difficult to localize," render articulate, and "manipulate into art." This is the phenomenology not of the visual, the auditory, the olfactory, or the gustatory, but rather of the comparatively dispersed, elusive, and subarticulate qualities of "feeling," embodied in Lingua and in Lingua's counterpart, the character Tactus, the sense of touch. Examining how "feeling" as a sensory-emotional phenomenon resisted full articulation and yet still managed, within as well as through the play, to evoke all manner of responses, will help us ultimately to reassess the status of spoken language and sensory experience in *Hamlet*.

From Nonsense to the Sixth Sense

Of all the creatures, the sense of tact is most exquisite in man.
—Alexander Ross, *Arcana microcosmi* (1651)[22]

The relationships between "feeling" and "feeling," outward "touch" and what Sidney called "inward tutch,"[23] were often central to explorations of affect in Renaissance dramas in ways that have become eclipsed by the more dominant critical attention to the historical phenomenology of the senses of vision and hearing. Histories of drama, following Andrew Gurr, regularly explore the sensory and aesthetic dimensions of what it meant to be "audience" and "spectator," and studies ranging from Bruce Smith's *The Acoustic World of Early Modern England* to Michael O'Connell's *The Idolatrous Eye* map out the historical contours of these particular sensory modes.[24] The sense of touch—occupying but one and a half pages of Caroline Spurgeon's early and seminal study *Shakespeare's Imagery*, in contrast has twenty-two pages on the senses of vision and hearing—has been relatively under examined, or indeed, under-articulated.[25] This is itself curious since drama as a medium was unique in staging characters who not only speak to and look at each other, but also touch each other in public. Indeed, the "lower" sense of touch, as well as the related senses of taste and smell, often emerged as dominant in Shakespearean tragedy: in *Titus Andronicus* we find bodies variously kissed, touched, tasted and indeed eaten; in *Hamlet* we find human remains touched and held close enough to smell ("And smelt so? Pah!"); in *King Lear* we find that the blind Gloucester might "smell his way to Dover" or come to "see feelingly," and in *The Winter's Tale*, we find Leontes's experience of a wife "too hot, too hot" resolve into the more temperate "Oh, she's warm!"[26]

Since antiquity, touch has been aligned with both human and animal capacities, and been contrasted with vision and hearing as senses integral to the ethical, intellectual, and even linguistic contours of what it means to be human.[27] So it is no surprise that sensory modes traditionally linked with the work of the mind are frequently privileged in discourses of historical phenomenology and even of audience response. Yet a word used as often as "spectator" and "audience" to describe playgoers in the Renaissance was "assembly," a word and concept that I will return to because it implied not only a coming together of persons but also a physically as well as emotionally charged touching of bodies in space. This fact alone underscores a need for a more full-bodied and extralinguistic approach to our understanding of theatrical experience, Renaissance aesthetics, and the representation of the senses themselves.[28] Given that touch was integral to humoral physiology (as touch detects temperatures and textures), to literary allegories of the senses, and to social rhetorics of persuasion, sexuality, affect, disease, and public health, this need may be considered acute.[29] So too, given the recent focus on the material object (as textual artifact, stage property, object of exchange, cultural spectacle, sumptuary habit),[30] we might consider what happens to the object in the domain of sensory perception. We might ask with the editors of *Subject and Object in Renaissance Culture* not only "*Where is the object?*" in histories of Renaissance subjectivity but also where is the object that is touched, caressed, taken in hand.[31] It is the hand that enables production, but it also touches—and is touched by—products. In Renaissance representations of touch, however, the question often becomes less "Where is the object?" than "Why *isn't* the object there?" Putting touch into a mix of material cultures, as we will see, gestures toward a kind of materialism without an object—or more precisely, without specific objects.

If the postulate of a sense without an object seems odd, it is because the material history of the senses has been, essentially, the history of their objectification. Expanding Marx's concern with economically manufactured sentience to consider sensuous experience more generally, for example, Elaine Scarry writes that the "socialization of sentience" marks a process in which "freestanding objects remake the live body" and "make sentience itself an artifact": "Such objects, by eliminating the limitations of sentience or, as it can with equal accuracy be phrased, magnifying its powers (the ear trumpet, hearing aid, sign language, telephone, songs, poetry, telegraph, victrola, stereo system, radio, tape recorder, sonar, acoustically precise symphony hall, and so forth all extend the range and acuity of the ear), make sentience itself an artifact."[32] The representation of sensory modes in the form of made objects, in other words, becomes inseparable from sensory perception, a feature of sensation that arguably makes writing about the senses *legible*. The clear relations between worlds of objects, mediation, and sense perception enable thinkers such as Jonathan Crary, among others, swiftly to posit visualization as "the site of certain practices, techniques, institutions, and procedures of subjectification."[33] While this chiasmus calls attention to the ways in which sensory "subjection" depends upon cultural models of representation, the emphasis on vision also suggests that some senses are easier to subject than others, and so are more accessible to a range of rational models of writing and thinking.

It is no coincidence, for example, that Raymond Williams opens his essay on the reification of "the medium" in aesthetic theory, "From Medium to Social Practice," with an example drawn from a Renaissance definition of *sight* from Burton's *The Anatomy of Melancholy* (1621): " 'To the Sight three things are required, the Object, the Organ and the Medium.' Here a description of the practical activity of seeing, which is a whole and complex process of relationship between the developed organs of sight and the accessible properties of things seen, is characteristically interrupted by the invention of a third term ('medium') which is given its own properties, in abstraction from the practical relationship. This general notion of intervening and in effect causal substances, on which various practical operations were believed to depend, had a long course in scientific thought."[34] This example marks, for Williams, an early history of the objectification of "process" by a focus on mediation, in which "a constitutive human activity is . . . abstracted and objectified" (158). Williams's sense that the priority of the medium for communications theory marks a dangerous reification suggests also something about the priority of the medium in the construction of the "hierarchy of the senses." Yet "touch occurs by direct contact," wrote Aristotle, "and that is why it has its name. The other sense organs perceive by contact too, but through a *medium*."[35] This gives rise to a central question: How does one write or speak or even think clearly about a sense without a medium? In contrast to vision and hearing (or optics and acoustics), which are made legible by abstract logics of mediation, organization, and objectification, touch is interesting and complex—and a form of sensory experience wedded to the inarticulate—precisely because it resists reification.[36]

From antiquity to the Renaissance, the five senses were classically defined by specific organs, mediums, and objects (for example, eye, air, and celestial objects, respectively).[37] As Helkiah Crooke put it in *Mikrokosmographia: A Description of the Body of Man* (1615), "Sense is a knowledge or discerning of the obiect receyued formally in the Organ," and "in euery Sense there be three things especially to be stood vpon, the Object, the *Medium* and the Organ" (653, 722). Touch, however, often eluded the specifics of all three categories, disrupting basic systems of classification that the senses "stood vpon." In terms of organs, from classical to Renaissance treatises on anatomy the entire body, the nerves, skin, fingertips, tongue, palms, and the region about the heart were alternatively imagined as the locus of touch.[38] "This sense is exquisite in men," writes Burton in *The Anatomy of Melancholy*, "and by his nerves dispersed all over the body."[39] Or as Crooke put it, "Al other Senses are restrayned within some small organ about the brayne, but the Touching is diffused through the whole body" (648). Whereas eyes, ears, nose, and tongue symbolize the modes of sensory perception they enable, touch was more difficult to represent, localize, and demonstrate.

Touch resisted, moreover, the very operations of representation so integral to early modern somatic symbolism: synecdoche and metonymy. This is not simply a theoretical point; it is integral to the representation of touch in the visual and verbal arts of the Renaissance.[40] Although one might think the human hand an easy metonymy for touch, this was not always or even usually the case. One early allegorical drama of the five senses features characters named Eye for vision, Ear for hearing, and Tongue for taste, but simply Touch for touch; in terms of basic forms of personification, here touch remains a sense without a synecdoche, a mode without a metonymy.[41] In *Lingua*, whereas Olfactus is represented by Odor (bearing Tobacco) and Auditus by Comedy and Tragedy (bearing music, poetry, and other acoustical artifacts), Tactus is represented by Mendacio (the lie), thus aligned from the first with qualities of elusiveness, communicative unreliability, and representational dispersion.

This sense without a synecdoche, this mode without a metonymy, itself becomes metonymic in much Renaissance drama for the psyche's approach to what the psyche cannot precisely locate, measure, or articulate. This is particularly marked in *Lingua*, which stages a microcosm (or little human body) suddenly and awkwardly confronting forces of tactile and emotional sensation that do not fit within the field of "common sense." The challenges posed by both Tactus and Lingua lead to a disrupted, but also to a potentially expanded, order of things. Lingua wants to expand the order of the sensorium itself to "make the Senses sixe" (A4v), and Tactus wants to expand the sensorium so that he may emerge as the dominant sense in the microcosm. Importantly, what each character brings into this world is a desire to make the body *feel*, or to acknowledge just how much it is capable of feeling, even or especially if that feeling seems to exceed ideals of articulate speech.

Let us begin with Lingua, who, as we have seen, sets the play set in motion by aspiring to be considered a legitimate sense, hoping to expand the sensorium to include language as a sense in its own right. If positing *language* as just as important as the five senses in the human body sounds utterly absurd, Lingua defends this view by observing that the senses are lodged in "present" experience, but "the tongue is able to recount thinges past, and often pronounce things to come" (F2v). Lingua alludes here, Folly-like, to the ecstatic experience of speaking in tongues, thus indexing the tongue's paradoxical power to communicate both extrasensory and extralinguistic perception. Language, moreover, can inform and alter the experience of sensation itself: "Oft haue I seasoned sauorie periods, / With sugred words, to delude *Gustus* taste, / And oft emblisht my entreatiue phrase / With smelling flowres of vernant Rhetorique, / Limming and flashing it with various Dyes, / To draw proud *Visus* to me by the eyes: / And oft with perfum'd my petitory stile, / With Ciuet-speach, t'entrap *Olfactus* Nose, / And clad my selfe in Silken Eloquence, / To allure the nicer touch of *Tactus* hand" (A4v). Lingua (grammatically gendered) thus enacts and alludes to her powers to touch the world around her, to mobilize sensation as communication. Here we *do* see how touch might find a medium: for language itself is the central medium through which touch might come into play as a mediated social force. Yet this very possibility is imagined, by the many inhabitants of Microcosmus, as an ultimate danger that could lead the body and psyche into utter chaos and disorganization, thus demanding repression by Auditus from the first.

As Lingua puts it, "all's become lost labour," since Auditus takes this tongue, pleading for recognition, to be but a "babling selfe" (A4v, A3v). As Auditus puts it, "prooue not starke madde, / Hopelesse to prosecute a haplesse sute: / For though (perchance) thy first straines pleasing are, / I dare ingage mine eares, the cloze will iarre" (A3r). Upon being debased by Auditus and blocked from "the eares of common Sense" (A4v), Lingua seems to have internalized the criticism of herself as capable only of "tunes without sense, words inarticulate." For she swiftly turns away from attempts to communicate (Lingua's "Nay good *Auditus* doe but heare me speake," is the opening line of the play) to a kind of self-talk, a muttering soliloquy: "Well then Ile goe, wither? nay what know I? / And do, in faith I will, the deuill knowes what, / What if I set them all at variance, / And so obteine to speake, it must be so, / It must be so, but how? There lyes the point: / How? thus: tut this deuise will neuer proue, / Augment it so; 'twill be too soon descried, / Or so, no so, 'tis too too dangerous, / Pish, none of these, what if I take this course? ha?" and so on (A4v). This scattered and self-doubting Lingua nevertheless decides upon a "point." She plots a "reuenge," plants a crown and robe for the senses to fight over in the quest for superiority, thus hoping to be able, ultimately, to speak on her own behalf and gain entrance into the ear and field of common sense.

The comedy of a tongue attempting to emerge as superior, above and beyond the senses and faculties within the human body—while rooted in Erasmus's own often hilarious treatment of the tongue in *Lingua, sive, de linguae usu atque abusu liber utilissimus*[42]—can also be visualized by recalling the emblem of the autonomous tongue, detached from the body of which it is a part (and pictured alongside the question "Wither will thou tendest?") in George Wither's collection of emblems (Figure 5).

This winged organ provides a nice image of Tomkis's Lingua, precisely because Lingua—as we saw in Chapter 3—speaks only to become detached

Figure 5. "Evill Tongue," George Wither, *A Collection of Emblemes, Ancient and Moderne, Quickened with Metricall Illustrations* (London, 1635). fSTC 25900a. Courtesy of the Houghton Library, Harvard College Library.

from the human body of which she is, otherwise, a part. Lingua, moreover, seems to become detached from reference as she attempts to assert superiority by speaking in no fewer than five tongues in a single sentence. All becomes "lost labour" indeed through Lingua's hilarious display of inarticulacy in a formal trial where she performs her powers to no effect, her speech reduced by others to a kind of material "lump"; "here's a Gallemaufry of speech indeed," says Common Sense, who likens Lingua's polyglot speech to the "language makers" of the day who "freezeth all Heterogeneall languages together, congealing English Tynne, Graecian Gold, Romaine Latine all in a lumpe" (F2r). Comments such as this pepper the play and make it clear that the misogyny operative in the gendering of speech is but a thin disguise for failures of humanism to cohere, to translate, indeed to speak from within, and on behalf of, the human body.

But at the same time, it is as if Lingua simply has *too much* sense to cram it all into a single language or indeed a coherent sentence—as she later puts it,— "I can neuer speake inough of the vnspeakeable praise of speech" (F3r). As John Davies wrote in his own *Microcosmos* (1603), the soul itself can become most inarticulate when "*strife* the *senses* frame doth so vnknit / That it confounds it, or distracts the *Wit* / . . . in this *moode* (though we esteeme it madd) / *Men* prophesie, and truely things foretell, / Speake diuerse *Tongues*, which erst they never had."[43] Such inarticulate potential grants validity to Lingua's quest to be considered a "sixth sense" of knowing or "prophesie" (to "pronounce things to come"), yet her auditors prove unwilling or unable to "esteeme" her quest as anything but "madd." Indeed, as potential plentitude becomes cast as a deranged deficit, largess as a "lumpe," a sixth sense to a non-sense, what is staged is a social process in which the demand for rational speech casts nonrational speech as utterly vacuous. The irony here is that Lingua is the star of the play, the element (language, speech, the tongue) without which the play could not exist. Moreover, Lingua's alienation from reference, from the possibility of affecting, contacting, and indeed touching the world she inhabits (alluring even "the nicer touch of *Tactus* hand"), informs the drama of revenge.

Lingua's equally dispersed and less than articulate parallel in the sensory domain of the play is Tactus, or touch, who is unable to abstract, generalize, or properly articulate himself through speech, extending, as he does, to not one, or two, or three, but to "euery particle of all the body" (I3r). If Lingua has words but lacks the power to make direct contact, Tactus can make direct contact but lacks the distance necessary for rhetorical coherence. This chiasmus emphasizes the problem of communication in a world, or microcosm, in which the relationship between language and "feeling," in both senses of the word, is attenuated. For no one seems to listen to Tactus when he says (in a speech directly following Lingua's claim to be able to simulate and stimulate touch) that he is *the* key to "feeling" in both senses of the word, to all of the senses as well as the emotions within the body: "the eyes do weepe; / The eares do feele, the tast's a kind of touching" (I3r). Indeed, despite his proclamations of centrality to the other sense organs, Tactus has a hard time entering into the field of legitimate discourse.

While Touch was traditionally aligned with the element of earth,[44] as is said of the personified Terra in *Lingua*, " 'twere an *indecorum Terra* should speake" (G1r). After the wonderful stage direction "*Terra comes to the midst of the Stage, stands stil a while, saith nothing, and steps back*," Common Sense observes what the audience already has: "Terra . . . can say—iust nothing" (G1r). The implication in this elemental allegory is that the entrance of the element of touch into social articulation is necessarily indecorous. Of all the pleasures of sensation, as Davies put it in his *Microcosmos*, "The vilst is that we *feele*, by that we *touch*; / Because it is the Earthli'st *sense* of all" (101). This follows Aristotle's sense that touch is worthy of "reproach . . . because it attaches to us not as men but as animals. So to enjoy such sensations and find the greatest satisfaction in them is brutish."[45] The motif of the earth as a locus of both debased and illegitimate forms of "feeling," we might observe, is a central theme of *Hamlet*. For Hamlet loathes the earth as rank and base (1.2.129–37) yet ultimately throws himself into it, at Ophelia's burial, at the *very* moment he becomes capable of direct public expression in the matter of feeling (5.1.276–80). Hamlet's earthly expressivity is itself hastily "esteemed," by both Claudius and Gertrude, to be "mad," "mere madness" (5.1.264–66, 276–80). While madness is a valid enough postulate, since Hamlet brings to the burial his own inappropriate feelings of competition with Laertes—for they battle somewhat absurdly over who can be buried more deeply in the earth—it also suggests how quickly the direct expression of feelings are debased and buried in Hamlet's social world. Even at a funeral, even, or especially, in the bowels of the earth, it seems, " 'twere an indecorum" for Hamlet to speak.

In *Lingua*, " 'twere an indecorum" for the element of touch to speak in basic representational as well as moral terms, since touch, as Aristotle stressed, lacked a proper medium, or medium proper, to speak of (or through). This problem clearly informs one of Tactus's apparent failures: to articulate himself properly. Although he longs to be understood as a principle of communication as well as of felt experience, his words fall on deaf ears. In the formal competition for the crown, judged by Common Sense, each sense puts on a show featuring its respective organ and the "objects" its brings into this little human world. Tactus, when asked to signify his "dignity by relation" (I2v), first locates himself in that Galenic "instrument of instruments, the hand"; he is "*Psyches* great Secretarie, the dumb's eloquence." But he quickly dislocates himself both rhetorically and conceptually: for his "power / Extends itself as far as our Queene [Psyche] commands, / Through all the parts and climes of *Microcosme*. / I am the roote of life, spreading my vertue / By sinewes that extend from head to foote / To euery liuing part" (I2v–I3r).

His narrative disperses as he proceeds to speak about every known medical and scientific commonplace about the necessity of touch, from protecting the body from danger to enabling it to feel a kiss, until Common Sense abruptly says, "*Tactus*, stand aside," and proceeds to judge on behalf of those senses nearer to the brain. Tactus's access to public expression, even in and through the necessary synesthesia through which eyes "do weepe" and ears "do feele," is cut off as he is relegated to the category of the "lower" sensorium. This parallels the restriction of Lingua's sensory and sensual words from public access, for she too is relegated to the lower sensorium, to base and earthly forms of materiality. Lingua's words are but a "lumpe," she is a "common whore" who "lets euery one lie with her," and she has "made Rhetorique wanton, Logicke to bable" (F3v).

Such criticisms of Tactus and Lingua are par for the course in a humanist-scholastic academic drama. For these two characters violate all manner of principles: rhetorical decorum, social moderation, civil conversation, stylistic discrimination, and common decency. Yet what is also on display here are the limits of both humanist and scholastic assumptions about what counts as knowledge and communication, and about eloquence and reason as the preeminent coordinates of social cohesion. As a drama, *Lingua* of course thrives on the very qualities that Tactus and Lingua bring into the little human world. Tactus and Lingua, figures of enormous if often inarticulate vitality, form the very basis of dramatic intrigue and entertainment. Their censure thus constitutes not only anxieties about embodiment, sexuality, and the experience of strong feeling but also about the power of theater to expose fissures within humanist ideals of self-fashioning. Indeed, the willful exclusion of touch from the domain of speech ("*Tactus*, stand aside") and of speech from the domain of touch ("common whore") dramatizes the self-repressive principles of a body aiming to keep itself, above and beyond anything else, intact. The very concept of a world that is whole or intact implies a word detached from the complexities of touch. The derivation of the word "intact" comes from the Latin *in* (not) and *tactus* (touched). As early as 1450 it meant "untouched; not affected by anything that injures, diminishes, or sullies; kept or left entire; unblemished; unimpaired."[46] Hamlet's "Oh that this too too sullied flesh would melt" (1.2.129) evinces a powerful internalization of the very principles of rational order and integrity that Tomkis stages.

Tomkis (like Shakespeare), however, stages a world, uneasily and momentarily, in touch with itself. Tactus's argument that "the eyes do weepe; / The eares do feele, the tast's a kind of touching" underscores not only the tactile substrate of all sensory perception, following Aristotle and others, but also the tactile substrate of all emotion (I3r), from "melancholie" (B3r) to outright "anger" (I2v).[47] Interestingly, Tactus's relationship to the expression of feeling is most visible when he *cannot* represent himself directly. For when it comes to staging the power of touch as mediated through "objects," and through the art of theater itself, we seem to see Tactus on the brink of disaster. "What in such anger, Tactus," asks Common Sense, "What's the Matter?" Tactus responds, "My Lord I had thought as other Senses did, / By sight of obiects to haue prou'd my worth," staging "a Gentleman enamored, / With his sweete touching of his Mistresse lippes, / And gentle griping of her tender hands, / And diuers pleasant relishes of touch," but his mistress has such a complex costume that after five hours "shee is scarse drest to the girdle." The representational hold up appears, at first, to be a conventionally misogynist diatribe:

> Thus 'tis, fiue houres agoe I set a douzen maides to attire a boy like a nize Gentlewoman: but there is such doing with their looking-glasses, pinning, vnpinning, setting, vnsetting, formings and conformings, painting blew vaines, and cheekes, such stirre with Stickes and Combes, Cascanets, Dressings, Purles, Falles, Squares, Buskes, Bodies, Scarffes, Neck laces . . . Borders, Tires, Fannes, Palizadoes, Puffes, Ruffes, Cuffes, Muffes, Pussles, Fussles, Partsets, Frislets, Bandlets, Fillets, Croslets, Pendulets, Amulets, Annulets, Bracelets, and so many lets, that yet shee is scarse drest to the girdle: and now there's such calling for Fardingales, Kirtlets, Busk-points, shootyes &c. that seauen Pedlers shops, nay all

Sturbridge Faire will scarse furnish her: a Ship is sooner rigd by farre,
then a Gentlewoman made ready. (I2v)

The lexical heap of absent objects clearly displaces the representational problems of touch onto the female sex. The character Fantasy responds, "Tis
strange, that women being so mutable, / Will neuer change in changing their
apparell," a comment that informs Patricia Parker's correct suggestion that the
play stages male anxieties about the effeminizing potential of representation.[48]

But there is another realm of signification at work, for this lavish insult
backfires in a particularly effective way. As with the logic of the excessive insult, where terms of abuse pile up, become detached from specific contexts,
and ultimately refer to the insulter rather than the insulted, so here imagined
objects accumulate to the point of being detached from both the specifically
gendered world and, more important, the specifically material world. If particular forms of feeling, to recall Davies, are "better *felt then showne*," it is only
appropriate that Tactus can't "show" himself. Although Tactus should be undermined by so many absent objects, in fact the unrepresented dimensions of
touch works as a brilliant form of self-reference, a demonstration of the plentitude, indeed the infinite diversity, of touch, which subtends (and yet is not
limited to) the entire world of drama. Through the absent materialization of
a kiss and a couple gently touching, and the infinite world of props and objects that touch the actor's body, Tactus at once suggests his lack of dependence on any specific domain of "objects" and asserts the dependence on *him*
of the other senses at play in the theater. That is, through their absence, the
missing lovers and the missing objects evoke conceptions of touch subtending the domain of "show." The proliferation of word sounds, moreover, including "Puffes, Ruffes, Cuffes, Muffes, Pussles, Fussles . . . Amulets,
Annulets, Bracelets, and so many lets," manifests a principle of ear-tingling
plentitude that, however comically, indexes extralinguistic dimensions of
feeling.

Although Tactus may be too indecorous for words or indeed for "show,"
the sense of feeling that he embodies is aligned with a knowing form of extralinguistic perception. The limitations on touch to enter into the field of
legitimate representation have an equal and opposite side: touch proves a
canny sense, able to know things that others cannot. Drawing from the commonplace fantasy in medical literature of a man made of glass, Tactus imagines himself as such: his "Breast was like a windowe," he says, so others may

understand, "Through which I plainely did perceiue my heart: / In whose two Concaues I discernd my thoughts, / Confus'dly lodged in great multitudes" (B4r). Tactus, while claiming, Hamlet-like, knowledge of "that within which passes show,"[49] is in this scene feigning madness, hoping to remain an undetected threat to the microcosm as he covets and hides the crown and robe now in his possession. He here utters the melancholic conceit, "Mans life is wonderous brittle," ponders things "past imagination" such as how the dead "haue beene metamorphosed, /To stranger matters and more vncoth formes," and speaks only to break off with a tenable silence, "And yet me thinks, I speake as I was wont /And —" (B3v). He thus succeeds in appearing to his companions as "melancholly," "mad," "feeble," a veritable candidate for "Bedlam" (B3r). But even in this feigning of madness, Tactus gestures toward a phenomenology of himself, toward at least the possibility of an alternative way of perceiving one's "heart" and acknowledging "confus'd" thoughts "lodged in great multitudes"—the inarticulate because inchoate and not typically visible substrate or interior of the self.

Touch was to an extent imagined as not only disabling ways of classifying knowledge but also opening up new possibilities for understanding the sense of things. While direct contact was integral to medical explanations of touch, the idea of touch in literature often stretched the domain of the tactile beyond the bounds of the body itself, implying conditions of hyperawareness and hypersensitivity. The commonplace iconography of the spider as a representative of touch, for example, is worth exploring in this respect because it expands the realm of sensitivity from body to environment. Davies wrote in *Nosce Teipsum* (1599) that touch, "*the Feeling power* . . . Much like a subtill Spider, which doth sit / In middle of her Web, which spreadeth wide, / If ought do touch the vtmost threed of it, / She feeles it instantly on euery side."[50] This passage has often been read as alluding to the spread of nerves throughout the body. But the simile also relocates touch from the physically proximate to the relatively distant space of environment, perhaps providing the closest Renaissance analogy to the contemporary notion of the sixth sense, that eerily inexplicable receptivity to seemingly undetectable environmental stimuli.

Francis Bacon would liken excess emotional receptivity to a whole environment of cobwebs. "*A Gentlemans honor*," he wrote, citing an earlier commonplace, "*should bee, De telâ crassiore*, of a good strong warppe or webbe that euery little thing should not catch in it, when as now it seemes they are but of cobwebbe lawne . . . so tender that it feeles euery thing."[51] If English laws were to sanction such hypersensitivity, to cater to "euery touch or light blow of the person," the state itself, Bacon stressed, would suffer from a web of its own making, "so tender" as to feel "euery thing" (20v–21r). Given such a postulate, one might consider Leontes's famous allusion to having "drunk and seen the spider" in *The Winter's Tale* as much in terms of his inexplicable oversensitivity to the environment *around* him as of his consciousness of feeling a poison *within* him.[52] It is as if only he can detect the erotic touch of the world around him: "Is whispering nothing? / Is leaning cheek to cheek? is meeting noses? / Kissing with inside lip? . . . wishing clocks more swift? Hours, minutes? noon, midnight? and all eyes / Blind with the pin and web, but theirs; theirs only" (1.2.284–92). This is a king with a kingdom perhaps as sensitive, as fragile, and ultimately as small as a web of his own making: "If I mistake," says Leontes of his jealous thoughts, "In those foundations which I build upon, / the center is not big enough to bear / A school-boy's top" (2.1.100–103). His "second sense" or perhaps sixth sense, while understandable given Hiermione's verbal heat and affection for his rival, becomes antithetical to communal acknowledgment and thus linguistic intelligibility, leading to linguistic involutions that critics still scratch their heads over while attempting to discern meaning.[53]

While spiders make webs to protect themselves and entrap others, what makes them a powerful paradigm of "sensing" in this period is that they can feel without direct contact. The "extrasensory" powers of touch as an alternative mode of receiving information are in fact highlighted by Tomkis's *Tactus*, where the spider works as a simile of tactile sensitivity but also a condition of knowing. "For as a suttle Spider closely sitting, / In the center of her web that spreddeth round: / If the least Flie but touch the smallest thred, / Shee feels it instantly; so doth my selfe" (I3r). The analogy between nerves and the webbed texture of the spider is expanded out from the domain of the physical body and into the untouchable realms of the cosmos. In one passage, Tactus is portrayed as having commanded a whole "troupe" of spiders to spin a chord with their own "gutts," spinning a "cordage fine" through which one might "scal[e]" and experience "the heauens" themselves (E2r). What is suggested here, however comically, is a vivid form of "gut" knowledge, or what David Hillman has called "visceral knowledge," at odds with emergent forms of visual-scientific inquiry in the Renaissance.[54] The spiders "Of their owne gutts to spinne a cordage fine, / Whereof t'haue fram'd a net (O wondrous worke) / That fastned by the Concaue of the Moone, / Spreds downe it selfe to th'earths circumference" (E2r). "Cordage," invoking the Latin for "heart," joins the nerves and sinews in an unaccountable way of perceiving the world.[55] Yet this way of sensing is unaccountable—or in other words, suspect—because it is Mendacio, the lie, who represents Tactus's very "core" or "gut" knowledge in this instance.

Tactus and Lingua thus converge as figures through which alternative, extralinguistic forms of perception are gestured toward but also foreclosed. Touch, like Lingua, is unable fully to express himself, and indeed the power of the "heart" or "core" to others on stage. When Tactus alludes to his own interior, to his perception of the "heart" and confused "thoughts" within, even Olfactus laughs, "Ha ha ha ha. . . . / Thou'st make a passing liue Anatomie" (B4r). In some ways the joke is on Olfactus. For this Tactus is indeed less dead than the "liue Anatomies" that people so many Renaissance medical texts, who point to their own entrails without apparent concern, dangle their skin over a shoulder like a warm coat on a sunny day, or pose for a guide to the anatomy of the brain with a conspicuously halved cranium.[56] Unlike these anesthetized bodies that, as Jonathan Sawday has pointed out, demonstrate the extent to which "the body had become subject to the gaze,"[57] Tactus is less a numb body pointing at itself than a "liue Anatomie" trying to express itself from inside out.

The trajectory of this drama leads, for the sake of microcosmic integrity, to the reinstantiation of the hierarchy of the senses, with Visus on top, Tactus on the bottom. Interestingly, Tactus's ability to disrupt or alter the order of things fully diminishes as he becomes vulnerable to physical (as opposed to cognitive and linguistic) forces stronger than he is. His perceptual sensitivity is realized in the body as he is tickled: "Ha, ha, ha, fie, I pray you leaue, you tickle me so, oh, ah, ha, ha, take away your hands I cannot indure, ah you tickle me, ah, ha, ha, ha, ah" (M2v). "We see no *Man* can ticke himslelfe," wrote Bacon in *Sylua Syluarum*, "*Tickling* is euer Painfull, and not well endured."[58] Indeed, tickles quickly become unbearable, and the tactual takes a turn for the worse. Tactus is touched with a "pinch," a "pinne," and a "stab" (M4r) and is wracked with cramps: "O the crampe, the crampe, the crampe, my legge, my legge" (M2v). His powers are diminished to sheer reaction to the physical force of the world he now inhabits. Tactus is overwhelmed by a kind of burning heat as "poison" toxins infiltrate the body: "Oh what a wildfire creepes among my bowells: / Aetna's within my breast, my marrowe fries, / And runnes about my bones, oh my sides: / My sides, my raines, my head my raines, my head; / My heart, my heart, my liuer, my liuer, oh / I burne, I burne, I burne oh how I burne" (K4r). In this heartburn par excellence, Tactus becomes a kind of grotesque version of the self-demonstrating anatomy, reduced to locating his vulnerabilities in a series of individuated and hurt body parts: "heart," "brains," "breast," "marrowe," "bones," "sides," "raines." "My heart, my heart, my liuer, my liuer."

Such a quick journey from a richly textured realm of plotting, perceiving, and knowing to a self defined by a series of single hurt organs in "paine" (K4r), subject to anatomical investigation, helps bring the play to a close. For Elaine Scarry, the articulation of physical pain, as it works counterfactually ("I feel as if") can eclipse the experience of it. Physical pain, she writes, "is language-destroying" (19), or more specifically, pain "resists objectification in language" (5). Yet here we see an inverse principle at work, for the language of touch, so fruitfully resistant to "objectification in language" earlier in the play, now becomes all too subject to objectification in language. Touch here speaks, and speaks all too directly, providing an impoverished version of touch as an affective force through which a social as well as a psychological body might otherwise come to understand itself anew. For what might have been—to tweak Francis Barker's well-known phrase—a kind of tremulous public body becomes a spectacle of individually marked symptoms and vulnerabilities of physical touch.[59] The complex coordinates of sensory-emotional "feeling" give way to coordinates of a body that has become its own object.

Lingua, meanwhile, with "former plots dispurposed" in the final act, has in fact poisoned the ear, eye, and all the senses with wine "mingled with such hellish drugges and forcible wordes," so that the body might become "possest with an inraged and mad kinde of anger" (K1v). She confesses as much as she, like Lady Macbeth, both walks and talks in her sleep. After she utters the nonsense "mum mum mum mum,"[60] her mumbles speak truth: she confesses to having poisoned the senses and "made them as madde as—well, If I cannot recouer it—let it goe" (M4r), as if the proper gloss or correlative for "madde" (to be angry, also to be insane) is somehow beyond the reach of the tongue. This wonderful slip of the tongue, even as it loses track of itself, brings the inarticulate full circle, from a form of senseless "babbling" to a form of unconscious revelation. "Some body hath felt, and shall feele more, if I liue," she adds, expressing even in her dreams a desire to make the body "feele more" (M3r). Yet, like Tactus's movement from a principle of emotional and perceptual feeling to one of sheer physical reactivity, Lingua's punishment is as follows: Rather than function as an instrument that might make the body "feel more," she is imprisoned within the mouth to be guarded by Gustus (to be a mere organ of taste and touch) and the "30 tall watchmen" of the teeth, who threaten to clamp down on her should she dare to exit the mouth again (M4v).

Complex forms of vulnerability that arise when feeling poses a threat to the order of reason and eloquence become, in the end, not only simplified but also exiled through the specter of the body in pain: the body becoming its own object. Even in this comic drama, incorporation—to remember our formulation early in this chapter—marks the failure of introjection; the unbearable lightness of touch, the surprise of a tickle, a hint, or an unexpected twist, in rhetoric and logic as on stage, are extremely difficult—in Tactus's words—to "indure."[61]

Antitheatrical Tactics: From Audience to Assembly

> *For what clipping, what culling, what kissing and bussing, what*
> *smouching & slabbering one of another, what filthie groping and*
> *vncleane handling is not practiced euery wher in these dauncings? . . .*
> *Some haue broke their legs with skipping, leaping, turning, . . . and*
> *some haue come by one hurt, some by another but neuer any came from*
> *thence without some parte of his minde broken and lame; such a*
> *wholsome exercise it is!*
> —Phillip Stubbes, *The Anatomie of Abuses* (1583)[62]

The reduction of "touch" as a sensitive and affective form of response to a bodily act, process, or habit was a recurrent feature of early treatises against the stage. For many antitheatricalists, dramatic tactics are dangerous precisely because they are tactile: poets in theaters, wrote Stephen Gosson in 1579, produce "consortes of melodie to tickle the eare, costly apparrell to flatter the sight, effeminate gesture to ravish the sence, and wanton speache to whette desire to inordinate lust."[63] Acoustics touch the ear into whispers of sensation, costumes visually "flatter" (a word deriving from touch, " 'to flatten down'; hence 'to stroke with the hand, caress' ")[64] or "touch" the eye, gestures "ravish" the sense, and words induce states of physiological arousal. Here the senses of hearing and vision, as vehicles of perception, become aligned with the sense of touch.

Although we alternately imagine theater-going collectives as "audiences" and "spectators,"[65] it is actually the sense of touch that consistently informs both modes of sensory reception in antitheatrical treatises (which may call for more attention to that third term of persons coming together, "assembly"). Words touch skin, blood, and bone and enter the bodily interior as a kind of liquid physiology, altering the substance of heart and mind: "By the privy entries of the eare [words] sappe downe into the heart, and with gunshotte of affection gaule the mind, where reason and vertue should rule the roste."[66] What is suggestive is not simply that touch encodes a logic of contagion, or that touch results in disrupted boundaries between bodies, but that it disrupts the boundaries between the senses themselves—leading to a confusion between sense and sense and a disarticulation of reason and virtue from the language of the stage. Indeed, what often emerges in such early accounts of audience response is the very phenomenon of synesthetic disorder featured elsewhere in the rhetoric and epistemology of touch and its relationship to the other senses.[67] Although Aristotle would single out touch and taste, as distinct from the other senses, as "brutish" pleasures linked with intemperance, antitheatricalists consistently expand the dangers of all forms of sensory perception by aligning them with the sense of touch.[68]

The tactile substrate of sensory perception and emotional experience was integral to a number of early theories of sense. Despite what Burton and others called the "distance" between "organ and obiect" required for visual apprehension, for example, the debate about whether eyes emanated rays or received particles through the air when visualizing objects speaks to a material process of visualization at the most basic physiological level.[69] So too acoustics was commonly imagined in tactile terms: tickling the ear, the touch of sweet harmony, or, as in George Chapman's translation of Homer: "Hard it is, in such a great concourse, (Though hearers eares be nere so sharpe) to touch at all things spoke."[70] Considering the literal possibility of hearing through touch, Sir Thomas Browne noted the classical conception that "When our cheeke burneth or ear tingleth, wee usually say that some body is talking of us; which is an ancient conceit, . . . a conceit hardly to be made out without the concession of a signifying Genius, or universall Mercury, conducting sounds unto their distant subiects, and teaching us to heare by touch."[71]

The confluence of hearing and touching (and indeed tasting) emerged largely from the domain of music, where the "soft touch" of fingers on a harp produced "sweet sounds," or where music could be ravishing, soothing, the food of love. As Bruce Smith has put it, in this period "the word 'voice' meant, first and foremost, a concatenation of bodily members: muscles, gristly tissues, fluids," so that " 'voice' never loses its physiological grounding."[72] But exactly what that "physiological grounding" was is anything but clear. Even as late as Thomas Blount's 1656 *Glossographia* one might note a kind of synesthetic slip-page in the domain of speech. "Oral," according to Blount, is defined by reference to at least three kinds of physiological ground: "(from *os, oris*) pertaining to the mouth, visage, face, look, savour, or voice."[73] Similarly, in Thomas Cooper's earlier *Thesavrvs Lingvae Romanae & Britannicae* (1578), "Os, oris" is defined similarly as "The mouth: the visage or countenance: The proportion of all the bodie. Presence. Language. Audacitie, boldenesse or hardinesse."[74] The rich textures of orality produce an overflow of sense, not only in the domain of rhetoric and theater but also in the very definition of the word.

But importantly, in antitheatrical discourse the synesthetic pleasures of theater that "move" typically become "flattened" in a largely specular economy of bodies engaged in physical acts. Richard Brathwait's treatise on the senses draws on the metaphor of theater to emphasize the shaming gaze: touch is the "Theater of shame if abused, but the eminent passage from a pilgrimage to a permanent Citie, if rightly employed."[75] And for Stephen Gosson, this conceit is fully articulated when he famously reimagines the audience as a spectacle of conspicuously touching bodies:

> In our assemblies at playes in *London*, you shall see such heauing and shoouing, such ytching and shouldring to sitte by women; Suche care for their garments that they be trode on: Such eyes to their lappes that no chippes light in them; such pillowes to their backes that they take no hurt: Such masking in their eares, I know not what: Suche geving them Pipins to passe the time: Suche playing at foote Saunt without Cardes: Such tick[l]ing, such toying, such smiling, such winking, and such manning them home when the sportes are ended, that it is a right Comedie to marke their behauiour, to watch their conceites, . . . or follow aloofe by the printe of their feete, and so discover by slotte where the Deare taketh soyle.[76]

Again this passage speaks to the relevance of "assemblies" as a third term in the sensory triad of audience, spectator, and assembly. According to *The Oxford English Dictionary*, "assembly" in the Renaissance could suggest a physical, military, and sexual as well as a spatial joining of persons: "To join together, unite (two things or persons, one thing to or with another)"; "To couple (sexually)"; "To come together into one place or company; to gather together, congregate, meet," and "To meet in fight; to join battle, make an attack or charge." Gosson's "assemblies" fits perfectly with the tactile surround of the term (where no one seems to be hearing or watching the play). So, too, all of these meanings converge in John Northbrooke's antitheatrical treatise (c. 1577), in which the theater is a place where people "are so fleshlye ledde, to see what rewarde there is giuen to suche Crocodiles, whiche deuoure the pure chastitie, bothe of single and maried persons, men and women, when as in their Playes you shall learne all things that appertayne to crafte, mischiefe, deceytes, and filthinesse. &c. If you will learne howe to bee false, and deceyue your husbandes, or husbandes their wyues, howe to playe the harlottes, to obtayne ones loue, howe to rauishe, howe to beguyle, howe to betraye, to flatter, lye, sweare, forsweare, howe to allure to whoredome, howe to murther, howe to poyson, . . . to mooue to lusts," and so on.[77]

This might seem a most excellent advertisement for assembling, but, like Gosson's catalogue of tickling, shouldering, itching, and the like, Northbrooke's list ultimately anatomizes specific forms of touch in order to subject the whole domain of "touch" to a shaming gaze: "*Vitanda ergo spectacula omnia*, All suche spectacles and shewes . . . are therefore to bee auoyded, not onelye bicause vices shall not enter our heartes and breastes, but also least the custome of pleasure sholde touche vs, and conuerte vs thereby both from God and good workes."[78] The affective power of plays to "touche" and "enter our heartes and breastes" is thus localized and contained in specific scenes of shame in Northbrooke's theologically coded anatomy theater. Importantly, what Northbrooke is trying to kill off is far more complex than any kind of physical or even moral touch: it is something perhaps at the core of "touch" as a condition of emotional receptivity, of allowing one's self to be "entered" by simply being curious. Following his diatribe, he reasons: "Therefore great reason it is that women (especiallye) sholde absent themselues from such Playes. What was the cause why Dina was rauished? was it not hir curiositie? the Mayden woulde go forth, and vnderstande the manners of other folkes. Curiositie then no doubt did hurt hir" (68). This logic typifies the representation of touch in antitheatrical rhetoric, which restricts the power of affect and the power of words to assemble people and ideas in new ways by foregrounding the body as the site of touch and extreme vulnerability to harm.

Much like the trajectories explored here, revenge dramas of the Renaissance often shift from an exploration of touch as a facet of affect or cognition to a restriction of tactile economies in the body subject to harm. In *Hamlet*, to take a case in point, Hamlet goes from being "touched" (or pretending he is) to being "touched" (and dead).[79] In the language of the play, touching shifts from the domain of rhetorical pointing to a single moment of fatal bodily contact. Hamlet's "I, there's the point" of the 1603 Quarto (uttered after "To be or not to be") returns materially and conceptually in the final act as he is fatally "touched" with Laertes's "point," "the point envenom'd too!" (5.2.327).[80] The first "there's the point" is drawn from the rhetoric of reading, in a reference both to oral performance (as the rhetorician used his finger to point to visual information, on a chart or an outline on his other hand), and to silent reading (with pointing fingers lining the margins of early books to indicate relevant textual moments).[81] "There's the point" either functions as an acoustical sign, a commonplace detached even from its own manual origins, or accompanies a visual gesture: Hamlet pointing to the very book he holds in his hand.[82]

Although this may seem a small point, in fact the detachment of a body from itself and its deployment for the operations of metaphor is the dominant concern of the opening act of *Hamlet*, marked by the phenomenon of the ghost. "Horatio says 'tis but our fantasy, / And will not let belief take hold of him, / Touching this dreaded sight twice seen of us," says Marcellus in the opening moments (1.1.26–28). "Touching this vision here," says Hamlet after his encounter with Old Hamlet, "It is an honest ghost, that let me tell you" (1.5.143–44). Touching, meaning "concerning, or pertaining to," is here a conceptual gesture as detached from the domain of physical touch as the ghost himself.[83] These early moments return in the form of a single bodily reference as Hamlet is touched with a point: nothing, says Laertes, "Under the moon, can save the thing from death / That is but scratch'd withal. I'll touch my point / With this contagion, that if I gall him slightly, / It may be death" (4.7.144–47). And later during the duel, upon the first point of contact, the Second Quarto reads: "A touch, a touch, I do confesse," and the Folio reads: "I, I grant, a tuch, a tuch." The term "touche," which acknowledges a solid conversational point, in fact originates from physical contact; the English word "touch" derives from the Old French *toucher*, "to touch," or the Italian *tocca*, "stroke, blow, touch" and *toccare*, "to hit, strike."[84] But in *Hamlet*, the trajectory reverses, and the conversational becomes the contactual; not only is

Hamlet touched to the quick, the effect of such a touch is located physiologically in his own heart: "Now cracks a noble heart" (5.2.364).

The heart is of course a particularly resonant locus of touch and vulnerability: "The *Hart* is such a powreful *thing*," wrote Davies, "My *hart* desires to touch it feelingly: / . . . for the *Hart* doth *paine* or *pleasure* bring."[85] For Aristotle in *De sensu* the sense of touch was somatically dispersed and peripherally epidermal, but it was ultimately localized in the region of the heart. Although this locus of touch in the body was much debated, it informs the somatization of heartbreak, or scenes of cardiac arrest, on the Renaissance stage; a topos that amounts to a kind of emotional open-heart surgery in John Ford's *'Tis Pity She's a Whore*. If Hamlet's immediate response to the ghost's narrative is: "Hold, hold, my heart, / And you, my sinews, grow not instant old, / But bear me stiffly up" (1.5.93–95), the question is not only of the heart's stability but also of what the heart might hold, can hold, and if the heart can be held or beheld. These are questions at the core of revenge drama. Ford's play explores the question of what it might mean to hold someone's heart in one's hands (literally, as Giovanni touches the still steaming or imagistically *breathing* heart of his dead beloved); Kyd's *Spanish Tragedy* comes to a close with Hieronimo's disconcertingly tactile *Solimon and Perseda* and his own sense of psychophysiological rupture: "And now to express the rupture of my part / First take my tongue and afterward my heart."[86] So too, Hamlet's own "break, my heart" (1..2.158) becomes displaced outward onto his mother as he wonders if her heart is "made of penetrable stuff" that he might somehow "wring" or cleave, or if it is rather armored, impenetrable, covered with brass, "proof and bulwark against sense" (3.4.35–38).

In each of these plays, the heart shifts from the domain of signification as emblem, citational cliché, heard (or sonically imagined) pulses, breath, words, and feeling to a material entity that is subject to the physical properties of touch.[87] The physical concretization of sensory-emotional experience that transforms the body itself into its own object foregrounds the profound difficulty of sustaining concepts of "feeling" as complex modes of mediation. In tragedies, we often see how characters who can't "indure" the intensity of complex feelings turn to their bodies to control those feelings, transforming bodies into objects to express feelings but also to anaesthetize them. As Laertes says upon encountering the mad Ophelia, "O heat, dry up my brains" (4.5.154). And in *King Lear*, Lear attempts to manage his emotional pain by anatomizing it: "Let me have surgeons; I am cut to th'brains"

(4.6.190–91), and earlier, "Let them anatomize Regan, see what breeds about her heart" (3.6.74–75). If the blind Gloucester manages to "see . . . feelingly" (4.6.147), this very idea of a tactile-emotional consciousness is at odds with Lear's attempt to use physical pain to avoid emotional pain. While still out in the raging storm that "invades us to the skin" (3.6.6–7), Lear says: "This tempest will not give me leave to ponder / On things would hurt me more" (24–25).

Hamlet, whose name contains the word "ham" which meant not only "home" and "land" but also "*skin*"—from the Old English *hama*; Middle High German *hame* and *ham*; Old Norse *hams*, and Danish *ham* for "A covering, *esp.* a natural covering, integument; skin, membrane"[88]—is in many senses acutely aware of how the skin might serve as a cover story for deeper and less articulable injuries of the heart. As he tells Gertrude, her preoccupation with his "madness" rather than with her own inner life or the loss of her husband, "will but skin and film the ulcerous place, / While rank corruption, mining all within, infects unseen" (3.4.148–150). Given the etymological potential of Hamlet's name, it is almost as if Hamlet sees a deadened version of himself not only in his mother's thoughts but also wrapped around her insides, protecting her, if as a "bulwark against sense," from her own capacity to "feel" (78–81).[89]

"Has this fellow no feeling of his business a sings in the grave-making?" says Hamlet of the gravedigger, "Did these bones cost no more the breeding but to play at loggets with 'em? Mine ache to think on it" (5.1.65–66, 60–91). To have "no feeling" for the dead is of course entwined in Hamlet's mind with the callous treatment, in language, song, and action, of the bodies of others, but it is the unfortunate afterlife of skin that he focuses on most particularly. In a variant of Hieronimo's imagistic transformation of legal documents into human bodies in *The Spanish Tragedy*, Hamlet speaks of legal documents ("action of battery," "statutes," "recognizances, "double vouchers," "recoveries, and "conveyances") only to ask Horatio, "is not parchment made of sheepskins?" Horatio responds, "Ah, my lord, and of calveskins too" (5.1.101–13). "There are sheep and calves which seek out assurance in that" (114), imagines Hamlet, as if animals might possess the rights to the afterlife of their own skin.[90] Hamlet in some ways attempts the same. That he throws himself into Ophelia's grave in order to hold "her once more in mine arms," and that he hopes to make that hold permanent, fusing "the quick and dead" by being buried alive alongside her (5.1.242–44), speaks to his ongoing desire keep the touch of the dead alive. At the same time, we also see here in this suicidal fantasy Hamlet's equally ongoing desire to kill off the "inward tutch," as Sidney put it, of the genuinely grieving "hart."[91]

From Old Hamlet's account of his own skin at the outset of the play—his once "smooth body" made "vile and loathsome crust" through poison coursing from within (1.5.72–73)—skin in *Hamlet* becomes a curious object of horror and fascination, itself akin to language as a kind of screen covering over deeper injuries. Responding to Hamlet's query, "How long will a man lie i' th' earth ere he rot," the Gravedigger responds, "A tanner will last you nine year. . . . His hide is so tanned with his trade that a wil keep out water a great while, and your water is a sore decayer of your whoreson dead body" (5.1.158–66). The callous treatment of the slow decay of skin is swiftly inverted through Hamlet's mnemonic restoration of poor Yorick's skull as one that had skin that could kiss and be kissed and indeed a body that could touch and be touched: "He hath bore me on his back a thousand times, and now—how abhorred in my imagination it is. My gorge rises at it. Here hung those lips that I have kissed I know not how oft" (179–83). Home, land, skin, the meanings at the core of "Hamlet," converge as Hamlet finds, here within the bowels of the earth, itself the well known element of touch, that he is not at all at home in his own skin. His gorge rises at it.

As Claudia Benthien has put it in a book entitled *Skin*, "skin is used as a stand-in for 'person,' 'spirit,' 'body,' or 'life,' as a *pars pro toto* of the entire human being. On the other hand, and this is what makes skin so singular, it functions simultaneously as the other of the self, as its enclosure, prison, or mask."[92] In *Hamlet*, the haunt of a ghost imagined as a "spirit" as well as a skin-encrusted "person" caught in an intolerable "prison-house"[93] speaks to the eerie status of the skin as a sign of life and personhood as well as suffocating enclosure. Hamlet's desire to shed his *own* skin—famously wishing that "this too too sullied [or "solid"] flesh would melt" or that his "mortal coil" be "shuffle[d] off" in order for the "heart-ache" of emotional pain to come to an end (3.1.60–67)[94]—is of course entwined with his desire to kill off all that is contained within him. While betraying an over-identification with the ghost, Hamlet's sense of being locked within "*this*" skin signals his sense of the skin as being at once "the other of the self" and an entity less liquid or permeable than he would like.

Like language, skin is at once a boundary between the self and the world and an organ of sense perception through which the world can be let in:

"Language—the human essence, the skin of thought, more to the mind than light is to the eye."[95] If Hamlet encapsulates a tragedy of what it might mean not to be able to let others inside one's own skin, to touch others or fully be touched, that tragedy is implicit when he says to Horatio, "Give me that man / That is not passion's slave, and I will *wear* him / In my heart's core, ay, in my heart of heart" (3.2.71–73, emphasis added). This image of a heart that might "wear" another as if for protection or cover, while paralleling Hamlet's claim that his own soul has "seal'd" itself (65), is aggressively displaced, later in the same act, onto the image of Gertrude's own heart and soul hidden beneath a protective covering of "skin and film." In essence, Hamlet asks his mother to shed a "skin" that he has not been able to: for he has just killed Polonius without apparent concern, betraying a kind of "skin or film" covering his own "unseen" interior.[96] Interestingly, the less vulnerable Hamlet becomes from the inside-out, the more vulnerable he becomes from the outside-in. For it is no coincidence that Hamlet, who describes himself upon his return from sea as " 'Naked' " and " 'Alone' " (4.7.50–51)—which itself might evoke sympathy but for the fact that he has, by this point, already killed a number of people—is ultimately reduced to so much vulnerable skin. While he perspires, "fat and scant of breath" during the duel, so he swiftly expires through the penetrative touch of a single, poisoned point. It is as if the "inward tutch" or the felt rawness of a "vulture-gnawen heart" that might otherwise be "open" or somehow communicated to others becomes, over the course of the play, shrouded by the body's all too mortal coil.[97]

If there is any "touchstone" in *Hamlet*, it may well be the grief of Hamlet's own heart. Gertrude suggests as much, noting his "very madness" after killing Polonius "like some ore / Among minerals of base, / Shows itself pure—a weeps for what is done" (4.1.25–27). But this location of Hamlet's woe as touchstone cannot bear a moment's scrutiny: it is quickly picked up in Claudius's anxious response: "O Gertrude, come away. / The sun no sooner shall the mountains touch / But we will ship him hence" (28–30). No sooner than the sun might touch the mountains will the sun be banished from the scene, "shipped hence." The nonrecognition of interiority here extends into the realm of theology. The sense of being "touched" with guilt emerges three times (very like the ghost) in the play. As Hamlet puts it, "Your Majesty, and we that have free souls, it touches us not. Let the galled jade wince, our withers are unwrung," to which Guildenstern later adds, "I know no touch of it, my lord" (3.2.236–38, 347). And subsequently Claudius says to Laertes: "And they shall hear and judge 'twixt you and me. / If by direct or by collateral hand / They find us touch'd, we will our kingdom give" (4.5.202–4). These tactually inflected metaphors amount to a public and collective denial of self-touch. It is, to adopt the words of one seventeenth-century writer, "As if men had forgone all touches of humanity and were become a kind of walking-ghosts."[98] Hamlet, as both character and play, battles with these ghosts. In contrast to the humanist as well as the antitheatrical conflation of touch with moral and even physical death,[99] this play in fact calls for a more nuanced recognition of feeling, of being touched in its many senses, so that one can live—rather than only be touched in death.

This question of how people can touch others in a world where they are not recognized or do not recognize themselves is central to *Hamlet*, but also to *Lingua*. The ghosts in both plays are an embodiment of this. The ghost as a symptom of nonrecognition emerges in the opening scene of *Lingua*, as Auditus refuses to hear the words of Lingua, who then wishes the "houling of tortur'd Ghosts / Pursue thee still and fill thy amazed eares / With cold astonishment and horrid feares" (A3v). This frustrated speaker-revenger smacks of the very ghost of *Hamlet*, who emerges in a world where he has lost power to enter "the whole ear of Denmark"—which is "by a forged process of my death, / Rankly abus'd"—to seek revenge on Claudius, himself described as a "mildew'd ear."[100] Lingua, like Hamlet, has language but minimal power to move or "touch" the world she inhabits, and out of her frustration emerges this tortured ghost and her subsequent revenge. Ghosts here and in other Renaissance dramas become the mark of metaphor dead before its time. Lingua's art is cast as an art of arousal, of "titillation," and touching, but one that has become dissociated from her internal counterpart, the heart, and ultimately, from all of the perceptive capacities within the sensory realm. She can simulate and stimulate but has lost the capacity to "touch." She is both a sixth sense and no sense at all; halfway between the living and the dead, and her words—like those of Tactus—are denied integration into a community in which "tact" might be deemed necessary for individual and collective integration.

Indeed, as I have begun to suggest, *Hamlet* raises all of the issues explored in this chapter thus far (and in a broader sense, all of the issues raised in this book thus far).[101] While Hamlet's career of feigned and genuine madness parallels that of Tactus—in a play from exactly the same period and performed in the same place—so too in Hamlet's world touch is ultimately reduced to a contaminant, infection, plague, or the final "contagion" that marks his death. We see also the reduction of an "assembled" collective to a fatally toxic one—resulting, of course, in a stage littered with corpses, reduced to a "sight" (5.2.419). And finally, we see the dis-integration of spoken language fully enabled (as by Lingua in Tomkis's play) by Hamlet's function as an unsettling Echo figure in the world around him.[102] But *Hamlet* stages as well the dramatic potential of the disintegration of the senses, marked from the outset of the play, since the ghost is visible but inaudible to the guards, with Horatio urging him five consecutive times to "speak" (1.1.131–42).[103] This inaugural drama of the visual refusing to be verbal is soon replayed in Hamlet's encounter with Ophelia. As Ophelia—responding to Polonius's question "What said he?"—explains,

> He took me by the wrist and held me hard,
> Then goes he to the length of all his arm,
> And with his other hand thus o'er his brow
> He falls to such perusal of my face
> As a would draw it. Long stay'd he so.
> At last, a little shaking of mine arm,
> And thrice his head thus waving up and down,
> He rais'd a sigh so piteous and profound
> As it did seem to shatter all his bulk
> And end his being. (2.1.87–96)

In this response to "What said he?" we see that Hamlet has said nothing, yet has communicated feeling through an extended dumb show that strikes Ophelia as both "piteous" and "profound." The communicative work of gesture here, as well that of physical touch, while aligning Hamlet with the ghost, also exemplifies the potential for partial and extralinguistic expression to move characters within the play in ways in which direct expression cannot.

This brings us to one of the most dominant topoi in *Hamlet*, the inexpressibility topos, which is all the more curious in Shakespeare's longest play, overflowing as it is with "words, words, words."[104] Indeed, continual allusions to things unsayable or only half-said throughout *Hamlet* serve to amplify the expressive (or "piteous" and "profound") dimensions of unsaid or underarticulated words. If Hamlet famously expresses contempt for known conventions and modes of speech—implicit in his "Buzz, buzz" (2.2.389), in which he reduces speech to so much annoying noise in the ear—he as well as other characters in the play consistently attempts to reference meanings that might enter the minds and bodies of others without the benefit of direct expression. Laertes's words, following the news of Ophelia's death, for example—"I have a speech 'o fire that fain would blaze / But that this folly douts it" (4.7.188–89)— offer a striking parallel to the ghost's "eternal blazon" that can "not be" in his early speech to Hamlet: "I *could* a tale unfold whose lightest word / Would harrow up thy soul" (1.5.15–16, emphasis added). The ghost's undisclosing disclosure to an eager auditor (and auditory) is similarly replicated in Hamlet's letter to Horatio, "*I have words to speak in thine ear will make the dumb; yet are they much too light for the bore of the matter*" (4.6.22–24), and in Hamlet's dying words: "You that look pale and tremble at this chance, / That are but mutes or audience to this act, / Had I but time. . . .—O I could tell you—/ But let it be" (5.2.339–43). So too the distraught Ophelia "hems, and beats her heart, / . . . speaks things in doubt / That carry but half sense" (4.5.5–7). The ideal so central to late Tudor rhetoric that language should, first and foremost, be able to move, to touch and to stimulate the passions and senses of others,[105] indeed, as an actor might "drown the stage with tears," "cleave the general ear with horrid speech," and "amaze indeed / the very faculties of eyes and ears," set against the problem of one who can "say nothing" (2.3.556–64), leads to convolutions of communication that themselves have the power to produce horror.

All of these examples invoke the pathos of the unsaid. For a sense of what it means to be in a world *without* the power of speech fully to move an auditory itself has the power—as in the case of Ophelia, whose "speech is nothing, / Yet the unshaped use of it doth move / The hearers to collection"—to express a "mood" that "needs to be pitied" (4.5.3–9). Such pathos is felt even or especially when it cannot be fully translated: "The hearers" of Ophelia's speech, "aim at it, / And botch the words up to fit to their own thoughts, / Which, as her winks and nods and gestures yield them, / Indeed would make one think there might be thought, / Though nothing sure, yet much unhappily" (9–13). Ophelia's patches of "half-sense" and her language of the body with winks, nods, gestures, hems, and the beats of the "heart" manifest an internalization and externalization of Hamlet's "wild and whirling words" after encountering the ghost (1.5.139), his earlier dumb show of amorous passion (evidenced as well in his inarticulate love letter), and his sense of heartbreak combined with an inability to speak out: "But break, my heart, for I must hold my tongue" (1.2.158).

Indeed, while Ophelia disintegrates to the point of madness, almost everyone that Hamlet *touches,* including Ophelia, Gertrude, Polonius, Rosencrantz, Guildenstern, Laertes, and Claudius, dies. The "poison of deep grief," as

Claudius puts it (4.5.75), mutates from the possibility of collective vulnerability—for losses are experienced all around—to a reductive expression of that vulnerability in the heap of corpses at the play's close. That Hamlet does not manage to kill Horatio, a name that of course smacks of oratio, suggests something about the residual power of words to offer at least a retrospective account of all that has been unsaid. But as we saw in the case of Andrea in *The Spanish Tragedy*, and as is well known of Horatio's retrospective account, Horatio's narrative focuses precisely on the action of the play as opposed to the nuances, the half-saids, unsaids, and even the saids through which action itself has come to be riddled with complexity (5.2.385–91). That Hamlet speaks more words in this play than any other character, and that he is often eloquent in solitude, only further emphasizes the problem of how even a surfeit of "words, words, words" can call out for a kind of communication—and a recognition of "deep grief"—that is missing in the play. Hamlet famously throws words back onto recipients so that they might hear another "sense" of just what it is that they have said.[106] But even then he allows his own words to "carry but half sense," leading to a final pathos in which Hamlet is ordered by Fortinbras to be carried "like a soldier to the stage," where "the soldier's music and the rite of war" will "Speak loudly for him" (5.2.401–5). Here, Hamlet is "spoken for" one last time, situated as a kind of armed ghost of himself, and spoken for by a public voice of military mourning that is not at all his own. Shakespeare here undermines theatrical as well as political and public mechanisms that might "speak loudly for" a character who never himself spoke with such an amplified and coherent sense of self.

In his partial or truncated expressions, Hamlet becomes a variant of the ghost who "was about to speak when the cock crew" (1.1.152), who is unable fully to "tell the secretes of [his] prison-house" (1.5.14), and who, leaving Horatio without speaking to him, makes him "tremble & look pale" (1.1.56), as Hamlet hopes to leave his audience upon his death: "You that look pale and tremble at this chance, / That are but mutes or audience to this act." When Hamlet adds, "Had I but time. . . . O I could tell you—/ But let it be," he signals a residual but failed aspiration famously uttered at the end of act 1: "The time is out of joint. O cursed spite, / That I was ever born to set it right" (1.5.196–97). He is of course in the clutches of a time untold, departing himself, as the ghost did, "unhousel'd, disappointed, unanel'd," so many "un" words that pepper the play of tales untold. The telling of time and story is finally unjointed in Hamlet's final lines, "So tell him, with th'occurrents more and less / Which have solicited—the rest is silence" (5.2.366).

The famously inarticulate but precisely punctuated groan, "O, o, o, o," following "—the rest is silence" in the 1623 Folio, suggests a staccato effect, as if we might somehow hear the final pulse of the "noble heart" even as it "cracks." Yet the tragic or even metaphysical tenor of the final inarticulate *o*'s is potentially undermined because it brings to a close the *third* of Hamlet's death speeches. For these *o*'s issue from a man who has already proclaimed "I am dead" some two dozen lines earlier (5.2.343).[107] If the groans recall Hamlet's earlier sense of being unable to "reckon" his "groans" in his letter to Ophelia, they also make his final "silence" less quiet, less "noble," even less effective because he now speaks from within a body in pain, a body having been subject to a "hit, a most palpable hit" (5.2.282). "O, o, o, o," thus represents an impoverished variant of the more subtle forms of subarticulate expression through which the feelings of the living began, over the course of the play, to come to light. At the same time, this inarticulate expression, following the word "silence," encodes another kind of pathos because it further aligns (the already discursively dead) Hamlet with the ghost whose eternal blazon cannot be, and with the many ghosts said to howl without coherence, to "squeak and gibber" as if they are haunts of those inarticulate "thoughts beyond the reaches of our souls" (1.1.119, 1.4.56). It is the eerie haunt of the inarticulate that begins the play and ends Hamlet's life.

In between, Hamlet is not unlike the figure of Harpocrates-Hermes that we considered in the Introduction (see Figure 1). For he embodies neither speech nor silence but a volatile relationship between the two. Harpocrates was famously imagined with a finger on his lips, signifying, as Plutarch wrote, not simply silence but also the fact that "mens language as touching the gods" was as "yet new, unperfect, and not distinct nor articulate."[108] Hamlet, upon acknowledging the ghost as an index of "thoughts beyond the reaches of our souls," asks his companions, "still your fingers on your lips, I pray," and immediately curses his fate in being born, almost god-like, to set right a world "out of joint" (1.5.195–96). "Let it be tenable in your silence still," says Hamlet-Harpocrates to those who have witnessed the ghost: "Give it an understanding but no tongue" (1.2.248, 50). At the same time, as if in a volatile fusion of Harpocrates and Hermes, Hamlet will speak, but will strategically impregnate his speech with unknowable content, "by pronouncing of some doubtful phrase, / As 'Well, we know', or 'We could and if we would', / Or 'If we list to speak', or 'There be and if there might', / Or such ambiguous giving out" (182–87). As he "puts on this confusion" (3.1.2), he opens up spaces of potential meaning beyond communal comprehension but also beyond sheer madness: "what he spake, though it lack'd form a little, / Was not like madness. There's something in his soul / O'er which his melancholy sits on brood," says Claudius, "And I do [not] doubt the hatch and the disclose / Will be some danger" (3.1.165–69). Again the trope of the unsaid, the unhatched, or undisclosed, signals powerful emotional content capable of reaching others, as Ophelia experiences "woe" in the face of Hamlet's "sweet bells jangled and out of tune" (160).

Yet when Hamlet speaks rather more directly through the medium of "The Mousetrap," what was "not like madness" becomes deemed "madness" in fact (3.3.2). The same is the case at Ophelia's funeral, as we have seen, where his direct language of emotional expressiveness is deemed doubly "mad" by Gertrude and Claudius alike. Indeed, it is in the first scene of act 5 that Hamlet, most enmeshed with the element of earth, the element of touch, speaks with passionate *directness*. "We must speak by the card or equivocation will undo us" (133–34), he says in the gravedigger scene, and "I lov'd Ophelia," he proclaims without equivocation in the funeral scene (264). Yet in both cases Hamlet is repeatedly esteemed to be but "mad" (143, 146, 149, 150, 267, 279), so that his directness is recast as a kind of equivocation undone. It is as if his madness, to follow his own earlier metaphor, is itself but a "skin and film" through which others might lose access to the "inward tutch" of their own hearts. Indeed, the very use of the word "mad" in the play occludes a number of its other available meanings including "anger"—which is disavowed through the madness that is insanity or foolishness, a sign of suspended or destabilized judgment—and the "mad" that was also an "earth-worm," from the word for "A maggot, a grub. Also: an insect egg from which a maggot may hatch," related to Hamlet's sense of "politic worms" or "maggots" that eat the body that should be eating (4.3.19–25).[109] It is as if the "skin" of the word becomes calcified, concealing something in as well as under the "skin and film" of language. So it was for T. S. Eliot, who deemed Hamlet, as well as his creator, pathological: "In the character Hamlet it is the buffoonery of an emotion which can find no outlet in action; in the dramatist it is the buffoonery of an emotion which he cannot express in art. The intense feeling, ecstatic or terrible, without an object or exceeding its object, is something which every person of sensibility has known; it is doubtless a study to pathologists."[110]

Revisiting now the question of the "frustrated and inarticulate Shakespeare," we find Stephen Booth in "On the Value of Hamlet" aiming to call a halt to approaches to *Hamlet*—indebted to the innovations of Sigmund Freud, Ernest Jones, and T. S. Eliot—that found the play ultimately "incoherent" and the author "inarticulate" in the face of psychological depths to which he him-self did not have full access. Booth's resistance is, in part, as we have seen, to the influence of Eliot, who called *Hamlet* an "artistic failure," because "Ham-let (the man) is dominated by an emotion which is inexpressible, because it is in *excess* of the facts as they appear" and because the audience "should have to understand things which Shakespeare did not understand himself." "Why he attempted it at all is an insoluble puzzle," wrote Eliot of Shakespeare in "Ham-let and His Problems," "under compulsion of what experience he attempted to express the inexpressibly horrible, we cannot ever know" (101). It is not that Shakespeare "attempted to express the inexpressibly horrible"; rather, he at-tempted to express the horrors of inexpressibility. And in that respect his "artis-tic failure" was an aesthetic triumph. What I have been suggesting here is a version of the "inarticulate Shakespeare" who did understand, and whose play was precisely *about* the power of the inarticulate to index the failure of what Eliot called the "objective correlative" (100). Even in Claudius's experience of the play-within-the-play, if Hamlet believes he is "struck so to the soul," as he puts it, we don't know just what moved Claudius to leave the theater: the mir-ror of nature or the threat of regicide. Through *Hamlet*, precisely by resisting objective correlation, by resisting full articulation in the matter of "sensory experience"—particularly in the matter of what it meant to touch and be touched—Shakespeare produced a drama that would reflect upon aspects of "feeling" that were indeed "difficult to localize," and on the limits of sensory-emotional vocabularies of Hamlet's world, and his own.

As the publisher of the 1603 Quarto of *Hamlet*, Nicholas Ling, put it in 1598, "The sence of touching although it be the last, yet is it the ground of all the rest. / One may liue without sight, hearing, and smelling, but not with-out feeling."[111] If we consider "touch," like the word "feeling," in the sense current at the time, "to mooue or grieue," Ling's statement might well de-scribe the work of theater itself. For to speak and not to move, or to speak and not to be moved, is like being in conversation with someone (or oneself) who is "as the air, invulnerable" (*Hamlet*, 1.1.150). And it is this frustration of non-recognition that drives so much revenge drama of the Renaissance, with ghosts entering where words are dying off, hearts bleeding where love can't be acknowledged, and, in *Titus Andronicus*, hands circulating where touch has been cut off. But what these plays call attention to is the need for a kind of "vulnerable" space between persons, a reciprocal sensitivity to forms of touch that don't die the moment they are pinned down: in short, a social and cultural development of that sense "which is most exquisite in man," the sense of tact. To have "tact" is to have just the right touch, a manifest sensitivity to one's linguistic and social surrounds. And if it is tact, in every sense of the word, at work in the most powerful tragic dramas of the English Renaissance, it may deserve much more of the very recognition it gives.

While we have seen "the body in pain" emerge as a model that resists "objectification in language," this dissolution works, paradoxically, to reify touch as pain, substituting the aliveness of touch as an aspect of affect and knowledge to the conspicuous rupture of an otherwise intact body. This is all the more reason to take seriously the elusiveness of touch to communicative norms; for what is at stake is less the "socialization of sentience" in the Marxian sense than the sensitization of the social in the dramatically literary sense. The inarticulate Renaissance, when not pinned down to bodies in physical pain but opened up for the exploration of representationally resistant forms of individual and collective vulnerability, might lead scholars well beyond pathologies of spoken language as those pathologies helped to secure only emergent norms. It might lead us toward something more like a sense of what it might have meant to be alive in a period definable not simply by humanist and Reformation ideals of eloquence and plain speech, or by the skepticism about effective speech as a vehicle for deception, but by departures from linguistic fluency, clarity, and efficacy that, if and when acknowledged, could suggest other kinds of knowing, thinking, and feeling in the spaces between.

Just who had a Renaissance? The rustic Margorie Mumblecrust and other apparently disempowered speakers, including revengers, lovers, students, scholars, and finally the senses themselves, seem to have had a Renaissance of their own. If this Renaissance was less than articulate, it was all the more productive for those playwrights who would turn to the inarticulate to find something that they didn't already know. This Renaissance on stage allowed for new models of dramatic invention, but also for a variety of cultural phenomena of ineffectual language use to be heard, seen, and experienced by assemblies of people so that they might not simply judge but also learn to listen in new ways to the inarticulate dimensions both of others and of themselves. This inarticulate Renaissance could make the experience of feeling inarticulate less a source of shame or humiliation than a starting point for investigating the deep structure of those feelings, for understanding those feelings as shared, and for finding new ways to make those feelings matter.

NOTES

INTRODUCTION

1. Wayne Rebhorn encourages readers to understand the English and European Renaissance as an "age of rhetoric" rather than an "age of exploration" in *Renaissance Debates on Rhetoric* (Ithaca: Cornell University Press, 2000), 2. While Rebhorn emphasizes the diversity of approaches to the topic of rhetoric in the period (3), "the pursuit of eloquence," as John O. Ward puts it, was "the identifying characteristic of Renaissance humanism—itself the keynote of Renaissance culture" ("Renaissance Commentators on Ciceronian Rhetoric," in *Renaissance Eloquence: Studies in the Theory and Practice of Renaissance Rhetoric*, ed. James J. Murphy [Berkeley: University of California Press, 1983], 126–73, 126). Ward here alludes to Hanna H. Gray's seminal article, "Renaissance Humanism: The Pursuit of Eloquence," *Journal of the History of Ideas* 24, no. 4 (1963): 497–514. Thomas M. Conley's *Rhetoric in the European Tradition* (Chicago: University of Chicago Press, 1990) summarizes the pervasive view that the "interest in rhetoric, in true eloquence," was a "common denominator" of various strands of European humanism through the end of the sixteenth century (109). On the centrality of rhetoric and the pursuit of eloquence in Renaissance English and European culture, see especially Ward; Wayne Rebhorn, *The Emperor of Men's Minds: Literature and the Renaissance Discourse of Rhetoric* (Ithaca: Cornell University Press, 1995); Arthur F. Kinney, *Humanist Poetics: Rhetoric, Thought, and Fiction in Sixteenth-Century England* (Amherst: University of Massachusetts Press, 1986); Brian Vickers, *In Defence of Rhetoric* (Oxford: Oxford University Press, 1989); Vickers, "The Age of Eloquence," *History of European Ideas* 5 (1984): 427–37; Vickers, " 'The Power of Persuasion': Images of the Orator, Elyot to Shakespeare," in *Renaissance Eloquence*, 411–35, and Madeleine Doran, *Endeavors of Art: A Study of Form in Elizabethan Drama* (Madison: University of Wisconsin Press, 1954). For an excellent study of competing conceptions of "plain style," see Debora K. Shuger, *Sacred Rhetoric: The Christian Grand Style in the English Renaissance* (Princeton: Princeton University Press, 1999). See also Neil Rhodes, *The Power of Eloquence and English Renaissance Literature* (New York: St. Martin's Press, 1992), where a "belief in the power of eloquence is perhaps the defining characteristic of the English Literary Renaissance" (vii–viii), and Rhodes's *Shakespeare and the Origins of English* (Oxford:

Oxford University Press, 2004), where he writes that "if expression constitutes the persuasive power of rhetoric, it also constitutes the affective power of literature" (15). See also Russ McDonald, *Shakespeare and the Arts of Language* (Oxford: Oxford University Press, 2001): "The language Shakespeare learned," he writes, "was the language of Renaissance humanism. His artistic achievement was, in other words, the product of a century of self-conscious debate about the power of the word in general and specifically about the potentialities of English for promoting the humanist ideals of eloquence and persuasion" (28).

2. Questions surrounding the cultivation of coherence in oral and textual cultures of the period, I argue, spurred dramatic innovations in ways that have become obscured by the longstanding critical focus on the impact of rhetorical techniques and plain speech alike on developing literary forms. Even scholars focused upon late Renaissance skepticism—within culture and drama—about rhetoric as a vehicle for the common good have paid little attention to alternative forms of perception, expression, and agency that were occasioned by departures from verbal coherence and efficacy. My aims in this book thus also differ from a tradition of scholarship on Renaissance rhetoric that has focused on the ability of persuasion to lead (through *argumentum in utramque partem*, or arguing persuasively on both sides of a question) to the "moral cultivation of ambivalence" (Joel Altman, *Tudor Play of Mind: Rhetorical Inquiry and the Development of Elizabethan Drama* [Berkeley: University of California Press, 1978], chap. 2), as well as to late Renaissance skepticism concerning the injurious as well as palliative dimensions of effective speech. On late Renaissance skepticism about rhetoric's relation to the good, see especially Heinrich F. Plett, "Shakespeare and the *Ars Rhetorica*," in *Rhetoric and Pedagogy: Its History, Philosophy, and Practice: Essays in Honor of James J. Murphy*, ed. Michael Leff (Mahwah, N.J.: Lawrence Erlbaum, 1995), 243–59. On deliberative rhetoric and moral thought, see especially Victoria Kahn, *Rhetoric, Prudence, and Skepticism in the Renaissance* (Ithaca: Cornell University Press, 1985); Kenneth Graham, *The Performance of Conviction: Plainness and Rhetoric in the Early English Renaissance* (Ithaca: Cornell University Press, 1994), and Thomas O. Sloane, *Donne, Milton, and the End of Humanist Rhetoric* (Berkeley: University of California Press, 1985). On the dangers of persuasion in English drama, see especially Brian Vickers, "'The Power of Persuasion'"; Trevor McNeely, *Proteus Unmasked: Sixteenth-Century Rhetoric and the Art of Shakespeare* (Bethlehem, Pa.: Lehigh University Press, 2004); Steven Mullaney, *The Place of the Stage: License, Play, and Power in Renaissance England* (Ann Arbor: University of Michigan Press, 1995); Christy Desmet, *Reading Shakespeare's Characters: Rhetoric, Ethics, and Identity* (Amherst: University of Massachusetts Press, 1992); Peter G. Platt, "Shakespeare and Rhetorical Culture," in *A Companion to Shakespeare,* ed. David Scott Kastan (Oxford: Blackwell, 1999), 277–96.

3. For a different approach to problems of speech in drama that focuses on slander, gossip, and insults as forms of linguistic interference, see Kenneth Gross, *Shakespeare's Noise* (Chicago: University of Chicago Press, 2001). While my focus is on the inefficacy of speech, as opposed to slanderous speech, I take inspiration from Gross's explanation of his keyword,

"noise," associated with "news," which "helps suggest a theater in which the human voice takes shape from the way that language interferes with itself, assumes the power of its own disorder—especially if we recall the word's older associations with disturbance, quarrel, and scandal" (1). On the concept of interference in the domain of acoustics and the stage, with particular attention to the materiality of the actor's voice, see Gina Bloom, *Voice in Motion: Staging Gender, Shaping Sound in Early Modern England* (Philadelphia: University of Pennsylvania Press, 2007), and Bruce R. Smith, *The Acoustic World of Early Modern England: Attending to the O- Factor* (Chicago: University of Chicago Press, 1999). On the often confused and confusing contemporary critical vocabularies through which Renaissance literature has been filtered, see Stanley Stewart, *"Renaissance" Talk: Ordinary Language and the Mystique of Critical Problems* (Pittsburgh: Duquesne University Press, 1997). For important approaches to rhetoric and drama that foreground not the inarticulate but the often unsettling gendered, erotic, and political dimensions of speech, see especially Madhavi Menon, *Wanton Words: Rhetoric and Sexuality in English Renaissance Drama* (Toronto: University of Toronto Press, 2004); Anne Cotterill, *Digressive Voices in Early Modern English Literature* (Oxford: Oxford University Press, 2004); Dympna Callaghan, *Shakespeare Without Women: Representing Gender and Race on the Renaissance Stage* (New York: Routledge, 2000); *Embodied Voices: Representing Female Vocality in Western Culture*, ed. Leslie C. Dunn and Nancy Jones (Cambridge: Cambridge University Press, 1994); Elizabeth D. Harvey, *Ventriloquized Voices: Feminist Theory and English Renaissance Texts* (New York: Routledge, 1992); Patricia Parker, *Literary Fat Ladies: Rhetoric, Gender, Property* (London: Methuen, 1987); and Jane Donawerth, *Shakespeare and the Sixteenth-Century Study of Language* (Urbana: University of Illinois Press, 1984). For an impressive approach to problems of masculinity and rhetorical self-fashioning in Renaissance literature, see Lynn Enterline, *The Tears of Narcissus: Melancholia and Masculinity in Early Modern Writing* (Stanford: Stanford University Press, 1995), and on speech and embodiment, see her *The Rhetoric of the Body from Ovid to Shakespeare* (Cambridge: Cambridge University Press, 2005). On the folk and popular aspects of cultural "mingle-mangle" as it informed representational variety in English drama, see Robert Weimann, *Shakespeare and the Popular Tradition in the Theater: Studies in the Social Dimension of Dramatic Form and Function* (Baltimore: Johns Hopkins University Press, 1978), and "Bifold Authority in Shakespeare's Theatre," *Shakespeare Quarterly* 39, no. 4 (1998): 401–17. Weimann's influential excavation of a "crisis in representation" visible on the Renaissance stage, where a "hodge-podge of social interests" and a mingle-mangle of popular and aristocratic traditions came into explicit conflict ("Bifold Authority," 404), is an important precursor to *The Inarticulate Renaissance*. But whereas I aim to examine inarticulate speech in drama that could not be recuperated by old models of eloquence or emergent models of articulate speech, Weimann ultimately aims to recuperate models of "authority," "appropriation," and *"articulateness"* in the wake of the "crisis of representation," and to locate the Habermasian "project of modernity" in the proliferation of authoritative models of discourse in sixteenth and early seventeenth-century England ("Bifold Authority," 401–2, emphasis added). For another important precursor that focuses specifically on the question of

English dialects, to which I will return in the chapters ahead, see Paula Blank, *Broken English: Dialects and the Politics of Language in Renaissance Writings* (London: Routledge, 1996).

4. Peter Burke, *Languages and Communities in Early Modern Europe* (Cambridge: Cambridge University Press, 2004), 38. On xenophobia and nationalism in Renaissance English drama, see A. J. Hoenselaars, *Images of Englishmen and Foreigners in the Drama of Shakespeare and His Contemporaries: A Study of Stage Characters and National Identity in English Renaissance Drama* (Rutherford, N.J.: Fairleigh Dickinson University Press, 1992).

5. For a contrasting perspective, see Margreta de Grazia's influential "Shakespeare's View of Language: An Historical Perspective," *Shakespeare Quarterly* 29, no. 3 (Summer 1978): 374–88.

6. Plutarch, *The Philosophie, commonlie called, The Morals Vvritten By the learned Philosopher Plutarch of Chaeronea. Translated out of Greeke into English, and conferred with the Latine translations and the French, by Philemon Holland of Coventrie, Doctor in Physicke* (London, 1603), 573–74.

7. Plutarch, *The Philosophie*, 573–74. For sensate but "vnarticulate" creatures, see also John Case, *The Praise of Mvsicke: Wherein besides the antiquitie, dignitie, delectation, & vse thereof in ciuill matters, is also declared the sober and lawfull vse of the same in the congregation and Church of God* (London, 1586), 15; John Davies, *Microcosmos: The Discovery Of The Little World, with the government thereof* (London, 1603), 9, and also Plutarch, *The Philosophie*, 771, 788, and 838. For a later example of the "unarticulate voice," see Thomas Blount, *Glossographia, or, A dictionary interpreting all such hard words of whatsoever language now used in our refined English Tongue* (London, 1633): "*Spher* (Lat.) an Indian, and Aethiopian Beast, rough bodied like an Ape (of the kinde whereof he is) yet hairless between his Neck and Brest, round, but out-faced, and Brested like a woman, his unarticulate voice like that of a hasty speaker, more gentle and tameable then an ordinary Ape, yet fierce by nature, and revengefull, when he is hurt; having eaten meat enough, he reserves his Chaps full to feed on when he feels himself hungry again" (s.v. "Spher"). On Shakespeare in particular and the question of species distinctions, see Terence Hawkes, *Shakespeare's Talking Animals: Language and Drama in Society* (London: Arnold, 1973).

8. I am interested less in well-known, and well-studied, cultural and dramatic constructions of silence than in cultural and dramatic treatments of what a character in a late Tudor play called "tunes without sense, words inarticulate" (Thomas Tomkis, *Lingua: Or the Combat of the Tongue and the five Senses for Superiority* [c. 1602, first printed London, 1607], A4v).

9. Plutarch's allusion here is to Harpocrates. The full quotation reads, "We must not imagine him to be some yoong god, and not come to ripe yeeres, nor yet a man: but that he is the superintendant and reformer of mens language as touching the gods, being yet new, unperfect, and not distinct nor articulate; which is the reason, that he holdeth a seale-ring before his mouth, as a signe and marke of taciturnity and silence" (*The Philosophie*, 1313).

10. Nicholas Ling, *Politeuphuia Wits Common wealth* (London, 1597), 50v.

11. John King (archdeacon of Nottingham), *Lectvres Vpon Ionas Delivered At Yorke In the yeare of our Lorde 1594* (London, 1599), 326.

12. William Fulke, *Praelections vpon the Sacred and holy Reuelation of S. John, written in latine by William Fulke Doctor of Diuinitie, and translated into English by George Gyffard* (London, 1573), 63r. See also William Prynne, *Histrio-mastix. The Players Scourge, Or, Actors Tragaedie, Divided into Two Parts* (London, 1633). If Prynne is to be believed, the theater is the product of a devil who speaks through "*mens mouthes,*" "*send[ing] forth an uncertaine and unarticulate voice,*" capable of reducing actors and playgoers alike to "*Swine buried in the dirt, grunting*" (419–20).

13. The cultural uncertainty about the moral coordinates of indistinct speech are explored, in terms of what we might call "inarticulate vernacularism" and Tudor Protestant polemic, in the first two chapters of this book.

14. Thomas Elyot, *The boke named the Gouernour* (London, 1531). Despite this and other instances of the "articulate," this sense is dated later by the *Oxford English Dictionary* (s.vv. "articulate, a. and n" and "articulate, v." 5 and 6). On this sense of "articulate," see also Pierre de La Primaudaye, *The French Academie. . . . newly translated into English by T. B.* (London, 1586): "The philosophers . . . said that speech is made by aire, beaten and framed with articulate and distinct sound" (127); Nicholas Ling's *Politeuphuia Wits Common wealth* (London, 1597) registered this as a commonplace: "Eloquence is made by ayre; beaten & framed with articulate & distinct sound, yet the reason thereof is hard to bee comprehended by humane sence" (50v).

15. Richard Huloet, *Hvloets Dictionarie, newelye corrected, amended, Set In Order And Enlarged, with many names of Men, Townes, Beastes, Foules, Fishes, Trees, Shrubbes, Herbes, Fruites, Places, Instrumentes &c. And in eche place fit Phrases, gathered out of the best Latin Authors. Also the Frenche therevnto annexed, by vvhich you may finde the Latin or Frenche, of anye English woorde you will. By Iohn Higgins late student in Oxeforde* (London, 1572), C2v.

16. Shakespeare, *Hamlet*, Arden Shakespeare, ed. Harold Jenkins (London: Methuen, 1982), 1.5.196. Hamlet's famous imperative to "set it right" (that is, "the time" or the age, which is "out of joint"), famously invokes the metaphor of the bone setter.

17. See also *The Oxford English Dictionary*, s.v. "articular," first use cited between 1432 and 1450.

18. Ferdinand de Saussure, *Course in General Linguistics*, ed. Charles Bally and Albert Sechehaye, trans. Wade Baskin (New York: McGraw-Hill, 1966), 113. On the shift from eloquence to articulateness, see Neil Rhodes, *Shakespeare and the Origins of English*, which excavates the expressive power of "eloquence" in the Renaissance at times eclipsed in and through the rubric of the "articulate." Conversely, my book foregrounds the expressive power of ineloquence facilitated in and through "inarticulate" grammars, lexicons, and other cultural formations.

19. Philip Sidney, *An Apologie for Poetrie* (London, 1595), L1v. Given, as Derek Attridge puts it, "the intense degree of organization of Latin and Greek verse, by which every syllable was weighted and measured and given appropriate place in the line," vernacular

imitations and translations were "condemned to fall short" ("Puttenham's Perplexity: Nature, Art, and the Supplement in Renaissance Poetic Theory," in *Literary Theory/Renaissance Texts*, ed. Patricia Parker and David Quint [Baltimore: Johns Hopkins University Press, 1986]), 263. Philip Sidney, for one, inverts this logic, urging poets and writers in his *Apologie* to understand Latin as disarticulating ("the Tower of Babilons curse") and English, unleashed from grammatical rule, a generative basis for literary invention: "Whereto our language giveth us great occasion, being indeed capable of any excellent exercising of it. I know some will say it is a mingled language: And why not, so much the better, taking the best of both the other? Another will say, it wanteth Grammer. Nay truthly it hath that praise that it wants not Grammer; for Grammer it might have, but it needs it not, being so easie in it selfe, and so voyd of those cumbersome differences of *Cases, Genders, Moods, & Tenses*, which I think was a peece of the Tower of Babilons curse, that a man should be put to school to learn his mother tongue" (Liv). For an elaboration of Attridge's argument, see Richard Helgerson, *Forms of Nationhood: The Elizabethan Writing of England* (Chicago: University of Chicago Press, 1992), and Paula Blank, *Broken English*. On vernacular "barbarity" in Tudor England, see Richard Foster Jones, *The Triumph of the English Language* (Stanford: Stanford University Press, 1953); Mullaney, *The Place of the Stage,* esp. 60–87; Richard W. Bailey, *Images of English: A Cultural History of the Language* (Ann Arbor: University of Michigan Press, 1991); Juliet Fleming, "Dictionary English and the Female Tongue," in *Enclosure Acts: Sexuality, Property, and Culture in Early Modern England*, ed. Richard Burt and John Michael Archer (Ithaca: Cornell University Press, 1994), 290–325, and Wendy Wall, " 'Household Stuff': The Sexual Politics of Domesticity and the Advent of English Comedy," *English Literary History* 65, no. 1 (1998): 1–45. For a broader approach to vernacular and classical languages on stage, see Janette Dillon, *Language and Stage in Medieval and Renaissance England* (Cambridge: Cambridge University Press, 1998).

20. [Anon.,] *Narcissus: A Twelfe Night Merriment*, ed. Margaret L. Lee (London, 1893), 470, 466–67. "Grammer," as Thomas Wilson put the commonplace in *The rule of Reason, conteinyng the Arte of Logique* (London, 1551), "doth teach to vtter wordes" (B2r).

21. [Anon,]. *Heteroclitanomalonomia* (c. 1613), in *Jacobean Academic Plays*, ed. Suzanne Gossett and Thomas L. Berger, Malone Society Collections, vol. 14 (Oxford: Oxford University Press, 1988), 57–97, 41, 59–60.

22. See Terence Cave, *The Cornucopian Text: Problems of Writing in the French Renaissance* (Oxford: Clarendon Press, 1979); Patricia Parker, *Literary Fat Ladies* and *Shakespeare from the Margins: Language, Culture, Context* (Chicago: University of Chicago Press, 1996); Wayne Rebhorn, *The Emperor of Men's Minds* and " 'His Tail at Commandment': George Puttenham and the Carnivalization of Rhetoric," in *A Companion to Rhetoric and Rhetorical Criticism*, ed. Walter Jost and Wendy Olmsted (Oxford: Blackwell, 2004), 96–111; Cotterill, *Digressive Voices in Early Modern English Literature.*

23. On problems of self-expression in English poetry, see especially Heather Dubrow, *The Challenges of Orpheus: Lyric Poetry and Early Modern England* (Baltimore: Johns Hopkins University Press, 2007). On problems of expression with regard to Herbert's poetry in

particular, see Douglas Trevor, "George Herbert and the Scene of Writing," in *Historicism, Psychoanalysis and Early Modern Culture*, ed. Carla Mazzio and Douglas Trevor (New York: Routledge, 2000), 228–59; Michael Schoenfeldt, *Prayer and Power: George Herbert and Renaissance Courtship* (Chicago: University of Chicago Press, 1991); and Richard Strier, *Love Known: Theology and Experience in Herbert's Poetry* (Chicago: University of Chicago Press, 1983). On the necessity of speech as a cure for grief, as grief existed "amid the fecund incoherence with which early modern culture confronted the passions," see Michael Schoenfeldt, "'Give Sorrow Words': Emotional Loss and the Articulation of Temperament in Early Modern England," in *Dead Lovers: Erotic Bonds and the Study of Premodern Europe*, ed. Basil Dufallo and Peggy McCracken (Ann Arbor: University of Michigan Press, 2007), 143–64, 143.

24. Understanding the significance of inarticulacy *topoi* in literary texts—that is, the eloquent representation of one's own inability to speak well or speak at all—is one thing, as the well-known identification of Renaissance English poets and writers with Philomel, Orpheus, and others make plain. Understanding the inarticulate utterance without the recuperative if paradoxical power of these mythic figures is another. On the power of these classical figures in the English literary imagination, see especially Heather Dubrow, *The Challenges of Orpheus*; Lynn Enterline, *The Rhetoric of the Body from Ovid to Shakespeare*; Sean Keilen, *Vulgar Eloquence: On the Renaissance Invention of English Literature* (New Haven: Yale University Press, 2006); George Steiner, *Language and Silence: Essays on Language, Literature, and the Inhuman* (New Haven: Yale University Press, 1998); and Jonathan Goldberg, *Voice Terminal Echo: Postmodernism and English Renaissance Texts* (New York: Methuen, 1986). For a classically as well as psychoanalytically informed analysis of language failure and melancholy in Renaissance texts, see Lynn Enterline, *The Tears of Narcissus*, and on the eloquent potential of the melancholic speech for male writers and dramatic characters of the Renaissance—in contrast to the depressive "babble" often associated with female speakers and characters—see Juliana Schiesari, *The Gendering of Melancholia: Feminism, Psychoanalysis, and the Symbolics of Loss in Renaissance Literature* (Ithaca: Cornell University Press, 1992). On women and silence, see especially Suzanne W. Hull's important *Chaste, Silent, and Obedient: English Books for Woman, 1575–1640* (San Marino, Calif.: Huntington Library, 1982); Christina Luckyj, *"A Moving Rhetorick": Gender and Silence in Early Modern England* (Manchester: Manchester University Press, 2002); Peter Stallybrass, "Patriarchal Territories: The Body Enclosed," in *Rewriting the Renaissance: The Discourses of Sexual Difference in Early Modern Europe*, ed. Margaret W. Ferguson, Maureen Quilligan, and Nancy J. Vickers (Chicago: University of Chicago Press, 1986), 123–42; Tita French Baumlin, "'A good (wo)man skilled in speaking,'" in *Ethos: New Essays in Rhetorical and Critical Theory*, ed. James S. Baumlin and Tita French Baumlin (Dallas: Southern Methodist University Press, 1994), 229–64; and Danielle Clarke, "'Formed into words by your divided lips': Women, Rhetoric and the Ovidian Tradition," in *"This Double Voice": Gendered Writing in Early Modern England*, ed. Danielle Clarke and Elizabeth Clarke (Basingstoke: Macmillan Press, 2000), 61–87.

25. Abraham Fraunce, *The Lawiers Logike, exemplifying the praecepts of Logike by the practise of the common Lawe* (London, 1588), preface, 3v–4r.

26. Ibid., 3r–v, 119v. On Renaissance ABCs, see especially Elizabeth Eisenstein, "An Unacknowledged Revolution Revisited," *American Historical Review* 107, no. 1 (February 2002): 87–105. On Adrian Johns's suggestion, in *The Nature of the Book: Print and Knowledge in the Making* (Chicago: University of Chicago Press, 1998), that all early modern books, "from lowly almanacs to costly folios," "from the humblest ABC to the most elaborate encyclopedia," were "so unreliable that no reader would credit their contents without foreknowledge of the conditions under which they were printed," Eisenstein writes, "It is difficult to imagine real readers of ABC books being concerned about such matters. There is no evidence that they were" (88). For an analysis of conditions of book use as they led to problems as well as possibilities of cognitive coherence, see Bradin Cormack and Carla Mazzio, *Book Use, Book Theory: 1500–1700* (Chicago: University of Chicago Library, distributed by University of Chicago Press, 2005).

27. Edward Coke, *Le Quart Part Des Reportes Del Edward Coke Chiualier* (London, 1604), B3v (emphasis added).

28. On the power of printed commonplace books and the spread of reading practices focused on the gathering of textual parts to dislodge eloquence from an aristocratic milieu and enable "upward mobility in the newly bureaucratized state," see Mary Thomas Crane, *Framing Authority: Sayings, Self, and Society in Sixteenth-Century England* (Princeton: Princeton University Press, 1993), 43. For a complication of Crane's argument, see Rebecca W. Bushnell, *A Culture of Teaching: Early Modern Humanism in Theory and Practice* (Ithaca: Cornell University Press, 1996), which argues that the emergence of a neoclassical ideal of organic wholeness, unity, and order in late Tudor England rendered fragmentary reading "superfluous" (120).

29. On print culture and anxieties of oral performance in the Renaissance (and on orality as a back-formation), see my "Sins of the Tongue in Early Modern England," *Modern Language Studies* 28, no. 4 (Autumn 1998): 93–124, which is an expansion of "Sins of the Tongue," in *The Body in Parts: Fantasies of Corporeality in Early Modern Europe*, ed. David Hillman and Carla Mazzio (New York: Routledge, 1997), 53–79. On the interanimation of oral and textual communities in the premodern period, see especially Brian Stock, *Listening for the Text: On the Uses of the Past* (Philadelphia: University of Pennsylvania Press, 1997) and Martin Elsky, *Authorizing Words: Speech, Writing, and Print in the English Renaissance* (Ithaca: Cornell University Press, 1989).

30. For a seminal treatment of the spatial and ideological "place" of the Renaissance stage, see Mullaney, *The Place of the Stage*.

31. On Abraham Fraunce's *Victoria*, see especially Horst-Dieter Blume, ed., *Hymenaeus, Abraham Fraunce, Victoria, Laelia*, Renaissance Latin Drama in England series, vol. 13 (Hildesheim: Georg Olms Verlag, 1991), 29–48; G. C. Moore Smith, *Victoria, A Latin Comedy by Abraham Fraunce*, Materialien zur Kunde des älteren englischen Dramas series, vol. XIV (Louvain: A. Uystpruyst, 1906); and Frederick Boas, *University Drama in*

the *Tudor Age* (Oxford: Clarendon Press, 1914), 140–46. See also Abraham Fraunce, *Victoria (c. 1583): A Hypertext Critical Edition*, ed. and trans. Dana F. Sutton, *The Philological Museum* (Birmingham: Shakespeare Institute, University of Birmingham, 2001), at: www.philological.bham.ac.uk.

32. Abraham Fraunce, *Victoria*: ed. Sutton, "Vigilabo hac nocte usque ad gallicinium in pervolvendis Zwinggeri tabulis" (5.8.1910–11).

33. By 1586, Zwinger's *Theatrum* had quadrupled in size, gradually expanding into five separate volumes. On Zwinger, see Ann Blair, "Reading Strategies for Coping with Information Overload ca. 1550–1700," *Journal of the History of Ideas* 64, no. 1 (2003): 11–28. Dana F. Sutton (*Victoria*) reads Fraunce's invocation of Zwinger as an allusion to his *Morum philosopia poetica ex veterum utriusque linguae Poetarum thesaurus* (Basel, 1575), a book of poetic commonplaces, topically arranged.

34. The particular pedant singled out here was in fact Fraunce's single most significant addition to Luigi Pasqualio's Italian *Il Fidele* (1576), the play upon which *Victoria* was based.

35. Erving Goffman, *Interactional Ritual: Essays in Face to Face Behavior* (New York: Pantheon, 1967), 125.

36. Erving Goffman, *Forms of Talk* (Philadelphia: University of Pennsylvania Press, 1981), 85.

37. By examining the significance of speech as it departed from techniques of humanist persuasion and from Protestant plainness and bibliocentrism, I differ from scholarship that has postulated Tudor dramatic development as a product of one or both of these developing practices and ideologies. See especially Kent Cartwright's *Theatre and Humanism: English Drama in the Sixteenth Century* (Cambridge: Cambridge University Press, 1999), which argues for the centrality of persuasive affect within humanism as it gave rise to a new tradition of drama that departed from the didacticism of medieval drama; Lorna Hutson's scholarship on humanist and legal rhetoric on Tudor dramatic development ("Forensic Aspects of Renaissance Mimesis," *Representations* 94 [Spring 2006]: 80–109); and John N. King's work on Protestant drama, *English Reformation Literature: The Tudor Origins of the Protestant Tradition* (Princeton: Princeton University Press, 1986). For a broader approach to literature, humanism, and Reformation scripturalism that I depart from in Chapters 1 and 2, see Janel Mueller, *The Native Tongue and the Word: Developments in English Prose Style 1380–1580* (Chicago: University of Chicago Press, 1984).

38. *Precepts*, trans. Marcus Fabius Calvus (Rome, 1525), and Rodericus à Fonseca, *In Septem Aphorismum Hippocratis Libros Commentaria* (Venice, 1595), both cited in Jeffrey Wollock's invaluable history of speech disorders, *The Noblest Animate Motion: Speech, Physiology and Medicine in Pre-Cartesian Linguistic Thought* (Amsterdam: John Benjamins, 1997), 296, 252.

39. Jeffery Wollock, *The Noblest Animate Motion*. My book, however, explores how such interior states as fury and as-yet-unformulated thought can be registers of larger cultural uncertainties and tensions. This is not to say that speech disorders are not often

effects of individual biology and personal conditions, but rather to say that the writers and the dramatists I take up in the chapters that follow speak to a culture in which new patterns of inarticulacy and attendant affects were coming into view.

40. On learned ignorance in the Renaissance, see Rosalie L. Colie, *Paradoxia Epidemica: The Renaissance Tradition of Paradox* (Princeton: Princeton University Press, 1966).

41. See Herbert Marks, "On Prophetic Stammering," in *The Book and the Text: The Bible in Literary Theory*, ed. Regina Schwartz (Oxford: Blackwell, 1990), 60–80; Mark Shell, "Moses' Tongue," *Common Knowledge* 12, no. 1 (2006): 150–76, and *Stutter* (Cambridge, Mass.: Harvard University Press, 2006).

42. Giovanni Pico della Mirandola, "Letter to Ermolao Barbaro," in *Renaissance Debates on Rhetoric*, ed. Wayne Rebhorn (Ithaca: Cornell University Press, 2000), 62, 59.

43. Ibid., 61, 62.

44. Ibid., 66. See Cicero, *De inventione*, trans. H. M. Hubbell (Cambridge, Mass.: Harvard University Press, 1949), where "To me, at least, it does not seem possible that a mute and voiceless wisdom could have turned men suddenly from their habits and introduced them to different patterns of life" (1.2.2–3). See also Cicero, *De officiis*, or *On Duties*, ed. M. T. Griffin and E. M. Atkins, trans. Griffin (Cambridge: Cambridge University Press, 1991), where "it is better to speak at length, provided one does so wisely, than to think, however penetratingly, without eloquence. For speculation turns in on itself, but eloquence embraces those to whom we are joined by social life" (1.156). Cicero of course emphasizes the opposite as well; eloquence without wisdom can lead to the ruin of civilization: "If we bestow fluency of speech on persons devoid of those virtues [of wisdom], we shall not have made orators of them but shall have put weapons into the hands of madmen" (*De oratore*, ed. H. Rackham, trans. E. W. Sutton [Cambridge, Mass.: Harvard University Press, 1949], 3.14.55).

45. See Corinthians, "And I, brethren, when I came to you, came not with excellency of speech or of wisdom, declaring unto you the testimony of God" (2:1); "And my speech and my preaching was not with enticing words of man's wisdom, but in demonstration of the Spirit and of power" (2:4); "Howbeit we speak wisdom among them that are perfect: yet not the wisdom of this world, nor of the princes of this world, that come to nought'" (2:6); "But we speak the wisdom of God in a mystery, even the hidden wisdom, which God ordained before the world unto our glory" (2:7); and "But as it is written, Eye hath not seen, nor ear heard, neither have entered into the heart of man, the things which God hath prepared for them that love him" (2:9).

46. Erasmus, *Moriae Encomium* (1509); *The praise of Folie. Moriae encomivm a booke made in latine by that great clerke Erasmus Roterodame. Englisshed by sir Thomas Chaloner knight* (London, 1549), T3r. The full passage in the 1509 text reads: "Hoc igitur quibus sentire licuit contingit autem perpaucis ii patiuntur quiddam dementiae simillimum, *loquuntur quaedam non satis coherentia*, nec humano more, sed dant sine mente sonum, deinde subinde totam oris speciem vertunt. Nunc alacres, nunc dejecti, nunc lacrymant, nunc rident, nunc suspirant; in summa, vere toti extra se sunt. Mox ubi ad ses redierint, negant

se scire, ubi fuerint, utrum in corpore, an extra corpus, vigilantes an dormientes, quid au-
dierint, quid viderint, quid dixerint, quid fecerint, non meminerunt, nisi tamquam per
nebulam, ac somnium, tantum hoc scient se felicissimos fuisse, dum ita desiperent. Itaque
plorant sese resipuisse, nihilque omnium malint, quam hoc insaniae genus perpetua in-
snire. Atque haec est futurae felicitates tenuis quaedam degustatiuncula." In M. A. Screech,
Erasmus: Ecstasy and the Praise of Folly (New York: Penguin, 1980), Appendix A, 255
(Screech's addition of italics and parentheses have been deleted, my own italics added).
John Wilson's later translation of Erasmus follows Chaloner, particularly in his rendering
of "*loquuntur quaedam non satis coherentia*" (*coherentia* being "to cling together, be united,
hang together"); "they utter many things, that do not hang together, and that too, not after
the manner of men, but make a kind of sound, which they neither heed themselves, nor is
understood by others, and change the whole figure of their countenance" (Erasmus, *Moriae Encomivm; Or, The Praise of Folly* [London, 1668, 159]). As White Kennett renders it,
the Latin "*non satis cohaerentia*" becomes "inarticulate noise, without any distinguishable
sense, or meaning" (*Witt against Wisdom. Or, A Panegyrick Upon Folly: Penn'd in Latin by
Desiderius Erasmus, Render'd into English* [Oxford, 1683], 155). The text that precedes this
passage in Erasmus invokes Corinthians 2:9: "Hoc nimirum est quod pollicetur Propheta:
Oculus non vidit, nec auris audivit, nec in cor hominis adscenderunt, quae praeparavit
Deus diligentibus se" (255), or "This is surely what the prophet has promised: 'Eye hath
not seen, nor ear heard, neither have entered into the heart of man the things which God
hath prepared them that love him.'" For an intensive analysis of "ecstacy" in *The Praise of
Folly*, see Screech, esp. 130–222.

    47. See Erasmus's letter to Maarten Van Dorp in *Praise of Folly and Letter to Martin
Dorp 1515: Erasmus of Rotterdam,* ed. and trans. Betty Radice (New York: Penguin, 1982),
158. For recent approaches to Erasmus and Christian rhetoric, see especially Marjorie
O'Rourke Boyle, "A Conversation Opener: The Rhetorical Paradigm of John 1:1," in *A
Companion to Rhetoric and Rhetorical Criticism,* ed. Walter Jost and Wendy Olmsted (Oxford: Blackwell, 2004), 58–79, and Thomas O. Sloane, "Rhetorical Selfhood in Erasmus
and Milton," also in *A Companion to Rhetoric and Rhetorical Criticism,* 112–27.

    48. Erasmus, "An Exhortacion to the diligent studye of Scripture," prefaced to William
Tyndale's translation *The Newe Testament of oure Saueour Jesus Christ translated by M. Wil.
Tyndall, yet once agayno [sic] corrected with new annotacyons very necessary to better onderstondynge; where vnto is added an exhortacion to the same of Erasmus Rotero* (London, 1549), *B2v.
Indeed, "What is philosophy?" is a question leading to the fact that, for Erasmus, there is
only one "fruitful" kind: "This kind of philosophy doth rather consist in the affectes of the
mynde, then in sotle [subtle] reasons" (*B2v). The "darke misterie" of the word should be
encountered on its own terms, as "a liffe rather then a disputation," "an inspiracion rather
then a science," "rather a newe transformation then a reasonynge" (*B2v). Scripture, even
in translation, should "rauyshe & transforme," leaving readers "in another mynde then they
were before" (*A1v). See also Erasmus's *Paraclesis* (1516) in *The Praise of Folly and Other Writings,* ed. and trans. Robert M. Adams (New York: Norton, 1989), 118–27.

49. Erasmus, "An Exhortacion to the diligent studye of Scripture," *A4r, *C2r.

50. Erasmus, "The preface of Erasmus vnto his paraphrase vpon the ghospell of Luke," *The first tome or volume of the Paraphrase of Erasmus vpon the newe testamente*, ed. and trans. Nicholas Udall (London, 1548), Bb4r. See also Erasmus's dedication in *Paraphrasis in evangelium Lucae*, in *Opera Omnia*, 11 vols. (Leiden, 1703–6), 7:271–80. Drawing on Luke (17:5–6), Erasmus writes, "No power of humayne eloquence could this haue dooen: but the godlye power of the trueth was hable, whiche laye hidden in the graine of mustardsede," but elaborates: "Talke euangelicall is of a playne homely sorte, of no eloquent composyng" (Bb4r). Erasmus explicitly contrasts the syntactical and stylistic *discomposure* of evangelical writing with the eloquence of secular writing, challenging the civilizing potential of humanist rhetoric: "What a noumbre of thynges dooe the Euangelistes leat passe, howe manye thynges dooe they touche with three woordes and no more in how many places dooeth the ordre disagree, and in how many places dooe they appere to be one contrarie vnto another? It was possible that suche things should haue turned awaye the mynde of the reader from the readyng of it, and should haue caused it neuer to be beleued. Contrariwyse they that haue written stories of worldly affaires, how carefull are they wherof to make the first begynnyng of the matter, what labour & diligence do they bestowe, that thei maye not tell anye thyng otherwyse then is semyng, that they maye not tell any thyng vnlykely, that they maye not tell any thyng not standyng together, or any thynges contrary vnto reason?" (Bb4r). Here Erasmus defends the appearance of disarticulated, inconsistent, and indecorous evangelical composition precisely by pitting it against the rigor of secular humanist *imitatio*. Lauding a "homely" discourse of disagreeable "ordre" and unnamed "thynges" functions to counter intercultural as well as international difference, offering a vivid genealogy of invention that subtends Erasmus's sociopolitical radicalism: "And by what maner felowes at last dyd so great a chaunge of the worlde firste come vp? by meane of a fewe disciples beeyng menne vnknowen, men of lowe degree, men of pouertie, & vnlearned. To what purpose is it to speake of the rest, whan Peter the chiefe of them was a fisher, and of no ferther knowlage but his bare mother toungue, Paule a leather sewer, and not one of them all, a man of rychesse, or a man of power, or a ientle man? . . . And by what wayes was it possible for suche men to bryng so great a matier to passe?" (Bb4r).

The charismatic *vir bonus* of humanist oratorical force pales in comparison to the discoveries of great "matier" by the unlearned, the unknown, and the laboring poor. On Erasmus and ineloquence in secular as well as sacred matters, see especially "Herculei labores" ("the labors of Hercules"), in the *Adages*, trans. and annotated by R. A. B. Mynors, in *The Collected Works of Erasmus*, vol. 33 (Toronto: University of Toronto Press, 1992), 170–80. As Erasmus puts it here of his own disarticulated compositional process, "Cicero does not demand eloquence from a philosopher" (177), and "I am not too deeply moved by Horace's principle," for "he laid down a law for writers of poetry, in which, as Pliny tells us, the highest degree of eloquence is needed; I am making a collection of adages" (180). This entry positions scholarly labor as distinct from the eloquence of those who only pretend to learning. If such orators, Erasmus posits, "ever made an experiment to discover what it means to devote whole books" to commonplaces of antiquity, "perhaps they would recognize how inarticulate they are" and how eloquent classical authors are, rather than dismissing works as "tongue-tied, dumb and inarticulate in which they have not found their four precious words from Cicero" (178). Here Erasmus exposes how casting others persons or texts as "tongue-tied, dumb and inarticulate" functions as a way to disavow one's own ignorance and inarticulacy, yet he himself had no trouble raging against "inarticulate" others.

51. Gilles Deleuze and Félix Guattari, *What Is Philosophy?* (New York: Columbia University Press, 1991), 69.

52. Ibid., 55.

53. Ibid., 55.

54. Avital Ronell, *Stupidity* (Urbana: University of Illinois Press, 2003), 103. I thank Lauren Berlant for calling this book to my attention.

55. Ibid., 66.

56. Ibid., 103.

57. On "incoherence" made manifest through poststructuralist "theoretical discourse" (itself "at one with the demonstration of the necessary incoherence and impossibility of all thinking") see Frederic Jameson, *Postmodernism: Or, the Cultural Logic of Late Capitalism* (Durham: Duke University Press, 1991), 218.

58. In devotional terms, for Augustine, "superfluity of words" thwarts communication with God, for prayer "consists more in groaning than in speaking, in tears rather than in words" (465). See *Letters of St. Augustine*, Letter CXXX.19 in *Nicene and Post Nicene Fathers of the Christian Church*, vol. 1, trans. Rev. J. G. Cunningham, ed. Philip Schaff (Grand Rapids, Mich.: Eerdmans, 1956). On Paul and the inexpressibility *topos*, see Paul W. Gooch, "Margaret, Bottom, Paul and the Inexpressible," *Word and World* 6, no. 3 (June 1986): 313–26.

59. For a brilliant analysis of premature "modernity" in contemporary approaches to Shakespeare's *Hamlet* and Renaissance culture, see Margreta de Grazia, *Hamlet Without Hamlet* (Cambridge: Cambridge University Press, 2007).

60. As a medium uniquely suited to complex arrangements of classical and contemporary material, Tudor drama may seem to offer a particular nexus for scholars of the (retrospectively oriented) Renaissance and the (prospectively imagined) early modern. The inarticulate subject, the focus of this book, may well be understood as the hallmark of postmodern conceptions of subjectivity, be it in the form of Giorgio Agamben's *Infanzia e storia. Distruzione dell'esperienza e origine della storia* (Turin: Einaudi, 1978), where "infancy" (from *infans*, incapable of speech) becomes the key to experience mediated by language and history, or Slavoj Žižek's *The Indivisible Remainder: An Essay on Schelling and Related Matters* (London: Verso, 1996), where the inarticulate conditions narrative itself: "Every narrative eventually endeavors to provide an answer to the enigma of how things got out of joint, how the old 'authentic' ties disintegrated" (42). But such a totalizing theory of narrative presumes that, in Žižek's words, the "subject is in the most radical sense 'out of joint';

it constitutively lacks its own place" (43). This insight may well be anticipated in sacred discourses of the Renaissance (*memento mori* itself a constant reminder to forget one's place) and even be operative in early secular contexts, but just like eloquence, inarticulacy demands attention to the particular significance of time, place, and circumstance, as well as to genres, languages, and particular historical contexts, in the formation of the inarticulate subject. On the "disarticulation of language from 'historical and political systems,' from the syntax of the sentence from the syntax of the skeleton" (45) in early and postmodern contexts, see Marjorie Garber, "Out of Joint," in Hillman and Mazzio, *The Body in Parts*, 22–51.

61. Ronell, *Stupidity*, 147.

62. Marjorie Garber, seminar on Shakespeare, Renaissance Workshop, University of Chicago, April 26, 2007. On the problem of historicism as a default mode of literary study, see Carla Mazzio and Douglas Trevor, "Dreams of History," in *Historicism, Psychoanalysis, and Early Modern Culture* (New York: Routledge, 2000), 1–19, and Marjorie Garber, *A Manifesto for Literary Studies* (Seattle: University of Washington Press, 2003). As Stephen Greenblatt puts it in *Hamlet in Purgatory* (Princeton: Princeton University Press, 2001), "My profession has become so oddly diffident and even phobic about literary power, so suspicious and tense, that it risks losing sight of—or at least failing to articulate—the whole reason anyone bothers with the enterprise in the first place" (4).

63. Anthony Grafton and Lisa Jardine, *From Humanism to the Humanities: Education and the Liberal Arts in Fifteenth- and Sixteenth-Century Europe* (Cambridge, Mass.: Harvard University Press, 1986). Or as Richard A. Lanham puts it in *The Electronic Word: Democracy, Technology, and the Arts* (Chicago: University of Chicago Press, 1993), "The 'humanist' task may pass to other groups while the humanities dwindle into grumpy antiquarianism" (228). While I draw from Grafton and Jardine's complication of ideals of persuasion within humanist educational culture, I focus on the history of ineffectual language use and aim to demonstrate how problems of rhetorical coherence gave rise to possibilities of dramatic innovation. For challenges to Grafton and Jardine, see Paul F. Grendler on Italy, *Schooling in Renaissance Italy: Literacy and Learning, 1300–1600* (Baltimore: Johns Hopkins University Press, 1989), and Rebecca Bushnell on England, *A Culture of Teaching*.

64. For a sensitive approach to the distinction between "indeterminacy" and inarticulateness from an anthropological and literary perspective, see Kirsten Hastrup, "The Inarticulate Mind: The Place of Awareness in Social interaction," in *Questions of Consciousness*, ed. Anthony Cohen and Nigel Rapport (London, Routledge, 1995), 181–97.

65. Or conversely, in directing our concerns toward contemporary forms of *un*intelligibility through which literary study itself has appeared to many as a disturbingly "incoherent" set of practices, methods, and aims, we might focus more sharply on historical conditions informing incoherence-intolerance. For an early and classical approach to the "mythology of coherence" in historical method, see Quentin Skinner, "Meaning and Understanding in the History of Ideas," *History and Theory* 8 (1969): 3–53, and for a histori-

cal approach to methodological "incoherence" in literary study in particular, see Mary Poovey, "Beyond the Current Impase in Literary Studies," *American Literary History* 11, no. 2 (1999): 354–77.

Note to epigraph: Thomas Tomkis, *Lingua: Or The Combat of the Tongue, And the fiue Senses for Superiority. A pleasant Comoedie* (c. 1602, first printed, London, 1607), M2v.

1. John Jewel, *Oratio contra Rhetoricam* (c. 1548), or "Oration Against Rhetoric," in *Renaissance Debates on Rhetoric*, ed. and trans. Wayne Rebhorn (Ithaca: Cornell University Press, 1999), 162–72, 164. On the dating and tenor of Jewel's oration, see especially H. H. Hudson, "Jewel's Oration Against Rhetoric: A Translation," *Quarterly Journal of Speech*, 14 (1928): 374–92, and Brian Vickers's *In Defence of Rhetoric*, 3rd rev. ed. (Oxford: Oxford University Press, 1997), 188–89.

2. Thomas Wilson, *The Arte of Rhetorique* (London, 1553), Gg1r–v. I've added a hyphen in Wilson's original "propronounce," to emphasize my sense that it is not a typographic error (later corrected as such) but an attempt at comic, textual mispronunciation; Wilson, *The three Orations of Demosthenes chiefe orator among the Grecians, in Favor of the Olynthians . . . with those his four orations . . . Against King Philip of Macedonie* (London, 1570), 110–11.

3. See, for example, Wilson's *The Arte of Rhetorique* (esp. Gg1v–Gg2r); George Puttenham's *The Arte of English Poesie* (London, 1589), 120–21, and for a later aproach to pronunciation, see Alexander Gill's *Logonomia Anglica* (London, 1619). On harsh vocal sounds, heavied and slowed speech, and vowel pronunciation in speech affecting rusticity (that sounds less like oratory than the speech of "messores," farm laborers) in Cicero, see *De oratore*, ed. H. Rackham, trans. E. W. Sutton (Cambridge, Mass.: Harvard University Press, 1949) 3.40–45. In *Brutus*, as Brutus puts it, such alien enunciative habits necessitate a "purge of language" (*expurgandus est sermo*) and a grammatically based regulation of language "not subject to change," *Brutus*, ed. and trans. G. L. Hendrickson (Cambridge, Mass.: Harvard University Press, 1971), 258. On pronunciation in republican Rome, see Edwin S. Ramage, "Cicero on Extra-Roman Speech," *Transactions and Proceedings of the American Philological Association* 92 (1961): 481–94, and Louise Adam Holland, *Lucretius and the Transpadanes* (Princeton: Princeton University Press, 1979). For a broader perspective on Latin textuality and pronunciation, see Paul Saenger, *Space Between Words: The Origins of Silent Reading* (Stanford: Stanford University Press, 2000).

4. This chapter will focus in particular on John Jewel's engagement with early Latin Christianity. On Reformation approaches to spoken utterance more generally, see especially Ramie Targoff, *Common Prayer: The Language of Public Devotion in Early Modern England* (Chicago: University of Chicago Press, 2001), esp. 18, and on the reformation of the Word in speech and writing, see Janel Mueller, *The Native Tongue and the Word: Develop-*

ments in English Prose Style 1380–1580 (Chicago: University of Chicago Press, 1984). Also, in more positive terms, in Catholic and Reformation theology we find no dearth of attention to indistinct speech in the form of prophetic stammering or devotional utterances replaced by tears and groans. On stammering, see Herbert Marks, "On Prophetic Stammering," in *The Book and the Text: The Bible and Literary Theory*, ed. Regina Schwartz (Oxford: Blackwell, 1990), 60–80, and on prayer that "consists more in groaning than in speaking, in tears rather than in words," see *Letters of St. Augustine* in *Nicene and Post Nicene Fathers of the Christian Church*, vol. 1, trans. Rev. J. G. Cunningham, ed. Philip Schaff (Grand Rapids, Mich.: Eerdmans, 1956), Letter CXXX.19, 465. On Moses's slowness of speech in particular, see Mark Shell, "Moses' Tongue," *Common Knowledge* 12, no. 1: 150–76, and *Stutter* (Cambridge, Mass.: Harvard University Press, 2006).

5. John Jewel, *An Apologie or answere in defence of the Churche of Englande, with a briefe and plaine declaration of the true Religion professed and vsed in the same,* trans. Lady Anne Bacon (London, 1564), K6r–v. Jewel's *Apologie* was printed in Latin and English in 1562. Unless otherwise noted, I will be citing the revised translation by Lady Anne Bacon of 1564.

6. On the physiology of speech from antiquity to the Renaissance, see Jeffrey Wollock, *The Noblest Animate Motion: Speech, Physiology and Medicine in Pre-Cartesian Linguistic Thought* (Amsterdam: John Benjamins, 1997).

7. William Tyndale, *The obedie[n]ce of a Christen man* (Antwerp, 1528), B5v. On the first known use of "mumble vp," see F. J. Mozley, "The English *Enchiridion* of Erasmus, 1533," *The Review of English Studies*, 20, no. 78 (April 1944): 97–107, 106. Jewel's *Apologia Ecclesiae Anglicanae* (London, 1562), reads: "Vetus Imperator Iustinianus, iussit in sacro ministerio omnia clara, & quam maxime arguta & expressa uoce pronuntiari, ut fructus ex ea re aliquis ad populum redire posset. Isti ne quid populus intelligat, omnia sua non tantum obscura & summissa uoce, sed etiam aliena, & Barbara lingua mussitant," E5v–E6r. On "priuate Masses in euery cornere or that be mumbled vp" in "the holy seruice with a lowe voice and in an vnknowen language," see Jewel, *An Apologie* (1564), P6r.

8. See, for example, John Florio, *A Worlde of Wordes, Or Most copious, and exact Dictionarie in Italian and English* (London, 1598), s.v. "mussare."

9. Even contemporary translations rarely invoke "mumble": for an exception, see Job 27:4 in *God's Word* (Cleveland: God's Word to the Nations, 1995).

10. "To mumble" derives from the Middle Low German *mummelen*, German *mummeln*, and Middle Dutch *mommelen, mummelen* (Dutch *mommelen, mummelen*). See *Oxford English Dictionary*, s.v. "mumble."

11. On rhetorical self-fashioning, see Stephen Greenblatt, *Renaissance Self-Fashioning: More to Shakespeare* (Chicago: University of Chicago Press, 1980).

12. For one of the most influential challenges to Jacob Burckhardt's "rise of the individual," see Peter Stallybrass, "Shakespeare, the Individual and the Text," in *Cultural Studies*, ed. Lawrence Greenberg, Cary Nelson, and Paula Treichler (New York: Routledge, 1992), 593–612, esp. 606. See also David Aers, "A Whisper in the Ear of Early Modernists;

or, Reflections on Literary Critics Writing the 'History of the Subject,'" in *Culture and History, 1350–1600: Essays on English Communities, Identities and Writing*, ed. David Aers (Detroit: Wayne State University Press, 1992), 177–203. On the "individual," see especially Jacob Burckhardt, *The Civilization of the Renaissance in Italy* (London: Phaidon Press, 1960), and Max Weber, *The Protestant Ethic and the Spirit of Capitalism* (New York: Routledge, 2001).

13. Hugh Latimer (describing Catholic liturgical utterance), *27 sermons preached by the ryght Reuerende father in God* (London, 1562), B8r. On the relation between "Bible" and "Babel" potentially implied in early uses of "bibble-babble," see Janette Dillon, *Language and Stage in Medieval and Renaissance England* (Cambridge: Cambridge University Press, 1998), 27.

14. Thomas Becon, *The Jewel of Joy, in The Catechism . . . with other works written in the Reign of Edward VI*, ed. A. J. Ayre, Parker Society Publications, vol. 3 (Cambridge: Cambridge University Press, 1844), 414. On "Masse mumbling," see John Foxe, *The Pope Confuted. The holy and Apostolique Church confuting the Pope. The first Action. Translated out of Latine into English, by Iames Bell* (London, 1580), 11.

15. See Jewel, *An Apologie, or aunswer in defence of the Church of England, concerninge the state of Religion vsed in the same. Newly set forth in Latin, and nowe translated into Englishe* (London, 1562).

16. Thomas Harding, reprinted in Jewel, *A Defence of the Apologie of the Church of Englande, conteining an Answeare to a certaine Booke lately set foorthe by M. Hardinge, and Entituled, A Confutation of &c.* (London: 1567), 515, emphasis added. Unless otherwise noted, all citations from Harding, and responses by Jewel to Harding, refer to this edition.

17. As the 1562 translation reads, "That auncient Emperor Iustinian commaunded yt al things in the holy administration of the Church should be pronounced wt a clere, a loude, and an open voice, that some fruite might come therof to the people. These men, least the people should vnderstande somewhat, doe whysper al their holy misteries, not only with an vncertaine & a lowe voice, but also in a strange and a barbarouse tong" (43v).

18. Thomas Stapleton would call Jewel's prose "childish . . . rascall wrangling." Stapleton, *A Retur[ne of vn]truthes vpon [M. Jewel]les Replie Partly of such, as he hath Slaunderously charged Harding withal* (Antwerp, 1566), 121r–v.

19. *Murmurare* was indeed glossed in later bilingual dictionaries as a "mumble" or "mumbling," but the slight misfit between the two words, emphasized by Harding, is still worth exploring. See, for example, Peter Levens, *Manipvlvs Vocabvlorvm. A Dictionarie of English and Latine wordes* (London, 1570), s.v. "mumble"; a variant in Thomas Cooper, *Thesavrvs Lingvae Romanae & Britannicae* (London, 1584), s.v. "Immurmuro, immurmuras, pe. cor. Immurmurare," and Thomae Thomasii (Thomas Thomas), *Dictionarivm lingvae Latinae et Anglicanae. In hoc opere qvid sit præstitum, & ad superiores λεξικογραφονς adiectum, docebit epistola ad Lectorem* (London, 1587), s. vv. "demurmuro," "murmur," and "mussitatio."

20. "Protestantism had no monopoly on the Word," notes Felicity Heal, "but it re-

mained the faith that had to be proved by the authority of the text. For the learned and the ideologically committed this meant that words had to be pondered and weighed, debated, and referred to their linguistic roots as never before." "Mediating the Word: Language and Dialects in the British and Irish Reformations," *Journal of Ecclesiastical History* 56, no. 2 (April 2005): 261–86, 285.

21. Rita Copeland, *Rhetoric, Hermeneutics, and Translation in the Middle Ages: Academic Traditions and Vernacular Texts* (Cambridge: Cambridge University Press, 1991), 106. Harding and Jewel attack each other on the grounds of rhetorical and linguistic facility; where Harding challenges Jewel for misconstruing Justinian, Jewel fires back: what "M. Harding lacked in weight, he would needes make vp in tale: and so vseth this onely as a floorishe before the fight; & as a streame blowen vp with winde and weather carieth with it much frothe & filth by the very rage & drifte of the water: euen so M. Hardinge in this place flowinge, & wanderinge ouer the bankes with *Copia verborum* by the violence & force of his talke carieth a great deale of errour, & vntruthe alonge before him." John Jewel, *A Replie Vnto M. Hardinges Ansvveare: By perusinge whereof the discrete, and diligent Reader may easily see, the weake, and vnstable groundes of the Romaine Religion, whiche of late hath beene accompted Catholique* (London, 1565), 6.

22. "*In your late* Council of Colaine it is written thus," writes Jewel, "Vt Presbyteri Preces non tantùm Ore Murmurent, sed etiam Corde Persoluant nunquam à manibus eorum Liber Legis, hoc est, Biblia deponatur: *That the Priestes not onely* Mumble *vp theire Praiers, but also pronouace them from theire hartes, Let the* Booke of the Lavve, *that is to saie, the* Bible, *neuer be saide from theire handes. Likewise* Regino *reporteth the woordes of the* Council of Nantes, Ridiculum est, muris, aut parietibus Infusurrare ea, quae ad populum pertinent: *It is a peeuishe thinge,* to vvhisper *those thinges to the walles, that perteine vnto the people*" (*A Defence of the Apologie*, 1567: 516).

23. See especially John Rastell, *Beware of M. Iewel* (Antwerp, 1566), as well as the Stapleton and Harding texts cited above.

24. For a history of women in relation to the vernacular bible, see Shannon McSheffrey, *Gender and Heresy: Women and Men in Lollard Communities, 1420–1530* (Philadelphia: University of Pennsylvania Press, 1995).

25. See Erasmus, *Paraclesis,* in *The Praise of Folly and Other Writings*, ed. and trans. Robert M. Adams (New York: Norton, 1989), 121.

26. Catholics, as one text puts it, "tire their tongues with mumbling vaine, and endlesse pattering, / Or Coocoolike continually, one kinde of musike sing." Thomas Naogeorg, *The Popish Kingdome, or reigne of Antichrist*, trans. Barnabe Googe (London, 1570), 40r.

27. Often mumbling was aligned with missing teeth, which compromised both pronunciation and chewing. See *Oxford English Dictionary*, s.v. "mumble," and Randle Cotgrave, *A dictionarie of the French and English tongues* (London, 1611), who glosses "Mascher Mascher en belin," "To mumble like an old toothlesse beldame" (s.v. "mascher").

28. Erasmus, "The Paraphrase of Erasmus vpon the Gospel of St. John," in *The first*

tome or volume of the paraphrase of Erasmus vpon the newe testament, ed. Nicholas Udall, paraphrase on John trans. Mary Tudor and Nicholas Udall (London, 1548), fff5r.

29. On the democratic imperatives of clear (nonmumbled) pronunciation in eighteenth-century devotional contexts, see Vicki Tolar Burton, "John Wesley and the Liberty to Speak: The Rhetorical and Literary Practices of Early Methodism," *College Composition and Communication* 53, no. 1 (2001): 65–91.

30. P. Martin Duncan, *A Manual for the Classification, Training, and Education of the Feeble-Minded, Imbecile, & Idiotic* (London: Longmans, Green, 1866), 134.

31. Jonathan Dollimore, *Radical Tragedy: Religion, Ideology and Power in the Drama of Shakespeare and His Contemporaries* (Chicago: University of Chicago Press, 2004 [1984]), 193.

32. Robert Burton, *The Anatomy of Melancholy* (Oxford, 1621), 27.

33. Viktor Shklovsky, "On Poetry and Trans-Sense in Language," *October* 34 (1985): 3–24.

34. Toby Fulwiler and Bruce Petersen, "Toward Irrational Heuristics: Freeing the Tacit Mode," *College English* 43, no. 6 (October 1981): 621–29, 629. "Mumbling," they point out, "is seldom given the place it deserves in theoretical discussions of heuristics; the teacher of problem solving will not find a discussion of it in Moshe Rubenstein's *Patterns in Problem Solving* (1975), James Adams's *Conceptual Blockbusting* (1976), or Alexander Osborne's *Applied Imagination* (1953)," 622.

35. Ibid., 623.

36. I turn now, first, to the negative aspects of mumbling operative in medieval Catholicism, where missing a single syllable in the process of enunciation could have eschatological implications, and, second, to humanist and Reformation adaptations of what we might call the case of the missing syllable. Udall, I argue in the next chapter, draws on both traditions, reconfiguring them anew.

37. On mumbling as an acoustical push and pull in psychoanalysis, see Albert Rothenberg's "The Janusian Process in Psychoanalytic Treatment," *Contemporary Psychoanalysis* 27 (1991): 422–53. On mumbling as "expressive behavior rather than communication," a form of "manifest agressivity" (479), masking while signaling trauma in an analytic setting, see George Devereux, "Mumbling: The Relationship Between a Resistance and Frustrated Auditory Curiosity in Childhood," *Journal of the American Psychoanalytic Association* 14 (1966): 478–84.

38. [Anon.,] *Here after Folowith the boke callyd the Myrroure of Oure Lady very necessary for all relygyous persones* (c. 1420–1450, first printed London, 1530), F2v. All citations to the *Myrroure* are to this first printed edition.

39. [Anon.,] *Jacob's Well: An English Treatise on the Cleansing of Man's Conscience,* ed. Arthur Brandeis, The Early English Text Society (London: K. Paul, Trench, Trübner, 1900), 114–15. Brandeis dates the original text to the first quarter of the fifteenth century. See also T. F. Crane, "New Analogues of Old Tales," *Modern Philology* 10, no. 3 (January 1913): 301–16, esp. 305–6, where Crane locates multiple early variants of the phrase "De diabolo, qui fragmina psalmorum collegit."

40. Jacques de Vitry, *Sermones Vulgares* (c. 1220), cited in Margaret Jennings, "Tutivillus: The Literary Career of the Recording Demon," *Studies in Philology* 74, no. 5 (1977): 1–95.

41. *Here after Folowith the boke callyd the Myrroure of Oure Lady*, F2r–v. On the historical surround of the *Myrroure*, see especially Rebecca Krug, *Reading Families: Women's Literature Practice in Late Medieval England* (Ithaca: Cornell University Press, 2002), 159–204, and on Titivillus in medieval drama, see Kathleen M. Ashley, "Titivillus and the Battle of Words in Mankind," *Annuale Mediaevale* 16 (1975): 128–50.

42. John of Wales, *Tractatus de Poenitentia* (c. 1285), British Museum, MS Royal 4, D, IV, 257r, cited in Jennings, "Tutivillus," 16.

43. On "moterers and mumlers" in the grip of Titivillus, see manuscript addition to Richard Rolle's *The Form of Living* (Oxford: Bodleian Library, MS Douce 302), transcribed by Susanna Greer Fein in "A Thirteen-Line Alliterative Stanza on the Abuse of Prayer from the Audelay MS," in *Medium Aevum* 63 (1994): 61–74.

44. See [Anon.,] *Judicium*, in *The Towneley Plays*, ed. G. England and A. W. Pollard, Early English Text Society (London: Kegan Paul, Trench, Trübner, 1897).

45. On Titivillus as a figure for collected gossip, see especially Susan Phillips, *Transforming Talk: The Problem of Gossip in Late Medieval England* (University Park: Pennsylvania State University Press, 2007), and on "church-chattering," see Kathy Cawsey, "Tutivillus and the 'Kyrkchaterars': Strategies of Control in the Middle Ages," *Studies in Philology*, 102, no. 4 (2005): 443–51. In *Jacob's Well* these two traditions coincide, when the fiend's capture of the unsaid sounds of clerical error coincides with his capture of "idyl woordes" of the "peple" or parishoners (114–15).

46. On the "unspoken" grounds of historiography, see Michele de Certeau, *The Writing of History* (New York: Columbia University Press, 1988). On "incommunicability that shapes the public moment; a psychic obscurity that is formative for public memory," where the unsaid is attended to in order to disrupt theories of reification in aesthetic production, see Homi Bhabha, "The World and the Home," *Social Text: Third World and Postcolonial Issues* 31–32 (1992): 141–53, 143. See also Bhabha's development of this argument in *The Location of Culture* (New York: Routledge, 1993). On the production of literature and philosophy at the interstices of articulate and inarticulate speech, see Gilles Deleuze and Félix Guattari, *What Is Philosophy?* (New York: Columbia University Press, 1991), esp. 55, 69.

47. François Rabelais, *The Histories of Gargantua and Pantagruel*, trans. J. M. Cohen (New York: Penguin, 1955), 569.

48. As Krug puts it, "The nuns are warned to pronounce their words carefully when they read their service, because if they mumble or misspeak, they . . . deserve to be punished with death" (*Reading Families*, 171).

49. On Titivillus "whose special task is to record women gossips in the church, illustrating the extremes of which the female tongue is capable," see Cynthia Ho, "As Good as Her Word: Women's Language in *The Knight of the Tour d'Landry*," in *The Rusted Hauberk: Feudal Ideals of Order and Their Decline*, ed. Liam O. Purdon and Cindy L. Vitto (Gainesville: University Press of Florida 1994), 99–120, 107. On nuns and mumbling, see

Eileen Edna Power, *Medieval English Nunneries*, c. 1275–1535 (Cheshire, Conn.: Biblo and Tannen, 1988), 292–93. For the violence directed against women in debates about proper ecclesiastical language use, see especially Dillon, *Language and Stage*.

50. John Northbrooke, *Spiritus est Vicarius Christi in terra. The poore mans Garden wherein are flowers of the Scriptures, and Doctours, very necessarie and profitable for the simple and ignoraunt people to reade* (London, 1571), 21v.

51. [Anon.,] *Jacob's Well*, preface, viii.

52. Thomas Betson, *Here begynneth a ryght profytable treatyse co[m]pendiously drawen out of many [and] dyuers wrytynges of holy men, to dyspose men to be vertuously occupyed in theyr myndes [and] prayers* (Westminster: Wynkyn de Worde, 1500), B2v.

53. *Here after Folowith the boke callyd the Myrroure of Oure Lady*, F2v.

54. See my Introduction on "articulate" as an early English term for distinct pronunciation.

55. See, for example, [Anon.,] *Jacob's Well*, 114–15.

56. *Oxford English Dictionary*, s.v. "mum."

57. Rabelais, "Gargantua," in *The Works of the Famous Mr. Francis Rabelais Doctor in Physick Treating of the Lives, Heroick Deeds, and Sayings of Gargantua and his son Pantagruel*, trans. Thomas Urquhart (London, 1664; title pages of "Gargantua" and "Pantagruel" read 1653, and the two sections have separate pagination), 181. Urquhart follows Rabelais closely: "Ilz marmonnent grand renfort de legendes & pseaulmes nullement par eulx en, tenduz. Ilz content force patenostres entrelardées de longs Avemariaz, sans y penser ny entendre. Et ce ie appelle mocquedieu non oraison," and Cohen's translation follows closely as well: "[Monks] mumble through ever so many miracle stories and psalms which they don't in the least understand. They count over a number of Paternosters interlarded with long Ave-Marias, without understanding them or giving them so much as a thought; and that I call not prayer, but mockery of God" (126).

58. Mikhail Bakhtin, "Forms of Time and of the Chronotope in the Novel," in *The Dialogic Imagination: Four Essays*, ed. Michael Holquist, trans. Caryl Emerson and Michael Holquist (Austin: University of Texas Press, 1988), 185.

59. Friedrich Staphylus, *The Apologie of Fridericvs Staphylvs*, trans. Thomas Stapleton (Antwerp, 1565), 137r.

60. Becon, *The Jewel of Joy*, 414. Cited in Richard C. McCoy, *Alterations of State: Sacred Kingship in the English Reformation* (New York: Columbia University Press, 2002), 2. On "Masse mumbling," see also Foxe, *The Pope Confvted*, 11.

61. The passage from the Froben edition of the *Moriae Encomium* (1515) reads: "Nec saltem admonet eos uertex rasus sacerdotem omnibus huius mundi cupiditatibus liberum esse oportere, neque quidquam nisi caelestia meditari. Sed homines suaues se suo offiio probe perfunctos aiunt, si preculas illas suas utcumque permurmurarint, quas mehercule demiror si quis deus uel audiat uel intelligat, um ipsi ned audiant ne intelligant, tum cum eas ore perstrepunt" (60). Erasmus, *Stultitiae Laus*, ed. John F. Collins (Bryn Mawr: Bryn Mawr College Library, 1991), 52.

62. Jean Calvin, *The Institution of Christian Religion, vvrytten in Latine by maister Ihon Caluin, and translated into Englysh according to the authors last edition.* London, 1561), 89r. See also 59v–60r, and 216r–v.

63. Thomas Key, "The preface of the Translatour" of Erasmus's paraphrase on the Gospel of St. Mark, in Erasmus, *The first tome or volume of the Paraphrase of Erasmus vpon the newe testament,* IV.

64. Edward Cardwell, *Documentary Annals of the Reformed Church of England* (Oxford: Oxford University Press, 1839), I, 9, 13, 181, 186.

65. John Bale, *Yet a course at the Romyshe foxe. A dysclosynge or openynge of the Manne of synne, contayned in the late Declaratyon of the Popes olde faythe made by Edmonde Boner bysshopp of London. wherby wyllyam Tolwyn was than newlye professed at paules crosse openlye into Antichristes Romyshe relygyon agayne by a newe solempne othe of obedyence, notwythsta[n]dynge the othe made to hys prynce afore to the contrarye* (London, 1543), 88r–v.

66. "Individual," Peter Stallybrass has pointed out, meant at once separate and inseparable from, emphasizing less autonomy than the always ongoing dialectic between autonomy and dependence, selfhood and sociality. "Shakespeare, the Individual and the Text," 606.

67. Latimer, "The second sermon vpon the Lordes prayer," *27 sermons,* C2v–r.

68. Ann Moss, *Renaissance Truth and the Latin Language Turn* (Oxford: Oxford University Press, 2003), 4.

69. Tyndale, *The parable of the Wycked Mammon. Compiled in the yere of our Lorde, M.d.xxxvi.* (London, 1547), A3r.

70. George Puttenham, *The Arte of English Poesie* (London, 1589), 69. John Bale, *Scriptorum Illustrium Maioris Brytanniae* (1557), cited in *John Skelton: The Critical Heritage,* ed. Anthony S. G. Edwards (London: Routledge & Kegan Paul, 1981), 55. On Skeltonics and the poetics of protests, see Jane Griffiths, *John Skelton and Poetic Authority: Defining the Liberty to Speak* (Oxford: Oxford University Press, 2006).

71. John Bale, *An excellent and a right learned meditacion, compiled in two prayers most frutefull and necessary to be vsed and said of al ttue [sic] English men, in these daungerous daies of affliction, for the comfort and better stay of the christen co[n]science, bewailing the deserued plages of England* (London, 1554), B3v.

72. On Bale's use of rhyme, see especially Thora Balslev Blatt, *The Plays of John Bale: A Study of Ideas, Technique and Style* (Copenhagen: G. E. C. Gad, 1968).

73. John Bale, *A mysterye of inyquyte contayned within the heretycall genealogye of Ponce Pantolabus, is here both dysclosed & confuted by Iohan Bale* (Antwerp, 1545), 11r, 38v.

74. Ben Jonson, *The English Grammar . . . For the benefit of all Strangers, out of his observation of the English Language now spoken, and in use* (posthumously published in 1640), in *The Workes of Benjamin Jonson,* 2nd ed. (London, 1641), 33–84, 47.

75. Thomas Becon's complaint, to offer another example, that "we lived never so ungodly, through the popish prattling of monstrous monks, and the mumbling masses of those monstrous lazy soul-carriers. What trust we reposed in the masking masses of

momish mass-mongers," uses repetition to satirize the self-referential tongue-twisting iter-ation of "mumbling masses" but also relies on such strategies to a remarkable degree. Becon, *The Jewel of Joy*, 414. Cited in McCoy, *Alterations of State*, 2.

76. Tyndale, *The obedie[n]ce of a Christen man*, B5v–B6r, emphasis added.

77. On the interanimation of reading and listening in liturgical practice, see Targoff, *Common Prayer*, esp. 18. In Anglo-American contexts, see Lisa M. Gordis, *Opening Scrip-ture: Bible Reading and Interpretive Authority in Puritan New England* (Chicago: University of Chicago Press, 2003), which develops central insights found in Janice Knight: *Othodox-ies in Massachusetts: Rereading American Puritanism* (Cambridge, Mass.: Harvard Univer-sity Press, 1994), and David D. Hall, *Worlds of Wonder, Days of Judgment: Popular Religious Belief in Early New England* (New York: Knopf, 1989).

78. Tyndale's part in the Reformation, argues Stephen Greenblatt in *Renaissance Self-Fashioning*, inaugurated no less than "a turning point in human history" (97).

79. On Foxe and "Protestant bibliocentricity," see Alexandra Walsham, "Unclasping the Book? Post-Reformation English Catholicism and the Vernacular Bible," *Journal of British Studies* 42 (2003): 141–66, 143. Walsham examines the 1582 Douai-Rheims Catholic Bible as a way to counterbalance this longstanding bias. On print and orality in Reforma-tion contexts, see also Walsham, "Reformed Folklore? Cautionary Tales and Oral Tradition in Early Modern England," in *The Spoken Word*, ed. Adam Fox and Daniel Woolf (Man-chester: Manchester University Press, 2003), 173–88, and Julia Crick and Walsham, "Intro-duction: Script, Print and History," in *The Uses of Script and Print: 1300–1700*, ed. Crick and Walsham (Cambridge: Cambridge University Press, 2004), 1–28.

80. Nicholas Udall, "The preface vnto the Kynges Maiestee," *The first tome or volume of the Paraphrase of Erasmus vpon the newe testament*, B4r.

81. Thomas Drant, *A Sermon Preached at S. Maries Spittle*, in *Two sermons preached the one at S. Maries Spittle on Tuesday in Easter weeke 1570* (London, 1570), F8r.

82. Thomas Bilson, *The Trve Difference Betweene Christian Subiection and Vnchristian Rebellion: Wherein The Princes Lawfull power to commaund for trueth, and indepriuable right to beare the sword are defended against the Popes censures and the Iesuits sophismes vttered in their Apologie and Defence of English Catholikes. With a demonstration that the thinges re-fourmed in the Church of England by the Lawes of this Realme are truely Catholike, notwith-standing the vaine shew made to the contrary in their late Rhemish Testament* (Oxford, 1585).

83. As Thomas Harding puts it, "We wishe, that al the people vnderstoode al our praiers. But we thinke it not conuenient, in a common prophane tongue, to vtter high mysteries. Therefore we wishe, they would learne the mystical tongue, and gladly do we teach their children the same. S. Dionyse the Areopagite scholer to S. Paule, teacheth Timothe, and in him al vs . . . to communicate those thinges, whiche haue power to make men perfite, with them, who make men perfite: that is to saie, to publishe priestly office of Consecration, (for nothinge maketh vs more perfite) among them onely, who are Priestes, and not among others" (515). Harding's emphasis on learned mediators compli-cates but still marks his emphasis on the communicated and textual Word.

84. Rastell, *Beware of M. Iewel*, 60r.

85. Targoff, *Common Prayer*.

86. John Bossy, "The Mass as a Social Institution: 1200–1700," *Past and Present* (August 1983): 29–61, 60–61.

87. Thomas Becon, *The Displaying of the Popish masse vvherein thou shalt see, what a wicked Idoll the Masse is, and what great difference there is between the Lords Supper and the Popes Masse: againe, what Popes brought in every part of the Masse, and counted it together in such monstrous sort, as it is now used in the Popes Kingdome. Written by Thomas Becon; and published in the dayes of Queene Mary* (London, 1637), 271.

88. On Renaissance "inwardness" in English religious and theatrical culture, see especially Katharine Eisaman Maus, *Inwardness and Theater in the English Renaissance* (Chicago: University of Chicago Press, 1995). On the mystical dimensions of reformation thought, see also Debora K. Shuger, *Habits of Thought in the English Renaissance: Religion, Politics and the Dominant Culture*, new ed. (Toronto: University of Toronto Press, 1997).

89. See, for example, all responses to Jewel cited in this chapter.

90. See especially Ethan H. Shagan, *Popular Politics and the English Reformation* (Cambridge: Cambridge University Press, 2002), and *Catholics and the "Protestant Nation": Religious Politics and Identity in Early Modern England*, ed. Shagan (Manchester: Manchester University Press, 2005). On illiteracy and prayer, see Ian Green, *Print and Protestantism in Early Modern England* (Oxford: Oxford University Press, 2000), esp. 24–26.

91. Thomas Cranmer, *Articles To Be Inquired Of In The Visitation To Be Had in the byshopricke of Norwyche, now vacant in the fourth yere of our most drad souerayn Lorde Edwarde the sixte* (London, 1549), A1v–A2v, emphasis added.

92. Jonas Barish, *The Antitheatrical Prejudice* (Berkeley: University of California Press, 1981).

93. Jeffrey Knapp, *Shakespeare's Tribe: Church, Nation and Theater in Renaissance England* (Chicago: University of Chicago Press, 2004); Kent Cartwright, *Theater and Humanism: English Drama in the Sixteenth Century* (Cambridge: Cambridge University Press, 1999); and John N. King, *English Reformation Literature: The Tudor Origins of the Protestant Tradition* (Princeton: Princeton University Press, 1986). See especially David Bevington, *Tudor Drama and Politics: A Critical Approach to Topical Meaning* (Cambridge, Mass.: Harvard University Press, 1968). See also John D. Cox and David Scott Kastan, *A New History of Early English Drama* (New York: Columbia University Press, 1997).

94. Bruce R. Smith, "Hearing Green: Logomarginality in *Hamlet*," *Early Modern Literary Studies* 7, no. 1, special issue 8 (May 2001): 1:1–2. On theater, iconophobia and logophilia, see Michael O'Connell, *The Idolatrous Eye: Iconoclasm and Theater in Early Modern England* (Oxford: Oxford University Press, 2000).

95. Foxe, *The Pope Confvted*, 11.

96. Tyndale, *The obedie[n]ce of a Christen man*, O1r. The marginal gloss here further emphasizes "dumb": "The popes sacrementes are doume."

97. Further linking the clergical "mum" with "mymmynge," Tyndale writes: "What

helpeth it also that the prest when he goeth to masse disgiseth him selfe with a great parte of the passion of Christe and pleyeth out the rest vnder silence with signes and profers / with noddinge / beckinge and mowinge / as it were Iacke a napes / when nether he him selfe nether any man else woteth what he meaneth? not at all veryly / but hurteth and that exceadinghly. For as moch as it not only destroyeth the fayth and quencheth the love that sholde be geven vnto the commaundemente / and maketh the people thankefull / . . . it bringeth them into soch supersticionthat they that they haue done . . . ynough for God . . . yf they be present once in a daye at soch mummynge: But also maketh the infidels to mock vs and abhorre vs / in that they se nothinge but soch apes playe amonge vs / where of no man can geve a reason" (J5r–v).

98. A correlative to mumming and mumbling was "business" and "buszying." Hamlet's "buzze buzze" comes to mind in this respect. The 1603 Quarto of *Hamlet* reads: "*Cor.* The Actors are come hither, my lord. / *Ham.* Buz, buz. / *Cor.* The best Actors in *Christendome,* / Either for Comedy, Tragedy, Historie, Pastorall" (1440–44, emphasis added). The 1623 Folio reads, "*Pol.* The Actors are come hither my Lord. / *Ham.* Buzze, buzze. / *Pol.* Vpon mine Honor. / *Ham.* Then can each Actor on his Asse —— / *Polon.* The best Actors in the world, either for Trage- / die, Comedie, Historie, Pastorall: Pastoricall-Comicall- / Historicall-Pastorall: Tragicall-Historicall: Tragicall- / Comicall-Historicall-Pastorall: Scene indiuible: or Po- / em vnlimited. *Seneca* cannot be too heauy, nor *Plautus* too light, for the law of Writ, and the Liberty. These are / the onely men" (1440–50).

99. *Oxford English Dictionary*, s.v. "mum, v."

100. See G. R Owst, *Literature and Pulpit in Medieval England* (New York: Barnes and Noble, 1966): "Our medieval pulpit satire adequately explains alike the coarseness and acerbity of both the Humanist and the Reformer" (235).

101. Luke Shepherd, *Doctour Doubble ale* (London, 1548). Hans Sachs, *A goodly dysputacion betwene a Christen Shomaker / and a Popysshe Parson with two other parsones more, done within the famous Citie of Norembourgh*, trans. Anthony Scoloker (London, 1548).

102. Henri Bergson, "Laughter," in *Comedy*, ed. Wylie Sypher, trans. Fred Rothwell (New York: Doubleday, 1956), 67, emphasis added.

103. Jewel, *An Apologie or answere in defence* (1564), B1r.

104. See especially Richard Foster Jones, *The Triumph of The English Language* (Stanford: Stanford University Press, 1953).

105. Mueller, *The Native Tongue and the Word*, 293. On English, Latin, and Greek, see Wilson's *Three Orations*, "Yea, the more that I looke vpon this Orator to bring his sentences and wordes knowne to our common speach and language: the more doe I finde him harde and vnable to be translated, according to the excellencie of his tongue. And manye times I haue bene ashamed of my selfe, when I compared his Greeke and my English togither. And no marueyle neyther. For the Latine translatours being otherwise most excellent men, haue not alwayes satisfied themselues, much lesse aunswered to their charge and enterprise in the opinion of others that compared their doings and the Greeke togither" (prefatory epistle, *4v).

106. Udall, "Preface to the Translation, paraphrase of Erasmus vpon Luke," *The first tome or volume of the Paraphrase of Erasmus vpon the newe testament*, 5v.

107. For a recent complication of this critical commonplace with particular attention to Luther, however, see Richard Strier, "Martin Luther and the Real Presence in Nature," *Journal of Medieval and Early Modern Studies* 37, no. 2 (2007): 271–303.

108. William Fulke, *D. Heskins, D. Sanders, And M. Rastel, accounted (among their faction) three pillers and Archpatriarches of the Popish Synagogue (vtter enemies to the truth of Christes Gospell, and all that syncerely professe the same) ouerthrowne, and detected of their seuerall blasphemous heresies* (London, 1579), 710v. In a rather complicated formulation, Fulke is here responsing to Rastell's response to Jewel's response to Harding's response to Jewel's *Apologie.*

109. Thomas Cranmer, *A Defence of the Trve and Catholike doctrine of the sacrament of the body and bloud of our sauiour Christ with a confutacion of sundry errors concernyng the same* (London, 1550), 18v. The passage reads, "Who vnderstode the mynde of Christ better than S. Paule, to whom Christe shewed his moste secrete counsailes? And saint Paule is not afraide, for our better vnderstandinge of Christes wordes, somewhat to alter the same, *least we might stande stiffely in the letters and syllables, and erre in mistaking of Christes wordes.* For where as our sauiour Christ brake the bread and said, This is my body: S. Paule saith, that the bread which we breake, is the communion of Christes body. Christ said, his body: and saint Paule said, the communion of his body: meaning neuertheles both one thinge, that thei which eate the breade worthely, do eate spiritually Christes very body."

110. Jewel, *A Replie Vnto M. Hardinges Ansvveare*, 317v.

111. Joseph Farrell, *Latin Language and Latin Culture: From Antiquity to Modern Times* (Cambridge: Cambridge University Press, 2001), 2, 175.

112. See Udall's preface to Erasmus's Paraphrase of Luke, *The first tome or volume of the Paraphrase of Erasmus vpon the newe testament*, A3v.

113. On Tyndale and the Lollards, see especially John N. King, "'The Light of Printing': William Tyndale, John Fox, John Day, and Early Modern Print Culture," *Renaissance Quarterly* 54, no. 1 (2001): 52–85.

114. On charges against Lollard diction, see especially Dillon, *Language and Stage*, 19.

115. Simon Birckbek, *The Protestants Evidence Taken Ovt Of Good Records; Shewing that for Fifteene hundred yeares next after Christ, divers worthy guides of Gods Church, have in sundry weightie poynts of Religion, taught as the Church of England* (London, 1635), 85–86. Birckbek continues: "Some have conceited them to have beene called *Lollards* of *Lollium*, cockle or darnell, and so saith the glosse in Linwood; as also in the Squires prologue in Chaucer. *I smell a Loller in the winde (quoth hee) abideth for Gods digne passion, for mee shall have a predication, this Loller here will preach us somewhat——here shall hee not preach, here shall he no Gospell glose, ne teach; he beleeueth all in the great God (quoth he) he would sowne some difficulty, or spring cockle in our cleare corne.* But they were called Lollards from one *Raynard Lollard*, who at the first was a *Franciscan* Monke, and an enemy to the *Waldenses*, but yet a man carried with a sanctified desire to finde the way of salvation. Hee afterwards taught the doctrine of

the *Waldenses*, was apprehended in *Germany* by the Monkes Inquisitours, and being delivered to the secular power, was burnt at *Cologne*. He wrote a Commentary upon the *Apocalyps*, wherein he applied many things to the Pope as to the Roman *Antichrist*. This was he of whom the faithfull in *England* were called Lollards; where he taught, witnesse that Tower in London which at this present is called by his name Lollards Tower, where the faithfull that professed his religion were imprisoned. *Iohn le Maire* in the third part of the difference of Schismes, puts him in the ranke of those holy *men that have foretold by divine revelation many things that have come to passe in his time;* such as were *Boccace*, Saint *Vincent of Valence; of the order of preaching Friers; Ioachim Abbot of Galabria;* to them he adjoyneth the Frier *Reynard Lollard*" (85–86). See also Chaucer, "The Squires Tale," *The Works of Our Ancient, Learned, & Excellent English Poet, Jeffrey Chaucer* (London, 1687), 47.

116. William Langland, *Piers Plowman* (C.x.215), cited in *Oxford English Dictionary*, s.v. "loll."

117. "Inarticulate," as we saw in the Introduction, combined problems of syntax, or "joining," with those of pronunciation.

118. [Anon.,] *Judicium,* in *The Towneley Plays* (30:213). For early approaches to Titivillus's allusion to himself as "master lollar" by Raine, Skeat, Gayley, and Pollard, see Oscar Cargill, "The Authorship of the Secunda Pastorum," *PMLA* 41, no. 4 (1926): 810–31, esp. 812 n. 2.

119. On this moment as an attack on Lollardy, and on "jangling" translators, see Dillon, *Language and Stage*, 43, and also Cawsey, "Tutivillus," 446. For a broader approach to this as an instence of idle utterance, see Jennings, "Tutivillus," 60, and for an argument that the Lollards are here singled out for praise, see Martin Stevens, "Language as Theme in the Wakefield Plays," *Speculum* 52 (1977): 100–17, 106. Dillon insightfully sees this moment as a deflection of anxiety about a broad-based movement toward vernacular preference in devotional practice by othering the Lollard heretics (44), known as "'janglers,' abusers of the word and the Word" (14).

120. "The flyting of Dunbar and Kennedy" (London, 1508), 143.

121. John of Bromyard, *Summa Praedicantium* (first published Basle, c. 1484), British Museum MS. 7 E. IV, 394r, cited in *A Selection of Latin Stories, from Manuscripts of the Thirteenth and Fourteenth Centuries: A Contribution to the History of Fiction During the Middle Ages*, ed. Thomas Wright (London: Percy Society, 1842), 259–60. G. G. Coulton records the verse in English: "These are they who wickedly corrupt the holy psalms: the dangler, the gasper, the leaper, the galloper, the dragger, the mumbler, the foreskipper, the forerunner and the over leaper: Tittivillus collecteth the fragments of these men's words," *A Medieval Garner: Human Documents from the Four Centuries Preceding the Reformation* (London: Archibald Constable, 1910), 423.

122. *Songs, Carols and other Miscellaneous Poems*, ed. Roman Dybosky, Early English Text Society, o.s., 101 (1907), 137, cited in Cawsey, "Tutivillus,"

123. See A. W. Reed, "Nicholas Udall and Thomas Wilson," *Review of English Studies* 1, no. 3 (July 1925): 275–83.

124. The articles as well as the response by Nicholas Udall are transcribed in Nicholas Udall, "Answer to the Commoners of Devonshire and Cornwall," in *Troubles Connected with the Prayer Book of 1549*, ed. Nicholas Pocock (Westminster: Camden Society, 1884), 141–93, 169.

125. Paula Blank, *Broken English: Dialects and the Politics of Language in Renaissance Writings* (London: Routledge, 1996), 7.

126. Further, Rastell adds: "If an English man, knowing no other tounge byside his owne, and a Welshman, of ye like knowledge in his naturall tounge only, shoulde come together to Diuinitye Schole in Oxforde, and both of them vnderstand ye Kinges Reader, this were much to be wondred at: but if there come to Paules Crosse, out of eche Sheer in England, seueral persons, and vnderstand the Preachers English, doe they loke one vpon an other for it? do they wonder at the working sprite in him, and say: howe doe we heare, euery one of vs, this fellowe, whiche is borne an English man, to speake our Vulgar tounge? Yet no doubt there is a difference of speache, betwen English men of diuers Sheers" (65v).

127. On preacher-player relations after the advent of permanent playhouses in 1576, see Jeffrey Knapp, "Preachers and Players in Shakespeare's England," *Representations* 44 (Autumn 1993): 29–59.

128. Thomas Wilson, *The rule of Reason, conteinyng the Arte of Logique* 3rd ed. (London, 1553), 66.

129. *The Arte of Rhetorique*, as Pollard and Redgrave's *Short Title Catalogue* records, was printed in 1553, 1560, 1562, 1563, 1567, 1580, 1584, and 1585, but on another undated copy (c. 1561) discovered and acquired by Cornell University Library, see Russell H. Wagner, "The Text and Editions of Wilson's *Arte of Rhetorique*," *Modern Language Notes*, 44, no. 7 (Nov. 1929): 421–28, 428. It is interesting if incidental that Wilson would have known of Titivillus from *Ralph Roister Doister*, where "Titiuile" is mentioned at the outset, as I discuss in the next chapter.

130. Thomas Wilson, *The three orations of Demosthenes chiefe orator among the Grecians in Favor of the Olynthians . . . With Those His Four Orations . . . Against King Philip of Macedonie* (London, 1570), prefatory epistle to William Cecil (*4v).

131. Elevating Demosthenes over Cicero in *The three orations,* Wilson writes "I may boldly say, that Demosthenes hath more matter couched in a small roume, than Tullie hath in a large discourse, & that Demosthenes writing is more binding, more fast, firme, and more agreable to our common maner of speach, than Tullies Orations are. And who so speaketh now as Demosthenes doth, I doe thynke hee should be counted the wiser, the more temperate, and the more graue man a great deale, than if he wholy followed Tullie, and vsed his large veyne and vehement maner of eloquence. . . . *And were it not better & more wisedome to speake plainly & nakedly after the common sort of men in few words, than to ouerflowe wyth vnnecessarie and superfluous eloquence as Cicero is thought sometimes to doe? . . . But perhaps wheras I haue bene somewhat curious to followe Demosthenes naturall phrase, it may be thought that I doe speake ouer bare Englysh. Well I had rather follow his veyne, the whych was to speake simply and plainly to the common peoples vnderstanding, than to ouer-*

flouryshe wyth superfluous speach, although I might therby be counted equall with the best that euer wrate Englysh (The three orations, "Preface to the Reader," emphasis added).

132. G. H. Mair, ed., *Wilson's Arte of Rhetorique* (Oxford: Clarendon, 1909), xxx.

133. Wilson, *The three Orations,* epistle to Cecil, *1r.

134. Wilson, *The three Orations,* "Preface to the Reader," *3r.

135. Wilson, *The three Orations,* epistle to Cecil, *4v.

136. "Raids on the inarticulate," from T. S. Eliot's *Four Quartets,* used by Terence Hawkes in the context of colonial encounter, *Shakespeare's Talking Animals: Language and Drama in Society* (London: Arnold, 1973), 211.

137. See Benedict Anderson, *Imagined Communities: Reflections on the Origin and Spread of Nationalism,* rev. ed. (New York: Verso, 2006).

138. On Tudor antiquarianism and vernacular reform, see Sean Keilen's *Vulgar Eloquence: On the Renaissance Invention of English Literature* (New Haven: Yale University Press, 2006). On the uncommon or learned construction of standard vernacularsism, see Blank, *Broken English.*

139. Or those, in images we will revisit in Udall, who "settes forth their lippes two ynches good beyonde their teeth . . . talkes as thoughe their tongue went of patyns . . . showes al their teeth . . . speakes in their teeth altogether . . . leates their wordes fall in their lippes, scant openyng theim when they speake" (Gg2r).

140. Fulwiler and Petersen, "Toward Irrational Heuristics," 623, 622.

141. William Shakespeare, *The Tragedy of King Lear,* in *Mr. William Shakespeares Comedies, Histories, & Tragedies. Published according to the True Originall Copies* (London, 1623), 297, 297, 298, 298, 303, 304. See also *M. William Shak-speare: His True Chronicle Historie of the life and death of King Lear and his three Daughters. With the vnfortunate life of Edgar, sonne and heire to the Earle of Gloster, and his sullen and assumed humor of Tom of Bedlam: As it was played before the Kings Maiestie at Whitehall upon S. Stephans night in Christmas Hollidayes. By his Maiesties servants playing usually at the Gloabe on the Bancke-side* (London, 1608) for the following variants: "a lo lo lo" (G2r), "hay no on ny" (G2r), "still fy fo and fum" (G3r), and "fie, fie, fie, pah, pah" (I4r). I thank Peter Stallybrass for encouraging me to consider the prehistory of such sounds in *King Lear.* For if "the realme of *Albion,*" as the Fool puts it in the Folio, shall "come to great confusion" (297), what do we make of such "confusion" enacted at the level of the spoken word sound in this and earlier Renaissance dramas?

142. Thomas Kyd, *The Spanish Tragedy,* ed. J. R. Mulryne (London: A. and C. Black, 1989), 4.1.180.

CHAPTER 2. FROM FAULT TO FIGURE

1. Margreta de Grazia, "Shakespeare's View of Language: An Historical Perspective," *Shakespeare Quarterly* 29, no. 3 (Summer 1978): 374–88; 376–77, 379. This is an extremely important corrective to deconstructive Renaissance scholarship overinvested in the

reification of linguistic indeterminacy. For a development of de Grazia's argument, see Paula Blank, *Broken English: Dialects and the Politics of Language in Renaissance Writings* (London: Routledge, 1996), esp. 87–88. On the pursuit of eloquence as a dominant colonial ideology, see Stephen Greenblatt, "Learning to Curse: Aspects of Linguistic Colonialism in the Sixteenth-Century," *Learning to Curse: Essays in Early Modern Culture* (New York: Routledge, 1990), 16–39. For a more complicated analysis of "social dialogue" on stage, which draws on epistolary rhetoric of the Renaissance, see Lynne Magnusson, *Shakespeare and Social Dialogue* (Cambridge: Cambridge University Press, 1999). For an alternative approach to the concept of "error" in Renaissance literature and drama, see Julian Yates, *Error, Misuse, Failure: Object Lessons from the English Renaissance* (Minneapolis: University of Minnesota Press, 2003).

2. On the date of composition, see J. W. Hales, "The Date of the First English Comedy," *Englische Studien* 18 (1893), 408–21, and David Bevington, *Tudor Drama and Politics: A Critical Approach to Topical Meaning* (Cambridge, Mass.: Harvard University Press, 1968), 121, where the play is most convincingly situated in the early 1500s. *Ralph Roister Doister*, long thought to be the first "regular" English comedy (see, for example, Hales), was preceded by a number of others, notably Henry Medwall's *Fulgrens and Lucrece*, explored in Howard B. Norland, *Drama in Early Tudor Britain, 1485–1558* (Lincoln: University of Nebraska Press, 1995), 242.

3. A warrant by Queen Mary dated December 3, 1554, reads: "Wheras our welbeloved Nicolas Udall hath at soondrie seasons convenient heretofore shewed, and myndeth hereafter to shewe, his diligence in setting foorth of Dialogues and Interludes before us fo[r] ou[r] regell disporte and recreacion, to th[e] entent that he maye bee in the better readinesse at all time whan yt shall be our pleasure to call, we will and commaunde you, and every of you, that at all and every such tyme and tymes, so oft and whan soever he shall nede and require yt, for shewing of any thing before us, ye deliver or cause to bee delivered to the said Udall, or to the bringer herof in his name, out of our office of revelles, such apparell for his use as he shal thinke necessarie and requisite for the furnisshinge and condigne setting forthe of his devises before us, and suche as maze be semely to bee shewed in our royall presence, and the same to be restored and redelivered by the said Udall into yo[ur] handes and custodie again. And that ye faile not thus to dooe from time to time as ye tendre oure pleasure, till ye shall receive expresse commaundement from us to the contrary herof. And this shal be your sufficient waraunte in this behalf." "A Warrant dormer from Mary the Queen, addressed to the Master and Yeoman of her Revels," cited in T. H. Vail Motter, *The School Drama in England* (London: Longmans, Green, 1929), 56–57.

4. On Erasmus and the limits of rhetoric, see my Introduction.

5. From Nicholas Udall, *What Creature is in health, eyther yong or olde* (London, 1566), 7r. The Short Title Catalogue title refers to the first words of Udall's opening poem. All citations of *Ralph Roister Doister* are from this edition.

6. See my Chapter 1 where I quote Tyndale, "Antychristes Bisshopes preach not and

their sacrementes speake not, but as the disgysed Bisshopes mum, so are their supersticious sacrementes doume," and my note 97 in Chapter 1, where I quote him writing against liturgical "mummynge" (*The obedie[n]ce of a Christen man*, O1r, J5r–v, and M1r–v).

7. Udall, Preface to Erasmus's Paraphrase on Luke, *The first tome or volume of the Paraphrase of Erasmus vpon the newe testament*, ed. Nicholas Udall, trans. Nicholas Udall, Thomas Key, Mary Tudor and others (London, 1548), A4v. On idolatry, see especially Nicholas Udall, "Answer to the Commoners of Devonshire and Cornwall," in *Troubles Connected with the Prayer Book of 1549*, ed. Nicholas Pocock (Westminster: Camden Society, 1884), 141–93.

8. Janel Mueller, *The Native Tongue and the Word: Developments in English Prose Style 1380–1580* (Chicago: University of Chicago Press, 1984). On Mueller and "Scripturalism," see my Chapter 1.

9. On Tudor translation and the status of the vernacular, see Richard Foster Jones, *The Triumph of the English Language* (Stanford: Stanford University Press, 1953), and Janette Dillon, *Language and Stage in Medieval and Renaissance England* (Cambridge: Cambridge University Press, 1998).

10. Nicholas Udall, "The preface to the Jentle christian reader," *The first tome or volume of the Paraphrase of Erasmus vpon the newe testament*, B6v.

11. Ann Moss, *Renaissance Truth and the Latin Language Turn* (Oxford: Oxford University Press, 2003), 6.

12. See, for example, Raphael Falco, "Medieval and Reformation Roots," in *A Companion to Renaissance Drama*, ed. Arthur F. Kinney (Oxford: Blackwell, 2002), 252. For a challenge to earlier conceptions of the drama as the "first English comedy," or the first comedy in five acts, see Norland, *Drama in Early Tudor Britain*, 267–72.

13. See especially Alan Stewart's discussion of the play in *Close Readers: Humanism and Sodomy in Early Modern England* (Princeton: Princeton University Press, 1997), and Elizabeth Pittenger, " 'To Serve the Queere': Nicholas Udall Master of Revels," in *Queering the Renaissance*, ed. Jonathan Goldberg (Durham: Duke University Press, 1994), 162–89. For earlier approaches to this topic, see William Edgerton, *Nicholas Udall* (New York: Twayne, 1965) and John Franceschina, *Homosexualities in the English Theatre: From Lyly to Wilde* (Westport, Conn.: Greenwood Press, 1997), esp. 21, 30, 36, 55–56, 195.

14. Peter Martyr, *A discourse or traictise of Petur Martyr Vermilla Flore[n]tine, the publyqe reader of diuinitee in the Uniuersitee of Oxford wherein he openly declared his whole and determinate iudgemente concernynge the Sacrament of the Lordes supper in the sayde Uniuersitee*, trans. Nicholas Udall (London, 1550).

15. On the treatment of women in the play, see especially Kent Cartwright, *Theatre and Humanism: English Drama in the Sixteenth Century* (Cambridge: Cambridge University Press, 1999), 81, 138, 142, 145, and Bevington, *Tudor Drama and Politics*, esp. 121–24, and Pittenger, " 'To Serve the Queere.' "

16. Joel Altman, *Tudor Play of Mind: Rhetorical Inquiry and the Development of Elizabethan Drama* (Berkeley: University of California Press, 1978), 150, and Lorna Hutson,

246 NOTES TO PAGES 63–68

The Usurer's Daughter: Male Friendship and Fictions of Women in Sixteenth-Century England (New York: Routledge, 1997), 189–90.

17. Royster, "A swaggering or blustering bully; a riotous fellow; a rude or noisy reveller" (*Oxford English Dictionary*, s.v. "Roister, n.")

18. Donatus, *Commentum Terenti*, ed. Paul Wessner, 3 vols. (Leipzig 1902–8), 1:21.

19. See the typographical corrections (including "married" for the two "marrieb") by Edward Arber in his early edition of *Roister Doister* (London, 1869).

20. Erasmus, *Apophthegmes that is to saie, prompte, quicke, wittie and sentencious saiynges, of certain Emperours, Kynges, Capitaines, Philosophiers and Oratours, aswell Grekes, as Romaines, bothe veraye pleasaunt [et] profitable to reade, partely for all maner of persones, [et] especially Gentlemen*, trans. Nicholas Udall (London, 1542), 245r. I differ from the transcription of the text available at *Early English Books Online*; from what I can glean, the word is not "bille" but "bible."

21. See my Chapter 1, and also Thomas Wilson, *The Arte of Rhetorique* (London, 1553), where what Wilson calls a "mynstrelles elocution, talkyng matters altogether in rime," is pitched against the "noise" of Popish "rime" (108v).

22. Samuel Daniel would still be defending rhyme in 1603 against charges that it was "grosse, vulgar and barbarous," claiming that "wee are no longer the slaues of Ryme, but we make it a most excellent instrument to serue vs." See *A Panegyrike Congratulatorie Deliuered To The Kings Most Excellent Maiestie At Bvrleigh Harrington in Rvtlandshire. By Samuel Daniel. Also Certaine Epistles, With A Defence Of Ryme Heretofore Written, And Now Pvblished By The Author* (London, 1603).

23. Richard Sherry, *A Treatise of the Figures of Grammer and Rhetorike* (London, 1555), B4r–5r.

24. See Liana De Girolami Cheney, "The Oyster in Dutch Genre Paintings: Moral or Erotic Symbolism," *Artibus et Historiae* 8, no. 15 (1987): 135–58.

25. *Oxford English Dictionary*, s.v. "oyster, n.," 9a–c.

26. Nicholas Udall, *Flovres for Latine Spekynge selected and gathered oute of Terence, and the same translated in to Englysshe, together with the exposition and setting for the as welle of such latyne wordes, as were throught nedefull to be annoted, as also of dyuers grammatical rules, very profytable [and] necessarye for the expedite knowledge in the lating tongue* (London, 1534), 144r–v. Udall is here drawing from Terence's *Heautontimoroumenos*. Or, as Udall puts it of Terence's *Eunuchus*, he "that hath no wisedome, nor witte, nor no grace nor good facion neither in wordes, nor gesture, nor otherwyse in his behauoure . . . it is largely shewed and declared in the thyrde scene of the seconde acte of this same comedie" (*Flovres*, 111r).

27. Shakespeare, *Romeo and Juliet*, ed. Dympna Callaghan (Boston: Bedford, 2003), 3.5.173.

28. On transubstantiation in the play, see Frederick S. Boas, *Cambridge History of English Literature*, 15 vols. (London: G. P. Putnam's Sons, 1910), 5:120.

29. Erasmus, "The Paraphrase of Erasmus vpon the Gospel of St. John," *The first tome or volume of the Paraphrase of Erasmus vpon the newe testament*, fff5r.

30. Thomas Geminum's 1445 *Compendiosa totius anatomie delineatio*, trans. Nicholas Udall et al. (London, 1553), B4r.

31. As a mid-Tudor homily against "mummishe massyng" and the proper reception of the sacrament reads, "It is well knowen, that the meate we seeke for in this supper, is spirituall foode, the nourishment of our soule, a heauenlye refection, and not earthly, an unuisible meate, and not bodyly, a ghostly substaunce, and not carnall: so that to thinke that without fayth we may enioye the eatynge and drinkyng thereof, or that, that is the fruition of it, is but to dreame a grosse carnell feedyng, basely abiectinge, and byndinge our selues to the elementes and creatures" ("The firste part of the Sermon of the worthy receauing of the Sacrament," in *The seconde tome of homelyes of such matters as were promised and intituled in the former part of homelyes, set out by the aucthoritie of the Quenes Maiestie: and to be read in euery paryshe churche agreablye* [London, 1563], fff1r–v, fff3r). On the status of metaphor in the controversy over the Real Presence, see especially Judith H. Anderson, "Language and History in the Reformation: Cranmer, Gardiner, and the Words of Institution," *Renaissance Quarterly* 54, no. 1 (Spring 2001): 20–51; Catherine Gallagher and Stephen Greenblatt, *Practicing New Historicism* (Chicago: University of Chicago Press, 2000), esp. 141; Julia Houston, "Transubstantiation and the Sign: Cranmer's Drama of the Lord's Supper," *Journal of Medieval and Renaissance Studies* 24 (1994): 113–30; David Aers, "New Historicism and the Eucharist," *Journal of Medieval and Early Modern Studies* 33 (2003): 241–59; and Tracey Sedinger, "'And yet woll I stiell saye that I am I': *Jake Juggler*, the Lord's Supper, and Disguise," *English Literary History* 74, no. 1 (Spring 2007): 239–69.

32. On toothlessness as a common sign of lack of disciplinary and discursive restraint, see Carla Mazzio, "Sins of the Tongue," in *The Body in Parts: Fantasies of Corporeality in Early Modern Europe*, ed. David Hillman and Carla Mazzio (New York: Routledge, 1997), 53–79, 67.

33. See, for example, Karen Cunningham, *Imaginary Betrayals: Subjectivity and the Discourse of Treason in Early Modern England* (Philadelphia: University of Pennsylvania Press, 2001), who argues for the problematic logic of female chastity being subject to male testimony, esp. 61–65.

34. Cartwright, *Theatre and Humanism*, 81, 138, 142, 145. Bevington, *Tudor Drama and Politics*, 121–24. Bevington suggests that the play was composed for choristers just before or just after Mary's coronation (121), that "Custance's story of feminine courage, charity and firm maternalism is calculated to warm Mary's heart" (121), and that the play upholds "feminine values of concord, domesticity, and forbearance" with a "harmless ending in a banquet" suggesting "social reconciliation that Mary so earnestly desired" (124). It is these last two arguments that my reading will put significant pressure on, as well as the place of festive (detoxified) anti-Catholicism in a play possibly composed for Mary. Whereas Bevington stresses plot and character, my differing viewpoints on both the religious dimension of the play and the play's comic closure (which indexes an important form of harm) emerge from attention to verbal structures in (and around) the play.

35. See especially Patricia Parker, *Literary Fat Ladies: Rhetoric, Gender, Property* (London: Methuen, 1987), usefully excerpted in *Feminism and Renaissance Studies*, ed. Lorna Hutson (Oxford: Oxford University Press, 1999), and Peter Stallybrass, "Patriarchal Territories: The Body Enclosed," in *Rewriting the Renaissance: The Discourses of Sexual Difference in Early Modern Europe*, ed. Margaret W. Ferguson, Maureen Quilligan, and Nancy J. Vickers (Chicago: University of Chicago Press, 1986), 123–42.

36. Walter J. Ong, "Latin Language Study as a Renaissance Puberty Rite," *Studies in Philology* 56 (1959): 103–24. Thomas Elyot writes, "Hit shall be expedient / that a noble-mannes sonne in his infancie haue with hym continually / only suche as may accustome hym by litle and litle to speake pure and elegant latin. Semblably the nourises and other women aboute [an infant or young boy] / if it be possible, to [speake pure and elegant latin], or at the leaste way / that they speke none englisshe but that / which is cleane / polite / perfectly / and articulately pronounced / omittinge no lettre or sillables as folisshe women often times do of a wantonnesse / whereby diuers noble men / and gentilmennes chyldren (as I do at this daye knowe) haue attained corrupte and foule pronunciation." *The boke named the Governour* (London, 1531), L3v. Elyot goes on to suggest that at the age of seven, "I holde it expedient that he be taken from the company of women: save yere or two at the most / an aunciant and sad matrone attendyng on hym in his chambre / which shall nat haue any young woman in her company" (L4r). On the dangers of the "nurse" in England with regard to language acquisition, and on women, humanism and English comedy with a focus on *Gammer Gurton's Needle* and *Merry Wives of Windsor*, see Wendy Wall, " 'Household Stuff': The Sexual Politics of Domesticity and the Advent of English Comedy," *English Literary History* 65, no. 1 (1998): 1–45, and *Staging Domesticity* (Cambridge: Cambridge University Press, 2006), esp. 59–93 and 127–60.

37. Erasmus, *Apophthegmes*, 307v. Here Erasmus is drawing on the sayings of Cicero. See also Wilson's treatment of *"Imbecillitas naturae"* in *The rule of Reason* (1551), where "some men are so sicke in their braine, that thei are neuer wise, some are capons by kynd, and some so blunt by nature, that no arte can whet them" (D1r).

38. Lauren Berlant, "The Female Complaint," *Social Text* 19–20 (Autumn 1988): 237–59. See also *The Female Complaint: The Unfinished Buisiness of Sentimentality in American Culture* (Durham: Duke University Press, 2008).

39. John Farmer, ed., *The Dramatic Writings of Nicholas Udall* (London: Early English Drama Society, 1906), 136.

40. Latimer, *A notable Sermo[n] of ye reuerende father Maister Hughe Latemer, whiche he preached in ye Shrouds at paules churche in London on the xviii. daye of Januarye. 1548* (London, 1548), D2v; Latimer, *27 sermons preached by the ryght Reuerende father in God* (London: 1562), M1v.

41. See, for example, Juan Luis Vives, *A very frutefull and pleasant boke called the Instruction of a Christian Woman . . . turned out of Laten into Englysshe by Rycharde Hyrde* (London, 1529), E4r–v.

42. Anthony Grafton and Lisa Jardine, *From Humanism to the Humanities: Education*

and the Liberal Arts in Fifteenth- and Sixteenth-Century Europe (Cambridge, Mass.: Harvard University Press, 1986). On Grafton and Jardine, see my Introduction.

43. On Ralph's amorous misfires as a send-up of early sonneteers looking to Petrarch for inspiration, see Norland, *Drama in Early Tudor Britain*, 272.

44. On *Ralph Roister Doister* composed for Queen Mary, see Susanne Westfall, "The Boy Who Would Be King: Court Revels of King Edward VI, 1547–1553," *Comparative Drama*, 35, no. 3 (September 2001): 271–91; on Mary's possible attendance alongside the anti-Catholic send-ups in the play, see David Loewenstein and Janel Mueller, eds., *The Cambridge History of Early Modern English Literature* (Cambridge: Cambridge University Press, 2002), 244–45.

45. On Katherine Parr and Nicholas Udall, see especially Susan E. James, *Kateryn Parr: The Making of a Queen* (Brookfield, Vt.: Ashgate, 1999).

46. Richard Tottell, *Songes and sonettes* (London, 1557), A1v.

47. See Udall's use of "nycibecetours" (for dainty "dames") in Erasmus, *Apophthegmes* (120v), and of "*Inopis te miserescat mei*" or "Haue thou pitie or compassion vpon me, beinge a pore felow, and without any maner helpe" in *Flovres* (197v).

48. Thomas Wilson, *The rule of Reason, conteinyng the Arte of Logique*, 3rd ed. (London, 1553), 66, emphasis added.

49. Nicholas Udall, *Republica: An Interlude for Christmas 1553, Attributed to Nicholas Udall*, ed. W. W. Greg (Oxford: Oxford University Press, 1952), xi.

50. See Stewart, *Close Readers*.

51. Custance would make the same suggestion to Tibet, but her social position grants her vocal authority which for Madge becomes the occasion for imagined punishment based on presumed indecorousness.

52. "*Adulari*," writes Udall in *Flovres*, "is to flater an other man in humblyng them selfes and beinge seruiceable about hym, and to labour by suche facions to wyn & get his fauor, whether it be by voyce and wordes, orels by gesture of the body, or by any other way and meane what so euer it be. *Nonius Marc.* sayth thus: *Adulatio est proprie canum blandimentum, quod ad homines consuetudine translatum est*, Adulation proprely signifieth the fauning and leapinge of dogges vppon their maisters, from whiche propretie by translation it is applied to men onely by use of spekynge, and not by the propre signification of the worde" (67v).

53. In response to Ralph's looming lips and his statement "I vse to kisse all them that I loue to God I vowe," Tibet asks: "I pray you when dyd you last kisse your cowe" (7v).

54. Even before this, though, we see Madge attempting to find ways to separate herself from Ralph. When he asks her to dance, she says, "Nay I will by myne owne selfe foote the song," and follows with a more tentative "perchaunce."

55. Udall has here done three things in this scene alone: unmoored talkativeness from female "wontonnesse" or promiscuity (Tibet Talk Apace does not "kisse men"), recuperated "smatches of country phrases" in the name of female agency (Madge directs Ralph toward another object), and finally, expanded upon the theologically inflected "mumbling"

(associated above with verbal indistinction, superstition, and heretical self-talk) from Mumblecrust, who is poor and uneducated but capable of canniness, who is comic but self-aware, Catholic but God-fearing, and, without money, between a rock and a hard place.

56. On legal jurisdiction and gendered violence with regard to *Othello*, see especially Nancy Seuffert, "Domestic Violence, Discourses of Romantic Love, and Complex Personhood in the Law," *Melbourne University Law Review* 23, no. 1 (1999): 211–40, and Katharine Eisaman Maus, "Proof and Consequences: Othello and the Crime of Intention," in *Inwardness and Theater in the English Renaissance* (Chicago: University of Chicago Press, 1995), 104–27. On broader problems of legal jurisdiction operative in late medieval and Renaissance literature and culture, see especially *Boundaries of the Law: Gender, Geography and Jurisdiction in Medieval and Early Modern Europe*, ed. Anthony Musson (Aldershot: Ashgate, 2005), R. S. White, *Natural Law in English Renaissance Literature* (Cambridge: Cambridge University Press, 1996), and Bradin Cormack, *A Power to Do Justice: Jurisdiction, English Literature and the Rise of Common Law, 1509–1625* (Chicago: University of Chicago Press, 2007).

57. For the strongest case for Udall's authorship, see Udall, *Respublica*, viii–xx.

58. Udall, *Respublica*, esp. xiv and 3.3.646–52.

59. See Udall's profuse letter of apology for the accusation of "buggery," in Sir Henry Ellis's *Original Letters of Eminent Literary Men: Of the Sixteenth, Seventeenth and Eighteenth Centuries* (London: J. B. Nichols and Son, 1843), 1–7.

60. Motter, *The School Drama in England*, 53.

61. As Udall puts it, "For wete ye well (good countrymen) that two sorts of beasts there be (for I should name them wrong to call them men) that are the chief causes of this tumultuous business. The one idle, loitering ruffians that will not labour ne can by any other ways get anything to maintain them withal but by an open and common spoil. . . . The other sort is of rank Papists, which could none other ways work their malicious and devilish disturbing of God's glory but by the mean of sedition, which could not have had any entrye except it were by them craftily and subtilly conveyed. These under the colour and name of the commonwealth first reysed the simple people, persuading them to be for a good and godly purpose" ("Answer," 146).

62. On female credibility as the deliberative issue of the play, see Altman, *Tudor Play of Mind*, 150, and Hutson, *The Usurer's Daughter*, 189–90.

63. Ovid, *The xv. Bookes of P. Ouidius Naso, entytuled Metamorphosis*, trans. Arthur Golding (London, 1567), 73r–74r.

64. But so too Custance internalizes the logic of Ralph's mythic counterpart: "I had rather be torne in pieces and flaine" than be wedded to him (25r).

65. The letter, later read with different stops, reads as the opposite: "Swéete mistresse, where as I loue you, nothing at all / Regarding your richesse and substance: chiefe of all / For your personage, beautie, demeanour and wit/ I commende me vnto you: Neuer a whitte / Sory to heare reporte of your good welfare./ For (as I heare say) suche your con-

ditions are, / That ye be worthie fauour: Of no liuing man / To be abhorred: of euery honest man / To be taken for a woman enclined to vice . . . / . . . yf ye will be my wife, / Ye shall be assured for the time of my life, / I wyll kéepe you right well: from good raiment and fare, / Ye shall not be kept: but in sorowe and care / Ye shall in no wyse lyue: at your owne libertie, / Doe and say what ye lust: ye shall neuer please me / But when ye are merrie: I will bée all sadde / When ye are sorie: I wyll be very gladde / When ye seeke your heartes ease: I wyll be vnkinde / At no time: in me shall ye muche gentlenesse finde. / But all things contrary to your will and minde / Shall be done otherwise: I wyll not be behynde /To speake: And as for all they that woulde do you wrong, / (I wyll so helpe and maintayne ye) shall not lyue long" (20r-v).

66. Pittenger, in " 'To Serve the Queere,' " calls this misogyny the "unconscious of the letter" (177).

67. Ralph's relative deafness to others is hilariously if subtly indexed as he wears a kitchen pot (in place of a military helmet) on his head as he prepares to wage war on the house of Custance.

68. Johan Huizinga, *Homo Ludens: A Study of the Play-Element in Culture*, trans. R. F. C. Hull (Boston: Beacon Press, 1950), esp. 1–28.

69. Shakespeare, *Love's Labour's Lost*, ed. H. R. Woudhuysen, Arden Shakespeare (Walton-on-Thames: Thomas Nelson and Sons, 1998), 5.1.36–37.

70. Jacques Rancière, *Dis-Agreement: Politics and Philosophy* (Minneapolis: University of Minnesota Press, 1998), 50.

CHAPTER 3. DISARTICULATING COMMUNITY

1. Thomas Kyd, *The Spanish Tragedy* (4.1.158). See also *The Spanish Tragedie, Containing the lamentable end of Don Horatio, and Bel-imperia: with the pittifull death of olde Hieronimo* (London, 1592). Unless otherwise noted, all citations of *The Spanish Tragedy* refer to the New Mermaid edition, ed. J. R. Mulryne (London: A. and C. Black, 1989). Subsequent references appear parenthetically within the text by act, scene, and line number.

2. Shakespeare, *Hamlet* (3.2.10–12). Unless otherwise noted, all citations of *Hamlet* refer to the Arden Shakespeare edition, ed. Harold Jenkins (London: Methuen, 1982). Subsequent references appear parenthetically within the text by act, scene, and line number.

3. John Jewel, *A Defence of the Apologie of the Churche of Englande, conteininge an Answeare to a certaine Booke lately set foorthe by M. Hardinge, and Entituled, A Confutation of &c.* (London, 1567), 517–18. On Hieronimo's name and St. Jerome see Frank Ardolino, "Hieronimo as St. Jerome in *The Spanish Tragedy*," *Etudes Anglaises* 36, no. 4 (1983): 435–37, and " 'Now I Shall See the Fall of Babylon': *The Spanish Tragedy* as a Reformation Play of Daniel," *Renaissance and Reformation* 14 (1990): 49–55, and Janette Dillon, *Language and Stage in Medieval and Renaissance England* (Cambridge: Cambridge University Press, 1998), 158. Although an analysis of Hieronimo/Jerome lies beyond the scope of this

chapter, it is worth observing that alongside the distinctly Protestant valorization of Jerome's vulgate stressed by Ardolino and Dillon was the centrality of Jerome to Spanish and Italian Catholicism, where the order of the Hieronymites emerged. For competing theological appropriations and attitudes toward St. Jerome in the Renaissance, see Eugene F. Rice, *Saint Jerome in the Renaissance* (Baltimore: Johns Hopkins University Press, 1985).

4. S. F. Johnson, "*The Spanish Tragedy*: Or Babylon Revisited," in *Essays on Shakespeare and Elizabethan Drama in Honor of Hardin Craig*, ed. Richard Holsley (London: Routledge and Kegan Paul, 1963), 23–36, 36.

5. On "Babylon-Spain," see Ardolino, " 'Now Shall I See the Fall of Babylon': *The Spanish Tragedy* as a Reformation Play of Daniel," 51. On Babel and *Soliman and Perseda*, see also Johnson, "*The Spanish Tragedy*: Or Babylon Revisited"; A. J. Hoenselaars, "Reconstructing Babel in English Renaissance Drama: William Haughton's *Englishmen for My Money* and John Marston's *Antonio and Mellida*," *Neophilologus* 76 (1992): 464–79, 465; Ardolino, "*Corrida* of Blood in *The Spanish Tragedy*: Kyd's Use of Revenge as National Destiny," *Medieval and Renaissance Drama in England* 1 (1984): 37–49, " 'Now Shall I See the Fall of Babylon': *The Spanish Tragedy* as Protestant Apocalypse," *Shakespeare Yearbook* 1 (1990): 93–116, and *Apocalypse and Armada in Kyd's* Spanish Tragedy (Kirksville, Mo.: Sixteenth-Century Journal Publishers, 1995). In *Apocalypse and Armada*, Hieronimo's allusion to the "fall of Babylon" informs Ardolino's reading of *Soliman and Perseda* as anti-Catholic, and of the four-act structure of Kyd's drama itself as based upon Protestant readings of the books of Revelation and Daniel. See also Dillon, *Language and Stage in Medieval and Renaissance England*, who alludes to the playlet in terms of Babel (158, 161–62, 184–85) but adds that "the confusion of languages" "mask[s] certain kinds of truth (narrative, political), while hinting at the existence of other, mythic truths that may lie deeper than language" (185).

6. M. C. Bradbrook, "St. George for Spelling Reform!" *Shakespeare Quarterly* 15, no. 3 (Summer 1964): 129–41, 129.

7. Kyd, *The Spanish Tragedy*, ed. David Bevington (Manchester: Manchester University Press, 1989), 9.

8. Jasper Heywood, *The Seconde Tragedie of Seneca entituled Thyestes faithfully Englished by Jasper Heywood fellowe of Alsolne College in Oxforde* (London, 1560), *5r.

9. This is to gesture not just toward the well-known matter of classical influence in the formation of English tragic drama but also toward the problem of "fruteles" speech that was understood by the earliest English translators of Seneca to be part and parcel of vernacular neoclassicism (Jasper Heywood, preface to *The Seconde Tragedie of Seneca entituled Thyestes*,*2v).

10. Ibid., *2v, and Jasper Heywood, preface to *The Sixt Tragedie of the most graue and prudent author Lucius, Anneus, Seneca, entituled Troas, with diuers and sundrye addicions to the same. Newly set forth in Englishe by Jasper Heywood student in Oxonforde* (London, 1559), A4r–v.

11. Heywood, *The Sixt Tragedie . . . entituled Troas*, A4r–v.

12. John Studley, preface to Seneca, *The Eyght Tragedie of Seneca. Entituled Agamemnon* (London, 1566), A3v.

13. Alexander Neville, preface to Seneca, *The Lamentable Tragedie of Oedipvs the Sonne of Laivs Kyng of Thebes out of Seneca* (London, 1563), A3r.

14. See my Chapters 1 and 2.

15. Shakespeare, *Hamlet* (2.2.555).

16. William Fullwood, *The Enemie of Idlenesse Teaching the maner and stile how to endite, compose, and wryte all sortes of Epistles and Letters: as wel by answer, as otherwise. Deuided into Foure bookes, no lesse pleasant than profitable* (London, 1571).

17. Richard Mulcaster, *The First Part Of The Elementarie Vvhich Entreateth Chefelie Of The right writing of our English tung* (London, 1582), 53, 78.

18. Samuel Daniel, *A Panegyrike Congratulatorie Deliuered To The Kings Most Excellent Maiestie At Bvrleigh Harrington in Rvtlandshire. By Samuel Daniel. Also Certaine Epistles, with A Defence Of Ryme, Heretofore Written, And Now Published By The Author* (London, 1603), I1v.

19. See Cheke's letter to Sir Thomas Hoby, printed at the end of Hoby's translation of Baldassare Castiglione, *The Covrtyer of Covnt Baldessar Castilio* (London, 1561), *1v.

20. The remainder of this first section of the chapter offers a revised account of my "Staging the Vernacular: Language and Nation in Thomas Kyd's *The Spanish Tragedy*," *Studies in English Literature* 38, no. 2 (Spring 1998): 207–32.

21. Robert Cawdrey, *A Table Alphabeticall, conteyning and teaching the true writing, and vnderstanding of hard vsuall English wordes, borrowed from the Hebrew, Greeke, Latine, or French, &c. With the interpretation thereof by plaine English words, gathered for the benefit & helpe of Ladies, Gentlewomen, or any other vnskilfull persons. Whereby they may the more easilie and better vnderstand many hard English wordes, vvhich they shall heare or read in scriptures, sermons, or elswhere, and also be made able to vse the same aptly themselues* (London, 1604), A3r. While Cawdrey does not acknowledge the debt, see Thomas Wilson, *The Arte of Rhetorique* (London, 1553), Y2v. For an earlier list of hard English words, see Mulcaster, *The First Part Of The Elementarie*, and for a more expansive glossary, see Edmund Coote, *The English schoole-maister teaching all his scholers, the order of distinct reading, and true writing our English tongue* (London, 1596).

22. Sir Philip Sidney, *An Apologie for Poetrie* (London, 1595), K2v.

23. Edward Phillips, *The New World Of English Words, Or, A General Dictionary: Containing the interpretations of such hard words as are derived from other Languages . . . Together with All those Terms that relate to the Arts and Sciences . . . : to which are added the significations of Proper Names, Mythology, and Poetical Fictions, Historical Relations, Geographical Descriptions of most Countries and Cities of the World . . . / Collected and published by E.P.* (London, 1658), C1v. I juxtapose Sidney and Phillips to emphasize the ongoing uneasiness about the condition of English.

24. See also Alexander Gill, *Logonomia Anglica*, ed. Bror Danielsson and Arvid Gabrielson, trans. Robin C. Alston (London, 1619; rprt. Stockholm: Almquist and Wiksell, 1972), where alien terms are called "monstrous," "illigitimate progeny," 82.

25. William Perkins, *Prophetica, Sive, De Sacra Et vnica ratione Concionandi Tractatus* (Cambridge, 1592), trans. as *The Arte Of Prophecying: Or A Treatise Concerning the sacred and onely true manner and methode of Preaching. First written in Latine by Master William Perkins; and now faithfully translated into English (for that it containeth many worthie things fit for the knowledge of men of all degrees) by Thomas Tuke* (London, 1607), K1r–v.

26. Wilson, *The Arte of Rhetorique*, Y3v.

27. See especially Richard Foster Jones, *The Triumph of the English Language* (Stanford: Stanford University Press, 1953); Sean Keilen, *Vulgar Eloquence: On the Renaissance Invention of English Literature* (New Haven: Yale University Press, 2006), which argues for the rise of a "vulgar eloquence" that signaled the Renaissance English "invention" of a national literature distinct from that of the classical past. On Protestant plain style, see my Chapters 1 and 2 in this book.

28. Thomas Heywood, *An Apology For Actors. Containing three brief Treatises. 1 Their Antiquity. 2 Their ancient Dignity. 3 The true vse of their quality* (c. 1607, printed London, 1612), F1r.

29. John Greene, *A Refvtation of the Apology for Actors. Diuided into three briefe Treatises . . . 1. Heathenish and Diabolical institution. 2. Their ancient and moderne indignitie. 3. The wonderfull abuse of their impious qualitie* (London, 1615), F2r–v.

30. As Steven Mullaney has noted, in Renaissance England the "voice of the Other, of the *barbaros*, sounded in the throat whenever the mother tongue was spoken; one's own tongue was strange yet familiar, a foreigner within, a quite literal *internal emigré*" ("Strange Things, Gross Terms, Curious Customs: The Rehearsal of Cultures in the Late Renaissance," in *Representing the English Renaissance*, ed. Stephen Greenblatt [Berkeley: University of California Press, 1988], 65–92, 80).

31. George Pettie, "To the Reader," in Stephen Guazzo, *The Civile Conuersation of M. Steeuen Guazzo written first in Italian, and nowe translated out of French by George Pettie, deuided into foure bookes* (London, 1581), *3v. The words I have just quoted introduce Pettie's English translation of a French translation of an Italian text on the art of conversation, which itself drew on classical Greek and Roman precedents to celebrate "diuersitie & varietie of . . . discourse" (16r).

32. Michael Hattaway, "*The Spanish Tragedy*: Architectonic Design," in *Elizabethan Popular Theatre: Plays in Performance* (London: Routledge, 1982), 101–28, 110. Hattaway goes on to suggest that Kyd was "trying to see whether he could employ a theater language that would, to the unlettered at least, communicate by mere sound" (110); I would argue to the contrary that Hieronimo's displacement of psychic alienation onto language functions as a kind of revenge on representation, a revenge that thwarts and exposes the rifts within communication rather than transcends them.

33. See Gordon Braden's discussion of Kyd in *Renaissance Tragedy and the Senecan Tradition* (New Haven: Yale University Press, 1985).

34. In *The Firste volume of the Chronicles of England, Scotlande, and Irelande. Conteyning, the Description and Chronicles of England, from the first inhabiting vnto the conquest*

(London, 1577), Holinshed writes: "No one speache vnder the sonne spoken in our time . . . hath or can haue more varietie of words and copie of phrases [than English]" (5:197). Also see Jones, *The Triumph of the English Language*, on the idealization of copia by Thomas Nashe, George Puttenham, Robert Parry, Holinshed, and John Florio.

35. On copia and its discontents in the Renaissance, see in particular Terence Cave, *The Cornucopian Text: Problems of Writing in the French Renaissance* (Oxford: Clarendon Press, 1979), and Patricia Parker, *Literary Fat Ladies: Rhetoric, Gender, Property* (London: Methuen, 1987).

36. See especially Paula Blank, *Broken English: Dialects and the Politics of Language in Renaissance Writings* (London: Routledge, 1996).

37. William Harrison, "The Description of Britain," in *The First and second volumes of Chronicles, comprising 1 The description and historie of England, 2 The description and historie of Ireland, 3 The description and historie of Scotland* (London, 1587), D1r, emphasis added.

38. On expanding commerce and the development of Renaissance aesthetics, see Lisa Jardine, *Wordly Goods: A New History of the Renaissance* (New York: W. W. Norton, 1998).

39. Philip Stubbes, *The Anatomie of Abuses: contayning, A Discouerie, Or Briefe Summarie of such Notable Vices and Imperfections, as now raigne in many countreyes of the worlde: but (especiallie) in a verie famous Ilande called Ailgna* (London, 1583), C2v, C6v, D6v.

40. Sartorial as well as linguistic "disorder" and "confusion" could of course compromise coordinates of both nation and degree, as the title of Queen Elizabeth's proclamation of 1566 made plain: *The Queenes Maiestie consideryng to what extremities a great number of her subiectes are growen, by excesse in apparell, both contrary to the lawes of the realme, and to the disorder and confusion of the degrees of all states.*

41. Joseph Hall, *Mvndvs Alter Et Idem* (London, 1605), A2r.

42. The word "translation" meant of course "altering, changing," as defined in Cawdrey's, *A table alphabeticall* (London, 1604).

43. Hieronimo's theater is literally and figuratively barbaric. As George Puttenham writes in *The Arte of English Poesie* (London, 1589), "When any straunge word not of the naturall Greeke or Latin was spoken, in the old time they called it *barbarisme*" (257). While "barbarous" was often invoked to describe discomfort with linguistic or dialectical otherness, it surfaces time and again in Renaissance texts to signify acts of savage, brutish, uncivilized violence. In John Lyly's *Midas*, for example, Sophronia wishes the gods would thrust "Martius, that soundest but bloud and terror, into those barbarous Nations, where nothing is to be found but bloud and terror" (2.1.102–3). Similarly, when Hieronimo confronts the spectacle of his son's dead body, he cries, "If this inhuman and barbarous attempt, . . . / Shall unrevealed and unrevenged pass, / How should we term your dealings to be just" (3.2.6–10). It is no coincidence that as part of his revenge, the learned Hieronimo makes the murderers inhabit theatrical identities that are—in every sense of the word—barbaric.

44. For a discussion of Kyd's reproduction of popular myths of Anglo-Spanish relations,

see Arthur Freeman, *Thomas Kyd: Facts and Problems* (Oxford: Clarendon Press, 1967). For an example of myths in circulation, see Christopher Ocland, *The Valiant Actes And victorious Battailes of the English nation: from the yeere of our Lord, one thousand threee hundred twentie and seven: being the first yeare of the raigne of the most mightie Prince Edward the third, to the year 1588. Also, Of The Peacable And quiet state of England, vnder the blessed gouernement of the most excellent and virtuous Princesse Elizabeth: a compendious declaration written by C. O. And newly translated out of Latin verse into English meeter. By J. S.* (John Sharrock), (London, 1585).

45. Freeman, *Thomas Kyd*, 54.

46. In terms of Spanish/Portuguese relations, the either/or structure which functions to differentiate Spain and Portugal from the first soon begins to collapse in the General's account of the battle: "Both furnished well, both full of hope and fear, / Both menacing alike with daring shows, / Both vaunting sundry colours of device, / Both cheerly sounding trumpets, drums and fifes, / Both raising dreadful clamours to the sky" (1.2.25–29). The differentiation between Spain and Portugal continues to collapse in his ensuing description of the leveling spectacle of mutilated bodies. Further, as Spain has just conquered Portugal, Hieronimo's historical masque implicitly equates Spanish with English military power, so that Kyd in effect says—if only for a moment—that England is Spain and Spain is England.

47. Hieronimo, "sounding the mystery" of his dumb show, explains that the "Earl of Gloucester . . . enforced the king [of Portugal] / To bear the yoke of English monarchy," and the "Earl of Kent . . . took the King of Portingale in fight," and "Brave John of Gaunt [who was 'as the rest a valiant Englishman'] . . . took our King of Castile prisoner" (1.4.140–67).

48. This aligns Hieronimo's deictic with the Viceroy's earlier verbal and gestural lament for the loss of a son who, at that point, was in fact alive and well: "Here let me lie, now am I at the lowest" (1.3.14), says the Viceroy, falling to the ground.

49. While following in a Senecan tradition of revengers who attempt to talk themselves into the "acting of revenge" (see, for example, Atreus's consistent turns to rhetoric to embolden him in his task to be revenged in Seneca's *Thyestes*), Hieronimo's repetitions betray the decline of his verbal skills.

50. Lukas Erne, *Beyond* The Spanish Tragedy: *A Study of the Works of Thomas Kyd* (Manchester: Manchester University Press, 2001), 72.

51. Pettie, "To the Reader," in Guazzo, *The civile Conuersation* (3v). The adjective "plain"—through the Anglo-Norman and Middle French *plain* or *plein* and the French *plain*—derived from the Latin *planus*, and the adjective "common" from the Old French *comun* and from the Latin *communi*. See *The Oxford English Dictionary*, s.vv. "plain" (adj.) and "common" (adj.).

52. For a suggestive psychoanalytic approach to verbs for speaking in *The Spanish Tragedy*, see Kay Stockholder, " 'Yet can he write': Reading the Silences in *The Spanish Tragedy*," *American Imago: A Psychoanalytic Journal for Culture, Science and the Arts* 47 (Summer 1990): 93–124.

53. Upon close listening, the haunt of an eerily dead yet undead judicial oratio can be heard in the very next scene: when Hieronimo thinks he sees his son's ghost and asks, "And art thou come, Horatio, from the depth, / To ask for justice in this upper earth?" (3.13.133–34), beyond the obvious haunt of an injustice not addressed, it is as if Hieronimo finds himself haunted by the ghost of oratio itself.

54. *The First Part of Hieronimo*, ed. Andrew S. Cairncross (Lincoln: University of Nebraska Press, 1967), 10.127–28. See Philip Henslowe's record of plays including "*spanes comodye donne oracioe*," "the *comodey of doneoracio*," and simply "*doneoracio*," *Henslowe's Diary*, ed. R. A. Foakes and R. T. Rickert (Cambridge: Cambridge University Press, 1961), 16–19. On the authorship debate around this play, see especially Erne, *Beyond* The Spanish Tragedy, 14–46.

55. Karl Kraus, from *Half-Truths and One-and-a-Half Truths: Karl Kraus, Selected Aphorisms*, ed. and trans. Harry Zohn (Montreal: Engendra Press, 1976), 67.

56. If, as Sidney put it of poetic verse in the *Apologie*, "*Oratio*, next to *Ratio*, Speech next to Reason, bee the greatest gyft bestowed vpon mortalitie" (G3r), this gift proves mortal in *The Spanish Tragedy*, dying along with Horatio. This point is emphasized by Isabella, Hieronimo's wife, earlier in act 3 when she aligns the death of Horatio with the loss of sweet sonic "harmony" on earth that "died, ay died a mirror in our days" (3.8.20–23). Without judicious harmony, Isabella's own sense of loss informs her repetitive "died, ay died a mirror," so that she holds a mirror up to nature that haunts rather than consoles.

57. Kyd, *The Spanish Tragedy*, ed. Mulryne, 133–35, emphasis added.

58. It is significant in this respect that Hieronimo is associated with Orpheus, a figure whose myth embodies the competing forces of integration and fragmentation. In Ovid's *Metamorphoses*, Orpheus, the Renaissance model for eloquence and civility, is torn limb from limb at the very moment he loses linguistic power. Appropriately, Hieronimo's response to the futility of language (literally, Hieronimo cannot get anyone at court to hear his plea for justice) is staged—in *Soliman and Perseda*—as a "scattering" of language and body.

59. The exact question that Hieronimo refuses to answer— "who were thy confederates in this?" (4.4.176) —has already been answered. This is demonstrated by the Viceroy's own comment: "That was thy daughter Bel-Imperia; / For by her hand my Balthazar was slain: / I saw her stab him" (4.4.177–79).

60. See additions in Kyd, *The Spanish Tragedy*, ed. Mulryne, 137.

61. A negative counterpart to Orpheus, Rufinus (who is, like Hieronimo, an official marshall of justice) is punished for his savage sins. The injustice of Claudian's Rufinus is ultimately revenged (Claudian, *The Second Book Against Rufinus*, trans. Maurice Platnauer [Cambridge, Mass.: Harvard University Press, 1922], 56–97): "All pierce him with their spears and tear quivering limb from limb. . . . They stamp on that face of greed and while yet he lives pluck out his eyes; others seize and carry off his severed arms. One cuts off his foot, another wrenches a shoulder from the torn sinews; one lays bare the ribs of the cleft spine, another his liver, his heart, his still panting lungs. . . . Come portion out Ruffinus' corpse among the lands he has wronged. Give the Thracians his head; let Greece have her

due his body. What shall be given the rest? Give but a limb apiece, there are not enough for the peoples he has ruined" (88–89).

62. John Weever, *Epigrammes in the oldest cut, and newest fashion* (London, 1599), C1.

63. Among many recapitulations of the myth that were available in sixteenth-century England is in Thomas Rogers, *A philosophicall discourse, Entituled, The Anatomie of the mind* (London, 1576): "But we wil bring forth examples of more straunge & wunderful Constancie. *Zeno* the Stoike beeing cruelly tormemted of a King of *Cypres* to vtter those things which the king was desiro[us] to know, at length because he would not satisfie his minde, bit of his owne toung, and spit the same in the tormentors face" (154r–v).

64. Plutarch, *De garrulitate*, in *Moralia*, vol. 6, trans. W. C. Hembold (Cambridge, Mass.: Harvard University Press, 1939), 415. Elsewhere Plutarch invokes the topos of heart and tongue to emphasize the relation between bodily fragmentation and spiritual cohesion: "Thus Zeno, the disciple of Parmenides . . . revealed when tried in the fire that the teaching of Parmenides in his heart was like the purest gold and equal to the proof, and demonstrated by the evidence of deeds that what a great man fears is shame, whereas pain is feared by children and weak women and men with such women's souls, for he bit off his tongue and spat it in the tyrant's face" (415).

65. Similarly, for Diogenes, Anaxarchus's self-mutilation in the literal face of an irrational tyrant functions to signify his detachment from the very tortures and threats of dismemberment that he (paradoxically) resists: Nicocreon "ordered him to be pounded to death with iron pestles. But he, making light of the punishment, made that well-known speech, 'Pound, pound the pouch containing Anaxarchus; ye pound not Anaxarchus.' And when Nicocreon commanded his tongue to be cut out, they say he bit it off and spat it at him" (Diogenes Laertius, *Lives of the Eminent Philosophers*, 2 vols., trans. R. D. Hicks (Cambridge, Mass.: Harvard University Press, 1925), 2:473.

66. Unlike his classical predecessor, Hieronimo has no secrets or "confederates" to betray. Although Johnson argues that the parallel with Zeno "serves to identify Hieronimo as admirably stoic" ("*The Spanish Tragedy*," 24), because Hieronimo lacks a logical motive, his self-mutilation actually inverts the neoclassical symbolics of autoglossotomy. Further, John Lyly writes in *Euphues and his England, Containing his voyage and aduentures, mixed with the sundry pretie discourses of honest Loue, the description of the countrey, the Court, and the manners of that Isle* (London, 1580) of "the patience yt *Zeno* taught *Eretricus* to beare and forbeare, neuer séeking reuenge" (118v–119r), which further establishes the contrast between the revenging Hieronimo and Zeno. See James R. Siemon, "Sporting Kyd," *English Renaissance Drama* 24, no. 3 (Autumn 1994): 553–82, where he writes: "Like his plays, [Hieronimo's] autoglossotomy is a work of conceptual performance, which forms the matter of his subjection into an assertion of transcendent distinction" (528). See also Siemon, "Dialogical Formalism: Word, Object, and Action in *The Spanish Tragedy*," *Medieval and Renaissance Drama in England* 5 (1991): 87–115.

67. Simplicius, *Simplicius on Aristotle's Physics 6*, trans. David Konstan (London: Duckworth, 1989).

68. Willy Maley, " 'This Sceptred Isle': Shakespeare and the British Problem," in *Shakespeare and National Culture*, ed. John J. Joughin (Manchester: Manchester University Press, 1997), 83–108, 85. The staged excision of the tongue, such a vital and symbolically charged corporeal part, would have had powerful analogies in the emergent national culture of England. The specter of a vulnerable or excised national tongue that haunts *The Spanish Tragedy* also haunts Mulcaster's *Elementarie*. Time and again, Mulcaster invokes analogies of the national body to emphasize the crucial "part" played by the tongue, which, if not tended to, would, according to the anatomical metaphorics at work throughout the text, either weaken the body of the nation or lead to its loss of voice (see especially the peroration, 250–91).

69. Sir John Fortescue, *A learned commendation of the politique lawes of Englande*, trans. Robert Mulcaster (London, 1567) 110r.

70. Miles Mosse, *The Arraignment And Conuiction Of Vsurie. That Is, The iniquitie, and vnlawfulnes of vsurie, displayed in sixe Sermons, preached at Saint Edmunds Burie in Suffolke, vpon Prouerb. 28.8. By Miles Mosse, Minister of the worde, and Bacheler of Diuinitie. Seene and allowed by authoritie* (London, 1595), 155.

71. Ann Moss, *Renaissance Truth and the Latin Language Turn* (Oxford: Oxford University Press, 2003), 3. On translation and empire, or *translatio imperii et studii*, see also Rita Copeland, *Rhetoric, Hermeneutics, and Translation in the Middle Ages: Academic Traditions and Vernacular Texts* (Cambridge: Cambridge University Press, 1991).

72. On rhetoric, legal argument, and dramatic development, see especially Eugene M. Waith, "Controversia in the English Drama: Medwall and Massinger," *PMLA* 68, no. 1 (March 1953): 286–303, Philip J. Finkelpearl, *Marston of the Middle Temple: An Elizabethan Dramatist in His Social Setting* (Cambridge, Mass.: Harvard University Press, 1969), and Joel Altman, *Tudor Play of Mind: Rhetorical Inquiry and the Development of Elizabethan Drama* (Berkeley: University of California Press, 1978). For more recent work on legal rhetoric and dramatic persuasion, see especially Lorna Hutson, "Forensic Aspects of Renaissance Mimesis," *Representations* 94 (Spring 2006): 80–109, and "Rethinking the Spectacle of the Scaffold," *Representations* 89 (Winter 2005): 30–58, and Luke Wilson, *Theaters of Intention: Drama and the Law in Early Modern England* (Stanford: Stanford University Press, 2000). On the performance of legal trials on stage and at the Inns of Court, see Subha Mukherji, *Law and Representation in Early Modern Drama* (Cambridge: Cambridge University Press, 2006). On the construction of agents and subjects in Renaissance law and literature, see especially Karen Cunningham, *Imaginary Betrayals: Subjectivity and the Discourse of Treason in Early Modern England* (Philadelphia: University of Pennsylvania Press, 2002), and Elizabeth Hansen, *Discovering the Subject in Renaissance England* (Cambridge: Cambridge University Press, 1998). Scholars have fruitfully examined how techniques of logical abstraction integral to hypothesis, inferential thinking, and the retrospective construction of causality functioned, in literary and legal rhetoric alike, to "produce accounts of human agency and subjectivity" (introduction to Victoria Kahn and Lorna Hutson, eds., *Rhetoric and Law in Early Modern Europe* [New Haven: Yale Uni-

versity Press, 2001], 1–27, 2); this excellent volume features contributions on law and rhet-
oric by Hutson and Kahn as well as by Barbara Shapiro, Luke Wilson, Peter Goodrich,
Annabel Patterson, and others. On "hypothesis" in law and drama, see Lorna Hutson, *The
Usurer's Daughter: Male Friendship and Fictions of Women in Sixteenth-Century England*
(New York: Routledge, 1997); see also Wilson, *Theaters of Intention*, Altman, *Tudor Play of
Mind*, and Waith, "Controversia in the English Drama." For a complication and expansion
of Altman's argument, see especially Steven Mullaney, *The Place of the Stage: License, Play, and
Power in Renaissance England* (Ann Arbor: University of Michigan Press, 1995).

73. Jordi Coral Escolà, "Vengeance Is Yours: Reclaiming the Social Bond in *The Spanish Tragedy* and *Titus Andronicus*," *Atlantis* 29, no. 2 (December 2007): 59–74, 59. If we
consider how the drama draws on Virgil, Ovid, and Seneca, and arguably Horace, Aristo-
phanes, and many others, and features a range of competing rhetorical personae, this point
may seem hard to refute.

74. Thomas McAlindon, "*Tamburlaine the Great* and *The Spanish Tragedy*: The Genesis of a Tradition," *Huntington Library Quarterly* 45, no. 1 (Winter 1982): 59–81, 73.

75. It is worth observing at this point that many revengers in Renaissance drama who
take language as well as justice into their own hands also happen to be scholars.

76. Roger Ascham, *The Scholemaster Or plaine and perfite way of teachyng children, to
vnderstand, write, and speake, the Latin tong but specially purposed for the priuate brynging
vp of youth in ientlemen and Noble mens houses, and commodious also for all such, as haue forgot the Latin tonge* (London, 1570), C2v.

77. Thomas Tomkis, *Lingua: Or The Combat of the Tongue, And the fiue Senses for Superiority. A pleasant Comoedie* (c. 1602, first printed London, 1607), F2r–F3r, E1r.

78. The gender politics of the grammatically gendered "Lingua" are crucial for understanding the rhetoric of displaced linguistic chaos in Tomkis's play but also a thin disguise
for anxieties about self-representation in a vernacular, as opposed to a Latin, university
drama. I here used the impersonal pronoun so as not to distract from the question of the
law that this tongue brings forth on a university stage. For more on *Lingua*, see my "Sins
of the Tongue in Early Modern England," *Modern Language Studies* 28, no. 4 (Autumn
1998): 93–124.

79. For Lingua opens the play by foregrounding the problem of "a plaintiffe [that]
cannot haue access" to the "ears of common Sense" or to the ears of the "Vice Gouenor,"
the principle of legal justice in the play (A3r–v). Lingua, like Hieronimo, moreover, is both
advocate and plaintiff, who suffers "without redress" and remains unheard by even the
"Heauens" (H1r). "Hopeless to prosecute a haplesse suit," we hear in the opening scene,
Lingua can only but "prooue . . . stark madde" (A3r). Like Hieronimo, Lingua takes revenge when she cannot get the justice desired.

80. Abraham Fraunce, *The Lawiers Logike, exemplifying the praecepts of Logike by the
practise of the common Lawe* (London, 1588), 3r.

81. On the extent to which juridical rhetoric could pose problems of coherence and
comprehensibility, see especially Fortescue, *A learned commendation*, 110r. For a brilliant

treatment of the linguistic history of the law, see Peter Goodrich, *Languages of Law: From Logics of Memory to Nomadic Masks* (London: Weidenfeld and Nicolson, 1990). See also Bradin Cormack, *A Power to Do Justice: Jurisdiction, English Literature and the Rise of Common Law, 1509–1625* (Chicago: University of Chicago Press, 2007).

82. Sir Thomas Smith, *De Repvblica Anglorvm The maner of Gouernement or policie of the Realme of England, compiled by the honorable man Thomas Smyth, Doctor of the ciuil lawes, knight, and principall Secretarie vnto the two most worthie princes, King Edwarde the sixt, and Queene Elizabeth* (London, 1583), 50–52.

83. "*Fides* in Latine," for example, writes Smith, "the Gothes comming into Italie and corrupting the language, was turned first into *fede*, and at this day in Italie they will say *in fide, en fede* or *ala fe*. And some vncunning Lawiers that would make a newe barbarous latine worde to betoken lande giuen *in fidem*, or as the Italian saith in *fede*, or *fe*, made it *in feudum* or *feodum*. The nature of the worde appeareth more euident in those which we call to *fef, feof* or *feoffees*, the one be *fiduciary possessores*, or *fidei commissarij*, the other is, *dare in fiduciam*, or *fidei commissum*, or more latinely, *fidei committere*. The same *Litleton* was as much deceiued in withernam, & diuerse other olde wordes. This withernam he interpreteth *vetitum nauium*, in what language I knowe not: whereas in trueth it is in plaine Dutche and in our olde Saxon language, *wyther nempt, alterum accipere, iterum rapere*, a worde that betokeneth that which in barbarous Latine is called *represalia*, when one taking of me a distresse, which in Latine is called *pignus*, or any other thing (*De Repvblica Anglorvm*, 112).

84. See Anne McLaren, "Reading Sir Thomas Smith's *De Republica Anglorum* as Protestant Apologetic," *Historical Journal* 42 (1999): 911–39.

85. Fraunce, *The Lawiers Logike*, B4r.

86. Bradin Cormack, "Practicing Law and Literature in Early Modern Studies," *Modern Philology* 101 (2003): 79–91, 80.

87. William J. Bouwsma, "Lawyers and Early Modern Culture," *American Historical Review* 78, no. 2 (1973): 303–27, 309, emphasis added.

88. For an account of the movement of law from oral to textual modes of transmission and reception, see Anthony Musson, "Law and Text: Legal Authority and Judicial Accessibility in the Late Middle Ages," in *The Uses of Script and Print: 1300–1700,* ed. Julia Crick and Alexandra Walsham (Cambridge: Cambridge University Press, 2004), 95–119. The power of print to serve as what David Zaret has called "democracy's handmaiden," in *Origins of Democratic Culture: Printing, Petitions and the Public Sphere in Early Modern England* (Princeton: Princeton University Press, 2000, 254), might be tempered by further attention to problems of communication and intelligibility that print could also induce.

89. Richard Mulcaster, *Positions, Wherin Those Primitive Circumstances Be Examined, Which Are Necessarie For The Training vp of children, either for skill in their booke, or health in their bodie* (London, 1581), 250–51.

90. William Fleetwood, *A Treatise vpon the Charters Liberties Lawes and Customes of all Forrestes Parkes Chases and Free Warrens* (Harvard Law School MS 15, 1581), 118V, cited

in Ian Lancashire, "Law and Early Modern English Lexicons," *Selected Proceedings of the 2005 Symposium on New Approaches in English Historical Lexis (HEL-LEX)*, ed. R. W. McConchie et al. (Somerville, Mass.: Cascadilla Proceedings Project, 2006), 8–23, 18. See also C. W. Brooks and Kevin Sharpe, "Debate: History, English Law and the Renaissance," *Past and Present*, 72 (1976): 133–42.

91. Thomas Egerton, "Proceedings in the Lords, 1597–98: October 24–February 9" in *Historical Collections: or, An exact Account of the Proceedings of the Four last Parliaments of Q. Elizabeth . . .* , ed. Heywood Townshend (London, 1680), 79–99, 81.

92. Kyd's father was a warden for the Company of Scriveners, which dealt centrally with the transcription of legal documents. On the Company of Scriveners and the status of scriveners in the late sixteenth and seventeenth centuries more generally, see especially Peter Beal, *In Praise of Scribes: Manuscripts and Their Makers in Seventeenth-Century England* (Oxford: Clarendon Press, 1998). According to Thomas Nashe, Kyd served in the trade as a scrivener as well, born as he was into the "the trade of Nouerint" ("To the Gentlemen Students of both Uniuersities," prefatory epistle to Robert Greene's *Menaphon Camillas alarum to slumbering Euphues, in his melancholie cell at Silexedra* [London, 1589], **3v). On Kyd as the object of Nashe's attack, see especially V. Østerberg, "Nashe's 'Kid in Aesop': A Danish Interpretation," *Review of English Studies* 18, no. 72 (October 1942): 385–94.

93. Sir Edward Coke, "The Preface," *La Sept Part Des Reports Sr. Edw. Coke Chiualer* (London, 1608), 5v, 6v.

94. On the circulation of letters in the play in terms of the legal status of epistolary evidence in the Scots trial, see Karen Cunningham, *Imaginary Betrayals*, 110–40. On delayed justice in the play (as in *Hamlet*) in terms of the increasingly bureaucratic structure of English law, see Peter Sacks, " 'Where Words Prevail Not': Grief, Revenge, and Language in Kyd and Shakespeare," *English Literary History* 49, no. 3 (Autumn 1982): 576–601. See also Sacks, *The English Elegy: Studies in the Genre from Spenser to Yeats* (Baltimore: Johns Hopkins University Press, 1985).

95. McAlindon, "*Tamburlaine the Great* and *The Spanish Tragedy*" 72.

96. On the "lawless" Hieronimo split off from his erstwhile position as knight marshall, see Marguerite A. Tassi, *The Scandal of Images: Iconoclasm, Eroticism, and Painting in Early Modern English Drama* (Selinsgrove, Pa.: Susquehanna University Press, 2005), 176, and on the moment in which Hieronio "abjures legal justice," see Frank Ardolino, "The Influence of Spenser's *Faerie Queene* on Kyd's *Spanish Tragedy*," *Early Modern Literary Studies* 7, no. 3 (January 2002): 4.1–70, 50. For a discussion about Hieronimo's presumed shift from legal advocate to outlaw, see also Escolà, "Vengeance Is Yours." Even through the playlet may seem to do justice, from a historical, international, and antirrhetic perspective, to Catholic Spain, Hieronimo is often interpreted as a character whose abandonment of civic speech constitutes his abandonment of the law.

97. On the legal history of *ejectio firmae*, see R. S. White, *Natural Law in English Renaissance Literature* (Cambridge: Cambridge University Press, 1996), 89–90.

98. The same may be the case in the petitioner who speaks of his "band" in the 1592 Quarto, typically glossed as "bond" or "legal writ," referring back to the "action of the case" (see Kyd, *The Spanish Tragedy*, ed. Mulryne, 88 n. 66), although the two words were often used interchangeably. If so, this resonates with Pedringano's unlearned hangman in a prior scene, who mispronounces his name as "Petergade" (3.7.20).

99. Mosse, *The Arraignment*, 155.

100. John Rastell, *The exposicions of [the] termys of [the] law of england [and] the nature of the writts with diuers rulys [and] principalles of the law as well out of the bokis of mayster littelton as of other bokis of the law* (London, 1523), A2r–v. On "Eieccione," see D1v.

101. John Rastell, *An exposition of certaine difficult and obscure words, and termes of the lawes of this realme* (London, 1579); see 7v and each of these terms glossed in the dictionary.

102. Shakespeare, *Hamlet*, 3.2.17–18. On *Hamlet* and the question of criminal "action" in legal cases, see Luke Wilson, "Hamlet, Hales V. Petit, and the Hysteresis of Action," *English Literary History* 60, no. 1 (Spring 1993): 17–55. Wilson complicates the idea of legal and dramatic action—functioning as "competing representational jurisdictions locked in a struggle for control"—by foregrounding the interanimated jurisdictions of Renaissance drama and law (36–37). For fuller account of drama and the law, see Wilson's *Theaters of Intention*.

103. On the Virgilian allusion to the drawing of lots and the image of Minos as he "drew forth" the "graven leaves" (1.1.36–37) from a pot or "urn," see Kyd, *The Spanish Tragedy*, ed. Mulryne, 7 n. 36.

104. Peter Sacks explains the "law's delay" in both *Hamlet* and *The Spanish Tragedy* in terms of the emergence of a legal bureaucracy in England: "By the mid-sixteenth century in England, parliament had taken responsibility for many judgments that had been previously left to the absolute monarch, thus introducing a sense of justice as a matter of interpretation and human vote, rather than heaven-sent verdicts. The judiciary itself had become far more bureaucratic, with a proliferation of courts and jurors, a kind of swell of mediations which delayed and made increasingly opaque the actual administration of justice" (" 'Where Words Prevail Not,' " 578).

105. For an acute analysis of legal rhetoric and the retrospective discernment of causality in matters of action in *Hamlet*, see Wilson, *Theaters of Intention*.

106. Sir Edward Coke, "To the Reader," *La Size Part Des Reports Sr. Edw. Coke Chiualier* (London, 1607), 10r–v. On the specifically oral dimensions of sixteenth-century legal training, see Paul Raffield, *Images and Cultures of Law in Early Modern England: Justice and Political Power, 1558–1660* (Cambridge: Cambridge University Press, 2004), 9–41; Peter Goodrich, *Law in the Courts of Love: Literature and Other Minor Jurisprudences* (London: Routledge, 1996), 72–94, and *Languages of Law*, chap. 3, and W. J. Loftie, *The Inns of Court and Chancery* (Southampton: Ashford Press, 1985).

107. Fraunce continues: "*Lyttleton* did what hée could in this behalfe, although it were

but litle, as in those his distinctions, Estate taile is generall or speciall: Dower is per le comen ley, per custom, *ad ostium ecclesiae, ex assensu patris,* de la pluis beale. Uillen per prescription ou confession: Item in gros ou regardant. Rent est rent seruice, charge, seck. Conditions in fayt, en ley. Garrantie, lineall, collaterall, perdisseisin, &c." (Q1r–v).

108. *The Spanish Tragedy* raises various questions about the "common law of arms" (1.3.47), about common law itself in which judges, at times, decided cases under the authority of the king, and about matters of "blood with blood" as well as "equity" at law (3.6.35, 3.13.54).

109. Peter Goodrich, "The Continuance of the Antirrhetic," *Cardozo Studies in Law and Literature* 4, no. 2 (Autumn 1992): 207–22, 209. As Goodrich further explains, "Even where the vernacular was used for commentary or elaboration, the reports, the rolls and the legislation remained in a tongue which would only serve the community of lawyers and not that of custom or populus" (212).

110. Goodrich, especially "The Continuance of the Antirrhetic."

111. Ibid., 207. Page numbers in the rest of this section refer to this article. On the antirrhetic, see also Goodrich, "*Ars Bablativa:* Ramism, Rhetoric, and the Genealogy of English Jurisprudence," in *Legal Hermeneutics,* ed. Gregory Leyh (Berkeley: University of California Press, 1992), 43–82, "Poor Illiterate Reason: History, Nationalism and Common Law," *Social and Legal Studies* 1, no. 1 (1992): 7–28, and *Oedipus Lex: Psychoanalysis, History, Law* (Berkeley: University of California Press, 1995).

112. On the sixteenth-century arts of logic, see especially Wilbur Samuel Howell, *Logic and Rhetoric in England, 1500–1700* (New York: Russell & Russell, 1961). See also Henry Turner, *The English Renaissance Stage: Geometry, Poetics, and the Practical Spatial Arts 1580–1630* (Oxford: Oxford University Press, 2006).

113. Wilson, *The rule of Reason, conteinyng the Arte of Logique,* Q6v.

114. Even at the height of his madness, when he bites out his tongue, Hieronimo says, "*First* take my tongue, and *afterwards* my heart" (4.4.191), foregrounding the telos of action as he would have it framed.

115. See especially Hutson, "Forensic Aspects of Renaissance Mimesis," where she argues that legal *narratio* enabled innovative forms of dramatic emplotment in Renaissance drama.

116. Ascham, *The Scholemaster,* 52r. So too the humanist and playwright William Gager would later recommend that students aiming to "practise their style either in prose or verse, be well acquainted with Seneca or Plautus, to try their voices and confirm their memories." Gager (Corpus Christi Archives, MS 352, 41–65), cited by John R. Elliott, "Early Staging in Oxford," in *A New History of Early English Drama,* ed. John D. Cox and David Scott Kastan (New York: Columbia University Press, 1997), 68–76, 68.

117. Martin Mueller, *Children of Oedipus and Other Essays on the Imitation of Greek Tragedy, 1550–1800* (Toronto: University of Toronto Press, 1980), 182.

118. Seneca, *Seneca: His Tenne Tragedies,* ed. Thomas Newton (London, 1581), A3v.

119. On judicial narratio and comic (as opposed to tragic) emplotment in the Renais-

sance, see Hutson, "Forensic Aspects of Renaissance Mimesis," 91. Judicial narratio, centered on the topics "who, what, with what help, why, how and when," writes Hutson, "was understood to be an innovative strategy of emplotment" (92–93).

120. Reviewing the critical tradition of situating English tragedy in terms of classical comedy, Lorna Hutson observes that as "T. S. Eliot, Alfred Harbage and, more recently, Lucas Erne have all pointed out, English Renaissance Tragedy (including Thomas Kyd, Shakespeare, Thomas Heywood, Thomas Middleton, and John Webster) is unlike Continental neoclassical tragedy precisely to the extent that its plots are less indebted to Seneca then to Latin intrigue comedy" ("Forensic Aspects of Renaissance Mimesis," 96).

121. Alexander Neville, preface to Seneca, *The Lamentable Tragedie of Oedipvs*, A3r.

122. John Studley, "Preface to the Reader," in Seneca, *The Eyght Tragedie of Seneca. Entituled Agamemnon*, A3v. Neville, preface to Seneca, *The Lamentable Tragedie of Oedipvs*, A5v.

123. Nashe, "To the Gentlemen Students of both Uniuersities," **3v–r.

124. On the way in which Hieronimo takes each quotation from Seneca out of context, reads three passages that are about tragic lamentation and self-destruction from *Agamemnon*, *Troades*, and *Oedipus*, and forces them into an agenda for revenge in which he will self-destruct, see Scott McMillin, "The Book of Seneca in *The Spanish Tragedy*," *Studies in English Literature* 14 (1974): 201–8.

125. Erne, *Beyond* The Spanish Tragedy, 81.

126. In Seneca, *Seneca. IX: Tragedies II*, ed. and trans. John G. Fitch (Cambridge, Mass.: Harvard University Press, 2004).

127. When Hieronimo offers what Mulryne calls a "loose translation" (85) from *Troades*, his English, while faithful to the Latin, is a bit awkward. Seneca's "*Fata si miseros juvant, habes salutem; / Fata si vitam negant, habes sepulchrum*" becomes "If destiny thy miseries do ease, / Then hast thou health, and happy shalt thou be; / If destiny deny thee life, Hieronimo, / Yet shalt thou be assured of a tomb" (3.13.12–17).

128. We might attend here to Hamlet's "To be or not to be" speech, spoken after he enters with a book in hand. This speech, as Robert Miola has argued in *Shakespeare and Classical Tragedy: The Influence of Seneca* (Oxford: Clarendon, 1992), draws explicitly from Senecan tragedy. But which Seneca? Heywood's Seneca or Seneca's Seneca? If we take seriously the 1603 Quarto of *Hamlet*, we might also consider a still largely eloquent Hamlet's sudden rhetorical halts and dialogic awkwardness: "To be, or not to be, I there's the point, / To Die, to sleepe, is that all? I all: / No, to sleepe, to dreame, I mary there it goes" (E1r–v). The rhetorical halting in both cases marks characters (Hieronimo and Hamlet) grappling with the Stoic and the tragic Seneca, but the presence of the book and awkward English calls for further attention to the "English *Seneca*" at stake in both plays.

129. Hieronimo and Revenge are not alone in using "plot" to supplant the function and complexity of communal speech; we find other characters turning away from shared language toward privatized plots. Kyd dramatizes not one but a remarkable proliferation of revenge plots, and each of these plots surfaces in an inappropriate context as an imagined solution to some failure of spoken language. Balthazar, Petrarchan lover lamenting

that his "words are rude and work her no delight," his "lines . . . but harsh and ill" (2.1.14–15), decides, rather indecorously, "I must take revenge, or die myself" (2.1.116). Lorenzo, his conspirator in plotting against Horatio (the more successful suitor to Bel-Imperia), states rather baldly, "Where words prevail not, violence prevails" (2.1.108), a sentence that informs his consistent self-image as an ingenious maker of "plot" and—as he shares that plot with Balthazar—"complot" (3.2.100, 3.4.40). The rhetoric of plot and the compensatory function of plot in relation to verbal inefficacy intensify as Isabella, mother of the now slain Horatio, believing that the King stands unmoved by words "to justice or compassion" (4.2.3), returns to the scene of the murderous "plot" and imitates it, leading to her own demise. Here Kyd draws on the dual meaning of "plot" in the period, meaning at once a piece of ground—Edward Hall writes of a burial plot, with carcasses "buried in a square plot of .xv.C. yardes"—and a "pattern of action." Converting the doubly emphasized "garden-plot" (12) and "Accursed complot of my misery" (13) into both burial and dramatic plot, Isabella enacts a tragedy of a tragedy, an action of an action, coercing mimesis into matricide, stabbing the "breast, / The hapless breast that gave Horatio suck" (37–38). See Edward Hall, *The Vnion of the two noble and illustre famelies of Lancastre [and] Yorke* (London, 1548), Iir, and *Oxford English Dictionary*, s.v. "plot."

130. R. L. Kesler, "Time and Causality in Renaissance Revenge Tragedy," *University of Toronto Quarterly* 59, no. 4 (Summer 1990): 474–97, 484.

131. That Bel-Imperia "improvises" her own death in *Soliman and Perseda* by sticking to, and subsuming herself within, Hieronimo's "plot" strikes Hieronimo as a surprise, an unexpected event beyond the frame of his revenge: "Poor Bel-Imperia missed her part in this: / For though the story saith she should have died, / Yet I of kindness, and of care to her, / Did otherwise determine of her end" (4.4.140–42). Bel-Imperia's "resolution" (145) to kill herself stands as a dramatic re-solution, a competing determination, of what an end should look like and who is the "author . . . in this tragedy" (147). This anticipates the final two scenes of the play, where first Hieronimo recapitulates the action (4.4.95–152) and then Andrea recapitulates it once more (4.5.3–11).

132. Heywood, *An Apology*, F1v.

133. See also Horatio's similarly reductive account of the play in terms of action in *Hamlet* (5.2.385–91).

134. Kyd, *The Spanish Tragedy*, ed. Mulryne, 122 nn. 1–2. Mulryne is here drawing on Barry B. Adams, "The Audiences of *The Spanish Tragedy*," *Journal of English and German Philology* 68 (1969): 221–36.

135. In the vision of the afterlife of the play, repetitive actions are contrasted with healing words, as Andrea aims to lead Hieronimo "where Orpheus plays" (4.5.23). While this might suggest an alternative classical tradition to counter the Senecan cycle of repetition, it is in and of itself a rather incongruous placement for a revenger who has, over the course of the play, torn representation to bits, composed a song without harmony, killed others, and bitten out his own tongue. The underworldy "plots" of the classical past are, even at the end, too restrictive for an adequate conclusion to Kyd's own play.

136. In Seneca's play, Thyestes did not merit the monstrous revenge exacted upon him by Atreus. Thyestes, having given up the court for a life in the country, poses no immediate threat to Atreus, though Atreus convinces himself otherwise. While Thyestes, in the prehistory of the play, did indeed sleep with Atreus's wife, steal a ram, and usurp political power, Atreus converts these sins, through his own preoccupation with paternity, into a justification for making Thyestes consume his own future by eating his sons. Heywood's conclusion—having Thyestes take further revenge upon himself—thus seems indecorous.

137. Just what the external audience is to take from the whole play's "end" has perplexed scholars for decades. Joel Altman, in *Tudor Play of Mind*, attempted to resolve the play's internal contradictions by arguing that Kyd put his audience in the difficult position of undertaking judicial inquiry and deliberation, ultimately coming toward a compassionate form of justice in evaluating Hieronimo. But this judicial role is complicated by the audience's invitation to inhabit and reconcile (at the very least) two contradictory frameworks for judgment; to identify with Hieronimo as an anti-Iberian, Anglophilic, and justly bereft revenger, and to dis-identify with him as someone as a native of Spain whose actions lead to the death of the innocent Castille, inadvertently enable Bel-Imperia's suicide, and potentially enable his wife's suicide—since while she kills herself he is busy working on the plot "already in [his] head" (4.1.51).

138. Seneca, *Thyestes* (1.1.195–96), in *Seneca: IX: Tragedies II*, ed. and trans. John G. Fitch, Loeb Classical Library (Cambridge, Mass.: Harvard University Press, 2004).

139. *Oxford English Dictionary*, s.v. "confusion," 7a.

140. For a fuller account of language diversity in the play, see my "Staging the Vernacular."

141. Kyd, *The Works of Thomas Kyd*, edited by Frederick S. Boas (Oxford: Clarendon Press, 1901).

142. While Kesler attempts to discern the rationality of plot in the play, Lucas Erne, noting Kyd's "well-wrought plot," argues that *The Spanish Tragedy*, though printed in four acts, was originally designed with a five-act structure: "Besides Seneca, New Comedy and neoclassical drama may also have suggested to Kyd the five-act structure to which *The Spanish Tragedy* conforms. In fact, the dramatic architecture of *The Spanish Tragedy* shows a careful five-act construction such as Kyd observed in Seneca" (*Beyond The Spanish Tragedy*, 67). Here we see Kyd being recuperated through the invocation of neoclassical plot arrangement, yet Kyd seems intent, as I have been arguing, on exposing the limits of writing for the plot.

143. Quentin Skinner, "Meaning and Understanding in the History of Ideas," *History and Theory* 16 (1969): 3–53. Skinner's "mythology of coherence" in modern historiography is the attempt to discern "coherence [in texts] which they may appear to lack" (16). Such a challenge has been a stimulus to a range of literary historians: Richard Strier, for example, calls for a vigorous resistance "against any sort of approach to texts that knows in advance what they will or must be doing or saying" (*Resistant Structures: Particularity, Radicalism, and Renaissance Texts* [Berkeley: University of California Press, 1995], 2).

144. F. J. Levy, *Tudor Historical Thought* (San Marino: Huntington Library, 1967). On "radical condensation" and principles of selection afforded by dramatic "construction," see especially xi, 237, 226–33; on "the principle of accretion" and the "vast quantities of miscellaneous information" in English chronicles, see especially 15, 167–68, 186. Of all English playwrights, Shakespeare emerges for Levy as a golden boy of historical discrimination: "The editors of the second edition of Holinshed had worked on a principle of agglomeration; Shakespeare used selection instead"; he "saw history in terms of the operation of ideas," and "because he was a dramatist, with only a brief space at his disposal, his selection had to be more rigorous" (233). Further, "to create order out of the confusion of the episodic chronicle play was the achievement of Shakespeare" (226). More generally, since Holinshed left "establishing causality" up to the reader, writes Levy, "this made him the ideal source for the playwrights; everything needful (and a great deal more) was included," but the "construction, the ordering of events, was left to others, who could thus make of the multitudinous facts what they would" (184). For a challenge to the assumption that chronicles provided "the raw material on which genius drew," see Annabelle M. Patterson, *Reading Holinshed's Chronicles* (Chicago: University of Chicago Press, 1994), 4.

145. Levy, *Tudor Historical Thought*, 168.

146. Patterson, *Reading Holinshed's Chronicles*, 32.

147. In a countervailing and contemporary assessment of Hall, Daniel Woolf writes: "Some chroniclers were not as literarily naive as we once thought. Edward Hall, for one, had a very clear unifying principle and a rhetorical strategy in mind when he cast his work both as annals and as a connected series of reigns leading to the titular Union of the two houses of York and Lancaster" ("Disciplinary History and Historical Discourse. A Critique of the History of History: The Case of Early Modern England," *Cromohs* 2 [1997]: 1–25, n. 35).

148. Richard Stanyhurst points out the historiographic impossibility of accommodating extant ideals of textual decorum and logical method: "If the historian be long, he is accompted a trifler: if he be short, he is taken for a summister," yet "the libertie of an historie requireth that all should be related, and nothing whusted" (Raphael Holinshed, *The Second volume of Chronicles: Conteining the description, conquest, inhabitation, and troublesome estate of Ireland; first collected by Raphaell Holinshed; and now newlie recognized, augmented, and continued* [London, 1586], 80, 81).

149. On the materiality of memory in *Lingua*, see Alan Stewart and Garrett A. Sullivan, " 'Worme-eaten, and full of canker holes': Materializing Memory in *The Faerie Queene* and *Lingua*," *Spenser Studies* 17 (2003): 215–38.

150. Holinshed, *The First and second volumes of Chronicles*, A1V. On "diversity of multivocality" in Holinshed's historiography, see Patterson, *Reading Holinshed's Chronicles*, 7. Patterson sanctions F. J. Levy's assessment that Holinshed left "the reader to be his own historian," but she revises Levy's conclusion to argue for Holinshed's "protoliberalism" and cultivation of a politics of dissent.

151. Patterson, *Reading Holinshed's Chronicles*.

152. Erving Goffman, *Interactional Ritual: Essays in Face to Face Behavior* (New York: Pantheon, 1967), 125.

153. Compare titles of editions from 1592, 1599, 1602, 1603, 1605, 1611, and 1615.

154. *Hamlet* is often singled out for its unique disruption of the logic of the revenge tragedy. See for example David Kastan, " 'His semblable in his mirror': *Hamlet* and the Imitation of Revenge," *Shakespeare Studies* 19 (1987): 111–24, and Helen Cooper, "*Hamlet* and the Invention of Tragedy," *Sederi* 7 (1996): 189–99. But here I am suggesting that Kyd's *Spanish Tragedy* anticipated Shakespeare's *Hamlet*, disrupting revenge tragedy in his own way and producing a backfiring comi-tragedy. Shakespeare would follow in Kyd's footsteps even as he produced something that may have *felt*, as we will see in the final chapter, a lot more like tragedy.

CHAPTER 4. ACTING IN THE PASSIVE VOICE

Note to epigraph: John Lyly, *Euphues and his England, Containing his voyage and aduentures, mixed with the sundry pretie discourses of honest Loue, the description of the countrey, the Court, and the manners of that Isle* (London, 1580), 87v.

1. Inarticulacy topoi could also be drawn from the tradition of Augustinian piety: the "inarticulate is that which is uttered in sighing, groning, and weeping," as George Downame put it, signifying the expressive, devotional "cry of the heart" (*A Godly And Learned Treatise Of Prayer; which both conteineth in it the Doctrine of Prayer, and also sheweth the Practice of it in the exposition of the Lords Prayer: By that faithfull and painfull servant of God George Downame, Doctr of Divinity, and late L. Bishop of Dery*, published posthumously, London, 1640), 127–28. On the voice in Reformation poetics, see especially Richard Strier, *Love Known: Theology and Experience in George Herbert's Poetry* (Chicago: University of Chicago Press, 1983), and Douglas Trevor, "George Herbert and the Scene of Writing," in *Historicism, Psychoanalysis and Early Modern Culture*, ed. Carla Mazzio and Douglas Trevor (New York: Routledge, 2000), 228–59. For a reassessment of tropes and conditions of melancholy in Renaissance England, see Douglas Trevor, *The Poetics of Melancholy in Early Modern England* (Cambridge: Cambridge University Press, 2004). On the more general trope of poetic production modeled on classical figures such as Philomel, Orpheus, and others, see especially Ann Rosalind Jones, "New Songs for the Swallow: Ovid's Philomela in Tullia d'Aragona and Gaspara Stampa," in *Refiguring Woman*, ed. Marilyn Migiel and Juliana Schiesari (Ithaca: Cornell University Press, 1991), 263–77; Jonathan Goldberg, *Voice Terminal Echo: Postmodernism and English Renaissance Texts* (New York: Methuen, 1986); Patricia Klindienst Joplin, "The Voice of the Shuttle Is Ours," *Stanford Literary Review* 1 (1984): 25–53; Lynn Enterline, *The Rhetoric of the Body from Ovid to Shakespeare* (Cambridge: Cambridge University Press, 2005), and Sean Keilen, *Vulgar Eloquence: On the Renaissance Invention of English Literature* (New Haven: Yale University Press, 2006).

2. Shakespeare, *Love's Labour's Lost* (3.1.177, 4.3.342–43), ed. Richard David, Arden

Shakespeare (London: Methuen, 1987). Unless otherwise noted, all citations to the play will refer to this edition.

3. Robert Burton, *The Anatomy of Melancholy*, ed. Lawrence Babb (Lansing: Michigan State University Press, 1965), 274. The link between the heart and the tongue was commonplace in a range of medical and poetic discourses, in which, to quote John Lyly, the "hart and tongue were twinnes, at once conceaued." See "My hart and tongue were twinnes, at once conceaued," in *The Complete Works of John Lyly* (Oxford: Clarendon Press, 1902), 12.

4. Baldassare Castiglione, *Il Cortegiano*, trans. Sir Thomas Hoby, *The Courtyer of Count Baldessar Castilio* (London, 1561), J3v.

5. Mary Thomas Crane, *Framing Authority: Sayings, Self, and Society in Sixteenth-Century England* (Princeton: Princeton University Press, 1993), 136. While Crane invokes this commonplace only to go on to challenge the notion of the "self" in the lyric tradition, I want to take issue with the vocal dimensions of love in particular. Indeed, tropes of vocal impairment are particularly marked in Petrarchan discourses of sixteenth-century England, where allegories of poetic muteness converge with increasingly commonplace tropes of the lover's silent or stammering tongue. On lyric and the problem of expression, see especially Heather Dubrow, *The Challenges of Orpheus: Lyric Poetry and Early Modern England* (Baltimore: Johns Hopkins University Press, 2007).

6. Amorous inarticulacy was of course not a new concept in this period. Indeed, the sense that one's heart belonged to another was frequently coupled with a sense that one's tongue was not one's own ("Then my tongue spoke," writes the love-struck Dante in *La vita nuova*, "almost as though moved of its own accord" [XIX]). Dante not only describes an act of poetic utterance as if words were being spoken through him, as though he has no control over his own voice or tongue, but also experiences a kind of "organ failure" in the very presence of Beatrice (XIV). *La vita nuova*, trans. Barbara Reynolds (New York: Penguin, 1969). But the diminishment of vocal agency in articulations of love, while integral to medieval courtly lyric from Dante's *La vita nuova* to Petrarch's *Rime Sparse*, became more and more commonplace in literary, medical, and educational treatments of love in sixteenth-century England. The vocal dispossession of the love melancholic becomes reanimated, as I argue over the course of this chapter, in contexts specific to the status of the voice in print.

7. John Florio, *Florio His firste Fruites: which yeelde familiar speech, merie Prouerbes, wittie Sentences, and golden Sayings. Also a perfect Induction to the Italian, and English tongues, as in the Table appeareth. The like heretofore, neuer by any man published* (London, 1578), S4r (cited in Frances Yates, *A Study of "Love's Labour's Lost"* [Cambridge: Cambridge University Press, 1936], 43). My work in this chapter is indebted to the early work of Frances Yates. But whereas Yates has located in the play a host of topical references to particular historical persons and court circles, arguing that the play is engaged with "anti-alien" (72) and "anti-pedagogical" (43) sentiments associated with Eliot and Florio, I want to argue that the play works in a broader sense to stage cultural anxieties, not so much about persons as about books, about the increasingly explicit interanimation of technologies of speaking, writing,

and print in a period of increased book production and public literacy. On important language debates in the play, see William C. Carroll, *The Great Feast of Language in* Love's Labour's Lost (Princeton: Princeton University Press, 1976), and for a summation of early critical perspectives on language in the play, see Louis Adrian Montrose, *"Curious-Knotted Garden": The Form, Themes, and Contexts of Shakespeare's* Love's Labour's Lost (Salzburg: Institut fur Englische Sprache und Literatur, U Salzburg, 1977), 49–66.

8. Juliana Schiesari, *The Gendering of Melancholia: Feminism, Psychoanalysis, and the Symbolics of Loss in Renaissance Literature* (Ithaca: Cornell University Press, 1992), 15. For an important psychoanalytic account of melancholia and masculinity in early modern literature, see Lynn Enterline, *The Tears of Narcissus: Melancholia and Masculinity in Early Modern Writing* (Stanford: Stanford University Press, 1995).

9. Henry Peacham, *Minerva Britanna Or A Garden Of Heroical Deuises furnished, and adorned with Emblemes and Impresa's of sundry natures, Newly devised, moralized, and published, by Henry Peacham, Mr. of Artes* (London, 1612), 126.

10. Schiesari, *The Gendering of Melancholia*, 48.

11. Margreta de Grazia, "Soliloquies and Wages in the Age of Emergent Consciousness," *Textual Practice* 9, no. 1 (1995): 67–92, 74.

12. Although in the sixteenth century, as Roger Chartier has observed in *The Order of Books: Readers, Authors and Libraries in Europe Between the Fourteenth and Eighteenth Centuries*, trans. Lydia G. Cochrane (Stanford: Stanford University Press, 1994), "the reading style implicit in a text, literary or not, was still often an oralization of the text," since texts were "addressed to the ear as much as the eye" (9); the activity of reading was often described in physiological terms as a dominance of heart and eye over tongue. We find this early, for example, in Augustine's description of St. Ambrose reading silently: "His eyes scanned the page, and his heart explored the meaning, but his voice was silent and his tongue was still" (Augustine, *Confessions*, trans. R. S. Pine-Coffin [Harmondsworth: Penguin Books, 1961], 114). And later, many symbolic accounts of the physiology of reading foregrounded the centrality of ocular and cardiac motion: Henry Peacham's emblem of "*Salomonis prudentia*" features an eye and heart floating above an open book (*Minerua Britanna*, 40).

13. Shakespeare, *Much Ado About Nothing*, ed. A. R. Humphreys, Arden Shakespeare (London: Routledge, 1988).

14. The sociolinguistic dimensions of love melancholy were frequently marked in send-ups of the speech pathologies of the lovesick, who were alternately mute or, to quote Nicholas Breton's *A floorish vpon fancie. As gallant a Glose vpon so triflinge a text, as euer was written . . .* (London, 1577), full of "straunge languages" leading them to "vtterly vndoe themselues" (Civ). John Eliot's 1593 satiric manual on English and French tongues, *Ortho-epia Gallica. Eliots frvits for the French: Enterlaced vvith a double nevv Inuention, vvhich teacheth to speake truely, speedily and volubly the French-tongue* (London, 1593), for example, features an extended dialogue about a lovesick versifier in order to expose deficiencies of speech; while he will "neuer speake to any bodie," he is "always

mumbling or recording some thing in English verse, that he hath made to his sweetheart and minion" (V4r).

15. On the "bibliographic ego," see Joseph Lowenstein, "The Script in the Marketplace," in *Representing the English Renaissance*, ed. Stephen Greenblatt (Berkeley: University of California Press, 1988), 265–78.

16. Sigmund Freud, "Mourning and Melancholia," in *The Standard Edition of the Complete Psychological Works*, trans. James Strachey (London: Hogarth, 1953–74), 14:243–58, 248.

17. George Whetstone, *An Heptameron of Ciuill Discourses* (London, 1582), reprinted as *A Critical Edition of George Whetstone's 1582 An Heptameron of Civill Discourses*, ed. Diana Shklanka, The Renaissance Imagination, vol. 35 (New York: Garland, 1987), 114.

18. Margreta de Grazia and Adrian Johns have recently explored the complex lexicon of "impression" in early modern England. See de Grazia, "Imprints: Shakespeare, Gutenberg, Descartes," in *Alternative Shakespeares*, vol. 2, ed. Terence Hawkes (London: Routledge, 1996), 63–94, and Johns, *The Nature of the Book: Print and Knowledge in the Making* (Chicago: University of Chicago Press, 1998), 380–443.

19. André Du Laurens, *A Discourse of the Preseruation of the Sight: of Melancholike diseases; of Rheumes, and of Old age. Composed by M. Andreas Laurentius, ordinarie Phisition to the King, and publike professor of phisicke in the Vniuersitie of Mompelier. Translated out of French into English, according to the last edition, by Richard Surphlet, practitioner in phisicke* (London, 1599), 96–97.

20. Jacques Ferrand, *Erotomania, Or A Treatise Discoursing of the Essence, Causes, Symptomes, Prognosticks, and Cure of Love or Erotique Melancholy* (Oxford, 1640), 259–60.

21. On metaphors of print at work in Falstaff's easy loving, see Elizabeth Pittenger, "Dispatch Quickly: The Mechanical Reproduction of Pages," *Shakespeare Quarterly* 42, no. 4 (Winter 1991): 389–408.

22. Timothy Bright, *A Treatise of Melancholy. Contayning the causes thereof, and reasons of the straunge effects it worketh in our minds and bodies: with the Phisicke cure, and spirituall consolation for such as haue thereto adioyned afflicted conscience. . . .* (London, 1586), A1r.

23. With a particular focus on print and attention to printed texts of the period that served as possible sources for the play (and that themselves addressed the problem of forms of speech too reliant on printed texts), my argument departs from that of Terence Hawkes, who focuses on scribal and oral practices in *Love's Labour's Lost* in "Shakespeare's Talking Animals," *Shakespeare Survey* 24 (1977): 47–54.

24. Julia Kristeva, *Tales of Love* (New York: Columbia University Press, 1987), 6.

25. Andrea Guarna, *Bellum grammaticale* (Cremona, 1511), translated into English by William Heyward as *Bellum Grammaticale, A discourse of gret war and dissention betwene two worthy Princes, the Noune and the Verbe, contending for the chefe place or dignitie in Oration* (London, 1569), D4v.

26. Michel de Montaigne, "On Schoolmasters' Learning," in *The Complete Essays*, trans. M. A. Screech (New York: Penguin, 1993), 156.

27. John Brinsley, *Ludus Literarius: Or, The Grammar Schoole; Shewing How To Proceede from the first entrance into learning, to the highest perfection required in the Grammar Schooles, with ease, certainty and delight both to Masters and Scholars* (London, 1612), 64.

28. William Salesbury, "Wyllym Salesbury to the Reader," in *A briefe and a playne introduction, teachyng how to pronounce the letters of the British tong, (now comenly called Walsh) wherby an English man shal not only w[ith] ease read the said tong rightly: but . . . attaine to the true and natural pronunciation of other expediente and most excellent languages set forth by D. Salesburye* (London, 1550). George Delamothe, "An Epistle to the Reader," in *The French Alphabeth [sic] Teaching In A Very Short Tyme, By a most easie way, to pronounce French naturally, to reade it perfectly, to write it truely, and to speake it accordingly* (London, 1592).

29. Erasmus, *De duplici copia verborum ac rerum commentarii duo* (1512), trans. Betty I. Knott, in *Collected Works of Erasmus: Literary and Educational Writings*, ed. Craig R. Thompson (Toronto: University of Toronto Press, 1978), 24:279–659, 492–93.

30. Leonard Hutten, *Bellvm Grammaticale, Sive, Nominum Verborumq[ue] discordia civilis Tragico-comoedia Summo cum applausu olim apud Oxonienses in scaenam producta, & nunc in omnium illorum qui ad Gra[m]maticam animos appellunt oblectamentum edita* (c. 1581, published London, 1635). Interestingly, one of the major changes Hutten made when adapting the Italian humanist Andrea Guarna's prose text *Grammaticale Bellum* (Cremona, 1511) for the stage was that he made Poeta a melancholy (rather than a military) figure. For the publication history and context of *Bellum Grammaticale*, see Frederick S. Boas, *University Drama in the Tudor Age* (Oxford: Clarendon Press, 1914), esp. 255–58. Guarna's text was translated into English, French, and Italian, circulated widely in the sixteenth century, translated into English by William Hayward in 1569, and first adapted for the stage by Hutten. Hutten's play was performed for Elizabeth at Christ's Church in September 1592 but was staged earlier as well: Boas notes Sir John Harington's reference to "our Cambridge Pedantius and the Oxford *Bellum Grammaticale*" in 1591 (Boas, *University Drama in the Tudor Age*, 255). See also Andrea Guarna, *Bellum grammaticale A discourse of gret war and dissention betweene two worthy princes, the noune and the verb[e contend]ing for the [chiefe place of dignitie in oration] . . . Turned into [English] by VV. H.* [William Hayward] (London, 1576), in *A Collection of Scarce and Valuable Tracts, on the Most Interesting and Entertaining Subjects*, edited by Sir Walter Scott, 13 vols, 2nd ed. (London, 1809), 1:533–54.

31. On this sacking of the "townes" of A, V, E, I and O, see Hayward's 1569 translation of *Bellum Grammaticale*, D3v. For a later variation of "Amo" as a character on stage and a principle of Latin grammar, see Samuel Shaw, *Words Made Visible, or, Grammar and Rhetorick Accommodated to the Lives and Manners of Men. Represented in a Country School for the Entertainment and Edification of the Spectators* (London, 1678).

32. Jacques Bellot, *Le maistre d'escole Anglois. Contenant plusieurs profitables preceptes pour les naturelz françois, et autres estrangers qui ont la langue françoise pour paruenir a la vraye prononciation de la langue Angloise. = The Englishe Scholemaister. Conteyning many profitable preceptes for the naturall borne french men, and other straungers that haue their*

French tongue, to attayne the true pronouncing of the Englishe tongue (London, 1580). See also Bellot, *Le Iardin de Vertv et Bonnes Moeurs Plain de Plusiers Belles Fleurs, & riches sentences auec le sens d'icelles, recueillies de plusiers autheurs, & mises en lumiere* (London, 1581).

33. For Nancy Vickers's most recent work on the anatomical blazon, see "Members Only: Marot's Anatomical Blazons," in *The Body in Parts: Fantasies of Corporeality in Early Modern Europe*, ed. David Hillman and Carla Mazzio (New York: Routledge, 1997), 1–23. Also, on the relationship between humanist and courtly models of "gathering and framing," see Mary Thomas Crane, *Framing Authority: Sayings, Self, and Society in Sixteenth-Century England* (Princeton: Princeton University Press, 1993).

34. While John Florio suggests that it is labor lost to speak of love, he nonetheless benefits from the words of "so many authores," deploying the poetics and textual commonplaces of love as a basis of knowledge and discourse for the purposes of translation and language learning. His English/Italian textbook, *Florios Second frvtes, To be gathered of twelue Trees, of diuers but delightsome tastes to the tongues of Italians and Englishmen. To which is annexed his Gardine Of Recreation yeelding six thousand Italian Prouerbs* (London, 1591), devotes an entire dialogue to the pros and cons of the anatomical blazon, as well as a dialogue to the "*discourse . . . of love*," which consists of a seemingly endless list of proverbs and commonplaces, loosely disguised as a conversation about love. So too, *Florio His firste Fruites* includes chapters on "Amarous talke"; "Discourses vpon Musicke and Loue"; "A discourse vpon Lust, and the force thereof"; "The opinion of Marcus Aurelius and Ovid, upon Loue, and what it is." Similarly, John Eliot's *Ortho-epia Gallica*—a language and pronunciation manual with English and French on facing pages—includes a dialogue about love melancholy, reproduces a supposedly authentic love letter, and features an extended example of the anatomical blazon (see especially 155–63).

35. Vickers, "Members Only." Also see Vickers, "Diana Described: Scattered Woman and Scattered Rhyme," *Critical Inquiry* 8 (1981): 265–80.

36. Vickers, "Members Only," 14.

37. On Holofernes as a send-up of Florio, see Yates, *A Study of "Love's Labour's Lost"* (following Warburton), esp. 35, 136.

38. A suggestive gloss to the spatial emphasis of being "in love" might be Thomas Blundeville's Ramist treatment of "passion," where emotion is represented diagrammatically on a single page, divided into categories, sets, and subsets in "The Table of Passion and passible qualitie": see Blundeville's wonderfully entitled *The Art Of Logike. Plainely taught in the English tongue, by M. Blundeuile of Newton Flotman in Norfolke, aswell according to the doctrine of Aristotle, as of all other moderne and best accounted authors thereof. A very necessarie booke for all young students in any profession to find out thereby the truth in any doubtfull speech, but specially for such zealous ministers as haue not beene brought vp in any Vniuersity, and yet are desirous to know how to defend by sound argumentes the true Christian doctrine, against all subtill sophisters, and cauelling schismatikes, [and] how to confute their false sillogismes, [and] captious arguments* (London, 1599), 31. The influence of Ramism in English texts on rhetoric and logic in the late sixteenth century, which I will discuss shortly,

may well inform Shakespeare's English play about a French academy where passion is, in a manner of speaking, put in its place.

39. Erasmus, *De duplici copia verborum ac rerum commentarii duo*, 321.

40. On oral culture and changing conditions of literacy and technologies of communication, see Adam Fox and Daniel Woolf, eds., *The Spoken Word: Oral Culture in Britain, 1500–1850* (Manchester: Manchester University Press, 2003), esp. 1–51.

41. Sidney, *An apologie for poetrie* (London, 1595), K4r.

42. Philip Sidney, *Syr P.S. His Astrophel and Stella Wherein the excellence of sweete poesie is concluded* (London, 1591), 9.

43. Peter Levens, "Preface to the Reader," in *Manipvlvs Vocabulorum. A Dictionarie of English and Latine wordes, set forthe in suche order, as none heretofore hath ben, the Englishe going before the Latine, necessary not onely for Scholers that wa[n]t varietis of words, but also for such as vse to write in English Meetre* (London, 1570). Importantly, Levens's text was the first dictionary published in England to be organized according to both alphabet and rhyme. Clearly designed for scholars and poets, it offers an early instance where the acoustical structure of rhyme is itself prescribed, visually organized, and made broadly available through the medium of print. It is no coincidence, in this respect, that the poem and the dictionary are never far apart in *Love's Labour's Lost*. While the bad poets Armado and Holofernes are famous for speaking in "strings of synonyms," Moth goes so far as to imagine his poem or "dangerous rhyme" as a veritable definition (1.2.86–101). The textual dimensions of the rhyme, and even the translation dictionary itself, are registered by Moth's plea in creating it: "My father's wit and my mother tongue assist me!" (89).

44. On the cognitive and graphic features of the list in cultures of writing and print, see Jack Goody, "What's in a List?", in *The Domestication of the Savage Mind* (Cambridge: Cambridge University Press, 1977), 74–111. "The list relies on discontinuity rather than continuity; it depends on physical placement, on location; it can be read in different directions, both sideways and downwards, up and down, as well as left and right. . . . Most importantly, it encourages the ordering of the items, by number, by initial sound, by category, etc." (81).

45. On the lack of an "oral equivalent" for lists, see Goody, "What's in a List?", 86–87.

46. [Anon.,] *A Very necessarye boke both in Englyshce & in Frenche wherein ye mayst learne to speake & wryte Frenche truly in a litle space yf thou gyue thy mynde and diligence there unto* (London, 1550).

47. For a categorical list of terms and phrases, see also Delamothe, *The French Alphabeth*.

48. Jacques Bellot, *Familiar Dialogues, For the Instruction of the[m], that be desirous to learne to speake English, and perfectlye to pronou[n]ce the same* (London, 1586).

49. See *Love's Labour's Lost*, ed. Richard David, 22 n. 81.

50. William Carroll, for example, writes that "[t]he songs throughout embody the fusion of Art and Nature in a perfect whole" (*The Great Feast of Language*, 220), and Thomas Greene reads the songs as "rhetorical touchstones by which to estimate the foregoing

abuses of language" (*"Love's Labor's Lost:* The Grace of Society," *Shakespeare Quarterly* 22 [1971], 315–328, 325).

51. Jacques Bellot, *The French Methode wherein is contained a perfite order of Grammer for the French tongue* (London, 1588), Aa1.

52. The text reads: "The fox, the ape, and the humble-bee, / Were still at odds, being but three" (3.1.85–86), a play with numbers that recurs when the "three" embarrassed lovers become "four" in the sonnet-reading scene: "The number now is even," says Dumain, to which the guilty Berowne responds, "True, true; we are four" (4.3.207–8).

53. On the movement of the lyric into print, see especially Wendy Wall, *The Imprint of Gender: Authorship and Publication in the English Renaissance* (Ithaca: Cornell University Press, 1993); Arthur Marotti, *Manuscript, Print, and the English Renaissance Lyric* (Ithaca: Cornell University Press, 1995), and Elizabeth Pomeroy, "England's Helicon: Music and Poetry in a Pastoral Anthology," in *Elizabethan Miscellanies: Development and Conventions* (Berkeley: University of California Press, 1973), 93–115. The detachment of lyric from its origins in music and oral performance was in many ways marked by the proliferation of poetry on the printed page, and by the increased attention to the visual structure of poetry in the 1580s and 1590s. As Diana E. Henderson writes, "With the rise of printing and the circulation of sonnet manuscripts and miscellanies; unlike the poetry of many early Tudor courtly makers, whose lyric compositions were often recited or set to lute music . . . many Elizabethan lyrics were addressed primarily to a reading audience" (*Passion Made Public: Elizabethan Lyric, Gender, and Performance* [Chicago: University of Illinois Press, 1995], 216).

54. In David Rowland's *A Comfortable ayde for Scholers full of varietie of Senences, gathered out of an Italian author* (London, 1568), a textbook treating vocabulary expansion through copious variation, we find in one section, and in good Erasmian form, nineteen consecutive variations on expressions of love (11–12). Armado's desire to perform his facility with superlatives and comparatives, poor substitutes for copious eloquence, smacks of the language lesson in Rowland (*"Amo te plurimum. / Amo te multum. / Amo te valde,"* 12) and elsewhere. Rowland's textbook itself closes with variations of the phrase "He is ouercomed, or he confesseth that he is ouercomed" (143).

55. Richard Tottel, *Tottel's Miscellany,* ed. Hyder E. Rollins, 2 vols. (Cambridge, Mass.: Harvard University Press, 1965), 2:108.

56. Eliot, *Ortho-epia Gallica,* V4r–v.

57. Eliot, *Ortho-epia Gallica,* A3v, C4v. As the latter passage in Eliot reads, *"The French vse in one period (if a word end with a consonant, and the next following begin with an open vowell or dipthongue, no point or comma comming betweene) to pronounce three, foure, or fiue words with a swift voice together, as,* Prins en amour ardant embrassoit vn image, sound, Preenzanamoorardantambrassoettewnneema²ieh, *as if it were all but one word*" ("To the Reader," C2v).

58. This lover is full of clichés, exalting in *"verses that Diana whom he loueth best: her haire is nothing but goldwire, her browes arches and vautes of Ebenus: her eies twinckling starres like Castor and Pollux, her lookes lightnings: her mouth Corall: her necke Orient-Pearle: her*

breath Baulme, Amber, and Muske: her throate of snow: her necke milke-white: her dugs that she hath on her brest, Mountains or Apples of Alablaster" (*Ortho-epia Gallica* V4v).

59. Andrew Gurr, *Playgoing in Shakespeare's London* (Cambridge: Cambridge University Press, 1987), 81.

60. On print and the visual orientation of Western culture, see especially Walter J. Ong, *Orality and Literacy: The Technologizing of the Word* (London: Methuen, 1982), *Rhetoric, Romance, and Technology* (Ithaca: Cornell University Press, 1971), and *Ramus, Method and the Decay of Dialogue* (Cambridge: Harvard University Press, 1958); and Marshall McLuhan, *The Gutenberg Galaxy: The Making of Typographic Man* (Toronto: University of Toronto Press, 1962).

61. Wall, *The Imprint of Gender*, 190–91 n. 40. As she writes in the same note, "If we consider this period a shift to an era in which plays are seen and reading is a private visual act, then the sonnets' preoccupation with seeing makes sense. Renaissance works generally exploit the destabilizing transition to a more sight-oriented culture." Similarly, in a discussion of the visual and magical dimensions of Renaissance love sonnets, Linda Woodbridge writes in *The Scythe of Saturn: Shakespeare and Magical Thinking* (Chicago: University of Illinois Press, 1994), "Sonnet readers brought with them a vast visual semiotics of sexuality and fertility and learned to apply it to the visual and imaginative experience of reading. The very exercise must have enhanced the powers of the eye. . . . When sonnets were printed, ancient fertility magic met modern technology, and their mutual ocularity multiplied their visual impact" (260).

62. "O! if the streets were paved with thine eyes, / Her feet were much to dainty for such tread" (4.3.274). Strikingly, Dumain responds by pointing out what an advantageous position this would be for a lover to see up his mistress's skirt as she walks "overhead" (4.3.274–76), quickly transforming a vivid antiblazon of the lover's own eyes into the lover's glimpse into "what upward lies," thereby reasserting the power of the gaze over (even as it is tread upon by) the female body.

63. While the king's expressions are described as marginalia (his "face's own margent did quote such amazes" [2.1.245]), the scholars themselves, variously described as "bookmen" (2.1.226), "book-mates" (4.1.101), and "men of note" (3.1.22), seem less an "academy" than a collection of books. Though Berowne says that bookishness is metonymic, that "learning is but an adjunct to ourself" (4.3.310), it is, in fact, synecdochal, and it is the textual parts that stand in for, and negotiate the identity of, the self. To be an academic as well as a lover in this world is literally to *embody* principles of textuality in a culture of print.

64. Shakespeare's "sonnet play," as Robert Giroux has called it, has often been read as a dramatization of tropes inherent in the Petrarchan lyric (*The Book Known as Q* [1982], 140–41, cited in *The Sonnets*, ed. G. Blakemore Evans, New Cambridge Shakespeare [Cambridge: Cambridge University Press, 1997], 5 n. 3). Carroll, for example, writes that "[t]he sonnet-reading scene indicates how in passages like these the linguistic dimension of the play finds an exact counterpart in the dramatic structure" (*The Great Feast of Language*, 69). And more recently, David Schalkwyk and Diana Henderson have explored the social

and political dynamics made explicit when sonnet turns plot; when monologue turns dialogue; when absent mistress materializes and now literally gazes at and through the poet, mocking and showing him up at every step. Schalkwyk, " 'She never told her love': Embodiment, Textuality, and Silence in Shakespeare's Sonnets and Plays," *Shakespeare Quarterly* 45 (1994): 381–407, and Henderson, *Passion Made Public.*

65. Wall, *The Imprint of Gender,* 179.

66. It is a wonderful irony in this respect that one of the first responses we have to *Love's Labour's Lost* should itself be written by a second-rate sonneteer and a self-professed melancholic: Robert Tofte's 1598 poem about *Love's Labour's Lost* was printed in his volume of love poems, *Alba: The Months Minde Of A Melancholy Louer, diuided into three parts* . . . (London, 1598). As one academic drama puts it, "sonnet-mungers" would "starue for conceits" were it not for the "multitude of Printers," issuing out formulae for "her hayre of Gold, her eyes of Diamond, her cheekes of Roses," and so forth. Thomas Tomkis, *Lingua: or The combat of the tongue, and the fiue senses for superiority. A pleasant comoedie* (c. 1602, published London, 1607), D2r–D3v.

67. Arthur Marotti, *John Donne: Coterie Poet* (Madison: University of Wisconsin Press, 1986), 3.

68. Thomas Nashe, *Pierce Penilesse his Supplication to the Diuell. Describing the ouerspreading of Vice, and suppression of Vertue. Pleasantly interlac't with variable delights: and pathetically intermixt with conceipted reproofes* (London, 1592), B2r.

69. Edmund Coote, *The English schoole-maister teaching all his schollers, the order of distinct reading, and true writing our English tongue* (London, 1596), A3. Like many other prefaces designed to appeal to a broad social spectrum, Coote invokes "scholar" to describe potential readers no less than thirteen times in the four-page preface. The book was extraordinarily popular, printed fifty-four times between 1596 and 1737.

70. Thomas O. Sloane, "The Crossing of Rhetoric and Poetry in the English Renaissance," in *The Rhetoric of Renaissance Poetry from Wyatt to Milton,* ed. Thomas O. Sloane and Raymond B. Waddington (Berkeley: University of California Press, 1974), 212–42, 231.

71. As Anthony Grafton and Lisa Jardine note in *From Humanism to the Humanities: Education and the Liberal Arts in Fifteenth- and Sixteenth-Century Europe* (Cambridge, Mass.: Harvard University Press, 1986), Ramus looked to poetry as a way to synthesize eloquence and philosophy, so much so that, as one French contemporary put it, "He holds that philosophy is far better taught from poets than from philosophers. In this obscure conjunction of philosophy and eloquence, he teaches no Aristotle, no philosophy, but pretty much poetry alone" (167).

72. Ong, *Ramus, Method, and the Decay of Dialogue,* 308.

73. Ibid., 289.

74. Ibid., 287 (also cited in Sloane, "The Crossing of Rhetoric and Poetry in the English Renaissance," 233).

75. Bruce Smith, "Prickly Characters," in *Reading and Writing in Shakespeare,* ed. David Bergeron (Newark: University of Delaware Press, 1996), 25–44, 27. See also Smith,

The Acoustic World of Early Modern England: Attending to the O-Factor (Chicago: University of Chicago Press, 1999), where he cautions against a proleptic account of print as an "agent of change" in early modern England: "We should be looking, not for evidence of type technology, but for all the ways in which that newly discovered resource was colonized by regimes of oral communication" (128). So, too, Marion Trousdale suggests that Shakespeare "reflects in his techniques as author the habits of an oral age" in which "language was speech" ("Shakespeare's Oral Text," *Renaissance Drama* 12 [1981]: 95–116, 105, 98). For a variation of this argument, see Trousdale's *Shakespeare and the Rhetoricians* (Chapel Hill: University of North Carolina Press, 1982), 55–64, and Jonathan Hope, "Shakespeare and Language: An Introduction," in *Shakespeare and Language*, ed. Catherine M. S. Alexander (Cambridge: Cambridge University Press, 2004), 1–17.

76. John Hart, *A Methode or comfortable beginning for all unlearned whereby they may be taught to read English, in a very short time, with pleasure* (London, 1570), in *John Hart's Works on English Orthography and Pronunciation*, ed. Bror Danielsson (Stockholm: Almquist & Wiksell, 1955), 235.

77. As Joseph Loewenstein suggests in "The Script in the Marketplace," "print stimulated a competitive relation between book and person, a competition for preeminence as the locus of intellectual summation" (265).

78. Coote, *The English schoole-maister*, preface.

79. [Anon.,] *Heteroclitanomalonomia* (c. 1613), in *Jacobean Academic Plays*, ed. Suzanne Gossett and Thomas L. Berger (Oxford: Oxford University Press, 1988), 57–97.

80. Shaw, *Words Made Visible*.

81. This is not to say that the play implicitly valorizes the "converse of breath" as *contrasted* to the world of reading and books, as Malcolm Evans and Terence Hawkes have argued, but rather that it draws attention to the interanimation of speech and silent reading which is a consequence of the increasing literacy of the late sixteenth century. See especially Evans, "The Converse of Breath," in *Signifying Nothing: Truth's True Contents in Shakespeare's Texts* (Athens: University of Georgia Press, 1986), 39–98, and "Mercury Versus Apollo: A Reading of *Love's Labor's Lost*," *Shakespeare Quarterly* 26 (1975): 113–27, and Hawkes, "Shakespeare's Talking Animals."

82. Shakespeare, *A Midsummer Night's Dream*, ed. Harold F. Brooks, Arden Shakespeare (London: Methuen, 1979), 3.

83. G. Blakemore Evans, ed., *The Riverside Shakespeare* (New York: Houghton Mifflin, 1997), 247.

84. Burton, *Philosophaster* (1606), trans. Paul Jordon Smith (Stanford: Stanford University Press, 1931), 19.

85. See my note 80, above.

86. Kenneth Muir, *Shakespeare's Comic Sequence* (New York: Barnes and Noble, 1979), 41.

87. Thomas Wilson, *The rule of Reason, conteinyng the Arte of Logique* (London, 1551), L4r–v.

88. Many critics have drawn on *The art of rhetorique* (1553), for example, to gloss

Armado's first letter (see Carroll, *The Great Feast of Language*, 48–49), but have glossed over a whole range of extraordinary and often tongue-twisting passages in *The rule of Reason* that seem to come alive over the course of *Love's Labour's Lost.*

89. As John Eliot's text reads, "*The Cookow and the Nightingale sing at one season of the yeare, to vvit, in the spring time, from the middest of Aprill to the end of May, or there-about. These two birds contended about the sweetnesse of their song, they seeke a iudge, and bi-cause their dispute was of notes, there was found fit to iudge this controuersie the Asse, vvho hath aboue all other beasts his eares long. The Asse hauing put backe the Nightingale, vvhose mu-sicke he sayd he did not vnderstand, iudged the victorie to the Cookow. The nightingale ap-pealed before man, vvhom vvhen she saw, she pleadeth her cause and singeth sweetly, to make her cause good, and to be reuenged of the vvrong that the Asse had offered her*" (150).

90. The final "You that way: we this way" was added to the 1623 Folio.

91. As Eliot emphasized, from a *comparative* perspective, one's own language could be reduced to "mere hybber-gybber," as when English is compared to French or reduced to "barbarous prittle-prattle," as "the Greeke, the Latine, the Italian, the Spanish, and the French" languages seem when compared to "Mexican tongues" (*Ortho-epia Gallica*, B2r, H3v). Phrases in Eliot's text such as "hybber-gybber," "prittle-prattle," and "ortho-epia" parody a tongue enriched by compounds while foregrounding the inarticulate speech that forms at the intersection of languages. If, as Richard Mulcaster put it in *The First Part Of The Elementarie* (London, 1582), "Ye shall sometime haue a word mungrell compound, half-foren, half English, *Headlong, wharfage, princelike*" (141), Eliot played upon the compound and the scene of linguistic hybridization for comic effect.

92. Shakespeare, *Love's Labour's Lost*, ed. G. R. Hibbard (Oxford: Clarendon Press, 1990), 57–59. Emphasis added.

93. The centrality of the book as a structuring mechanism for the play surfaces again and again in the descriptive language of critics of the play, who often imagine it less a play than a book: Granville-Barker writes about the "pages of pages of . . . smart repartee," and Samuel Johnson writes that there is not "any play that has more evident marks of the hand of Shakespeare" (both excerpted in *Shakespeare's Early Comedies*, ed. Pamela Mason [London: Macmillan Press, 1995], 194, 190). Yates imagines the play as a veritable "essay" (*A Study of* Love's Labour's Lost, 122), and Rosalie L. Colie refers to the play as "an anthology . . . a textbook of literary *copia* and resource"; she sees each character dressed in "linguistic garb, as fully identifying as his social role and costume" (*Shakespeare's Living Art* [Princeton: Princeton University Press, 1974], 49, 43).

94. *Love's Labour's Lost*, ed. Richard David, xvii.

95. Ibid.

96. Linda McJannet, *The Voice of Elizabethan Stage Directions: The Evolution of a The-atrical Code* (Newark: University of Delaware Press, 1999), 73. See also McJannet, "Eliza-bethan Speech Prefixes," in *Reading and Writing in Shakespeare*, ed. David M. Bergeron (Newark: University of Delaware Press, 1996), 45–63, 59–60.

97. McJannet, *The Voice of Elizabethan Stage Directions*, 73. On the expressive and

largely oral dimensions of printed plays, see also Anthony Graham White, *Punctuation and Its Dramatic Value in Shakespearean Drama* (Newark: University of Delaware Press, 1995).

98. Shakespeare, *Shakspere's Loves Labors Lost: The First Quarto, 1598, A Facsimile in Photo-Lithography*, ed. William Griggs and Frederick James Furnivall (London: W. Griggs, 1880).

99. The fact that the first woman Berowne converses with in the Quarto is not "*Ros*," as most modern editions suggest, but "*Kath*," is also suggestive in terms of the autonomy of voice and character in the play. Although I do not agree with Capell, who argued that Berowne here is and should be speaking to "*Kath*," it is suggestive that what seems to be a straightforward compositorial error itself anticipates the ultimate confusion of lover and beloved in the masque of the Muscovites, where Berowne thinks he speaks to "*Ros*." but in fact speaks to someone with a very different speech prefix. This gives a whole new meaning of being "woo'd by the sign of she." On the logic of Capell's reading, see *Love's Labour's Lost*, ed. Richard David, xx–xxi.

100. The idea of the material text surfaces again and again in the play to articulate a crisis of self-referential mediation, where desires articulated in and through visible texts are suspect at best. Rituals of courtship are marked by an embarrassingly graphic circulation of the love letter, which is amorous and alphabetic at once: "Ware pencils, ho! let me not die your debtor, / My red dominical, my golden letter: / O! that your face were not so full of O's," says Rosaline, in mock description that exposes the textual self-reference of the anatomical blazon (5.2.44–45).

101. Shakespeare, *Loues Labour's lost*, in *The First Folio of Shakespeare, 1623*, facsimile prepared and introduced by Doug Moston (New York: Applause, 1995), 131.

102. *O* and *I*, the two capital letters that most frequently stand alone in expressions of affective intensity throughout Shakespeare's plays, veritably seem to jump off the pages of the Quarto and Folio texts of *Love's Labour's Lost*, particularly in light of Rosaline's "literal" reading of Berowne's poem. But individuated letters that may visually enact elements of the plot are frequently modernized ("O" to "Oh," "L." to "Lord") by contemporary editors, and what is often edited out is the self-referential absurdity of the lover's alphabet. Berowne's speech in the Arden begins, "O! and I forsooth in love!" (3.1.168).

103. Phineas Fletcher, *The Purple Island, Or, The Isle Of Man Together With Piscatorie Eclogs And Other Poeticall Miscellanies* (London, 1633), K3r.

104. Robert Burton, *The anatomy of melancholy what it is. With all the kindes, causes, symptomes, prognosticks, and seuerall cures of it. In three maine partitions with their seuerall sections, members, and subsections. Philosophically, medicinally, historically, opened and cut vp . . .* , 2nd ed. (Oxford, 1624), 2.3.5 (Oo2r).

105. Shakespeare, *Romeo and Juliet*, in *The Riverside Shakespeare*, ed. G. Blakemore Evans (New York: Houghton Mifflin, 1997). I thank Coppélia Kahn for encouraging me to think twice about this particular list.

106. Shakespeare, Sonnet 23, in *Shakespeare's Sonnets*, ed. Stephen Booth (New Haven: Yale University Press, 1977), 23.

107. As an analogue to what I am suggesting about the curative dimensions of theater, the activity of talking was often prescribed as a cure for melancholia in early medical texts. As Du Laurens writes in *A Discourse of the Preseruation of the Sight*, because the love melancholic "loues silence out of measure," the physician "must first of all assay to draw him with fayre words from these fond and foolish imaginations" (122). If conversation with one individual fails, then "diuers men" should be called upon to perform a communal act of name calling; "calling his mistress light, inconstant, foolish, deuoted to varietie, mocking and laughing to scorne this his greife" (122–23). Though spoken words would ideally be "sufficient and able to cure this inchauntment" (123), often, confesses Du Laurens, words "can doe very little in [a] place where melancholike conceitedness hath taken roote" (123). In *Erotomania*, Ferrand, following Burton, goes so far as to recommend "Plaies" along with other distractions such as music and feasts as a cure for the melancholic (326). What I suggest here is a kind of "talking cure" that stages the process through which a kind of "melancholike conceitedness hath taken root," through which speakers are exposed as products of a printed world of melancholic conceits themselves.

CHAPTER 5. FEELING INARTICULATE

Note to epigraphs: Stephen Booth, "On the Value of Hamlet," in *Shakespeare: An Anthology of Criticism and Theory, 1945–2000*, edited by Russ McDonald (Oxford: Blackwell, 2004), 225–44, 228. T. S. Eliot, "Hamlet and His Problems," in *The Sacred Wood: Essays on Poetry and Criticism* (London: Methuen, 1922), 95–103, 100–101.

1. Eliot, "Hamlet and His Problems," 100. In addition to Stephen Booth's analysis of T. S. Eliot in "On the Value of Hamlet," see Margreta de Grazia, *Hamlet Without* Hamlet (Cambridge: Cambridge University Press, 2007), 108.

2. Eliot, "Hamlet and His Problems," 100–101, emphasis in original.

3. Benjamin Ifor Evans, *The Language of Shakespeare's Plays* (New York: Routledge, rprt. 2005), 97.

4. George Bernard Shaw, "To Arthur Bingham Walkley" (1903), dedicatory epistle, *Man and Superman: A Comedy and a Philosophy* (Cambridge: Mass.: Harvard University Press, 1914), v–xxxvii, xxi. On the "logocentrism" of Hamlet's soliloquies in contrast to the logo-marginal sounds in the world around him, see Bruce Smith "Hearing Green: Logo-marginality in *Hamlet*." *Early Modern Literary Studies* 7, no. 1, Special Issue 8 (May 2001), 41.1–5.6.

5. George Bernard Shaw, Untitled transcript on *Hamlet* (1937), cited in Bernard F. Dukore, "Shaw on 'Hamlet,'" *Educational Theatre Journal*, 23, no. 2 (May 1971), 152–59, 155.

6. Walter Murdoch, *Seventy-Two Essays: A Selection* (New York: Books for Library Press, 1970), 258. Murdoch brought to *Hamlet* a commonplace assumption about what constitutes "real literature": "The whole effort at the back of real literature is the effort to

be articulate, to be significant, to convey to other minds, with the utmost possible precision, a clear meaning" (159). On editorial practice and the construction of coherence and intelligibility in Shakespeare's *The Winter's Tale*, see Stephen Orgel, "The Poetics of Incomprehensibility," *Shakespeare Quarterly* 42 (1991), 431–37.

7. Hamlet is, without doubt, simultaneously a humanist and a counterhumanist, a university scholar who at once inhabits and resists a tradition within rhetoric and logic in which, as Ronald Knowles has rightly put it, "Stoic and Christian thought depreciates passion" (Knowles, "Hamlet and Counter-Humanism," *Renaissance Quarterly* 52 [1999]: 1046–69, 1046). But Hamlet's displays of inarticulacy have not yet been fully examined as a, or as the, central issue of the play.

8. Shakespeare, *Hamlet*, ed. Harold Jenkins, Arden Shakespeare (London: Methuen, 1982), 2.2.119–21. Unless otherwise noted, all references to *Hamlet* are to this edition. Writing of Hamlet's odd love letter to Ophelia, Benjamin Ifor Evans avowed the odd composition and phrasing of the letter as a "problem" in the construction of Hamlet as a character, but dismissed such a problem as a concern of the Shakespearean scholar in the study rather than for the audience in the theater: "In the theater the passage would raise no problems. It is appropriate that the verse of Hamlet's letter should be different from the verse of the play itself, just as the Play within the Play is different from the rest of the tragedy. There is deliberately a broader and cruder brush-work in such passages, and it is dangerous to examine too minutely in the study effects which have been designed for the conditions of the stage." Thus Hamlet is preserved by Evans as the "fastidious master of language" (*The Language of Shakespeare's Plays*, 97–98).

9. John Davies, *Microcosmos: The discovery Of The Little World, with the government thereof* (London, 1603), 166.

10. The subject position of the critic, encapsulated in Polonius (as in Holofernes in *Love's Labour's Lost*), generates sympathy for what is, by all accounts, including Hamlet's own account, an inarticulate expression of feeling. The subject position of the critic, encapsulated in Hamlet's own self-censure ("*I am ill at these numbers, I have not art to reckon my groans*"), evinces a desire for communication that does not depend upon the reckoning, or the rational narrative ordering, of groans.

11. I here allude to Nicholas Abraham and Maria Torok's theory of introjection and incorporation operative in melancholic speech. See especially *The Shell and the Kernel: Renewals of Psychoanalysis*, ed. and trans. Nicholas T. Rand (Chicago: University of Chicago Press, 1995), particularly Torok's chapter "The Illness of Mourning and the Fantasy of the Exquisite Corpse," translated from her original, "Maladie du deuil et fantasme du cadavre exquis," *Revue française de psychanalyse* 32, no. 4 (1968), 715–35.

12. Anne-Marie Smith, *Julia Kristeva: Speaking the Unspeakable* (London: Pluto Press, 1998), 39–40.

13. Michael Schoenfeldt, " 'Give Sorrow Words': Emotional Loss and the Articulation of Temperament in Early Modern England," in *Dead Lovers: Erotic Bonds and the Study of Premodern Europe*, ed. Basil Dufallo and Peggy McCracken (Ann Arbor: University of

Michigan Press, 2007), 143. Schoenfeldt demonstrates how this medical-literary alternative to the Protestant suppression of discourses of sorrow can help us understand the crucial function of giving "sorrow words" in Shakespeare's *Hamlet* and *The Winter's Tale*. On the religious treatment of grief with regard to *Hamlet*, see also Steven Mullaney, "Mourning and Misogyny: *Hamlet, The Revenger's Tragedy*, and the Final Progress of Elizabeth I, 1600–1607," *Shakespeare Quarterly* 45 (1994), 139–62.

14. Thomas Wright, *The Passions of the Minde* (London, 1601), emphasis added, cited in Schoenfeldt, " 'Give Sorrow Words,' " 144.

15. See my Chapter 4, "Acting in the Passive Voice," which is based on my earlier publication entitled "The Melancholy of Print: *Love's Labour's Lost*," in *Historicism, Psychoanalysis and Early Modern Culture*, ed. Carla Mazzio and Douglas Trevor (New York: Routledge, 2000), 186–227. I thank Michael Schoenfeldt for acknowledging this essay in " 'Giving Sorrow Words.' "

16. Thomas Tomkis, *Lingua: or The Combat of the Tongue, And the fiue Senses for Superiority. A pleasant Comoedie* (first performed, c. 1602, first published London, 1607). See F2r for internal evidence on the date of 1602.

17. As the title page to the 1603 Quarto of Hamlet reads, *The Tragicall Historie of Hamlet Prince of Denmarke, As it hath beene diuerse times acted by his Highnesse seruants in the Cittie of London: as also in the two Vniuersities of Cambridge and Oxford, and else-where* (London, 1603).

18. Thomas Cooper, *Thesavrvs Lingvae Romanae & Britannicae* (London, 1578), s.v. "tango."

19. Eve Kosofsky Sedgwick, *Touching Feeling: Affect, Pedagogy, Performativity* (Durham: Duke University Press, 2003), 14.

20. See, for perhaps the most famous example, G. W. F. Hegel's postulate that vision and hearing are the only "theoretical" senses (*Vorlesungen über die Ästhetik in Werke in zwanzig Bänden*, ed. E. Moldenhauer and K. M. Michel, 20 vols. [Frankfurt: Suhrkamp, 1970], 13:61).

21. Jean-Luc Nancy, "Corpus," in *Thinking Bodies*, ed. Juliet Flower MacCannell and Laura Zakarin (Stanford: Stanford University Press, 1994), 24.

22. Alexander Ross, *Arcana Microcosmi: Or, The hid Secrets of Man's Body discovered; In an Anatomial Duel between Aristotle and Galen* (London, 1665), 66.

23. Philip Sidney, *Syr P.S. His Astrophel And Stella Wherein the excellence of sweete Poesie is concluded* (London, 1591), 7.

24. On "audience" and "spectator," see Andrew Gurr, *Playgoing in Shakespeare's London* (Cambridge: Cambridge University Press, 1997), 86–105, and Jonathan Baldo, *The Unmasking of Drama: Contested Representation in Shakespeare's Tragedies* (Detroit: Wayne State University Press, 1997). On hearing, see Bruce R. Smith, *The Acoustic World of Early Modern England: Attending to the O-Factor* (Chicago: University of Chicago Press, 1999). On vision, see Bruce R. Smith, *The Key of Green: Passion and Perception in Renaissance Art* (Chicago: University of Chicago Press, 2009); Michael O'Connell, *The Idolatrous Eye:*

Iconoclasm and Theater in Early Modern England (Oxford: Oxford University Press, 2000); Jonathan Sawday, *The Body Emblazoned: Dissection and the Human Body in Renaissance Culture* (London: Routledge, 1995); Martin Jay, *Force Fields: Between Intellectual History and Cultural Critique* (New York: Routledge, 1993); and Barbara Freedman, *Staging the Gaze: Postmodernism, Psychoanalysis, and Shakespearean Comedy* (Ithaca: Cornell University Press, 1991). On the interanimation (as opposed to the isolation) of vision and hearing in this period, see Elizabeth L. Eisenstein, *The Printing Press as an Agent of Change: Communications and Cultural Transformations in Early Modern Europe* (Cambridge: Cambridge University Press, 1979).

25. Caroline Spurgeon, *Shakespeare's Imagery and What it Tells Us* (Cambridge: Cambridge University Press, 1935), 57–78, 82–83.

26. Shakespeare, *Hamlet*, 5.1.194; *King Lear*, ed. Kenneth Muir, Arden Shakespeare (London: Methuen, 1964), 3.7.92–93, 4.6.147; *The Winter's Tale*, ed. J. H. P. Pafford, Arden Shakespeare (London: Methuen, 1963). All references to *King Lear* and *The Winter's Tale* in this chapter are to these editions.

27. Aristotle, *Nicomachean Ethics*, trans. J. A. K. Thomson, ed. Jonathan Barnes (London: Penguin, 1955), 1976. Touch and taste, writes Aristotle, are "are concerned with such pleasures as are shared by animals too (which makes them regarded as low and brutish)" (137). For a conventional assessment of vision as the "most precious, and the best . . . by it we learn and discern all things," and of touch as the "most ignoble," see Robert Burton, *The Anatomy of Melancholy*, ed. Floyd Dell and Paul Jordan-Smith (London: Routledge, 1931), 138–39.

28. On the reification of "touch" in contemporary theoretical accounts of mediation and sensation, see Mark Hansen, *New Philosophies for New Media* (Cambridge, Mass.: MIT Press, 2004). On the need for further attention to "logomarginal" phenomena in Shakespeare Studies in particular, see Bruce Smith, "Hearing Green: Logomarginality in *Hamlet*," and on the place of the body and the extralinguistic aspects of sensory perception in early faculty psychology, see Katherine Park, "The Organic Soul," in *The Cambridge History of Renaissance Philosophy*, ed. Charles B. Schmitt (Cambridge: Cambridge University Press, 1988), 464–84.

29. For recent approaches to the phenomena of touch, see especially *The Book of Touch*, ed. Constance Classen (Oxford: Berg, 2005); *Empire of the Senses: The Sensual Culture Reader*, ed. David Howes (Oxford: Berg, 2005), which includes my "The Senses Divided: Organs, Objects and Media in Early Modern England" (85–105); *Sensible Flesh: On Touch in Early Modern Culture*, ed. Elizabeth D. Harvey (Philadelphia: University of Pennsylvania Press, 2003), which includes my "Acting with Tact: Touch and Theater in the Renaissance" (159–86). Recent work on the body in contemporary literature and thought has also integrated "touch" as a technology drawing together bodies, minds, and cultures. While the French philosopher and psychoanalytic critic Didier Anzieu, in *The Skin Ego* (New Haven: Yale University Press, 1989) maps out a kind of thermal and tactual unconscious, other theorists of the body such as Jean Luc-Nancy (in "Corpus") and Elizabeth

286 NOTES TO PAGES 184–185

Grosz have turned to "touch" as a rich and largely neglected technology of perception. See, for example, Susan A. Stewart, *Poetry and the Fate of the Senses* (Chicago: University of Chicago Press, 2002); Elizabeth Grosz, *Volatile Bodies: Toward a Corporeal Feminism* (Bloomington: Indiana University Press, 1994); and Luce Irigaray's "The Sex Which Is Not One," in *New French Feminisms*, ed. Elaine Marks and Isabelle de Courtivron, trans. Claudia Reeder (Amherst: University of Massachusetts Press, 1980), 99–106.

30. On material objects and Renaissance drama, see especially Natasha Korda *Shakespeare's Domestic Economies: Gender and Property in Early Modern England* (Cambridge: Cambridge University Press, 2002); *Staged Properties in Early Modern English Drama*, ed. Jonathan Gil Harris and Natasha Korda (Cambridge: Cambridge University Press, 2002), and Peter Stallybrass and Ann Rosalind Jones, *Renaissance Clothing and the Materials of Memory* (Cambridge: Cambridge University Press, 2000). On the critical focus on material objects and the limits of material history, see especially Eric Wilson, "Abel Drugger's Sign and the Fetishes of Material Culture," in *Historicism, Psychoanalysis and Early Modern Culture*, ed. Carla Mazzio and Douglas Trevor (New York: Routledge, 2000), 110–35, and Douglas Bruster, *Shakespeare and the Question of Culture: Early Modern Literature and the Cultural Turn* (New York: Palgrave, 2003).

31. As Margreta de Grazia, Maureen Quilligan, and Peter Stallybrass, the editors of *Subject and Object in Renaissance Culture* (Cambridge: Cambridge University Press, 1996), ask: "In the period that has from its inception been identified with the emergence of the subject: *where is the object?*" (2).

32. Elaine Scarry, *The Body in Pain: The Making and Unmaking of the World* (Oxford: Oxford University Press, 1987), 255.

33. Jonathan Crary, *Techniques of the Observer: On Vision and Modernity in the Nineteenth Century.* (Cambridge, Mass.: MIT Press, 1990), 5. So too Walter Benjamin, in *Illuminations*, ed. Hannah Arendt, trans. Harry Zohn (New York: Schocken Books, 1968), wrote that "the camera introduces us to unconscious optics as does psychoanalysis to unconscious impulses" (237); and Jacques Lacan, in *The Four Fundamental Concepts of Psychoanalysis*, ed. Jacques-Alain Miller, trans. Alan Sheridan (New York: Norton, 1998), formulates his theory of the psyche in terms of optics, perspective, and mirrors.

34. Raymond Williams, "From Medium to Social Practice," *Marxism and Literature* (Oxford: Oxford University Press, 1990), 158. See Robert Burton, *The Anatomy of Melancholy, What It Is. With All The Kindes, Causes, Symptomes, Prognostickes, And Seuerall Cures Of It. In three maine partitions with their seuerall sections, members, and subsections. Philosophically, Medicinally, Historyically, Opened And Cvt Vp* (Oxford, 1621), 33.

35. Aristotle, *De anima*, trans. W. S. Hett (Cambridge, Mass.: Harvard University Press, 1986), 435a, 16–20 (emphasis added). On touch in Aristotle as a "contact" sense, see especially Richard Sorabji, "Aristotle on Demarcating the Five Senses," in *Essays on Aristotle, vol. 4: Psychology and Aesthetics*, ed. Jonathan Barnes, Malcolm Schofield, and Richard Sorabji (London: Duckworth, 1979), 76–92.

36. See, especially, W. J. T. Mitchell, *Iconology: Image, Text, Ideology* (Chicago: University of Chicago Press, 1986), 118–19.

37. Helkiah Crooke, *Mikrokosmographia: A Description of the Body of Man* (London, 1615).

38. This issue is still fully alive when Alexander Ross responds to ancient and contemporary medical writing in the mid-seventeenth century: "The sense of tact either hath no medium, or else we must make the skin the medium; and the flesh, membranes and nerves the organ" (*Arcana Microcosmi*, 66). The singular use of "organ" to encapsulate such complex and individuated parts of the body speaks to the extent to which the triad of organ, object, and medium, though insufficient, was nonetheless continually invoked to organize the sensory modes.

39. Burton, *The Anatomy of Melancholy* (1621), 139.

40. The representation of the palace of touch in Phineas Fletcher's *The Purple Island, Or, The Isle Of Man* (London, 1633), is relatively brief and vague in comparison with the other senses. Abram Barnett Langdale suggests that "Fletcher had no opportunity to be more courteous [in elaborating the specifics of both touch and taste], because touch and taste had to await Malpighi's microscope and genius" (*Phineas Fletcher, Man of Letters, Science and Divinity* [New York: Columbia University Press, 1937], 194; cited in Louise Vinge, *The Five Senses: Studies in a Literary Tradition* [Lund: Berlingska Boktryckeriert, 1975], 97).

41. For details on this morality drama, attributed to Jean Gerson and written between 1377 and 1384, see also Vinge's text and informative note, *The Five Senses*, 60 n. 27.

42. See Erasmus's *Lingua, sive, de linguae usu atque abusu liber utilissimus*, in *The Collected Works of Erasmus*, vol. 29, trans. Elaine Fantham, ed. Elaine Fantham and Erika Rummel (Toronto: University of Toronto Press, 1989).

43. Davies, *Microcosmos*, 51.

44. See Nicholas Ling on the commonplace, "The sence of touching, aunswereth the element of the earth; to the end it might agree better with those things that are to be felt thereby" (*Politeuphuia Wits Common wealth* [London, 1597], 190r–v).

45. Aristotle, *Nicomachean Ethics*, 137.

46. *Oxford English Dictionary*, s.v. "intact, a."

47. On the distinction as well as the relationship between touch as a contact and a feeling sense in Aristotle, see especially T. K. Johansen, *Aristotle on the Sense-Organs* (Cambridge: Cambridge University Press, 1998). On the body as a vehicle subject to human self-fashioning, through which passions as well as physiological health could be rendered temperate, see Michael Schoenfeldt, *Bodies and Selves in Early Modern England: Physiology and Inwardness in Spenser, Shakespeare, Herbert, and Milton* (Cambridge: Cambridge University Press, 2000).

48. Patricia Parker, "On the Tongue: Cross Gendering, Effeminacy, and the Art of Words," *Style* 23 (1989), 445–63.

49. Shakespeare, *Hamlet*, 1.2.85.

50. John Davies, *Nosce teipsum, This Oracle expounded in two Elegies, 1. Of Humane knowledge, 2. Of the Soule of Man, and the immortalitie thereof* (London, 1599), 45.

51. Francis Bacon, *The charge of Sir Francis Bacon Knight, his Maiesties Attourney generall, touching duells vpon an information in the Star-chamber against Priest and Wright. With the decree of the Star-chamber in the same cause* (London, 1614), 21r.

52. Shakespeare, *The Winter's Tale*, ed. J. H. P. Pafford, Arden Shakespeare (London: Methuen, 1963).

53. On editorial treatments of incomprehensible speech in *The Winter's Tale*, see Stephen Orgel, "The Poetics of Incomprehensibility." For a critical assessment of Orgel's argument about textual instability and indeterminate meaning subtending unintelligible language in *The Winter's Tale*, see David Laird, "Competing Discourses in *The Winter's Tale*," *Connotations* 4, no. 1–2 (1994–95), 25–43.

54. David Hillman, *Shakespeare's Entrails: Belief, Scepticism and the Interior of the Body* (New York: Palgrave Macmillan, 2007). See also Hillman, "Visceral Knowledge," in *The Body in Parts: Fantasies of Corporeality in Early Modern England*, ed. David Hillman and Carla Mazzio (New York: Routledge, 1997), 81–105.

55. The expanded sphere or "web" of perception enabled by touch in this passage foregrounds the centrality of touch in detecting temperature, climate, and the structure and motion of the cosmos. Given the lunar and astral forces at play, it is worth noting that in the Renaissance, the tactile operated under a very different sphere of influence (to be "touched," for example, as the "lunatic").

56. For a series of these "self-figuring" anatomical figures, see Sawday, *Body Emblazoned: Dissection and the Human Body in Renaissance Culture* (London: Routledge 1995) 38–39. On the optical fantasies of knowing oneself, see especially, 1–15.

57. Sawday, *Body Emblazoned*, 18.

58. Francis Bacon, *Sylua Syluarum: or A Naturall Historie In ten Centuries* (London, 1627), 198.

59. See Francis Barker, *The Tremulous Private Body: Essays on Subjection*, rev. ed. (Ann Arbor: University of Michigan Press, 1995).

60. See F. S. Boas, " 'Macbeth' and 'Lingua,' " *Modern Language Review* 4, no. 4 (July 1909), 517–20. Boas suggested that the string of "mums" are a possible parody of Lady Macbeth's "come, come, come, come" (520).

61. This shift in imagination from the body as a perceptive organism to a body subject to hurt, with pain now defining individuated parts, is parodied in a stage direction where hearing and smelling enter at each other's "throats": enter "Avditvs, *pulling* Olfactvs *by the nose*, and Olfactvs *wringing* Auditvs *by the eares*": "AVD: Oh mine eares, mine eares, mine eares. / OLF: Oh my nose, my nose, my nose" (K3). Even "*Visus* hath broke his forehead against the oake yonder" (K3). In a flash these disintegrating senses are "bound" by Somnus, the immobilizing force of sleep and dream. Indeed, any merit to Tactus's resistance to rational, quantitative, and indeed scopic regimes is undermined by the localization of touch in the manifestly vulnerable body. When Tactus comes to his senses, he explains to Common Sense that it was wine that "made our braynes, somewhat irregular" (M3).

62. Phillip Stubbes, *The Anatomie of Abuses: Contayning, A Discouerie, Or Briefe Sum-*

marie of such Notable Vices and Imperfections, as now raigne in many Christian Countreyes of the worlde: but (especiallie) in a verie famous Ilande called Ailgna (London, 1583), M8r-v.

63. Stephen Gosson, *The Schoole of Abuse, Conteining a plesaunt inuectiue against Poets, Pipers, Plaiers, Iesters, and such like Caterpillers of a Cōmonwelth* (London, 1579); reprinted as *The Schoole of Abuse* in *Early Treatises on the Stage* (London: Shakespeare Society, 1853), 22.

64. From the French "*flatar;* the primary meaning of this word is believed to be 'to flatten down, smooth'; hence 'to stroke with the hand, caress' " (*Oxford English Dictionary*, s.v. "flatter").

65. On "audience" and "spectator," see Gurr, *Playgoing in Shakespeare's London*, 86–105.

66. Gosson, *Schoole of Abuse*, 22.

67. On Aristotle's understanding of touch as a sense integral to vision, hearing, tasting and smelling ("For without a sense of touch it is impossible to have any other sensation" [*De anima*, 435a, 13–14]), Helkiah Crooke, for example, evinced nervousness about the possibility of sensory confusion if such a postulate were taken too seriously or too literally. For if touch were indeed a central facet of all the senses, Crooke observes, "The Foote would see, and the Elbow would heare, and the sides would smell, and the crowne would taste, if in these parts there wer[e] a disposition to receiue the objects of these Senses" (*Mikrokosmographia*, 725). If Aristotle was correct that no sense can "subsist without Touching," moreover, then the absence of touch would, Crooke reasons, extinguish *all* possibilities of sense, at once conceptual and cultural, including "all the Artes both Liberall and Mechanicall" (649). Aiming to banish the taxonomical (and synesthetic) confusion from his own anatomy text, Crooke points out: "Aristotle doth oftentimes affirm that all sense is a kinde of Touching; from whence it would as well follow that there is but one Sense, that is, the Touch, then which nothing can be more absurd" (716). In the more local matter of distinguishing taste from touch, Renaissance medical texts frequently cited Aristotle on the debate about whether taste and touch were one and the same (see *De anima*, especially 423a, 19–20 and 434b, 22). Crooke argued vigorously for an affinity rather than an equivalence between the two senses: "if hee [Aristotle] had meant that the Tast and the Touch did not differ in *Specie*, hee would neuer haue sayd that *Gustus* was *Tactus quidam*, but simply and plainly *Gustus* is *Tactus*, hee would not have sayd that Tast is a kinde of Touch, but that Tast is a Touch" (716). Aristotle's distinction is crucial here for Crooke as a way of maintaining that these two must be "esteemed distinct Senses."

68. Aristotle, *Nicomachean Ethics*, 137.

69. Burton, *The Anatomy of Melancholy* (1621), 33. As Burton puts it, "Betwixt the Organ and Obiect a true distance is required, that it be not too neere, or too farre of. Many excellent questions appertaine to this sense, discussed by Philosophers, as whether this sight bee caused *Intra mittendo, vel extra mittendo, &c.* By receauing in the visible Species, or sending of them out, which *Plato, Plutarch, Macrobius, Lactantius*, and others dispute. And besides it is the subiect of the *Perspectiues*, of which *Alhasen* the *Arabian, Vitell, Roger*

Bacon, Baptista Porta, Guidus Vbaldus, &c. haue written whole volumes" (33–34). And elsewhere Burton writes that the "other senses, hearing, touching, may much penetrate and affect, but none so much, none so forcible as Sight" (555). On the materiality of vision, see especially Sergei Lobonov-Rostovsky, "Taming the Basilisk," in *The Body in Parts: Fantasies of Corporeality in Early Modern Europe,* ed. Hillman and Mazzio, 195–220. In slightly different terms, that optic window to the soul was also, of course, a particularly vulnerable muscle subject to involuntary motion. To describe the glazy look of love, Jaques Ferrand draws on André Du Laurens, nothing that "our Moderne Anatomists call that Muscle, which is the Instrument by which this Love-looke is caused, *Musculus Amorosus"* (*Erotomania Or A Treatise Discoursing of the Essence, Causes, Symptoms, Prognosticks, and Cure of Love, Or Erotiqve Melancholy* [Oxford, 1640], 107).

70. George Chapman, translator, *The Iliads of Homer Prince of Poets. Neuer before in any languag truely translated. With a Co[m]ment vppon some of his chiefe places; Donne according to the Greeke By Geo: Chapman* (London, 1611), 269 (see also *OED,* s.v. "touch," 17a).

71. Sir Thomas Browne. *Pseudodoxia Epidemica: or, Enquiries Into Very many received Tenents, And commonly presumed Truths* (London, 1646), 265.

72. Smith, *The Acoustic World of Early Modern England,* 101.

73. Thomas Blount, *Glossographia: Or A Dictionary, Interpreting all such Hard Vvords, Whether Hebrew, Greek, Latin, Italian, Spanish, French, Teutonick, Belgick, British or Saxon; as are now used in our refined English tongue* (London, 1656), Ee3r.

74. Cooper, *Thesavrvs Lingvae Romanae & Britannicae* (1578), s.v. "os."

75. Richard Brathwaite, *Essaies Vpon the Five Senses, Revived by a new Supplement; with a pithy one upon Detraction. Continued Vvith sundry Christian Resolves, and divine Contemplations, full of passion and devotion; purposely composed for the zealously-disposed* (London, 1635), 37. See also Brathwaite's, *Essaies Vpon the Fiue Senses with a pithie one vpon Detraction* (London, 1620).

76. Gosson, *Schoole of Abuse,* 25.

77. John Northbrooke, *Spiritus est vicarius Christi in terra. A Treatise wherein Dicing, Dauncing, Vaine playes or Enterluds with other idle pastimes [et]c. commonly vsed on the Sabboth day, are reproued by the Authoritie of the word of God and auntient writers. Made Dialoguewise by Iohn Northbrooke Minister and Preacher of the word of God* (London, c. 1577), 67–68.

78. Ibid., 62.

79. Robert Burton registers the commonplace of melancholy as a condition of being "touched": "And who is not a foole, who is free from Melancholy? who is not touched more or lesse in habite or in disposition?" (*The Anatomy of Melancholy* [1621], 15).

80. Shakespeare, *The Tragicall Historie of Hamlet Prince of Denmarke* (1603), D3.

81. For an illustrated history of the relationship between hands, books, and memory systems, Claire Richter Sherman, *Writing on Hands: Memory and Knowledge in Early Modern Europe* (Washington, D.C.: Folger Shakespeare Library, 2001).

82. On the possibility that this soliloquy is *read* from a book, see Margreta de Grazia,

"Soliloquies and Wages in the Age of Emergent Consciousness," *Textual Practice* 9, no. 1 (1995), 67–92, 74.

83. "Touching" was used interchangably with terms for "concerning" and "of," as in Bacon's *A Briefe Discovrse, Touching the Happie Vnion of the Kindomes of England, and Scotland* (London, 1603), and his *Considerations Touching A Warre With Spaine* (London, 1629). The contemporary analogue to this use of "touching" is now generally "with regard to" or "with respect to," each a visual rather than tactile metaphor.

84. *Oxford English Dictionary*, s.v. "touch."

85. Davies, *Microcosmos,* 52.

86. Thomas Kyd, *The Spanish Tragedy*, ed. J. R. Mulryne (London: A and C Black, 1989), see 1602 additions, 129.

87. This shift is in many ways analogous to what Rosalie L. Colie termed the process of "unmetaphorization" in Shakespearean drama, where clichés and symbols become animated as part of the theatrical action. What is striking is the attention in Renaissance drama to the specifically sensory dimensions of this process. Indeed, it might well be said that tragic drama itself is marked by a trajectory of "touch" from a metaphoric, mobile, and emotional phenomenon to "touch" as a kind of metaphor deadened through literalization. See Colie, *Shakespeare's Living Art* (Princeton: Princeton University Press, 1974).

88. For "home" from the Old English *hám*, see *Oxford English Dictionary*, s.v. "ham, n^3"; for "land" from the Late German *hamm* or "piece of enclosed land," see *OED*, s.v. "ham, n^2"; and for "skin" see OED, s.v. "hame^1." On the much neglected thematics of land and earth as a clues to Hamlet's lost inheritance, see Margreta de Grazia, "Weeping for Hecuba," in *Historicism, Psychoanalysis and Early Modern Culture*, ed. Carla Mazzio and Douglas Trevor (New York: Routledge, 2000), 350–75, and *Hamlet Without* Hamlet.

89. Indeed, although Gertrude claims that Hamlet has "cleft [her] heart in twain," what concerns her is not her own actions or inner life but, as we see in the next scene, the fact that her son is "Mad as the sea and wind when both contend" (4.1.7–8).

90. Harold Jenkins glosses "assurance" as "(1) certainty of possession; (2) legal deed securing this" (383, n. 114). For a possible extension of this legal pun, see *Oxford English Dictionary*, s.v. "hamald, hamelt, hamel," where "hamald, haimhald v. (*Old Sc. Law*)" is "to prove (something withholden or claimed by another) to be one's own property."

91. Sidney, *Astrophel and Stella*, 7, 9. That Hamlet has killed off parts of his own "inward tutch" is all too manifest in his treatment of the dead body of Polonius, in which he seems to have (as he says of the Gravedigger), "no feeling of his business" (5.1.65).

92. Claudia Benthien, *Skin: On the Cultural Border Between Self and World* (New York: Columbia University Press, 2004), 13.

93. Shakespeare, *Hamlet*, 1.5.9, 1.3.244, 1.5.14.

94. Harold Jenkins glosses "coil" not simply as "body," as many other commentators have, but a nautical word signifying "something wound round us like a rope" (*Hamlet*, 278, n. 67).

95. Richard Lederer, *The Miracle of Language* (New York: Simon & Schuster, 1991).

96. For Hamlet has just killed Polonius without apparent concern, betraying a kind of "skin or film" covering his own "unseen" interior.

97. Sidney, *Astrophel and Stella*, 7, 9, 69.

98. John Goodman, *The Penitent Pardoned: Or, A Discourse of the Nature of Sin, And The Efficacy of Repentance: Under the Parable Of The Prodigal Son* (London, 1679). Claudius's denial of feeling touched here contrasts with his later aside, in which he privately acknowledges "how smart a lash" Polonius's speech about the performance of devotion "doth give my conscience" (3.1.48–50).

99. On the relationship between touch and physical death in rhetoric and treatises on the plague, see especially Margaret Healy, "Anxious and Fatal Contacts: Taming the Contagious Touch," in *Sensible Flesh: On Touch in Early Modern Culture*, ed. Elizabeth Harvey (Philadelphia: University of Pennsylvania Press, 2003), 22–38.

100. Shakespeare, *Hamlet*, 1.5.36–38; 3.4.63. On the dominance of "hair-heir-here-hear" homonymns in *Hamlet*, see Helge Kökeritz, *Shakespeare's Pronunciation* (New Haven: Yale University Press, 1953), 90–91; and on "ear" as part of this homonymic cluster, see Philippa Berry, "Hamlet's Ear," in *Shakespeare and Language*, ed. Catherine M. S. Alexander (Cambridge: Cambridge University Press, 2004), 201–12. On hearing problems in *Hamlet*, see Peter Cummings, "Hearing in *Hamlet*: Poisoned Ears and the Psychopathology of Flawed Audition," *Shakespeare Yearbook* 1 (1990), 81–92.

101. By this I allude to the questions, raised in *Hamlet*, of Protestant and Catholic approaches to language and meaning; of words cast as mumbling as in Hamlet's famous "buzz buzz"; of verbal excess integral to legal as well as courtly rhetoric; of the challenges to speech in scholarly and heavily textualized contexts; of the revenge "plot" that palls to produce another effect; and, finally, the issue of inarticulate love (in gesture as in writing).

102. On Hamlet as an Echo and Narcissus figure at once, see Berry, "Hamlet's Ear."

103. On the relationship between the senses of vision and hearing in *Hamlet*, see especially Paul A. Kottman, "Sharing Vision, Interrupting Speech: *Hamlet's* Spectacular Community," *Shakespeare Studies* (Shakespeare Society of Japan) 36 (1998), 29–57, and Don Parry Norford, " 'Very Like a Whale': The Problem of Knowledge in *Hamlet*," *English Literary History* 46, no. 4 (Winter 1979), 559–76.

104. For a suggestive treatment of "narrative abruption" and mortality in *Hamlet*, see Michael Neill, *Issues of Death: Mortality and Identity in English Renaissance Tragedy* (Oxford: Oxford University Press, 1999), 216–42.

105. On the centrality of emotional contact or "movement" to Renaissance rhetoric, or the "the increasing stress on persuasion via the passions" that "led to a readjustment of emphasis within rhetoric" so that *movere* became predominant, see Brian Vickers, "On the Practicalities of Renaissance Rhetoric," in *Rhetoric Revalued*, ed. Brian Vickers (Binghampton, N.Y.: Center for Medieval and Early Renaissance Studies, 1982), 136.

106. T. S. Eliot read Hamlet's word-play as a species of Shakespeare's own pathology: "The levity of Hamlet, his repetition of phrase, his puns, are not part of a deliberate plan of dissimulation, but a form of emotional relief. . . . It often occurs in adolescence: the or-

dinary person puts these feelings to sleep, or trims down his feeling to fit the business world; the artist keeps it alive by his ability to intensify the world to his emotions. The Hamlet of Laforgue is an adolescent; the Hamlet of Shakespeare is not, he has not that explanation and excuse. We must simply admit that here Shakespeare tackled a problem which proved too much for him" ("Hamlet and His Problems," 101).

107. For Bruce Smith, the series of O sounds in the Folio marks the "inexorable disintegration of the speaking 'I'" and calls attention to the logo-marginal texture of speech in the play more generally ("Hearing Green," 4.3–4.4).

108. Plutarch, *The Philosophie, commonlie called, The Morals Vvritten By the learned Philosopher Plutarch of Chaeronea. Translated out of Greeke into English, and conferred with the Latine translations and the French, by Philemon Holland of Coventrie, Doctor in Physicke* (London, 1603), 1313.

109. *Oxford English Dictionary*, s.vv. "mad," "mathe."

110. Eliot, "Hamlet and His Problems," 101.

111. Nicholas Ling, *Politeuphuia Wits Common wealth* (London, 1598), 190v. This particular allusion to Aristotle was added to this second edition of *Politeuphuia*, though the Latin quotation to follow was included in the first (1597) edition as well: "*Nos Aper auditu, Linx visu, Simia gustu, / Vultur odoratu, nos vincit Aranea tactu*" (190v). Ling, we recall, was the publisher of the 1603 *Hamlet*.

SELECTED BIBLIOGRAPHY

PRIMARY SOURCES

Alighieri, Dante. *La Vita Nuova*. Translated by Barbara Reynolds. New York: Penguin, 1969.

Aristotle. *De anima*. Translated by W. S. Hett. Cambridge, Mass.: Harvard University Press, 1986.

———. *Nicomachean Ethics*. Translated by J. A. K. Thomson, edited by Jonathan Barnes. London: Penguin, 1955.

Ascham, Roger. *The Scholemaster Or plaine and perfite way of teachyng children, to vnderstand, write, and speake, the Latin tong but specially purposed for the priuate brynging vp of youth in ientlemen and Noble mens houses, and commodious also for all such, as haue forgot the Latin tonge*. London, 1570.

Augustine. *Confessions*. Translated by R. S. Pine-Coffin. Harmondsworth: Penguin Books, 1961.

———. *Letters of St. Augustine*. In *Nicene and Post Nicene Fathers of the Christian Church*, vol. 1. Translated by Rev. J. G. Cunningham, Edited by Philip Schaff. Grand Rapids, Mich.: Eerdmans, 1956.

Bacon, Francis. *A Briefe Discovrse, Touching the Happie Vnion of the Kindomes of England, and Scotland*. London, 1603.

———. *The charge of Sir Francis Bacon Knight, his Maiesties Attourney generall, touching duells vpon an information in the Star-chamber against Priest and Wright. With the decree of the Star-chamber in the same cause*. London, 1614.

———. *Considerations Touching A Warre With Spaine*. London, 1629.

———. *Sylua Syluarum: Or A Naturall Historie In ten Centuries*. London, 1627.

Bale, John. *An excellent and a right learned meditacion, compiled in two prayers most frutefull and necessary to be vsed and said of al ttue [sic] English men, in these daungerous daies of affliction, for the comfort and better stay of the christen co[n]science, bewailing the deserued plages of England*. London, 1544.

———. *A mysterye of inyquyte contayned within the heretycall genealogye of Ponce Pantolabus, is here both dysclosed & confuted by Iohan Bale*. Antwerp, 1545.

————. *Yet a course at the Romyshe foxe. A dysclosynge or openynge of the Manne of synne, contayned in the late Declaratyon of the Popes olde faythe made by Edmonde Boner bysshopp of London. wherby wyllyam Tolwyn was than newlye professed at paules crosse openlye into Antichristes Romyshe relygyon agayne by a newe solempne othe of obedyence, notwythsta[n]dynge the othe made to hys prynce afore to the contrarye.* London, 1543

Becon, Thomas. *The Displaying of the Popish masse vvherein thou shalt see, what a wicked Idoll the Masse is, and what great difference there is between the Lords Supper and the Popes Masse: againe, what Popes brought in every part of the Masse, and counted it together in such monstrous sort, as it is now used in the Popes Kingdome. Written by Thomas Becon; and published in the dayes of Queene Mary.* London, 1637.

————. *The Jewel of Joy,* in *The Catechism . . . with other works written in the Reign of Edward VI.* Edited by A. J. Ayre. Parker Society Publications, vol. 3. Cambridge: Cambridge University Press, 1844.

Bellot, Jacques. *Familiar Dialogues, For the Instruction of the[m], that be desirous to learne to speake English, and perfectlye to pronou[n]ce the same.* London, 1586.

————. *The French Methode wherein is contained a perfite order of Grammer for the French Tongue.* London, 1588.

————. *Le Iardin de Vertv et Bonnes Moeurs Plain de Plusiers Belles Fleurs, & riches sentences auec le sens d'icelles, recueillies de plusiers autheurs, & mises en lumiere.* London, 1581.

————. *Le maistre d'escole Anglois. Contenant plusieurs profitables preceptes pour les naturelz françois, et autres estrangers qui ont la langue françoise pour paruenir a la vraye prononciation de la langue Angloise. = The Englishe Scholemaister. Conteyning many profitable preceptes for the naturall borne french men, and other straungers that haue their French tongue, to attayne the true pronouncing of the Englishe tongue.* London, 1580.

Betson, Thomas. *Here begynneth a ryght profytable treatyse co[m]pendiously drawen out of many [and] dyuers wrytynges of holy men, to dyspose men to be vertuously occupyed in theyr myndes [and] prayers.* Westminster: Wynkyn de Worde, 1500.

Bilson, Thomas. *The Trve Difference Betweene Christian Subiection and Unchristian Rebellion: Wherein The Princes Lawfull power to commaund for trueth, and indepriuable right to beare the sword are defended against the Popes censures and the Iesuits sophismes vttered in their Apologie and Defence of English Catholikes: With a demonstration that the thinges refourmed in the Church of England by the Lawes of this Realme are truely Catholike, notwithstanding the vaine shew made to the contrary in their late Rhemish Testament.* Oxford: 1585.

Birckbek, Simon. *The Protestants Evidence Taken Ovt Of Good Records; Shewing that for Fifteene hundred yeares next after Christ, divers worthy guides of Gods Church, have in sundry weightie poynts of Religion, taught as the Church of England.* London, 1635.

Blount, Thomas. *Glossographia: Or A Dictionary, Interpreting all such Hard Vvords, Whether Hebrew, Greek, Latin, Italian, Spanish, French, Teutonick, Belgick, British or Saxon; as are now used in our refined English tongue.* London, 1656.

Blundeville, Thomas. *The Art of Logike. Plainely taught in the English tongue, by M. Blundeuile of Newton Flotman in Norfolke, aswell according to the doctrine of Aristotle, as of all other moderne and best accounted authors thereof. A very necessarie booke for all young students in any profession to find out thereby the truth in any doubtfull speech, but specially for such zealous ministers as haue not beene brought vp in any Vniuersity, and yet are desirous to know how to defend by sound argumentes the true Christian doctrine, against all subtill sophisters, and cauelling schismatikes, [and] how to confute their false sillogismes, [and] captious arguments.* London, 1599.

Bocchi, Achille. *Symbolicarvm qvaestionvm, de vniverso genere, quas serio ludebat, libri qvinqve.* Bologna, 1574.

Brathwaite, Richard. *Essaies Vpon the Fiue Senses with a pithie one vpon Detraction.* London, 1620.

———. *Essaies Vpon the Five Senses, Revived by a new Supplement; with a pithy one upon Detraction. Continued Vvith sundry Christian Resolves, and divine Contemplations, full of passion and devotion; purposely composed for the zealously-disposed.* London, 1635.

Breton, Nicholas. *A floorish vpon fancie. As gallant a Glose Vpon so triflinge a text, as euer was written.* London, 1577.

Bright, Timothy. *A Treatise of Melancholy. Contayning the causes thereof, and reasons of the straunge effects it worketh in our minds and bodies: with the Phisicke cure, and spirituall consolation for such as haue thereto adioyned afflicted conscience.* London, 1586.

Brinsley, John. *Ludus Literarius: Or, The Grammar Schoole; Shewing How To Proceede from the first entrance into learning, to the highest perfection required in the Grammar Schooles, with ease, certainty and delight both to Masters and Schollars.* London, 1612.

Bromyard, John of. *Summa Praedicantium* (Basle: c. 1484). In *A Selection of Latin Stories, from Manuscripts of the Thirteenth and Fourteenth Centuries: A Contribution to the History of Fiction During the Middle Ages,* edited by Thomas Wright. London: Percy Society, 1842.

Browne, Thomas. *Pseudodoxia Epidemica: or, Enquiries Into Very many received Tenents. And commonly presumed Truths.* London, 1646.

Burton, Robert. *The Anatomy of Melancholy, What It Is. With All The Kindes, Causes, Symptomes, Prognostickes, And Seuerall Cures Of It. In Three Maine Partitions with their seuerall Sections, Members, and Subsections. Philosophically, Medicinally, Historically, Opened And Cvt Vp.* Oxford, 1621 and 1624.

———. *The Anatomy of Melancholy,* edited by Floyd Dell and Paul Jordan-Smith. London: Routledge, 1931.

———. *The Anatomy of Melancholy.* Edited by Lawrence Babb. Lansing: Michigan State University Press, 1965.

———. *Philosophaster* (1606). Translated by Paul Jordan Smith. Stanford: Stanford University Press, 1931.

Calvin, Jean. *The Institution of Christian Religion, vvrytten in Latine by maister Ihon Caluin, and translated into Englysh according to the authors last edition.* London, 1561.

Cardwell, Edward. *Documentary Annals of the Reformed Church of England.* Oxford: Oxford University Press, 1839.

Case, John. *The Praise of Mvsicke: Wherein besides the antiquitie, dignitie, delectation, & vse thereof in ciuill matters, is also declared the sober and lawfull vse of the same in the congregation and Church of God.* London, 1586.

Castiglione, Baldassare. *The Covrtyer of Covnt Baldessar Castilio.* Translated by Sir Thomas Hoby. London, 1561.

Cawdrey, Robert. *A Table Alphabeticall, conteyning and teaching the true writing, and vnderstanding of hard vsuall English wordes, borrowed from the Hebrew, Greeke, Latine, or French, &c. With the interpretation thereof by plaine English words, gathered for the benefit & helpe of Ladies, Gentlewomen, or any other vnskilfull persons. Whereby they may the more easilie and better vnderstand many hard English wordes, vvhich they shall heare or read in scriptures, sermons, or elswhere, and also be made able to vse the same aptly themselues.* London, 1604.

Chapman, George. Translator, *The Iliads of Homer Prince of Poets. Neuer before in any languag truely translated. With a Co[m]ment vppon some of his chiefe places; Donne according to the Greeke By Geo: Chapman.* London, 1611.

Chaucer, Geoffrey. *The Works of Our Ancient, Learned, & Excellent English Poet, Jeffrey Chaucer.* London, 1687.

Cicero. *Brutus.* Translated by G. L. Hendrickson. Loeb Classical Library. Cambridge, Mass: Harvard University Press, 1971.

———. *De inventione.* Translated by H. M. Hubbell. Loeb Classical Library. Cambridge, Mass.: Harvard University Press, 1949.

———. *De officiis,* or *On Duties.* Edited by M. T. Griffin and E. M. Atkins, translated by Griffin. Cambridge: Cambridge University Press, 1991.

———. *De oratore.* Edited by H. Rackham, translated by E. W. Sutton. Loeb Classical Library. Cambridge, Mass.: Harvard University Press, 1949.

Claudian. *The Second Book Against Rufinus.* Translated by Maurice Platnauer. Cambridge, Mass.: Harvard University Press, 1922.

Coke, Edward. *La Sept Part Des Reports Sr. Edvv. Coke Chiualer.* London, 1608.

———. *La Size Part Des Reports Sr. Edw. Coke Chiualer.* London, 1607.

———. *Le Quart Part Des Reportes Del Edward Coke Chiualier.* London, 1604.

Cooper, Thomas. *Thesavrvs Lingvae Romanae & Britannicae.* London, 1578.

———. *Thesavrvs Linguae Romanae & Britannicae.* London, 1584.

Coote, Edmund. *The English schoole-maister teaching all his scholers, the order of distinct reading, and true writing our English tongue.* London, 1596.

Cotgrave, Randle. *A Dictionarie of the French and English Tongves.* London, 1611.

Cranmer, Thomas. *Articles To Be Inquired Of In The Visitation To Be Had in the byshopricke of Norwyche, now vacant in the fourth yere of our most drad souerayn Lorde Edwarde the sixte.* London, 1549.

———. *A Defence of the Trve and Catholike doctrine of the sacrament of the body and bloud of our sauiour Christ with a confutacion of sundry errors concernyng the same.* London, 1550.

Crooke, Helkiah. *Mikrokosmographia: A Description of the Body of Man.* London, 1615.

Daniel, Samuel. *A Panegyrike Congratvlatorie Deliuered To The Kings Most Excellent Maiestie At Bvrleigh Harrington in Rvtlandshire. By Samuel Daniel. Also Certaine Epistles, With A Defence Of Ryme Heretofore Written, And Now Pvblished By The Avthor.* London, 1603.

Davies, John. *Microcosmos: The Discovery Of The Little World, with the government thereof.* London, 1603.

———. *Nosce teipsum. This Oracle expounded in two Elegies, 1. Of Humane knowledge, 2. Of the Soule of Man, and the immortalitie thereof.* London, 1599.

de La Primaudaye, Pierre. *The French Academie, wherein is discoursed the institution of manners . . . newly translated into English by T. B.* London, 1586.

Delamothe, George. *The French Alphabeth [sic] Teaching In A Very Short Tyme, By a most easie way, to pronounce French naturally, to reade it perfectly, to write it truely, and to speake it accordingly.* London, 1592.

Diogenes (Laertius). *Lives of the Eminent Philosophers.* 2 vols. Translated by R. D. Hicks. Cambridge, Mass.: Harvard University Press, 1925.

Donatus. *Commentum Terenti.* 3 vols. Edited by Paul Wessner. Leizpig, 1902–8.

Downame, George. *A Godly And Learned Treatise Of Prayer; Which both conteineth in it the Doctrine of Prayer, and also sheweth the Practice of it in the exposition of the Lords Prayer: By that faithfull and painfull servant of God George Downame, Doctr of Divinity, and late L. Bishop of Dery.* London, 1640.

Drant, Thomas. *A Sermon Preached at S. Maries Spittle.* In *Two Sermons preached the one at S. Maries Spittle on Tuesday in Easter weeke 1570.* London, 1570.

Du Laurens, André. *A Discourse of the Preseruation of the Sight: of Melancholike diseases; of Rheumes, and of Old age. Composed by M. Andreas Laurentius, ordinarie Phisition to the King, and publike professor of Phisicke in the Vniuersitie of Mompelier. Translated out of French into English, according to the last edition, by Richard Surphlet, practitioner in phisicke.* London, 1599.

Dunbar, William, and Walter Kennedy. "The flyting of Dunbar and Kennedy." London, 1508.

Duncan, P. Martin. *A Manual for the Classification, Training, and Education of the Feeble-Minded, Imbecile, & Idiotic.* London: Longmans, Green, 1866.

Egerton, Thomas. "Proceedings in the Lords, 1597–98: October 24–February 9." In *Historical Collections: or, An exact Account of the Proceedings of the Four last Parliaments of Q. Elizabeth.* Edited by Heywood Townshend, 79–99. London, 1680.

Eliot, John. *Ortho-epia Gallica. Eliots Frvits for the French: Enterlaced vvith a double nevv Inuention, vvhich teacheth to speake truely, speedily and volubly the French-tongue.* London, 1593.

Ellis, Henry. *Original Letters of Eminent Literary Men: Of the Sixteenth, Seventeenth and Eighteenth Centuries.* London: J. B. Nichols and Son, 1843.

Elyot, Thomas. *The boke named the Gouernour.* London, 1531.

Erasmus, Desiderius. *Adages.* In *The Collected Works of Erasmus*, vol. 33. Translated and edited by R. A. B. Mynors. Toronto: University of Toronto Press, 1992.

———. *Apophthegmes that is to saie, prompte, quicke, wittie and sentencious saiynges, of certain Emperours, Kynges, Capitaines, Philosophiers and Oratours, aswell Grekes, as Romaines, bothe veraye pleasaunt [et] profitable to reade, partely for all maner of persones, [et] especially Gentlemen.* Translated by Nicholas Udall. London, 1542.

———. *De duplici copia verborum ac rerum commentarii duo* (1512). In *Collected Works of Erasmus: Literary and Educational Writings.* Translated by Betty I. Knott, edited by Craig R. Thompson, 24: 279–659. Toronto: University of Toronto Press, 1978.

———. "An Exhortacion to the diligent studye of Scripture." In *The Newe Testament of oure Saueour Jesus Christ translated by M. Wil. Tyndall, yet once agayno [sic] corrected with new annotacyons very necessary to better onderstondynge; where vnto is added an exhortacion to the same of Erasmus Rotero.* London, 1549.

———. *The first tome or volume of the Paraphrase of Erasmus vpon the newe testamente.* Edited by Nicholas Udall and translated by Udall, et al. London, 1548.

———. *Lingua, sive, de linguae usu atque abusu liber utilissimus.* In *The Collected Works of Erasmus*, vol. 29. Translated by Elaine Fantham and edited by Elaine Fantham and Erika Rummel. Toronto: University of Toronto Press, 1989.

———. [*Moriae Encomium*] *The praise of Folie. Moriae encomivm a booke made in latine by that great clerke Erasmus Roterodame. Englisshed by sir Thomas Chaloner knight.* Translated by Thomas Chaloner. London, 1549.

———. *Moriae Encomivm; Or, The Praise of Folly.* Translated by John Wilson. London, 1668.

———. [*Moriae Encomium*] *Witt against Wisdom. Or A Panegyrick Upon Folly: Penn'd in Latin by Desiderius Erasmus, Render'd into English.* Translated by White Kennett. Oxford, 1683.

———. *Moriae Encomium.* In M. A. Screech, *Erasmus: Ecstasy and The Praise of Folly*, Appendix A (New York: Penguin, 1980).

———. [*Moriae Encomium*] *Praise of Folly and Letter to Martin Dorp 1515: Erasmus of Rotterdam.* Edited and translated by Betty Radice. New York: Penguin, 1982.

———. [*Moriae Encomium*] *Stultitiae Laus*, edited by John F. Collins. Bryn Mawr: Bryn Mawr College Library, 1991.

———. *Paraclesis. In The Praise of Folly and Other Writings.* Edited and translated by Robert M. Adams. New York: Norton, 1989, 118–27.

———. *Paraphrasis in evangelium Lucae.* In *Opera Omnia*, vol. 7. Leiden, 1703–6.

Ferrand, Jacques. *Erotomania, Or A Treatise Discoursing of the Essence, Causes, Symptomes, Prognosticks, and Cure of Love, Or Erotiqve Melancholy.* Oxford, 1640.

Fletcher, Phineas. *The Purple Island, Or, The Isle Of Man Together With Piscatorie Eclogs And Other Poeticall Miscellanies.* London, 1633.

Florio, John. *Florio His firste Fruites: which yeelde familiar speech, merie Prouerbes, wittie Sentences, and golden Sayings. Also a perfect Induction to the Italian, and English*

tongues, as in the Table appeareth. The like heretofore, neuer by any man published.
London, 1578.

———. *Florios Second Frvtes, To be gathered of twelue Trees, of diuers but delightsome tastes to the tongues of Italians and Englishmen. To which is annexed his Gardine Of Recreation yeelding six thousand Italian Prouerbs.* London, 1591.

———. *A Worlde of Wordes, Or Most copious, and exact Dictionarie in Italian and English.* London, 1598.

Fortescue, John. *A learned commendation of the politique lawes of Englande.* Translated by Robert Mulcaster. London, 1567.

Foxe, John. *The Pope Confvted. The holy and Apostolique Church confuting the Pope. The first Action. Translated out of Latine into English, by Iames Bell.* London, 1580.

Fraunce, Abraham. *The Arcadian rhetorike: or The praecepts of rhetorike made plaine by examples Greeke, Latin, English, Italian, French, Spanish, out of Homers Ilias, and Odissea, Virgils Aeglogs, [. . .] and Aeneis, Sir Philip Sydnieis Arcadia, songs and sonets.* London, 1588.

———. *The Lawiers Logike, exemplifying the praecepts of Logike by the practise of the common Lawe.* London, 1588.

———. *Victoria, A Latin Comedy by Abraham Fraunce.* Edited by G. C. Moore Smith. Materialien zur Kunde des Älteren Englischen Dramas Series 14. Louvaine: A. Uystpruyst, 1906.

———. *Victoria.* In *Hymenaeus—Victoria—Laelia*, edited by Horst-Dieter Blume. Renaissance Latin Drama in England Series 13. Hildesheim: Georg Olms Verlag, 1991.

———. *Victoria (c. 1583): A Hypertext Critical Edition.* Edited and translated by Dana F. Sutton, *The Philological Museum,* The Shakespeare Institute, University of Birmingham, 2001. Available at www.philological.bham.ac.uk.

Freud, Sigmund. *The Standard Edition of the Complete Psychological Works.* Translated by James Strachey. London: Hogarth, 1953–74.

Fulke, William. *D. Heskins, D. Sanders, And M. Rastel, accounted (among their faction) three pillers and Archpatriarches of the Popish Synagogue (vtter enemies to the truth of Christes Gospell, and all that sincerely professe the same) ouerthrowne, and detected of their seuerall blasphemous heresies.* London, 1579.

———. *Praelections vpon the Sacred and holy Reuelation of S. John, written in latine by William Fulke Doctor of Diuinitie, and translated into English by George Gyffard.* London, 1573.

Fullwood, William. *The Enemie of Idlenesse Teaching the maner and stile how to endite, compose, and wryte all sortes of Epistles and Letters: as wel by answer, as otherwise. Deuided into foure Bookes, no lesse pleasant than profitable.* London, 1571.

Geminum, Thomas. *Compendiosa totius anatomie delineation.* Translated by Nicholas Udall, et al. London, 1553.

Gill, Alexander. *Logonomia Anglica* (London, 1619). Translated by Robin C. Alston, edited by Bror Danielsson, Arvid Gabrielson. Stockholm: Almqvist & Wiksell, 1972.

Goodman, John. *The Penitent Pardoned: Or, A Discourse of the Nature of Sin, And The Ef-ficacy of Repentance, Under the Parable Of The Prodigal Son.* London, 1679.

Gosson, Stephen. *The Schoole of Abuse, Conteining a plesaunt inuectiue against Poets, Pipers, Plaiers, Iesters, and such like Caterpillers of a Cŏmonwelth.* London, 1579. Reprinted as *The Schoole of Abuse* in *Early Treatises on the Stage.* London: Shakespeare Society, 1853.

Greene, John. *A Refvtation of the Apology for Actors. Diuided into three briefe Treatises . . . 1. Heathenish and Diabolical institution. 2. Their ancient and moderne indignitie. 3. The wonderfull abuse of their impious qualitie.* London, 1615.

Guarna, Andrea. *Grammaticale Bellum.* Cremona, 1511.

———. *Bellum Grammaticale, A discourse of gret war and dissention betwene two worthy Princes, the Noune and the Verbe, contending for the chefe place or dignitie in Oration* [William Heyward]. London, 1569 and 1576.

———. *Bellum grammaticale A discourse of gret war and dissention betweene two worthy princes, the noune and the verb[e contend]ing for the [chiefe place of dignitie in oration]. . . Turned into [English] by VV. H.* [William Hayward]. London, 1576. In *A Collection of Scarce and Valuable Tracts, on the Most Interesting and Entertaining Subjects,* 2nd ed., edited by Sir Walter Scott, 13 vols. London, 1809.

Guazzo, Stephen. *The Civile Conuersation of M. Steeuen Guazzo written first in Italian, and nowe translated out of French by George Pettie, deuided into foure bookes. In the first is conteined in generall, the fruites that may bee reaped by conuersation. . . . In the second, the manner of conuersation. . . . In the third is perticularly set foorth the orders to bee ob-serued in conuersation within doores, betwéene the husband and the wife. . . . In the fourth, the report of a banquet.* London, 1581.

Hall, Edward. *The Vnion of the two noble and illustre fameilies of Lancastre [and] Yorke.* London, 1548.

Hall, Joseph. *Mvndvs Alter Et Idem.* London, 1605.

Hansen, Mark. *New Philosophies for New Media.* Cambridge, Mass.: MIT Press, 2004.

Harding, Thomas. See John Jewel, *A Defence of the Apologie of the Churche of Englande, Conteininge an Answeare to a certaine Booke lately set foorthe by M. Hardinge, and En-tituled, A Confutation of &c.* London, 1567.

Harrison, William. "The Description of Britain." In *The First and second volumes of Chron-icles, comprising 1 The description and historie of England, 2 The description and histo-rie of Ireland, 3 The description and historie of Scotland.* London, 1587.

Hart, John. *A Methode or comfortable beginning for all unlearned whereby they may be taught to read English, in a very short time, with pleasure* (London, 1570). In *John Hart's Works on English Orthography and Pronunciation,* edited by Bror Danielsson. Stockholm: Almquist & Wiksell, 1955.

Henslowe, Philip. *Henslowe's Diary,* edited by R. A. Foakes and R. T. Rickert. Cambridge: Cambridge University Press, 1961.

Herbert, J. A. *Catalogue of Romances in the Department of MSS in the British Museum.* London, 1910.

Here after Folowith the boke callyd the Myrroure of Oure Lady very necessary for all relygyous persones. London, 1530.

Heteroclitanomalonomia (c. 1613). In *Jacobean Academic Plays.* Edited by Suzanne Gossett and Thomas L. Berger. Malone Society Collections, vol. 14, 57–97. Oxford: Oxford University Press, 1988.

Heywood, Jasper. Preface, *The Seconde Tragedie of Seneca entituled Thyestes faithfully Englished by Jasper Heywood fellowe of Alsolne College in Oxforde.* London, 1560.

———. Preface, *The Sixt Tragedie of the most graue and prudent author Lucius, Anneus, Seneca, entituled Troas, with diuers and sundrye addicions to the same. Newly set forth in Englishe by Jasper Heywood student in Oxonforde.* London, 1559.

Heywood, Thomas. *An Apology For Actors. Containing three brief Treatises. 1 Their Antiquity. 2 Their ancient Dignity. 3 The true vse of their quality.* London, 1612.

Holinshed, Raphael. *The First and second volumes of Chronicles comprising 1 The description and historie of England, 2 The description and historie of Ireland, 3 The description and historie of Scotland: First collected and published by Raphaell Holinshed, William Harrison, and others: Now newlie augmented and continued.* London, 1587.

———. *The Firste volume of the Chronicles of England, Scotlande, and Irelande. Conteyning, the Description and Chronicles of England, from the first inhabiting vnto the conquest.* London, 1577.

———. *The Second volume of Chronicles: Conteining the description, conquest, inhabitation, and troublesome estate of Ireland; first collected by Raphaell Holinshed; and now newlie recognized, augmented, and continued.* London, 1586.

Huloet, Richard. *Hvloets Dictionarie, newelye corrected, amended, Set In Order And Enlarged, with many names of Men, Townes, Beastes, Foules, Fishes, Trees, Shrubbes, Herbes, Fruites, Places, Instrumentes &c. And in eche place fit Phrases, gathered out of the best Latin Authors. Also the Frenche thereunto annexed, by vvhich you may finde the Latin or Frenche, of anye English woorde you will. By Iohn Higgins late student in Oxeforde.* London, 1572.

Hutten, Leonard. *Bellvm Grammaticale, Sive, Nominum Verborumq[ue] discordia civilis Tragico-comoedia Summo cum applausu olim apud Oxonienses in scaenam producta, & nunc in omnium illorum qui ad Gra[m]maticam animos appellunt oblectamentum edita.* London, 1635.

Jacob's Well: An English Treatise on the Cleansing of Man's Conscience. Edited by Arthur Brandeis. The Early English Text Society. London: K. Paul, Trench, Trübner, 1900.

Jewel, John. *Apologia Ecclesiae Anglicanae.* London, 1562.

———. *An Apologie, or aunswer in defence of the Church of England, concerninge the state of Religion vsed in the same. Newly set forth in Latin, and nowe translated into Englishe.* London, 1562.

———. *An Apologie or answere in defence of the Churche of Englande, with a briefe and plaine declaration of the true Religion professed and vsed in the same.* Translated by Lady Anne Bacon. London, 1564.

————. *A Defence of the Apologie of the Churche of Englande, conteininge an Answeare to a certaine Booke lately set foorthe by M. Hardinge, and Entituled, A Confutation of &c.* London, 1567.

————. *Oratio contra Rhetoricam*, "Oration Against Rhetoric." In *Renaissance Debates on Rhetoric*, edited and translated by Wayne Rebhorn, 162–72. Ithaca: Cornell University Press, 1999.

————. *A Replie Vnto M. Hardinges Ansvveare: By perusinge whereof the discrete, and diligent Reader may easily see, the weake, and vnstable groundes of the Romaine Religion, whiche of late hath beene accompted Catholique.* London, 1565.

Jonson, Ben. *The English Grammar . . . For the benefit of all Strangers, out of his observation of the English Language now spoken, and in use.* In *The Workes of Benjamin Jonson*, 33–84. London, 1641.

————. *Poetaster.* Edited by Tom Cain. Manchester: Manchester University Press: 1995.

Key, Thomas. "The preface of the Translatour." In Erasmus, *The first tome or volume of the Paraphrase of Erasmus vpon the newe testament.* London, 1548.

King, John. *Lectvres Vpon Ionas Delivered At Yorke In the yeare of our Lorde 1594.* London, 1599.

Kyd, Thomas. *The Spanish Tragedie, Containing the lamentable end of Don Horatio, and Belimperia: with the pittifull death of olde Hieronimo.* London, 1592.

————. *The Spanish tragedie, or, Hieronimo is mad againe. Containing the lamentable end of Don Horatio, and Belimperia; with the pittifull death of Hieronimo.* London, 1615.

————. *The Spanish Tragedy.* Edited by David Bevington. Manchester: Manchester University Press, 1989.

————. *The Spanish Tragedy.* Edited by J. R. Mulryne. London: A. and C. Black, 1989.

————. *The Works of Thomas Kyd.* Edited by Frederick S. Boas. Oxford: Clarendon Press, 1901.

Latimer, Hugh. *A notable Sermo[n] of ye reuerende father Maister Hughe Latemer, whiche he preached in ye Shrouds at paules churche in London on the xviii. daye of Januarye. 1548.* London, 1548.

————. *27 sermons preached by the ryght Reuerende father in God.* London, 1562.

Levens, Peter. *Manipvlvs Vocabvlorvm. A Dictionarie of English and Latine wordes, set forthe in suche order, as none heretofore hath ben, the Englishe going before the Latine, necessary not onely for Scholers that wa[n]t varietis of words, but also for such as vse to write in English Meetre.* London, 1570.

Ling, Nicholas. *Politeuphuia Wits Common wealth.* London, 1597.

Lyly, John. *Euphues and his England, Containing his voyage and aduentures, mixed with the sundry pretie discourses of honest Loue, the description of the countrey, the Court, and the manners of that Isle.* London, 1580.

————. "My hart and tongue were twinnes at once conceaued." In *The Complete Works of John Lyly.* Edited by Richard W. Bond, 12. Oxford: Clarendon Press, 1902.

Martyr, Peter. *A discourse or traictise of Petur Martyr Vermilla Flore[n]tine, the publyqe reader of diuinitee in the Uniuersitee of Oxford wherein he openly declared his whole and deter-minate iudgemente concernynge the Sacrament of the Lordes supper in the sayde Uniuer-sitee.* Translated by Nicholas Udall. London, 1550.

Montaigne, Michel de. *The Complete Essays.* Translated by M. A. Screech. New York: Penguin, 1993.

Mosse, Miles. *The Arraignment And Conuiction Of Vsurie. That Is, The iniquitie, and vnlawfulnes of vsurie, displayed in sixe Sermons, preached at Saint Edmunds Burie in Suffolke, vpon Prouerb. 28.8. By Miles Mosse, Minister of the worde, and Bacheler of Diuinitie. Seene and allowed by authoritie.* London, 1595.

Mulcaster, Richard. *The First Part Of The Elementarie Vvhich Entreateth Chefelie Of The right writing of our English tung.* London, 1582.

———. *Positions, Wherin Those Primitive Circumstances Be Examined, Which Are Necessarie For The Training vp of children, either for skill in their booke, or health in their bodie.* London, 1581.

Naogeorg, Thomas. *The Popish Kingdome, or reigne of Antichrist.* Translated by Barnabe Googe. London, 1570.

Narcissus: A Twelfe Night Merriment. Edited by Margaret L. Lee. London, 1893.

Nashe, Thomas. *Pierce Penilesse his Supplication to the Diuell. Describing the ouer-spreading of Vice, and suppression of Vertue. Pleasantly interlac't with variable delights: and pathetically intermixt with conceipted reproofs.* London, 1592.

———. "To the Gentlemen Students of both Uniuersities." In Robert Greene, *Menaphon Camillas alarum to slumbering Euphues, in his melancholie cell at Silexedra.* London, 1589.

Neville, Alexander. Preface, *The Lamentable Tragedie of Oedipvs the Sonne of Laivs Kyng of Thebes out of Seneca.* Translated by Alexander Neville. London, 1563.

Newton, Thomas. Preface, *Seneca: His Tenne Tragedies.* Edited by Thomas Newton. London, 1581.

Northbrooke, John. *Spiritus est vicarius Christi in terra. A Treatise wherein Dicing, Dauncing, Vaine plays or Enterluds with other idle pastimes [et]c. commonly vsed on the Sabboth day, are reproued by the Authoritie of the word of God and auntient writers. Made Dialoguewise by Iohn Northbrooke Minister and Preacher of the word of God.* London, c. 1577.

———. *Spiritus est Vicarius Christi in terra. The poore mans Garden wherein are flowers of the Scriptures, and Doctours, very necessarie and profitable for the simple and ignoraunt people to reade.* London, 1571.

Ocland, Christopher. *The Valiant Actes And victorious Battailes of the English nation: from the yeere of our Lord, one thousand threee hundred twentie and seven: being the first yeare of the raigne of the most mightie Prince Edward the third, to the year 1588. Also, Of The Peacable And quiet state of England, vnder the blessed gouernement of the most excellent and virtuous Princesse Elizabeth: a compendious declaration written by C. O. And newly translated out of Latin verse into English meeter. By J. S.* Translated by John Sharrock. London, 1585.

Ovid. *The. xv. Bookes of P. Ouidius Naso, entytuled Metamorphosis.* Translated by Arthur Golding. London, 1567.

Peacham, Henry. *Minerva Britanna Or A Garden Of Heroical Deuises furnished, and adorned with Emblemes and Impresa's of sundry natures, Newly devised, moralized, and published, by Henry Peacham, Mr. of Artes.* London, 1612.

Perkins, William. *The Arte Of Prophecying: Or A Treatise Concerning the sacred and onely true manner and methode of Preaching. First written in Latine by Master William Perkins; and now faithfully translated into English (for that it containeth many worthie things fit for the knowledge of men of all degrees) by Thomas Tuke.* London, 1607.

———. *Prophetica, Sive, De Sacra Et vnica ratione Concionandi Tractatus.* Cambridge, 1592.

Phillips, Edward. *The New World Of English Words, Or, A General Dictionary: Containing the interpretations of such hard words as are derived from other Languages . . . Together with All those Terms that relate to the Arts and Sciences . . . : to which are added the significations of Proper Names, Mythology, and Poetical Fictions, Historical Relations, Geographical Descriptions of most Countries and Cities of the World . . . / Collected and published by E.P.* London, 1658.

Pico della Mirandola, Giovanni. "Letter to Ermolao Barbaro." In *Renaissance Debates on Rhetoric,* edited and translated by Wayne Rebhorn, 58–67. Ithaca: Cornell University Press, 2000.

Plutarch. *De Garrulitate.* In *Moralia,* vol. 6, translated by W. C. Hembold. Cambridge, Mass.: Harvard University Press, 1939.

———. *The Philosophie, commonlie called, The Morals Vvritten By the learned Philosopher Plutarch of Chaeronea. Translated out of Greeke into English, and conferred with the Latine translations and the French, by Philemon Holland of Coventrie, Doctor in Physicke.* London, 1603.

Price, Owen. *The Vocal Organ, Or A new Art of teaching the English Orthographie.* London, 1665.

Prynne, William. *Histrio-mastix. The Players Scourge, Or, Actors Tragaedie, Divided into Two Parts.* London, 1633.

Puttenham, George. *The Arte of English Poesie. Contriued into three Bookes: the first of Poets and Poesie, the second of Proportion, the third of Ornament.* London, 1589.

Rabelais, François. *The Histories of Gargantua and Pantagruel.* Translated by J. M. Cohen. New York: Penguin, 1955.

———. *The Works Of The Famous Mr. Francis Rabelais Doctor in Physick Treating of the Lives, Heroick Deeds, and Sayings of Gargantua and his son Pantagruel.* Translated by Thomas Urquhart. London, 1664.

Rastell, John. *Beware of M. Iewel.* Antwerp, 1566.

———. *An exposition of certaine difficult and obscure words, and termes of the lawes of this realme.* London, 1579.

———. *The exposicions of [the] termys of [the] law of england [and] the nature of the writts with diuers rulys [and] principalles of the law as well out of the bokis of mayster littelton as of other bokis of the law.* London, 1523.

Rogers, Thomas. *A philosophicall discourse, Entituled, The Anatomie of the mind.* London, 1576.

Rowland, David. *A Comfortable ayde for Scholers, full of varietie of Sentences, gathered out of an Italian Authur.* London, 1568.

Ross, Alexander. *Arcana Microcosmi: Or, The hid Secrets of Man's Body discovered; In an Anatomical Duel between Aristotle and Galen.* London, 1652.

Sachs, Hans. *A goodly dysputacion betwene a Christen Shomaker / and a Popysshe Parson with two other parsones more, done within the famous Citie of Norembourgh.* Translated by Anthony Scoloker. London, 1548.

Salesbury, William. *A briefe and a playne introduction, teachyng how to pronounce the letters of the British tong, (now comenly called Walsh) wherby an English man shal not only w[ith] ease read the said tong rightly: but markyng ye same wel, it shal be a meane for him with one labour and diligence to attaine to the true and natural pronuncation of other expediente and most excellente languages.* London, 1550.

Seneca. *Agamemnon.* In *Seneca. IX: Tragedies II.* Edited and translated by John G. Fitch. Loeb Classical Library. Cambridge, Mass.: Harvard University Press, 2004.

———. *The Eyght Tragedie of Seneca. Entituled Agamemnon.* Translated by John Studley. London, 1566.

———. *The Lamentable Tragedie of Oedipvs the Sonne of Laivs Kyng of Thebes out of Seneca.* Translated by Alexander Neville. London, 1563.

———. *The Seconde Tragedie of Seneca entituled Thyestes faithfully Englished by Jasper Heywood fellowe of Alsolne College in Oxforde.* London, 1560.

———. *Seneca His Tenne Tragedies.* Edited by Thomas Newton. London, 1581.

———. *The Sixt Tragedie of the most graue and prudent author Lucius, Anneus, Seneca, entituled Troas, with diuers and Sundrye addicions to the same. Newly set forth in Englishe by Jasper Heywood student in Oxonforde.* London, 1559.

Shakespeare, William. *[Hamlet] The Tragicall Historie of Hamlet Prince of Denmarke, As it hath beene diuerse times acted by his Highnesse seruants in the Cittie of London: as also in the two Vniuersities of Cambridge and Oxford, and else-where.* London, 1603.

———. *Hamlet.* Edited by Harold Jenkins. Arden Shakespeare. London: Methuen, 1982.

———. *[King Lear] M. William Shak-speare: His True Chronicle Historie of the life and death of King Lear and his three Daughters. With the vnfortunate life of Edgar, sonne and heire to the Earle of Gloster, and his sullen and assumed humor of Tom of Bedlam: As it was played before the Kings Maiestie at Whitehall vpon S. Stephans night in Christmas Hollidayes. By his Maiesties seruants playing vsually at the Gloabe on the Bancke-side.* London, 1608.

———. *King Lear.* Edited by Kenneth Muir. Arden Shakespeare. London: Methuen, 1964.

———. *[Love's Labour's Lost] A Pleasant Conceited Comedie Called, Loues labors lost.* London, 1598.

———. *Shakspere's Loves Labors Lost: The First Quarto, 1598, A Facsimile in Photo-Lithography.* Edited by William Griggs and Frederick James Furnivall. London: W. Griggs, 1880.

———. *Loues Labour's Lost.* In *The First Folio of Shakespeare, 1623.* Facsimile prepared and introduced by Doug Moston. New York: Applause, 1995.

———. *Love's Labour's Lost.* Edited by Richard David. Arden Shakespeare. London: Methuen, 1987.

———. *Love's Labour's Lost.* Edited by G. R. Hibbard. Oxford: Clarendon Press, 1990.

———. *Love's Labour's Lost..* Edited by H. R. Woudhuysen. Arden Shakespeare. Walton-on-Thames: Thomas Nelson and Sons, 1998.

———. *A Midsummer Night's Dream.* Edited by Harold F. Brooks. Arden Shakespeare. London: Methuen, 1979.

———. *Mr. William Shakespeares Comedies, Histories, & Tragedies. Published according to the True Originall Copies.* London, 1623.

———. *Much Ado About Nothing.* Edited by A. R. Humphreys. Arden Shakespeare. London: Routledge, 1988.

———. *Romeo and Juliet.* Edited by G. Blakemore Evans. The Riverside Shakespeare. New York: Houghton Mifflin, 1997.

———. *Romeo and Juliet.* Edited by Dympna Callaghan. Boston: Bedford, 2003.

———. *Shake-speares sonnets Neuer before Imprinted.* London, 1609.

———. *Shakespeare's Sonnets.* Edited by Stephen Booth. New Haven: Yale University Press, 1977.

———. *The Sonnets.* Edited by G. Blakemore Evans. New Cambridge Shakespeare. Cambridge: Cambridge University Press, 1997.

———. *The Winter's Tale.* Edited by J. H. P. Pafford. Arden Shakespeare. London: Methuen, 1963.

Shaw, Samuel. *Words Made Visible, or, Grammar and Rhetorick Accommodated to the Lives and Manners Of Men. Represented in a Country School for the Entertainment and Edification of the Spectators.* London, 1678.

Shepherd, Luke. *Doctour Doubble ale.* London, 1548.

Sherry, Richard. *A Treatise of the Figures of Grammer and Rhetorike.* London, 1555.

Sidney, Philip. *An Apologie for Poetrie.* London, 1595.

———. *Syr P.S. His Astrophel And Stella. Wherein the excellence of sweete Poesie is concluded.* London, 1591.

Simplicius. *Simplicius on Aristotle's Physics 6.* Translated by David Konstan. London: Gerald Duckworth, 1989.

Smith, Thomas. *De Repvblica Anglorvm The maner of Gouernement or policie of the Realme of England, compiled by the honorable man Thomas Smyth, Doctor of the ciuil lawes, knight, and principall Secretarie vnto the two most worthie princes, King Edwarde the sixt, and Queene Elizabeth.* London, 1583.

Staphylus, Friedrich. *The Apologie of Fridericvs Staphylvs.* Translated by Thomas Stapleton. Antwerp, 1565.

Stapleton, Thomas. *A Retur[ne of Vn]truthes Vpon [M. Jewel]les Replie Partly of such, as he hath Slaunderously charged Harding withal.* Antwerp, 1566.

Stubbes, Phillip. *The Anatomie of Abuses: Contayning, A Discouerie, Or Briefe Summarie of such Notable Vices and Imperfections, as now raigne in many Christian Countreyes of the worlde: but (especiallie) in a verie famous Ilande called Ailgna.* London, 1583.

Studley, John. Preface, *The Eyght Tragedie of Seneca. Entituled Agamemnon.* London, 1566.

Thomasii, Thomae. *Dictionarivm lingvae Latinae et Anglicanae. In hoc opere qvid sit præstitum, & ad superiores λεξικογραφονς adiectum, docebit epistola ad Lectorem.* London, 1587.

Tofte, Robert. *Alba, The Months Minde Of A Melancholy Louer, diuided into three parts.* London, 1598.

Tomkis, Thomas. *Lingua: Or The Combat of the Tongue, And the fiue Senses for Superiority. A pleasant Comoedie* (c. 1602). London, 1607.

Tottell, Richard. Preface. *Songes and sonettes.* London, 1557.

———. Preface. *Tottel's Miscellany.* Edited by Hyder E. Rollins. Cambridge: Harvard University Press, 1965.

The Towneley Plays. Edited by G. England and A. W. Pollard. The Early English Text Society, London: Kegan Paul, Trench, Trübner, 1897.

Tyndale, William. *The obedie[n]ce of a Christen man.* Antwerp, 1528.

———. *The parable of the Wycked Mammon. Compiled in the yere of our Lorde, M.d.xxxvi.* London, 1547.

Tyndale, William, translator. *The Newe Testament of oure Saueour Jesus Christ translated by M. Wil. Tyndall, yet once agayno [sic] corrected with new annotacyons very necessary to better onderstondynge; where vnto is added an exhortacion to the same of Erasmus Rotero.* London, 1549.

Udall, Nicholas. "Answer to the Commoners of Devonshire and Cornwall." In *Troubles Connected with the Prayer Book of 1549,* edited by Nicholas Pocock. Westminster: Camden Society, 1884.

———. *The Dramatic Writings of Nicholas Udall.* Ed. John Farmer. London: Early English Drama Society, 1906.

———. *Flovres for Latine Spekynge selected and gathered oute of Terence, and the same translated in to Englysshe, together with the exposition and settinge for the as welle of such latyne wordes, as were throught nedefull to be annoted, as also of dyuers grammatical rules, very profytable [and] necessarye for the expedite knowledge in the lating tongue.* London: 1534.

———. [*Ralph Roister Doister*] *What Creature is in health, eyther yong or olde.* London, 1566.

———. *Respublica: An Interlude for Christmas 1553, Attributed to Nicholas Udall.* Edited by W. W. Greg. Oxford: Oxford University Press, 1952.

Udall, Nicholas, translator. Erasmus, *Apophthegmes that is to saie, prompte, quicke, wittie and sentencious saiynges, of certain Emperours, Kynges, Capitaines, Philosophiers and Or-*

atours, aswell Grekes, as Romaines, bothe veraye pleasaunt [et] profitable to reade, partely for all maner of persones, [et] especially Gentlemen. London, 1542.

———. Thomas Geminum, *Compendiosa totius Anatomie delineatio.* London, 1553.

———. Peter Martyr, *A discourse or traictise of Petur Martyr Vermilla Flore[n]tine, the publyqe reader of diuinitee in the Uniuersitee of Oxford wherein he openly declared his whole and determinate iudgemente concernynge the Sacrament of the Lordes supper in the sayde Uniuersitee.* London, 1550.

Udall, Nicholas, editor and translator. Erasmus, *The first tome or volume of the Paraphrase of Erasmus vpon the newe testamente.* London, 1548.

A Very necessarye boke both in Englyshce & in Frenche wherein ye mayst learne to speake & wryte Frenche truly in a litle space yf thou gyue thy mynde and diligence there unto. London, 1550.

Vives, Juan Luis. *A very frutefull and pleasant boke called the Instruction of a Christian Woman . . . turned out of Laten into Englysshe by Rycharde Hyrde.* London, 1529.

Weever, John. *Epigrammes in the Oldest Cut, and Newest Fashion.* London, 1599.

Whetstone, George. *An Heptameron of Ciuill Discourses.* London, 1582.

———. *A Critical Edition of George Whetstone's 1582* An Heptameron of Civill Discourses, ed. Diana Shklanka, *The Renaissance Imagination*, vol. 35. New York: Garland, 1987.

Wilson, Thomas. *The Arte of Rhetorique for the vse of all suche as are studious of Eloquence, sette forth in English.* London, 1553.

———. *The rule of Reason, conteinyng the Arte of Logique.* London, 1551 and 1553.

———. *The three Orations of Demosthenes chiefe orator among the Grecians, in Favor of the Olynthians . . . with those his four Orations . . . Against King Philip of Macedonie.* London, 1570.

———. *Wilson's Arte of Rhetorique.* Edited by G. H. Mair. Oxford: Clarendon, 1909.

Wither, George. *A Collection of Emblemes, Ancient and Moderne, Quickened With Metricall Illustrations.* London, 1635.

Wright, Thomas. *The Passions of the Minde.* London, 1601.·

Zwinger, Theodor. *Theatrum Vitae Humanae.* Basel, 1565, 1571, 1586, 1604.

SECONDARY SOURCES

Abraham, Nicholas, and Maria Torok. *The Shell and the Kernel: Renewals of Psychoanalysis.* Edited and translated by Nicholas T. Rand. Chicago: University of Chicago Press, 1995.

Adams, Barry B. "The Audiences of *The Spanish Tragedy.*" *Journal of English and German Philology* 68 (1969): 221–36.

Aers, David. "New Historicism and the Eucharist." *Journal of Medieval and Early Modern Studies* 33 (2003): 241–59.

———. "A Whisper in the Ear of Early Modernists; or, Reflections on Literary Critics Writing the 'History of the Subject.'" In *Culture and History, 1350–1600: Essays on En-*

glish Communities, Identities and Writing, edited by David Aers, 177–203. Detroit: Wayne State University Press, 1992.

Agamben, Giorgio. *Infanzia e storia. Distruzione dell'esperienza e origine della storia*. Turin: Einaudi, 1978.

Altman, Joel. *Tudor Play of Mind: Rhetorical Inquiry and the Development of Elizabethan Drama*. Berkeley: University of California Press, 1978.

Anderson, Benedict. *Imagined Communities: Reflections on the Origin and Spread of Nationalism*. Rev. ed. New York: Verso, 2006.

Anderson, Judith H. "Language and History in the Reformation: Cranmer, Gardiner, and the Words of Institution." *Renaissance Quarterly* 54, no. 1 (Spring 2001): 20–51.

Anzieu, Didier. *The Skin Ego*. New Haven: Yale University Press, 1989.

Ardolino, Frank. *Apocalypse and Armada in Kyd's* Spanish Tragedy. Kirksville, Mo.: Sixteenth-Century Journal Publishers, 1995.

———. "*Corrida* of Blood in *The Spanish Tragedy*: Kyd's Use of Revenge as National Destiny." *Medieval and Renaissance Drama in England* 1 (1984): 37–49.

———. "Hieronimo as St. Jerome in *The Spanish Tragedy*." *Etudes Anglaises* 36, no. 4 (1983): 435–37.

———. "The Influence of Spenser's *Faerie Queene* on Kyd's *Spanish Tragedy*." *Early Modern Literary Studies* 7, no. 3 (January 2002): 41–70.

———. " 'Now Shall I See the Fall of Babylon': *The Spanish Tragedy* as Protestant Apocalypse." *Shakespeare Yearbook* 1 (1990): 93–116.

———. " 'Now I Shall See the Fall of Babylon': *The Spanish Tragedy* as a Reformation Play of Daniel." *Renaissance and Reformation* 14 (1990): 49–55.

Ashley, Kathleen M. "Titivillus and the Battle of Words in Mankind." *Annuale Mediaevale* 16 (1975): 128–50.

Attridge, Derek. "Puttenham's Perplexity: Nature, Art, and the Supplement in Renaissance Poetic Theory." In *Literary Theory/Renaissance Texts*, edited by Patricia Parker and David Quint, 257–79. Baltimore: Johns Hopkins University Press, 1986.

Bailey, Richard W. *Images of English: A Cultural History of the Language*. Ann Arbor: University of Michigan Press, 1991.

Bakhtin, Mikhail. "Forms of Time and of the Chronotope in the Novel." In *The Dialogic Imagination: Four Essays* edited by Michael Holquist, translated by Caryl Emerson and Michael Holquist. Austin: University of Texas Press, 1988.

Baldo, Jonathan. *The Unmasking of Drama: Contested Representation in Shakespeare's Tragedies*. Detroit: Wayne State University Press, 1997.

Barish, Jonas. *The Antitheatrical Prejudice*. Berkeley: University of California Press, 1981.

Barker, Francis. *The Tremulous Private Body: Essays on Subjection*. Rev. ed. Ann Arbor: University of Michigan Press, 1995.

Baumlin, Tita French. " 'A good (wo)man skilled in speaking.' " In *Ethos: New Essays in Rhetorical and Critical Theory*, edited by James S. Baumlin and Tita French Baumlin, 229–64. Dallas: Southern Methodist University Press, 1994.

Beal, Peter. *In Praise of Scribes: Manuscripts and Their Makers in Seventeenth-Century England.* Oxford: Clarendon Press, 1998.

Benarz, James P. *Shakespeare and the Poets' War.* New York: Columbia University Press, 2001.

Benjamin, Walter. *Illuminations.* Edited by Hannah Arendt, translated by Harry Zohn. New York: Schocken Books, 1968.

Benthien, Claudia. *Skin: On the Cultural Border Between Self and World.* New York: Columbia University Press, 2004.

Bergson, Henri. "Laugher." In *Comedy,* edited by Wylie Sypher, translated by Fred Rothwell, 61–190. New York: Doubleday, 1956.

Berlant, Lauren. *The Female Complaint: The Unfinished Buisiness of Sentimentality in American Culture.* Durham: Duke University Press, 2008.

———. "The Female Complaint." *Social Text* 19–20 (Autumn 1988): 237–59.

Berry, Philippa. "Hamlet's Ear." In *Shakespeare and Language,* edited by Catherine M. S. Alexander, 201–12. Cambridge: Cambridge University Press, 2004.

Bevington, David. *Tudor Drama and Politics: A Critical Approach to Topical Meaning.* Cambridge, Mass.: Harvard University Press, 1968.

Bhabha, Homi. *The Location of Culture.* New York: Routledge, 1993.

———. "The World and the Home." *Social Text: Third World and Postcolonial Issues* 31–32 (1992): 141–53.

Blair, Ann. "Reading Strategies for Coping with Information Overload ca. 1550–1700." *Journal of the History of Ideas* 64, no. 1 (2003): 11–28.

Blank, Paula. *Broken English: Dialects and the Politics of Language in Renaissance Writings.* London: Routledge, 1996.

Blatt, Thora Balslev. *The Plays of John Bale: A Study of Ideas, Technique and Style.* Copenhagen: G. E. C. Gad, 1968.

Bloom, Gina. *Voice in Motion: Staging Gender, Shaping Sound in Early Modern England.* Philadelphia: University of Pennsylvania Press, 2007.

Brooks, C. W., and Kevin Sharpe. "Debate: History, English Law and the Renaissance." *Past and Present* 72 (1976): 133–42.

Boas, Frederick S. *Cambridge History of English Literature.* 15 vols. London: G. P. Putnam's Sons, 1910.

———. " 'Macbeth' and 'Lingua.' " *Modern Language Review* 4, no. 4. (July 1909): 517–20.

———. *University Drama in the Tudor Age.* Oxford: Clarendon Press, 1914.

Booth, Stephen. "On the Value of Hamlet." In *Shakespeare: An Anthology of Criticism and Theory, 1945–2000,* edited by Russ McDonald, 225–44. Oxford: Blackwell, 2004.

Bossy, John. "The Mass as a Social Institution: 1200–1700." *Past and Present* (August 1983): 29–61.

Bouwsma, William J. "Lawyers and Early Modern Culture." *American Historical Review* 78, no. 2 (1973): 303–27.

Boyle, Marjorie O'Rourke. "A Conversation Opener: The Rhetorical Paradigm of John

1:1." In *A Companion to Rhetoric and Rhetorical Criticism*, edited by Walter Jost and Wendy Olmsted, 58–79. Oxford: Blackwell, 2004.

Bradbrook, M. C. "St. George for Spelling Reform!" *Shakespeare Quarterly* 15, no. 3 (Summer, 1964): 129–41.

Braden, Gordon. *Renaissance Tragedy and the Senecan Tradition.* New Haven: Yale University Press, 1985.

Bruster, Douglas. *Shakespeare and the Question of Culture: Early Modern Literature and the Cultural Turn.* New York: Palgrave, 2003.

Burckhardt, Jacob. *The Civilization of the Renaissance in Italy.* London: Phaidon Press, 1960.

Burke, Peter. *Languages and Communities in Early Modern Europe.* Cambridge: Cambridge University Press, 2004.

Burton, Vicki Tolar. "John Wesley and the Liberty to Speak: The Rhetorical and Literary Practices of Early Methodism." *College Composition and Communication* 53, no. 1 (2001): 65–91.

Bushnell, Rebecca W. *A Culture of Teaching: Early Modern Humanism in Theory and Practice.* Ithaca: Cornell University Press, 1996.

Callaghan, Dympna. *Shakespeare Without Women: Representing Gender and Race on The Renaissance Stage.* New York: Routledge, 2000.

Cargill, Oscar, "The Authorship of the Secunda Pastorum." *PMLA* 41, no. 4 (1926): 810–31.

Carroll, William C. *The Great Feast of Language in* Love's Labour's Lost. Princeton: Princeton University Press, 1976.

Cartwright, Kent. *Theatre and Humanism: English Drama in the Sixteenth Century.* Cambridge: Cambridge University Press, 1999.

Cave, Terence. *The Cornucopian Text: Problems of Writing in the French Renaissance.* Oxford: Clarendon Press, 1979.

Cawsey, Kathy. "Tutivillus and the 'Kyrkchaterars': Strategies of Control in the Middle Ages." *Studies in Philology* 102, no. 4 (2005): 443–51.

Cercignani, Fausto. *Shakespeare's Works and Elizabethan Pronunciation.* Oxford: Clarendon Press, 1981.

Chartier, Roger. *The Order of Books: Readers, Authors and Libraries in Europe Between the Fourteenth and Eighteenth Centuries.* Translated by Lydia G. Cochrane. Stanford: Stanford University Press, 1994.

Cheney, Liana De Girolami. "The Oyster in Dutch Genre Paintings: Moral or Erotic Symbolism." *Artibus et Historiae* 8, no. 15 (1987): 135–58.

Clarke, Danielle. " 'Formed into Words by Your Divided Lips': Women, Rhetoric and the Ovidian Tradition." In *"This Double Voice": Gendered Writing in Early Modern England*, edited by Danielle Clarke and Elizabeth Clarke, 61–87. Basingstoke: Macmillan Press, 2000.

Classen, Constance, editor. *The Book of Touch.* Oxford: Berg, 2005.

Colie, Rosalie L. *Paradoxia Epidemica: The Renaissance Tradition of Paradox.* Princeton: Princeton University Press, 1966.

———. *Shakespeare's Living Art.* Princeton: Princeton University Press, 1974.

Conley, Thomas M. *Rhetoric in the European Tradition.* Chicago: University of Chicago Press, 1990.

Cooper, Helen. "*Hamlet* and the Invention of Tragedy." *Sederi* 7 (1996): 189–99.

Copeland, Rita. *Rhetoric, Hermeneutics, and Translation in the Middle Ages: Academic Traditions and Vernacular Texts.* Cambridge: Cambridge University Press, 1991.

Cormack, Bradin. *A Power to Do Justice: Jurisdiction, English Literature and the Rise of Common Law, 1509–1625.* Chicago: University of Chicago Press, 2007.

———. "Practicing Law and Literature in Early Modern Studies." *Modern Philology* 101 (2003): 79–91.

Cormack, Bradin, and Carla Mazzio. *Book Use, Book Theory: 1500–1700.* Chicago: University of Chicago Library, 2005.

Cotterill, Anne. *Digressive Voices in Early Modern English Literature.* Oxford: Oxford University Press, 2004.

Coulton, G. G. *A Medieval Garner: Human Documents from the Four Centuries Preceding the Reformation.* London: Archibald Constable, 1910.

Crane, Mary Thomas. *Framing Authority: Sayings, Self, and Society in Sixteenth-Century England.* Princeton: Princeton University Press, 1993.

Crane, T. F. "New Analogues of Old Tales." *Modern Philology* 10, no. 3 (January 1913): 301–16.

Crary, Jonathan. *Techniques of the Observer: On Vision and Modernity in the Nineteenth Century.* Cambridge, Mass.: MIT Press, 1990.

Crick, Julia, and Alexandra Walsham, editors. *The Uses of Script and Print: 1300–1700.* Cambridge: Cambridge University Press, 2004.

Cummings, Peter. "Hearing in *Hamlet*: Poisoned Ears and the Psychopathology of Flawed Audition." *Shakespeare Yearbook* 1 (1990): 81–92.

Cunningham, Karen. *Imaginary Betrayals: Subjectivity and the Discourse of Treason in Early Modern England.* Philadelphia: University of Pennsylvania Press, 2002.

de Certeau, Michel. *The Writing of History.* New York: Columbia University Press, 1988.

de Grazia, Margreta. *Hamlet Without Hamlet.* Cambridge: Cambridge University Press, 2007.

———. "Homonyms Before and After Lexical Standardization." *Shakespeare Jahrbuch* (1990), 143–56.

———. "Imprints: Shakespeare, Gutenberg, Descartes." In *Alternative Shakespeares*, vol. 2, edited by Terence Hawkes, 63–94. London: Routledge, 1996.

———. "Shakespeare's View of Language: An Historical Perspective." *Shakespeare Quarterly* 29, no. 3 (Summer 1978): 374–88.

———. "Soliloquies and Wages in the Age of Emergent Consciousness." *Textual Practice* 9, no. 1 (1995): 67–92.

————. "Weeping for Hecuba." In *Historicism, Psychoanalysis and Early Modern Culture*, edited by Carla Mazzio and Douglas Trevor, 350–75. New York: Routledge, 2000.

de Grazia, Margreta, Maureen Quilligan and Peter Stallybrass, editors. *Subject and Object in Renaissance Culture*. Cambridge: Cambridge University Press, 1996.

Deleuze, Giles, and Félix Guattari. *What Is Philosophy?* New York: Columbia University Press, 1991.

Desmet, Christy. *Reading Shakespeare's Characters: Rhetoric, Ethics, and Identity*. Amherst: University of Massachusetts Press, 1992.

Devereux, George. "Mumbling: The Relationship Between a Resistance and Frustrated Auditory Curiosity in Childhood." *Journal of the American Psychoanalytic Association* 14 (1966): 478–84.

Dillon, Janette. *Language and Stage in Medieval and Renaissance England*. Cambridge: Cambridge University Press, 1998.

Dollimore, Jonathan. *Radical Tragedy: Religion, Ideology and Power in the Drama of Shakespeare and His Contemporaries*. Chicago: University of Chicago Press, 2004.

Donawerth, Jane. *Shakespeare and the Sixteenth-Century Study of Language*. Urbana: University of Illinois Press, 1984.

Doran, Madeleine. *Endeavors of Art: A Study of Form in Elizabethan Drama*. Madison: University of Wisconsin Press, 1954.

Dubrow, Heather. *The Challenges of Orpheus: Lyric Poetry and Early Modern England*. Baltimore: Johns Hopkins University Press, 2007.

Dukore, Bernard F. "Shaw on 'Hamlet.'" *Educational Theatre Journal* 23, no. 2 (May 1971): 152–59.

Dunn, Leslie C., and Nancy Jones, editors. *Embodied Voices: Representing Female Vocality in Western Culture*. Cambridge: Cambridge University Press, 1994.

Edgerton, William. *Nicholas Udall*. New York: Twayne, 1965.

Edwards, Anthony S. G., editor. *John Skelton: The Critical Heritage*. London: Routledge and Kegan Paul, 1981.

Eisenstein, Elizabeth. *The Printing Press as an Agent of Change: Communications and Cultural Transformations in Early Modern Europe*. Cambridge: Cambridge University Press, 1979.

————. "An Unacknowledged Revolution Revisited." *American Historical Review* 107, no. 1 (2002): 87–105.

Eliot, T. S. "Hamlet and His Problems." In *The Sacred Wood: Essays on Poetry and Criticism*. London: Methuen, 1922.

Elliott, John R. "Early Staging in Oxford." In *A New History of Early English Drama*, edited by John D. Cox and David Scott Kastan, 68–78. New York: Columbia University Press, 1997.

Elsky, Martin. *Authorizing Words: Speech, Writing, and Print in the English Renaissance*. Ithaca: Cornell University Press, 1989.

Enterline, Lynn. *The Rhetoric of the Body from Ovid to Shakespeare*. Cambridge: Cambridge University Press, 2005.

————. *The Tears of Narcissus: Melancholia and Masculinity in Early Modern Writing*. Stanford: Stanford University Press, 1995.

Erne, Lukas. *Beyond* The Spanish Tragedy: *A Study of the Works of Thomas Kyd*. Manchester: Manchester University Press, 2001.

Escolà, Jordi Coral. "Vengeance Is Yours: Reclaiming the Social Bond in *The Spanish Tragedy* and *Titus Andronicus*." *Atlantis* 29, no. 2 (December 2007): 59–74.

Evans, Benjamin Ifor. *The Language of Shakespeare's Plays*. New York: Routledge, reprint, 2005.

Evans, Malcolm. "The Converse of Breath." In *Signifying Nothing: Truth's True Contents in Shakespeare's Texts*, 39–98. Athens: University of Georgia Press, 1986.

————. "Mercury Versus Apollo: A Reading of *Love's Labor's Lost*." *Shakespeare Quarterly* 26 (1975): 113–27.

Falco, Raphael. "Medieval and Reformation Roots." In *A Companion to Renaissance Drama*, edited by Arthur F. Kinney, 239–56. Oxford: Blackwell, 2002.

Farmer, John, editor. *The Dramatic Writings of Nicholas Udall*. London: Early English Drama Society, 1906.

Farrell, Joseph. *Latin Language and Latin Culture: From Antiquity to Modern Times*. Cambridge: Cambridge University Press, 2001.

Fein, Susanna Greer. "A Thirteen-Line Alliterative Stanza on the Abuse of Prayer from the Audelay MS." *Medium Aevum* 63 (1994): 61–74.

Fineman, Joel. *Shakespeare's Perjured Eye: The Invention of Poetic Subjectivity in the Sonnets*. Berkeley: University of California Press, 1986.

Finkelpearl, Philip J. *Marston of the Middle Temple: An Elizabethan Dramatist in His Social Setting*. Cambridge, Mass.: Harvard University Press, 1969.

Fleming, Juliet. "Dictionary English and the Female Tongue." In *Enclosure Acts: Sexuality, Property, and Culture in Early Modern England*, edited by Richard Burt and John Michael Archer, 290–325. Ithaca: Cornell University Press, 1994.

Folkwerth, Wes. *The Sound of Shakespeare*. London: Routledge, 2002.

Franceschina, John. *Homosexualities in the English Theatre: From Lyly to Wilde*. Westport, Conn.: Greenwood Press, 1997.

Freedman, Barbara. *Staging the Gaze: Postmodernism, Psychoanalysis, and Shakespearean Comedy*. Ithaca: Cornell University Press, 1991.

Freeman, Arthur. *Thomas Kyd: Facts and Problems*. Oxford: Clarendon Press, 1967.

Fulwiler, Toby, and Bruce Petersen. "Toward Irrational Heuristics: Freeing the Tacit Mode." *College English* 43, no. 6 (1981): 621–29.

Fumerton, Patricia. *Cultural Aesthetics: Renaissance Literature and the Practice of Social Ornament*. Chicago: University of Chicago Press, 1991.

Gallagher, Catherine, and Stephen Greenblatt. *Practicing New Historicism*. Chicago: University of Chicago Press, 2000.

Garber, Marjorie. *A Manifesto for Literary Studies*. Seattle: University of Washington Press, 2003.

———. "Out of Joint." In *The Body in Parts: Fantasies of Corporeality in Early Modern Europe*, edited by David Hillman and Carla Mazzio, 22–41. New York: Routledge, 1997.

———. *Shakespeare's Ghost Writers: Literature as Uncanny Causality*. New York: Methuen, 1987.

Goffman, Erving. *Forms of Talk*. Philadelphia: University of Pennsylvania Press, 1981.

———. *Interactional Ritual: Essays in Face to Face Behavior*. New York: Pantheon, 1967.

Goldberg, Jonathan. *Voice Terminal Echo: Postmodernism and English Renaissance Texts*. New York: Methuen, 1986.

Gooch, Paul W. "Margaret, Bottom, Paul and the Inexpressible." *Word and World* 6, no. 3 (June 1986): 313–26.

Goodrich, Peter. "*Ars Bablativa:* Ramism, Rhetoric, and the Genealogy of English Jurisprudence." In *Legal Hermeneutics,* edited by Gregory Leyh, 43–82. Berkeley: University of California Press, 1992.

———. "The Continuance of the Antirrhetic." *Cardozo Studies in Law and Literature* 4, no. 2 (Autumn 1992): 207–22.

———. *Languages of Law: From Logics of Memory to Nomadic Masks*. London: Weidenfeld and Nicolson, 1990.

———. *Law in the Courts of Love: Literature and Other Minor Jurisprudences*. London: Routledge, 1996.

———. *Oedipus Lex: Psychoanalysis, History, Law*. Berkeley: University of California Press, 1995.

———. "Poor Illiterate Reason: History, Nationalism and Common Law." *Social and Legal* Studies 1, no. 1 (1992): 7–28.

Goody, Jack. "What's in a List?" In *The Domestication of the Savage Mind*, 74–111. Cambridge: Cambridge University Press, 1977.

Gordis, Lisa M. *Opening Scripture: Bible Reading and Interpretive Authority in Puritan New England*. Chicago: University of Chicago Press, 2003.

Grafton, Anthony, and Lisa Jardine. *From Humanism to the Humanities: Education and the Liberal Arts in Fifteenth- and Sixteenth-Century Europe*. Cambridge, Mass.: Harvard University Press, 1986.

Graham, Kenneth. *The Performance of Conviction: Plainness and Rhetoric in the Early English Renaissance*. Ithaca: Cornell University Press, 1994.

Gray, Hanna H. "Renaissance Humanism: The Pursuit of Eloquence." *Journal of the History of Ideas* 24, no. 4 (Oct. –Dec. 1963), 497–514.

Green, Ian. *Print and Protestantism in Early Modern England*. Oxford: Oxford University Press, 2000.

Greenblatt, Stephen. *Hamlet in Purgatory*. Princeton: Princeton University Press, 2001.

———. *Learning to Curse: Essays in Early Modern Culture*. New York: Routledge, 1990.

———. *Renaissance Self-Fashioning: More to Shakespeare*. Chicago: University of Chicago Press, 1980.

Greene, Thomas. "*Love's Labour's Lost:* The Grace of Society." *Shakespeare Quarterly* 22 (1971): 315–28.

Grendler, Paul F. *Schooling in Renaissance Italy: Literacy and Learning, 1300–1600.* Baltimore: Johns Hopkins University Press, 1989.

Griffiths, Jane. *John Skelton and Poetic Authority: Defining the Liberty to Speak.* Oxford: Oxford University Press, 2006.

Gross, Kenneth. *Shakespeare's Noise.* Chicago: University of Chicago Press, 2001.

Grosz, Elizabeth. *Volatile Bodies: Toward a Corporeal Feminism.* Bloomington: Indiana University Press, 1994.

Gurr, Andrew. *Playgoing in Shakespeare's London.* Cambridge: Cambridge University Press, 1996.

Hales, J. W. "The Date of the First English Comedy." *Englische Studien* 18 (1893): 408–21.

Hall, David D. *Worlds of Wonder, Days of Judgment: Popular Religious Belief in Early New England.* New York: Knopf, 1989.

Hansen, Elizabeth. *Discovering the Subject in Renaissance England.* Cambridge: Cambridge University Press, 1998.

Hansen, Mark. *New Philosophies for New Media.* Cambridge, Mass.: MIT Press, 2004.

Harris, Jonathan Gil, and Natasha Korda, editors. *Staged Properties in Early Modern English Drama.* Cambridge: Cambridge University Press, 2002.

Harvey, Elizabeth, D. *Ventriloquized Voices: Feminist Theory and English Renaissance Texts.* New York: Routledge, 1992.

Harvey, Elizabeth, D., editor, *Sensible Flesh: On Touch in Early Modern Culture.* Philadelphia: University of Pennsylvania Press, 2003.

Hastrup, Kirsten. "The Inarticulate Mind: The Place of Awareness in Social Interaction." In *Questions of Consciousness*, edited by Anthony Cohen and Nigel Rapport, 181–97. London: Routledge, 1995.

Hattaway, Michael. "*The Spanish Tragedy:* Architectonic Design." In *Elizabethan Popular Theatre: Plays in Performance,* 101–28. London: Routledge, 1982.

Hawkes, Terence. *Shakespeare's Talking Animals: Language and Drama in Society.* London: Arnold, 1973.

———. "Shakespeare's Talking Animals." *Shakespeare Survey* 24 (1977): 47–54.

Heal, Felicity. "Mediating the Word: Language and Dialects in the British and Irish Reformations." *Journal of Ecclesiastical History* 56, no. 2 (April 2005): 261–86.

Healy, Margaret. "Anxious and Fatal Contacts: Taming the Contagious Touch." In *Sensible Flesh: On Touch in Early Modern Culture*, edited by Elizabeth D. Harvey, 22–38. Philadelphia: University of Pennsylvania Press, 2003.

Helgerson, Richard. *Forms of Nationhood: The Elizabethan Writing of England.* Chicago: University of Chicago Press, 1992.

Henderson, Diana E. *Passion Made Public: Elizabethan Lyric, Gender, and Performance.* Chicago: University of Illinois Press, 1995.

Hillman, David. *Shakespeare's Entrails: Belief, Scepticism and the Interior of the Body.* New York: Palgrave Macmillan, 2007.

———. "Visceral Knowledge." In *The Body in Parts: Fantasies of Corporeality in Early Modern Europe*, edited by David Hillman and Carla Mazzio, 81–105. New York: Routledge, 1997.

Hillman, David, and Carla Mazzio, editors. *The Body in Parts: Fantasies of Corporeality in Early Modern Europe.* New York: Routledge, 1997.

Ho, Cynthia. "As Good as Her Word: Women's Language in *The Knight of the Tour d'Landry.*" In *The Rusted Hauberk: Fuedal Ideals of Order and Their Decline,* edited by Liam O. Purdon and Cindy L. Vitto, 99–120. Gainesville: University Press of Florida, 1994.

Hoenselaars, A. J. *Images of Englishmen and Foreigners in the Drama of Shakespeare and His Contemporaries: A Study of Stage Characters and National Identity in English Renaissance Drama.* Rutherford, N.J.: Fairleigh Dickinson University Press, 1992.

———. "Reconstructing Babel in English Renaissance Drama: William Haughton's *Englishmen for My Money* and John Marston's *Antonio and Mellida.*" *Neophilologus* 76 (1992): 464–79.

Holland, Louise Adam. *Lucretius and the Transpadanes.* Princeton: Princeton University Press, 1979.

Hope, Jonathan. "Shakespeare and Language: An Introduction." In *Shakespeare and Language*, edited by Catherine M. S. Alexander, 1–17. Cambridge: Cambridge University Press, 2004.

Houston, Julia. "Transubstantiation and the Sign: Cranmer's Drama of the Lord's Supper." *Journal of Medieval and Renaissance Studies* 24 (1994): 113–30.

Howell, Wilbur Samuel. *Logic and Rhetoric in England, 1500–1700.* New York: Russell & Russell, 1961.

Howes, David, editor. *Empire of the Senses: The Sensual Culture Reader.* Oxford: Berg, 2005.

Hudson, H. H. "Jewel's Oration Against Rhetoric: A Translation." *Quarterly Journal of Speech* 14 (1928): 374–92.

Huizinga, Johan. *Homo Ludens: A Study of the Play-Element in Culture.* Translated by R. F. C. Hull. Boston: Beacon Press, 1950.

Hull, Suzanne W. *Chaste, Silent, and Obedient: English Books for Women, 1575–1640.* San Marino, Calif.: Huntington Library, 1982.

Hutson, Lorna. "Forensic Aspects of Renaissance Mimesis." *Representations* 94 (Spring 2006): 80–109.

———. "Rethinking the Spectacle of the Scaffold." *Representations* 89 (Winter 2005): 30–58.

———. *The Usurer's Daughter: Male Friendship and Fictions of Women in Sixteenth-Century England.* New York: Routledge, 1997.

Irigaray, Luce. "The Sex Which Is Not One." In *New French Feminisms*, edited by Elaine Marks and Isabelle de Courtivron, translated by Claudia Reeder, 99–106. Amherst: University of Massachusetts Press, 1980.

James, Susan E. *Kateryn Parr: The Making of a Queen*. Brookfield, Vt.: Ashgate, 1999.

Jameson, Frederic. *Postmodernism: Or, the Cultural Logic of Late Capitalism*. Durham: Duke University Press, 1991.

Jardine, Lisa. *Wordly Goods: A New History of the Renaissance*. New York: W. W. Norton, 1998.

Jay, Martin. *Force Fields: Between Intellectual History and Cultural Critique*. New York: Routledge, 1993.

Jennings, Margaret. "Tutivillus: The Literary Career of the Recording Demon." *Studies in Philology* 74, no. 5 (1977): 1–95.

Johansen, T. K. *Aristotle on the Sense-Organs*. Cambridge: Cambridge University Press, 1998.

Johns, Adrian. *The Nature of the Book: Print and Knowledge in the Making*. Chicago: University of Chicago Press, 1998.

Johnson, S. F. "*The Spanish Tragedy*: Or Babylon Revisited." In *Essays on Shakespeare and Elizabethan Drama in Honor of Hardin Craig*, edited by Richard Holsey, 23–36. London: Routledge and Kegan Paul, 1963.

Jones, Ann Rosalind. "New Songs for the Swallow: Ovid's Philomela in Tullia d'Aragona and Gaspara Stampa." In *Refiguring Woman*, edited by Marilyn Migiel and Juliana Schiesari, 263–77. Ithaca: Cornell University Press, 1991.

Jones, Richard Foster. *The Triumph of the English Language*. Stanford: Stanford University Press, 1953.

Joplin, Patricia Klindienst. "The Voice of the Shuttle Is Ours." *Stanford Literary Review* 1 (1984): 25–53.

Kahn, Victoria. *Rhetoric, Prudence, and Skepticism in the Renaissance*. Ithaca: Cornell University Press, 1985.

Kahn, Victoria, and Lorna Hutson, editors. *Rhetoric and Law in Early Modern Europe*. New Haven: Yale University Press, 2001.

Kastan, David. "'His semblable in his mirror': *Hamlet* and the Imitation of Revenge." *Shakespeare Studies* 19 (1987): 111–24.

Keilen, Sean. *Vulgar Eloquence: On the Renaissance Invention of English Literature*. New Haven: Yale University Press, 2006.

Kesler, R. L. "Time and Causality in Renaissance Revenge Tragedy." *University of Toronto Quarterly* 59, no. 4 (Summer 1990): 474–97.

King, John N. *English Reformation Literature: The Tudor Origins of the Protestant Tradition*. Princeton: Princeton University Press, 1986.

———. "'The Light of Printing': William Tyndale, John Foxe, John Day, and Early Modern Print Culture." *Renaissance Quarterly* 54, no. 1 (2001): 52–85.

Kinney, Arthur F. *Humanist Poetics: Rhetoric, Thought, and Fiction in Sixteenth-Century England*. Amherst: University of Massachusetts Press, 1986.

Korda, Natasha. *Shakespeare's Domestic Economies: Gender and Property in Early Modern England*. Cambridge: Cambridge University Press, 2002.

Kottman, Paul A. "Sharing Vision, Interrupting Speech: *Hamlet*'s Spectacular Community." *Shakespeare Studies* (Shakespeare Society of Japan) 36 (1998): 29–57.

Knapp, Jefferey. "Preachers and Players in Shakespeare's England." *Representations* 44 (Autumn 1993): 29–59.

———. *Shakespeare's Tribe: Church, Nation and Theater in Renaissance England.* Chicago: University of Chicago Press, 2004.

Knight, Janice. *Orthodoxies in Massachusetts: Rereading American Puritanism.* Cambridge, Mass.: Harvard University Press, 1994.

Knowles, Ronald. "Hamlet and Counter-Humanism." *Renaissance Quarterly* 52 (1999): 1046–69.

Kökeritz, Helge. *Shakespeare's Pronunciation.* New Haven: Yale University Press, 1953.

Kraus, Karl. *Half-Truths and One-and-a-Half Truths: Karl Kraus, Selected Aphorisms.* Edited and translated by Harry Zohn. Montreal: Engendra Press, 1976.

Kristeva, Julia. *Tales of Love.* New York: Columbia University Press, 1987.

Krug, Rebecca. *Reading Families: Women's Literature Practice in Late Medieval England.* Ithaca: Cornell University Press, 2002.

Lacan, Jacques. *The Four Fundamental Concepts of Psychoanalysis.* Edited by Jacques-Alain Miller, translated by Alan Sheridan. New York: Norton, 1998.

Laird, David. "Competing Discourses in *The Winter's Tale*." *Connotations* 4, no. 1–2 (1994–95): 25–43.

Lancashire, Ian. "Law and Early Modern English Lexicons." In *Selected Proceedings of the 2005 Symposium on New Approaches in English Historical Lexis (HEL-LEX),* edited by R. W. McConchie et al., 8–23. Somerville, Mass.: Cascadilla Proceedings Project, 2006.

Lanham, Richard A. *The Electronic Word: Democracy, Technology, and the Arts.* Chicago: University of Chicago Press, 1993.

Lederer, Richard. *The Miracle of Language.* New York: Simon and Schuster, 1991.

Levy, F. J. *Tudor Historical Thought.* San Marino: Huntington Library, 1967.

Lobonov-Rostovsky, Sergei "Taming the Basilisk." In *The Body in Parts: Fantasies of Corporeality in Early Modern Europe,* edited by David Hillman and Carla Mazzio, 195–220. New York: Routledge, 1997.

Loewenstein, David, and Janel Mueller, editors. *The Cambridge History of Early Modern Literature.* Cambridge: Cambridge University Press, 2002.

Loewenstein, Joseph. "The Script in the Marketplace." In *Representing the English Renaissance,* edited by Stephen Greenblatt, 265–78. Berkeley: University of California Press, 1988.

Loftie, W. J. *The Inns of Court and Chancery.* Southampton: Ashford Press, 1985.

Luckyj, Christina. *"A Moving Rhetorick": Gender and Silence in Early Modern England.* Manchester: Manchester University Press, 2002.

Magnusson, Lynne. *Shakespeare and Social Dialogue.* Cambridge: Cambridge University Press, 1999.

Maley, Willy. "'This Sceptred Isle': Shakespeare and the British Problem." In *Shakespeare and National Culture*, edited by John J. Joughin, 83–108. Manchester: Manchester University Press, 1997.

Marks, Herbert. "On Prophetic Stammering." In *The Book and the Text: The Bible and Literary Theory*, edited by Regina Schwartz, 60–80. Oxford: Blackwell, 1990.

Marotti, Arthur. *John Donne: Coterie Poet*. Madison: University of Wisconsin Press, 1986.

———. *Manuscript, Print, and the English Renaissance Lyric*. Ithaca: Cornell University Press, 1995.

———. "Shakespeare's Sonnets as Literary Property." In *Soliciting Interpretation: Literary Theory and Seventeenth-Century English Poetry*, edited by Elizabeth D. Harvey and Katharine Eisaman Maus, 143–73. Chicago: University of Chicago Press, 1990.

Mason, Pamela, editor. *Shakespeare's Early Comedies*. London: Macmillan Press, 1995.

Masten, Jeffrey, "Pressing Subjects; Or, The Secret Lives of Shakespeare's Compositors." In *Language Machines: Technologies of Literary and Cultural Production*, edited by Jeffrey Masten, Peter Stallybrass, and Nancy J. Vickers, 75–107. New York: Routledge, 1997.

Maus, Katharine Eisaman. *Inwardness and Theater in the English Renaissance*. Chicago: University of Chicago Press, 1995.

Mazzio, Carla. "Acting with Tact: Touch and Theater in the Renaissance." In *Sensible Flesh: On Touch in Early Modern Culture*, edited by Elizabeth D. Harvey, 159–86. Philadelphia: University of Pennsylvania, 2003.

———. "Anatomy of a Ghost: History as Hypothesis." In *Literature Compass* 3, no. 1 (January 2006): 3–17.

———. "The Melancholy of Print: *Love's Labour's Lost*." In *Historicism, Psychoanalysis and Early Modern Culture*, edited by Carla Mazzio and Douglas Trevor, 186–227. New York: Routledge, 2000.

———. "The Senses Divided: Organs, Objects and Media in Early Modern England." In *Empire of the Senses: The Sensual Culture Reader*, edited by David Howes, 85–105. Oxford: Berg, 2005.

———. "Sins of the Tongue." In *The Body in Parts: Fantasies of Corporeality in Early Modern Europe*, edited by David Hillman and Carla Mazzio, 53–79. New York: Routledge, 1997.

———. "Sins of the Tongue in Early Modern England." *Modern Language Studies* 28, no. 4 (Autumn 1998): 93–124.

———. "Staging the Vernacular: Language and Nation in Thomas Kyd's *The Spanish Tragedy*." *Studies in English Literature* 38, no. 2 (Spring 1998): 207–32.

Mazzio, Carla, and David Hillman. "Individual Parts." In *The Body in Parts: Fantasies of Corporeality in Early Modern Europe*. Edited by Hillman and Mazzio, xi–xxix. New York: Routledge, 1997.

Mazzio, Carla, and Douglas Trevor, "Dreams of History." In *Historicism, Psychoanalysis, and Early Modern Culture*. Edited by Mazzio and Trevor, 1–19. New York: Routledge, 2000.

McAlindon, Thomas. "*Tamburlaine the Great* and *The Spanish Tragedy*: The Genesis of a Tradition." *Huntington Library Quarterly* 45, no. 1 (Winter 1982): 59–81.

McCoy, Richard, C. *Alterations of State: Sacred Kingship in the English Reformation*. New York: Columbia University Press, 2002.

McDonald, Russ. *Shakespeare and the Arts of Language*. Oxford: Oxford University Press, 2001.

McJannet, Linda. "Elizabethan Speech Prefixes." In *Reading and Writing in Shakespeare*, edited by David M. Bergeron, 45–63. Newark: University of Delaware Press, 1996.

———. *The Voice of Elizabethan Stage Directions: The Evolution of a Theatrical Code*. Newark: University of Delaware Press, 1999.

McLaren, Anne. "Reading Sir Thomas Smith's *De republica Anglorum* as Protestant Apologetic." *Historical Journal* 42 (1999): 911–39.

McLuhan, Marshall. *The Gutenberg Galaxy: The Making of Typographic Man*. Toronto: University of Toronto Press, 1962.

McMillin, Scott. "The Book of Seneca in *The Spanish Tragedy*." *Studies in English Literature* 14 (1974): 201–8.

McNeely, Trevor. *Proteus Unmasked: Sixteenth-Century Rhetoric and the Art of Shakespeare*. Bethlehem, Pa.: Lehigh University Press, 2004.

McSheffrey, Shannon. *Gender and Heresy: Women and Men in Lollard Communities, 1420–1530*. Philadelphia: University of Pennsylvania Press, 1995.

Menon, Madhavi. *Wanton Words: Rhetoric and Sexuality in English Renaissance Drama*. Toronto: University of Toronto Press, 2004.

Miola, Robert. *Shakespeare and Classical Tragedy: The Influence of Seneca*. Oxford: Clarendon, 1992.

Mitchell, W. J. T. *Iconology: Image, Text, Ideology*. Chicago: University of Chicago Press, 1986.

Montrose, Louis Adrian. *"Curious-Knotted Garden": The Form, Themes, and Contexts of Shakespeare's Love's Labour's Lost*. Salzburg: Institut für Englische Sprache und Literatur, U Salzburg, 1977.

Moss, Ann. *Renaissance Truth and the Latin Language Turn*. Oxford: Oxford University Press, 2003.

Motter, T. H. Vail. *The School Drama in England*. London: Longmans, Green, 1929.

Mozley, F. J. "The English *Enchiridion* of Erasmus, 1533." *Review of English Studies* 20, no. 78 (1944): 97–107.

Mueller, Janel. *The Native Tongue and the Word: Developments in English Prose Style, 1380–1580*. Chicago: University of Chicago Press, 1984.

Mueller, Martin. *Children of Oedipus and Other Essays on the Imitation of Greek Tragedy, 1550–1800*. Toronto: University of Toronto Press, 1980.

Muir, Kenneth. *Shakespeare's Comic Sequence*. New York: Barnes and Noble, 1979.

Mukherji, Subha. *Law and Representation in Early Modern Drama*. Cambridge: Cambridge University Press, 2006.

Mullaney, Steven. "Mourning and Misogyny: *Hamlet, The Revenger's Tragedy,* and the Final Progress of Elizabeth I, 1600–1607." *Shakespeare Quarterly* 45 (1994): 139–62.

———. *The Place of the Stage: License, Play, and Power in Renaissance England.* Ann Arbor: University of Michigan Press, 1995.

———. "Strange Things, Gross Terms, Curious Customs: The Rehearsal of Cultures in the Late Renaissance." In *Representing the English Renaissance,* edited by Stephen Greenblatt, 65–92. Berkeley: University of California Press, 1988.

Murdoch, Walter. *Seventy-Two Essays: A Selection.* New York: Books for Library Press, 1970.

Musson, Anthony. "Law and Text: Legal Authority and Judicial Accessibility in the Late Middle Ages." In *The Uses of Script and Print: 1300–1700,* edited by Julia Crick and Alexandra Walsham, 95–119. Cambridge: Cambridge University Press, 2004.

Musson, Anthony, editor. *Boundaries of the Law: Gender, Geography and Jurisdiction in Medieval and Early Modern Europe.* Aldershot: Ashgate, 2005.

Nancy, Jean-Luc. "Corpus." In *Thinking Bodies,* edited by Juliet Flower MacCannell and Laura Zakarin. Stanford: Stanford University Press, 1994.

Neill, Michael. *Issues of Death: Mortality and Identity in English Renaissance Tragedy.* Oxford: Oxford University Press, 1999.

Norford, Don Parry. " 'Very Like a Whale':The Problem of Knowledge in *Hamlet.*" *English Literary History* 46, no. 4 (Winter 1979): 559–76.

Norland, Howard B. *Drama in Early Tudor Britain, 1485–1558.* Lincoln: University of Nebraska Press, 1995.

O'Connell, Michael. *The Idolatrous Eye: Iconoclasm and Theater in Early Modern England.* Oxford: Oxford University Press, 2000.

Ong, Walter J. "Latin Language Study as a Renaissance Puberty Rite." *Studies in Philology* 56 (1959): 103–24.

———. *Orality and Literacy: The Technologizing of the Word.* London: Methuen, 1982.

———. *Ramus, Method, and the Decay of Dialogue.* Cambridge, Mass.: Harvard University Press, 1958.

———. *Rhetoric, Romance, and Technology.* Ithaca: Cornell University Press, 1971.

Orgel, Stephen. "The Poetics of Incomprehensibility." *Shakespeare Quarterly* 42 (1991): 431–37.

Østerberg, V. "Nashe's 'Kid in Aesop': A Danish Interpretation." *Review of English Studies* 18, no. 72 (1942): 385–94.

Owst, G. R. *Literature and Pulpit in Medieval England.* New York: Barnes and Noble, 1966.

Park, Katherine. "The Organic Soul." In *The Cambridge History of Renaissance Philosophy.* Edited by Charles B. Schmitt, 464–84. Cambridge: Cambridge University Press, 1988.

Parker, Patricia. *Literary Fat Ladies: Rhetoric, Gender, Property.* London: Methuen, 1987.

———. "On the Tongue: Cross Gendering, Effeminacy, and the Art of Words." *Style* 23 (1989): 445–63.

————. *Shakespeare from the Margins: Language, Culture, Context*. Chicago: University of Chicago Press, 1996.

Patterson, Annabelle M. *Reading Holinshed's Chronicles*. Chicago: University of Chicago Press, 1994.

Phillips, Susan. *Transforming Talk: The Problem of Gossip in Late Medieval England*. University Park: Pennsylvania State University Press, 2007.

Pittenger, Elizabeth. "Dispatch Quickly: The Mechanical Reproduction of Pages." *Shakespeare Quarterly* 42, no. 4 (Winter 1991): 389–408.

————. "'To Serve the Queere': Nicholas Udall Master of Revels." In *Queering the Renaissance*, edited by Jonathan Goldberg, 162–89. Durham: Duke University Press, 1994.

Platt, Peter G. "Shakespeare and Rhetorical Culture." In *A Companion to Shakespeare*, edited by David Scott Kastan, 277–96. Oxford: Blackwell, 1999.

Plett, Heinrich F. "Shakespeare and the *Ars Rhetorica*." In *Rhetoric and Pedagogy: Its History, Philosophy, and Practice: Essays in Honor of James J. Murphy*, edited by Michael Leff, 243–59. Mahwah, N.J.: Lawrence Erlbaum, 1995.

Pomeroy, Elizabeth. "England's Helicon: Music and Poetry in a Pastoral Anthology." In *Elizabethan Miscellanies: Development and Conventions*, 93–115. Berkeley: University of California Press, 1973.

Poovey, Mary. "Beyond the Current Impasse in Literary Studies." *American Literary History* 11, no. 2 (1999): 354–77.

Power, Eileen Edna. *Medieval English Nunneries, c. 1275–1535*. Cheshire, Conn.: Biblo and Tannen, 1988.

Rabkin, Norman, editor. *Reinterpretations of Elizabethan Drama: Selected Papers from the English Institute*. New York: Columbia University Press, 1969.

Raffield, Paul. *Images and Cultures of Law in Early Modern England: Justice and Political Power, 1558–1660*. Cambridge: Cambridge University Press, 2004.

Ramage, Edwin S. "Cicero on Extra-Roman Speech." *Transactions and Proceedings of the American Philological Association* 92 (1961): 481–94.

Rancière, Jacques. *Dis-Agreement: Politics and Philosophy*. Minneapolis: University of Minnesota Press, 1998.

Rebhorn, Wayne. *The Emperor of Men's Minds: Literature and the Renaissance Discourse of Rhetoric*. Ithaca: Cornell University Press, 1995.

————. "'His Tail at Commandment': George Puttenham and the Carnivalization of Rhetoric." In *A Companion to Rhetoric and Rhetorical Criticism*, edited by Walter Jost and Wendy Olmsted, 96–111.Oxford: Blackwell, 2004.

Rebhorn, Wayne, editor. *Renaissance Debates on Rhetoric*. Ithaca: Cornell University Press, 2000.

Reed, A. W. "Nicholas Udall and Thomas Wilson." *Review of English Studies* 1, no. 3 (1925): 275–83.

Rhodes, Neil. *The Power of Eloquence and English Renaissance Literature*. New York: St. Martin's Press, 1992.

————. *Shakespeare and the Origins of English*. Oxford: Oxford University Press, 2004.

Rice, Eugene F. *Saint Jerome in the Renaissance*. Baltimore: Johns Hopkins University Press, 1985.

Ronell, Avital. *Stupidity*. Urbana: University of Illinois Press, 2003.

Rothenberg, Albert. "The Janusian Process in Psychoanalytic Treatment." *Contemporary Psychoanalysis* 27 (1991): 422–53.

Sacks, Peter. *The English Elegy: Studies in the Genre from Spenser to Yeats*. Baltimore: Johns Hopkins University Press, 1985.

————. " 'Where Words Prevail Not': Grief, Revenge, and Language in Kyd and Shakespeare." *English Literary History* 49, no. 3 (Autumn 1982): 576–601.

Saenger, Paul. *Space Between Words: The Origins of Silent Reading*. Stanford: Stanford University Press, 2000.

Saussure, Ferdinand de. *Course in General Linguistics*. Translated by Wade Baskin, edited by Charles Bally and Albert Sechehaye. New York: McGraw-Hill, 1966.

Sawday, Jonathan. *The Body Emblazoned: Dissection and the Human Body in Renaissance Culture*. London: Routledge, 1995.

Scarry, Elaine. *The Body in Pain: The Making and Unmaking of the World*. Oxford: Oxford University Press, 1987.

Schalkwyk, David. " 'She never told her love': Embodiment, Textuality, and Silence in Shakespeare's Sonnets and Plays." *Shakespeare Quarterly* 45 (1994): 381–407.

Schiesari, Juliana. *The Gendering of Melancholia: Feminism, Psychoanalysis, and the Symbolics of Loss in Renaissance Literature*. Ithaca: Cornell University Press, 1992.

Schoenfeldt, Michael. *Bodies and Selves in Early Modern England: Physiology and Inwardness in Spenser, Shakespeare, Herbert, and Milton*. Cambridge: Cambridge University Press, 2000.

————. " 'Give Sorrow Words': Emotional Loss and the Articulation of Temperament in Early Modern England." In *Dead Lovers: Erotic Bonds and the Study of Premodern Europe*, edited by Basil Dufallo and Peggy McCracken, 143–64. Ann Arbor: University of Michigan Press, 2007.

————. *Prayer and Power: George Herbert and Renaissance Courtship*. Chicago: University of Chicago Press, 1991.

Screech, M. A. *Erasmus: Ecstasy and the Praise of Folly*. New York: Penguin, 1980.

Sedgwick, Eve Kosofsky. *Touching Feeling: Affect, Pedagogy, Performativity*. Durham: Duke University Press, 2003.

Sedinger, Tracy. " 'And yet woll I stiell saye that I am I': *Jake Juggler*, the Lord's Supper, and Disguise." *English Literary History* 74, no. 1 (2007): 239–69.

Seuffert, Nancy. "Domestic Violence, Discourses of Romantic Love, and Complex Personhood in the Law." *Melbourne University Law Review* 23, no. 1 (1999): 211–40.

Shagan, Ethan H. *Popular Politics and the English Reformation*. Cambridge: Cambridge University Press, 2002.

Shagan, Ethan H., editor. *Catholics and the "Protestant Nation": Religious Politics and Identity in Early Modern England.* Manchester: Manchester University Press, 2005.

Shell, Mark. "Moses' Tongue." *Common Knowledge* 12, no. 1 (2006): 150–76.

———. *Stutter.* Cambridge, Mass.: Harvard University Press, 2006.

Sherman, Claire Richter. *Writing on Hands: Memory and Knowledge in Early Modern Europe.* Washington, D.C.: Folger Shakespeare Library, 2001.

Shklovsky, Viktor. "On Poetry and Trans-Sense in Language." *October* 34 (1985): 3–24.

Shuger, Debora K. *Habits of Thought in the English Renaissance: Religion, Politics and the Dominant Culture.* New ed. Toronto: University of Toronto Press, 1997.

———. *Sacred Rhetoric: The Christian Grand Style in the English Renaissance.* Princeton: Princeton University Press, 1999.

Siemon, James R. "Dialogical Formalism: Word, Object, and Action in *The Spanish Tragedy.*" *Medieval and Renaissance Drama in England* 5 (1991): 87–115.

———. "Sporting Kyd." *English Renaissance Drama* 24, no. 3 (Autumn 1994): 553–82.

Skinner, Quentin. "Meaning and Understanding in the History of Ideas." *History and Theory* 8 (1969): 3–53.

Sloane, Thomas O. "The Crossing of Rhetoric and Poetry in the English Renaissance." In *The Rhetoric of Renaissance Poetry from Wyatt to Milton*, edited by Thomas O. Sloane and Raymond B. Waddington, 212–42. Berkeley: University of California Press, 1974.

———. *Donne, Milton, and the End of Humanist Rhetoric.* Berkeley: University of California Press, 1985.

———. "Rhetorical Selfhood in Erasmus and Milton." In *A Companion to Rhetoric and Rhetorical Criticism*, edited by Walter Jost and Wendy Olmsted, 112–27. Oxford: Blackwell, 2004.

Smith, Anne-Marie. *Julia Kristeva: Speaking the Unspeakable.* London: Pluto Press, 1998.

Smith, Bruce R. *The Acoustic World of Early Modern England: Attending to the O-Factor.* Chicago: University of Chicago Press, 1999.

———. "Hearing Green: Logomarginality in *Hamlet.*" *Early Modern Literary Studies* 7, no. 1, Special Issue 8 (May 2001): 4.1–5.6.

———. *The Key of Green: Passion and Perception in Renaissance Art.* Chicago: University of Chicago Press, 2009.

———. "Prickly Characters." In *Reading and Writing in Shakespeare*, edited by David Bergeron, 25–44. Newark: University of Delaware Press, 1996.

Sorabji, Richard. "Aristotle on Demarcating the Five Senses." In *Essays on Aristotle*, vol. 4, *Psychology and Aesthetics*, edited by Jonathan Barnes, Malcolm Schofield, and Richard Sorabji, 76–92. London: Duckworth, 1979.

Spurgeon, Caroline. *Shakespeare's Imagery and What It Tells Us.* Cambridge: Cambridge University Press, 1935.

Stallybrass, Peter. "Patriarchal Territories: The Body Enclosed." In *Rewriting the Renaissance: The Discourses of Sexual Difference in Early Modern Europe*, edited by Margaret W. Ferguson, Maureen Quilligan, and Nancy J. Vickers, 123–42. Chicago: University of Chicago Press, 1986.

———. "Shakespeare, the Individual and the Text." In *Cultural Studies*, edited by Lawrence Greenberg, Cary Nelson, and Paula Treichler, 593–612. New York: Routledge, 1992.

Steiner, George. *Language and Silence: Essays on Language, Literature, and the Inhuman.* New Haven: Yale University Press, 1998.

Stevens, Martin. "Language as Theme in the Wakefield Plays." *Speculum* 52 (1977): 100–117.

Stewart, Alan. *Close Readers: Humanism and Sodomy in Early Modern England.* Princeton: Princeton University Press, 1997.

Stewart, Alan, and Garrett A. Sullivan. " 'Worme-eaten, and full of canker holes': Materializing Memory in *The Faerie Queene* and *Lingua.*" *Spenser Studies* 17 (2003): 215–38.

Stewart, Stanley. *"Renaissance" Talk: Ordinary Language and the Mystique of Critical Problems.* Pittsburgh: Duquesne University Press, 1997.

Stewart, Susan A. *Poetry and the Fate of the Senses.* Chicago: University of Chicago Press, 2002.

Stock, Brian. *Listening for the Text: On the Uses of the Past.* Philadelphia: University of Pennsylvania Press, 1997.

Stockholder, Kay. " 'Yet can he write': Reading the Silences in *The Spanish Tragedy.*" *American Imago: A Psychoanalytic Journal for Culture, Science and the Arts* 47 (1990): 93–124.

Strier, Richard. *Love Known: Theology and Experience in George Herbert's Poetry.* Chicago: University of Chicago Press, 1983.

———. "Martin Luther and the Real Presence in Nature." *Journal of Medieval and Early Modern Studies* 37, no. 2 (2007): 271–303.

———. *Resistant Structures: Particularity, Radicalism, and Renaissance Texts.* Berkeley: University of California Press, 1995.

Targoff, Ramie. *Common Prayer: The Language of Public Devotion in Early Modern England.* Chicago: University of Chicago Press, 2001.

Tassi, Marguerite A. *The Scandal of Images: Iconoclasm, Eroticism, and Painting in Early Modern English Drama.* Selinsgrove, Pa.: Susquehanna University Press, 2005.

Trevor, Douglas. "George Herbert and the Scene of Writing." In *Historicism, Psychoanalysis and Early Modern Culture*, edited by Carla Mazzio and Douglas Trevor, 228–59. New York: Routledge, 2000.

———. *The Poetics of Melancholy in Early Modern England.* Cambridge: Cambridge University Press, 2004.

Trousdale, Marion. *Shakespeare and the Rhetoricians.* Chapel Hill: University of North Carolina Press, 1982.

———. "Shakespeare's Oral Text." *Renaissance Drama* 12 (1981): 95–116.

Turner, Henry. *The English Renaissance Stage: Geometry, Poetics, and the Practical Spatial Arts, 1580–1630.* Oxford: Oxford University Press, 2006.

Vickers, Brian. "The Age of Eloquence." *History of European Ideas* 5 (1984): 427–37.

———. *In Defence of Rhetoric.* Rev. ed. Oxford: Oxford University Press, 1989.

———. "On the Practicalities of Renaissance Rhetoric." In *Rhetoric Revalued*, edited by Brian Vickers, 133–41. Binghampton, N.Y.: Center for Medieval and Early Renaissance Studies, 1982.

———. " 'The Power of Persuasion': Images of the Orator, Elyot to Shakespeare." In *Renaissance Eloquence: Studies in the Theory and Practice of Renaissance Rhetoric*, edited by James J. Murphy, 411–35. Berkeley: University of California Press, 1984.

Vickers, Nancy. "Diana Described: Scattered Woman and Scattered Rhyme." *Critical Inquiry* 8 (1981): 265–80.

———. "Members Only: Marot's Anatomical Blazons." In *The Body in Parts: Fantasies of Corporeality in Early Modern Europe*, edited by David Hillman and Carla Mazzio, 1–23. New York: Routledge, 1997.

Vinge, Louise. *The Five Senses: Studies in a Literary Tradition.* Lund: Berlingska Boktryckeriert, 1975.

Wagner, Russell H. "The Text and Editions of Wilson's *Arte of Rhetorique.*" *Modern Language Notes* 44, no. 7 (November 1929): 421–28.

Waith, Eugene M. "Controversia in the English Drama: Medwall and Massinger." *PMLA* 68, no. 1 (March, 1953): 286–303.

Wall, Wendy. " 'Household Stuff': The Sexual Politics of Domesticity and the Advent of English Comedy." *English Literary History* 65, no. 1 (Spring 1998): 1–45.

———. *The Imprint of Gender: Authorship and Publication in the English Renaissance.* Ithaca: Cornell University Press, 1993.

———. *Staging Domesticity.* Cambridge: Cambridge University Press, 2006.

Walsham, Alexandra. "Reformed Folklore? Cautionary Tales and Oral Tradition in Early Modern England." In *The Spoken Word*, edited by Adam Fox and Daniel Woolf, 173–88. Manchester: Manchester University Press, 2003.

———. "Unclasping the Book? Post-Reformation English Catholicism and the Vernacular Bible." *Journal of British Studies* 42 (2003): 141–66

Ward, John O. "Renaissance Commentators on Ciceronian Rhetoric." In *Renaissance Eloquence: Studies in the Theory and Practice of Renaissance Rhetoric*, edited by James J. Murphy, 126–73. Berkeley: University of California Press, 1983.

Weber, Max. *The Protestant Ethic and the Spirit of Capitalism.* New York: Routledge, 2001.

Weimann, Robert. "Bifold Authority in Shakespeare's Theatre." *Shakespeare Quarterly* 39, no. 4 (1988): 401–17.

———. *Shakespeare and the Popular Tradition in the Theater: Studies in the Social Dimension of Dramatic Form and Function.* Baltimore: Johns Hopkins University Press, 1978.

Westfall, Susanne. "The Boy Who Would Be King: Court Revels of King Edward VI, 1547–1553." *Comparative Drama* 35, no. 3 (September 2001): 271–91.

White, Anthony Graham. *Punctuation and Its Dramatic Value in Shakespearean Drama.* Newark: University of Delaware Press, 1995.

White, R. S. *Natural Law in English Renaissance Literature.* Cambridge: Cambridge University Press, 1996.

Williams, Raymond. "From Medium to Social Practice." In *Marxism and Literature,* 158–64. Oxford: Oxford University Press, 1990.

Wilson, Eric. "Abel Drugger's Sign and the Fetishes of Material Culture." In *Historicism, Psychoanalysis and Early Modern Culture,* edited by Carla Mazzio and Douglas Trevor, 110–35. New York: Routledge, 2000.

Wilson, Luke. "Hamlet, Hales V. Petit, and the Hysteresis of Action." *English Literary History* 60, no. 1 (Spring 1993): 17–55.

———. *Theaters of Intention: Drama and the Law in Early Modern England.* Stanford: Stanford University Press, 2000.

Wollock, Jefferey. *The Noblest Animate Motion: Speech, Physiology and Medicine in Pre-Cartesian Linguistic Thought.* Amsterdam: John Benjamins, 1997.

Woodbridge, Linda. *The Scythe of Saturn: Shakespeare and Magical Thinking.* Urbana: University of Illinois Press, 1994.

Woolf, Daniel. "Disciplinary History and Historical Discourse. A Critique of the History of History: The Case of Early Modern England." *Cromohs* 2 (1997): 1–25.

Yates, Frances. *A Study of "Love's Labour's Lost."* Cambridge: Cambridge University Press, 1936.

Yates, Julian. *Error, Misuse, Failure: Object Lessons from the English Renaissance.* Minneapolis: University of Minnesota Press, 2003.

Zaret, David. *Origins of Democratic Culture: Printing, Petitions and the Public Sphere in Early Modern England.* Princeton: Princeton University Press, 2000.

Žižek, Slavoj. *The Indivisible Remainder: An Essay on Schelling and Related Matters.* London: Verso, 1996.

INDEX

Page numbers for illustrations are indicated in italics.

Hansen, Mark, 285 n.28

Harding, Thomas, 23, 24, 231 n.16, 232 n.21, 237 n.83; Latin Mass defended by, 38–39, 237 n.83; philology and, 40

Harpocrates (god), 4, 211, 218 n.9

Harrison, William, 103

Hart, John, 163

Harvey, Elizabeth, 217 n.3, 285 n.29

Hattaway, Michael, 102, 254 n.32

Hawkes, Terence, 243 n.126, 272 n.23, 279 n.81

Heal, Felicity, 231–32 n.20

Healy, Margaret, 292 n.99

hearing, sense of, 3, 143, 183, 185, 198, 199; incomplete comprehension and, 27 (*see also* mumbling), Protestantism and, 37, 51, 54, 237 n.77; in *Ralph Roister Doister,* 63, 78, 80, 81, 90–93

Hebrew language, 23, 40, 45, 99

Helgerson, Richard, 220 n.19

Henderson, Diana E. 276 n.53, 277–78 n.64

Henry VIII, King, 58

Henslowe, Philip, 108

Heptameron (Whetstone), 146

hermeneutics, 4, 68

Hermes (god), 4, *4,* 211

Heteroclitanomalonomia (academic drama), 6, 164

heuristics, 27, 54

Heywood, Jasper, 97, 128, 134, 135, 137–38

Heywood, Thomas, 101, 132

Hibbard, G. R., 168

Hillman, David, 195

Hippocrates, 14, 16

historiography, 1, 11–13, 180; chronicle, 11, 12, 137–40; distortions of Reformation polemic and, 40; logic and, 125–26; playwrights and, 137–38; "unspoken" grounds of, 234 n.46

Hoby, Sir Thomas, 143

Hoenselaars, A. J., 218 n.4

Holinshed, Raphael, 139–40, 253–54 n.34, 268 n.144

Holland, Philemon, 3

homiletic tradition, 61, 62, 74, 247 n.31

Houston, Julia, 247 n.31

Howell, Samuel Wilbur, 264 n.112

Huizinga, Johan, 91, 251 n.68

Hull, Suzanne W., 221 n.24

Huloet, Richard, 5, 219 n.15

humanism, 1, 10, 11, 18, 55, 180; Catholic humanism of Erasmus, 16, 57; historiography and, 138; gender and, 71–78; humanities and, 17–18; languages and, 98, 113; law and, 112–26; limits of, 55, 61, 75, 122; oratory and, 161; persuasion and, 2, 223 n.37; pronunciation and, 20; Protestant humanism, 44–47, 58, 59; rhetoric of civic agency and, 13; self-fashioning and, 55, 61, 71, 74–75, 77, 191; sensory perception and, 189; touch sense and, 182, 207

Hutson, Lorna, 63, 223 n.37, 245–46 n.16, 250 n.62, 259–60 n.72, 264 n.115, 265 n.120

Hutten, Leonard, 149, 273 n.30

ideologies, 1, 18, 25, 27, 46, 52, 112

The Idolatrous Eye (O'Connell), 183

idolatry, 35, 36, 58, 59, 66; erotic and religious, 66; in *Ralph Roister Doister,* 71, 72, 75

ignorance, learned, 14, 16

imperialism, 94, 103, 104

inarticulateness (incoherence), 2, 5, 12, 17; aesthetics of, 176, 180; affect (emotion) and, 3, 14, 111–12, 142–47, 178, 270 n.6, 271 n.14; Augustinian piety and, 16, 233 n.34, 269 n.1, 271 n.12, 227 n.58; classical tropes of, 221 n.24; cognitive processes and, 27, 54–55, 195, 233 n.34; dramatic representation of, 13, 56, 95, 114–15, 120, 122–23, 143–47, 172, 178–79, 189, 191, 195; Erasmus on, 15, 16, 226–27 n.50; etymology of *articulate,* 5–6, 219 nn.14–18; interior of the self and, 194; internalized feelings of, 3, 178; of legal discourse, 7, 112–26; literary criticism/theory and, 227 n.57, 227–28 n.60, 228 n.62, 228–29 n.65; pathos of, 6, 14, 111–12, 120, 178–79; problem solving and, 54, 55, 93; Shakespeare's, 175–76; tacit knowledge and, 27, 54–55, 178, 233 n.34; talking cures and, 171–73, 179, 282 n.107; touch sense and, 181–82. *See also* Babel; babbling; barbarism; gibberish; inexpressibility; mumbling; "murmuring"; stammering; stuttering; unsaid; whispering

incorporation (psychoanalytic concept), 179, 198

ACKNOWLEDGMENTS

A NUMBER OF ENORMOUSLY ARTICULATE FRIENDS and colleagues helped to create the conditions in which the inarticulate could be, for me, a subject of critical inquiry, historical investigation, and personal curiosity. From the outset, I thank Marge Garber as well as Jeff Masten and Derek Pearsall, whose brilliance, intellectual generosity, and extraordinary humor made the inarticulate easier to talk about than it might otherwise have been. I also thank Anne Lake Prescott for her intimate wit and loving support, and Stephen Greenblatt as well for inspiring an early essay, "Sins of the Tongue," that was published in a volume that I edited with David Hillman, entitled *The Body in Parts*. Although that essay is not used here in large measure, it marked the first stage of my thinking about pathologies of speech in the Renaissance as indices of larger historical issues and cultural transformations.

The Inarticulate Renaissance took its current shape over the past few years while I was teaching at the University of Chicago. I am enormously grateful to those at Chicago who read and commented on a number of chapters in substantial ways, including David Bevington, Bradin Cormack, Janice Knight, Michael Murrin, Christina von Nolcken, Lisa Ruddick, Josh Scodel, and Richard Strier, and all of my colleagues at Chicago who encouraged me, often choosing just the right words along the way, especially Lauren Berlant, Bill Brown, Jim Chandler, Jackie Goldsby, Elaine Hadley, Miriam Hansen, Tom Mitchell, Debbie Nelson, Sandra McPherson, Eric Slauter, and Bob Von Hallberg. Judith Anderson and Diana Robin also read and commented on parts of the book in brilliant and encouraging ways. Elizabeth Chandler made me laugh when the inarticulate seemed most grave, and a number of friends and colleagues, particularly Janice Knight and Lisa Ruddick, lifted my spirits and stimulated my intellect when the "inarticulate" seemed an elusive subject of history, or alternatively, a subject too close to home in the present day.

Indeed, for helping me to see that subjects seemingly too close to home are often the ones that can, if acknowledged, drive critical innovation, I thank in particular Valerie Traub and Peter Stallybrass. In addition to their capacity for staggering insight informing all of our conversations, both brought their analytic intensity and thoughtfulness to their reading of my work in ways for which I will always remain grateful. Most of all, I thank David Hillman, who, since we conspired on *The Body in Parts* in graduate school, has been my steadfast collaborator in friendship and intellectual mischief in ways that have given me, and continue to give me, enormous joy.

So too, for their fiery intellects, sustaining friendships, and forms of collegial vitality, I am deeply grateful to a number of cherished friends and colleagues. These include Linda Gregerson, Elizabeth Harvey, Bill Ingram, Betty Ingram, Mike Schoenfeldt, Steven Mullaney, as well as those who have worked with me in a variety of ways on other projects, including Mary Thomas Crane, Tom Conley, Bill Germano, Margreta de Grazia, John Guillory, Ann Rosalind Jones, Sergei Lobanov-Rostovsky, Katy Park, Gail Kern Paster, Curtis Perry, Katherine Rowe, Kathryn Schwarz, Scott Stevens, Libby Spiller, Kristen Poole, Linda Schlossberg, Doug Trevor, Nancy Vickers, James Boyd White, and Eric Wilson. Many of my graduate students, now colleagues, proved stimulating interlocutors as they responded, if not always to the chapters of this book, to the central ideas contained within it; my thanks especially to Gina Bloom, Aiden Johnson, Aaron Kitch, Stephanie Murray, Caryn O'Connell, Jeff Rufo, Adam Rzepka, Hristomir Stanev, and Jason Yost. It is these and other students who have long made the study of Renaissance literature, for me, a continuous labor of love.

Without support from the National Endowment for the Humanities to do research at the Newberry Library and from the Andrew W. Mellon Foundation to do research for a glorious summer at the Huntington Library, this book, which was composed alongside a number of other projects, would not have been possible. Jim Grossman, Paul Gale, Paul Saenger, and Carla Zecher at the Newberry Library, Roy Ritchie, Susi Krasnoo, and Mona Schulman at the Huntington Library, and Alice Schreyer at the University of Chicago's Special Collections Library all provided an enormous amount of intellectual stimulation and good fun that enriched my experience of research and writing. Completion of the final draft took place at the Radcliffe Institute for Advanced Study at Harvard University, and I am especially grateful to my phenomenal research assistant, Paris Spies-Gans, for helping me to dot my i's when I might have crossed them and for helping me track down out-of-the-way texts for fact-checking. Magda Teter also read portions of the final manuscript and caught, with her eagle eye, typos within early modern orthography, and she along with Lisa Bielawa and Judy Vichniac provided a great deal of support and intellectual stimulation throughout the final year. Elizabeth Harvey and David Howes provided feedback on early and skeletal versions of Chapter 5, published in their respective volumes, *Sensible Flesh: On Touch in Early Modern Culture* (Philadelphia: University of Pennsylvania Press, 2003) and *Empire of the Senses* (Oxford: Berg, 2005). I am grateful to both of them, and to members of the Department of English at the University at Buffalo as well, for responding with vigor and brilliance to a version of that chapter as well. I also thank Routledge for permission to reprint material from my essay "The Melancholy of Print," published in *Historicism, Psychoanalysis and Early Modern Culture* (2000), a book that I edited with Douglas Trevor, in my current Chapter 4.

Without the scholars cited in the text, notes, and bibliography, this book would not exist. Even as economic conditions of publication demand the slimming of endnotes, I thank Jerry Singerman, my editor at the University of Pennsylvania Press, for allowing me to include a selected bibliography, itself but a small testament to the vast and enormously rich field of scholarship upon which the book is based. Jerry has been a model of wit and sagacity, and those at Penn involved in the preparation of this book, including copyeditor, Otto Bohlmann, and Mariana Martinez, Noreen O'Connor-Abel, Will Boehm, and the press readers who offered incisive commentary, all deserve my infinite gratitude. A special thanks as well to Mary C. Foltz, who provided invaluable support and assistance during the proof reading stage.

For their longstanding friendship, I am especially grateful to Alex Ashline, whose brilliance and kindness made what could have been a difficult year more like a year of opportunities for reflection and growth, and Joe Blackmore, Andrea Henderson, Tiffany Holmes, Paula McEvoy, Sharonda Moscol, Andrew Damien Pratt, and Tina Richardson. Mary Poovey in particular provided an enormous amount of support and encouragement during the final stages of this book's preparation. I thank her for her presence in my life and for the ways in which she helped me to approach the inarticulate in ways that go well beyond this book. For helping me to say "go little book" and allow the inarticulate to speak, I thank Hilary Bracken and Terry Scherling. And finally, for her gift of the gab, her love of words, and her hard-earned ability to acknowledge the textures in between, I thank my loving "mum," Paula Collins Mazzio.